Are We There Yet?

Are We There Yet?

By Pat Oliphant

**Andrews McMeel
Publishing**

Kansas City

─── ATTENTION: SCHOOLS AND BUSINESSES ───

Andrews McMeel books are available at quantity discounts with bulk purchase for educational, business, or sales promotional use. For information, please write to: Special Sales Department, Andrews McMeel Publishing, 4520 Main Street, Kansas City, Missouri 64111.

February 10, 1997

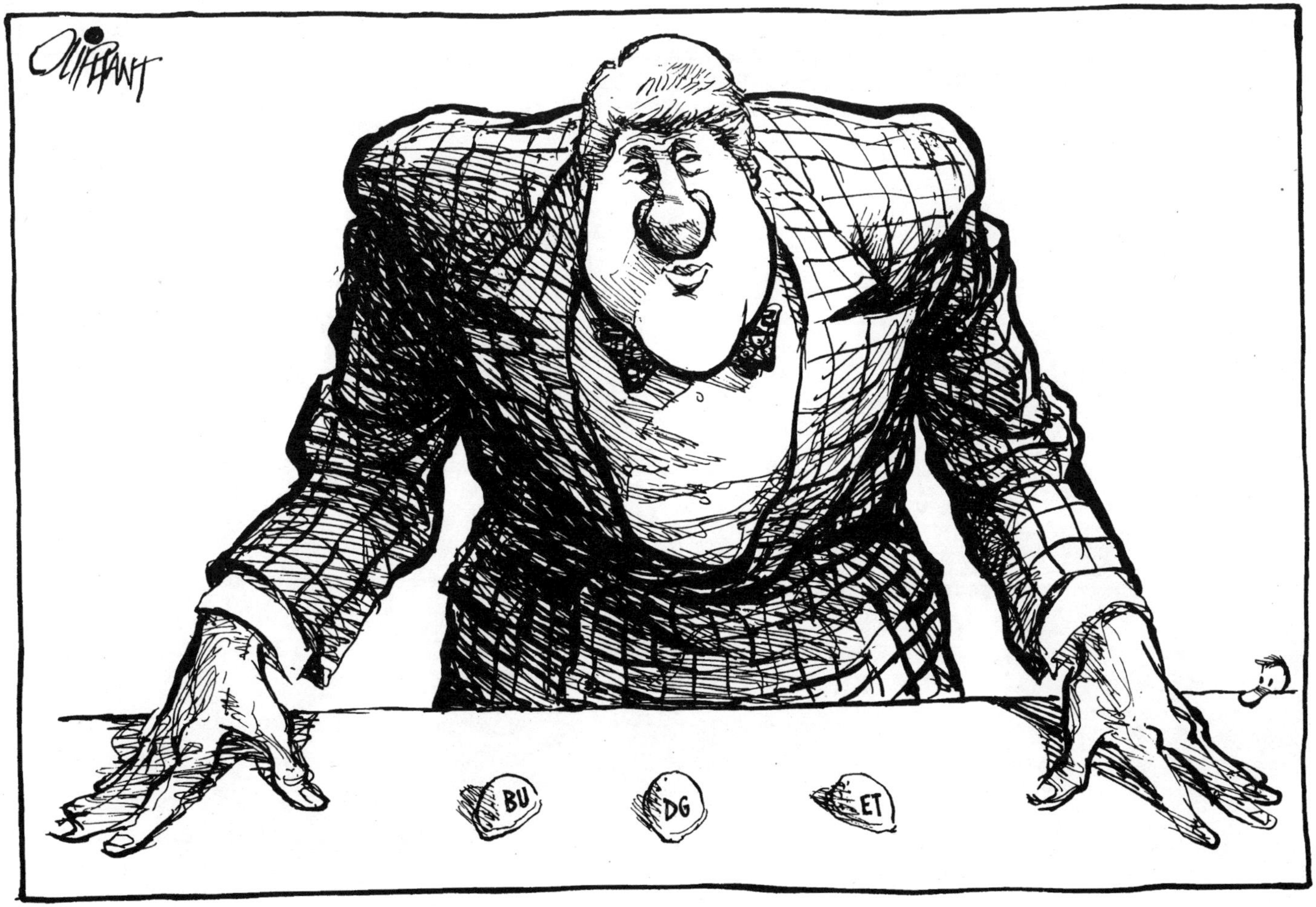
OLIPHANT
BU
DG
ET

February 11, 1997

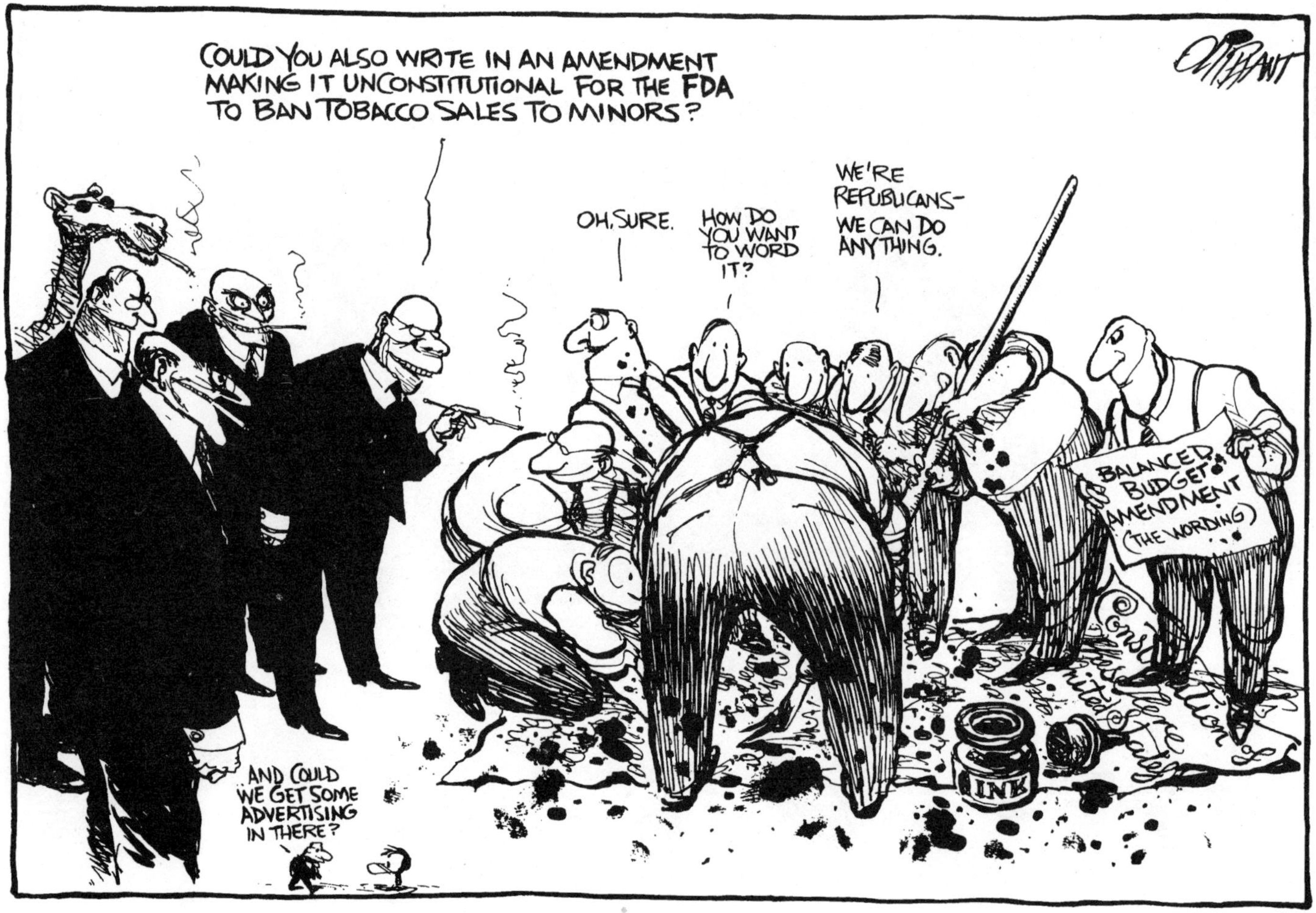
COULD YOU ALSO WRITE IN AN AMENDMENT MAKING IT UNCONSTITUTIONAL FOR THE FDA TO BAN TOBACCO SALES TO MINORS?
OH, SURE.
HOW DO YOU WANT TO WORD IT?
WE'RE REPUBLICANS- WE CAN DO ANYTHING.
BALANCED BUDGET AMENDMENT (THE WORDING)
INK
AND COULD WE GET SOME ADVERTISING IN THERE?
OLIPHANT

February 13, 1997

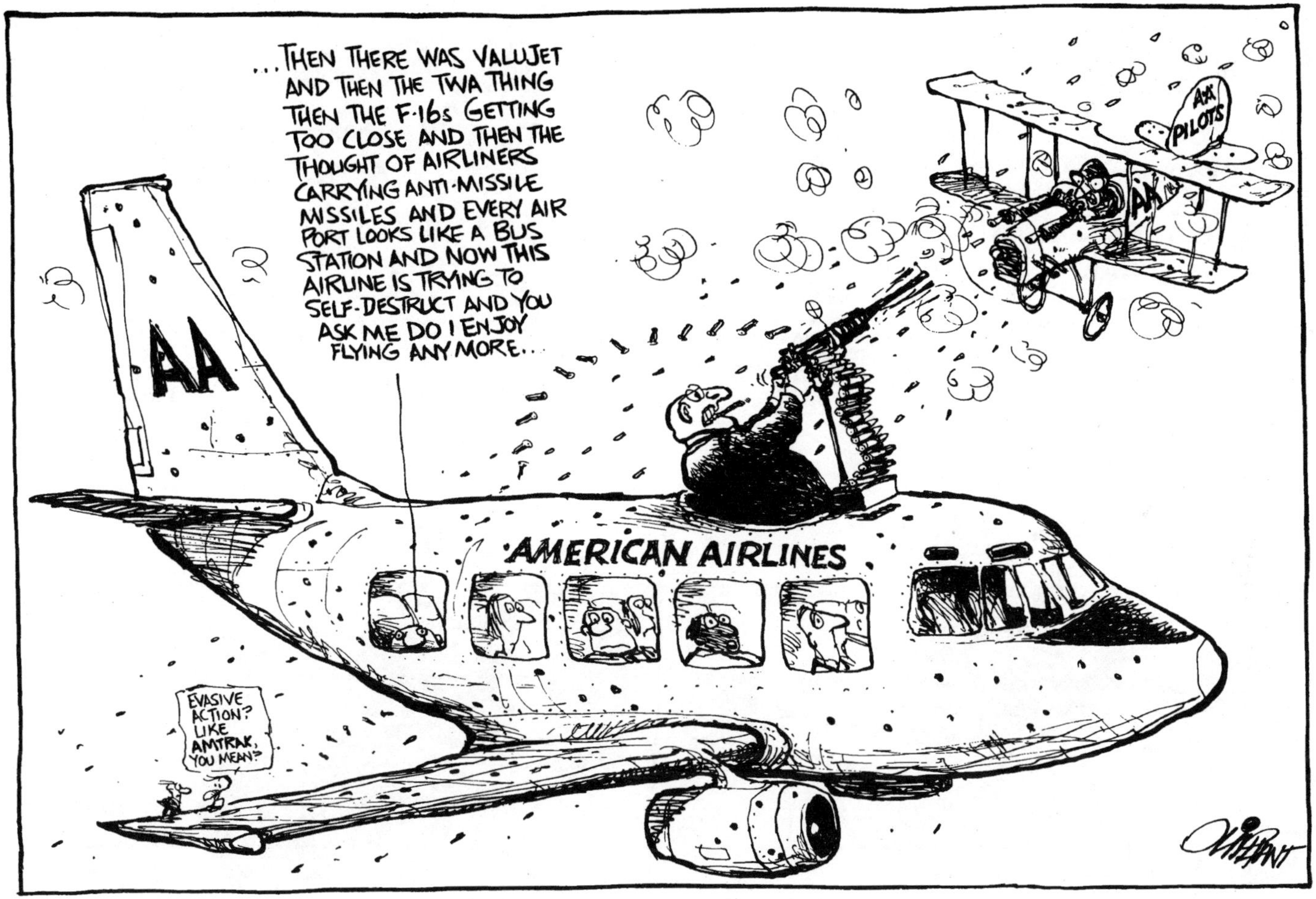
...THEN THERE WAS VALUJET AND THEN THE TWA THING THEN THE F-16s GETTING TOO CLOSE AND THEN THE THOUGHT OF AIRLINERS CARRYING ANTI-MISSILE MISSILES AND EVERY AIR PORT LOOKS LIKE A BUS STATION AND NOW THIS AIRLINE IS TRYING TO SELF-DESTRUCT AND YOU ASK ME DO I ENJOY FLYING ANY MORE...
AA PILOTS
AA
AA
AMERICAN AIRLINES
EVASIVE ACTION? LIKE AMTRAK, YOU MEAN?
OLIPHANT

February 18, 1997

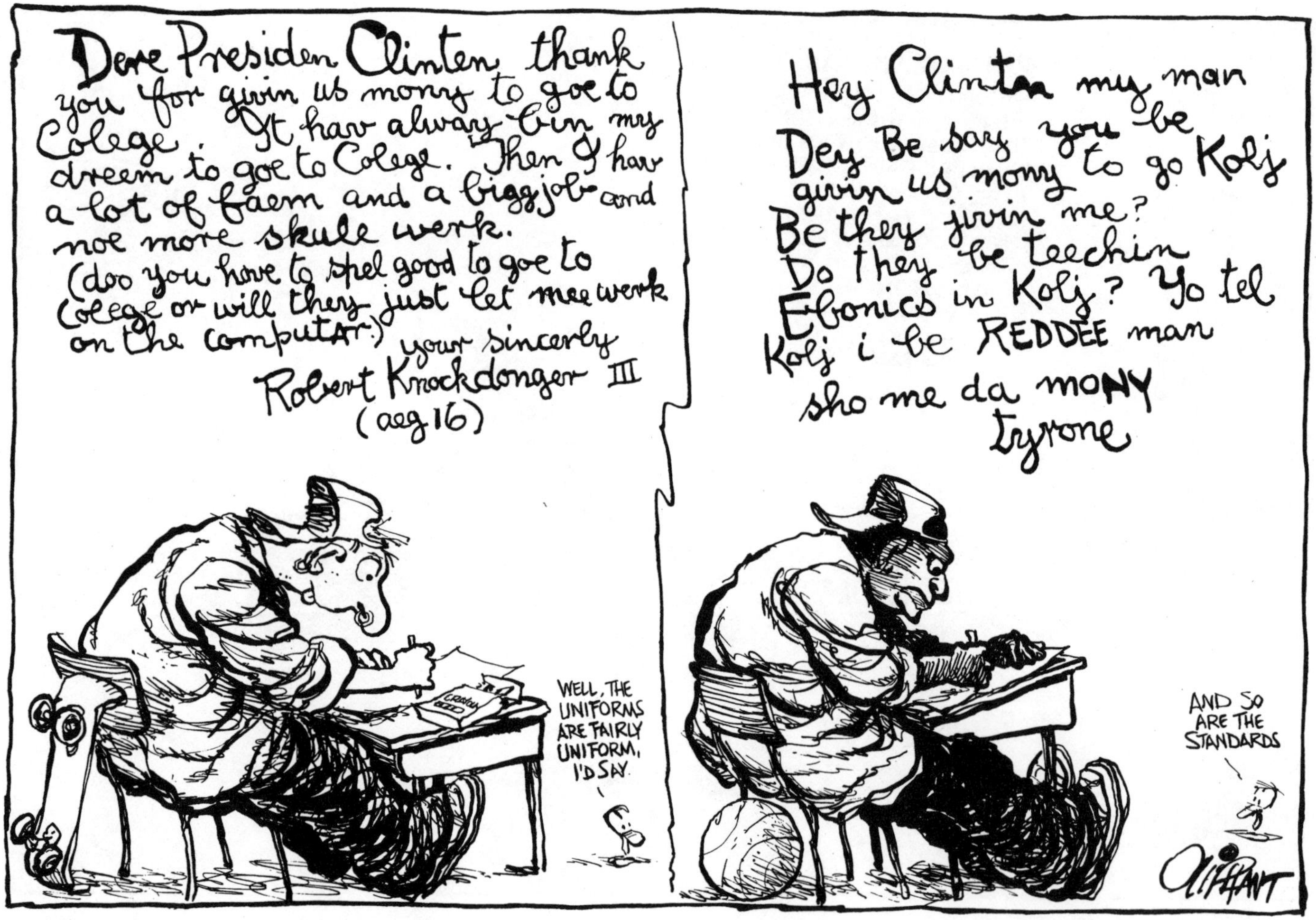

February 25, 1997

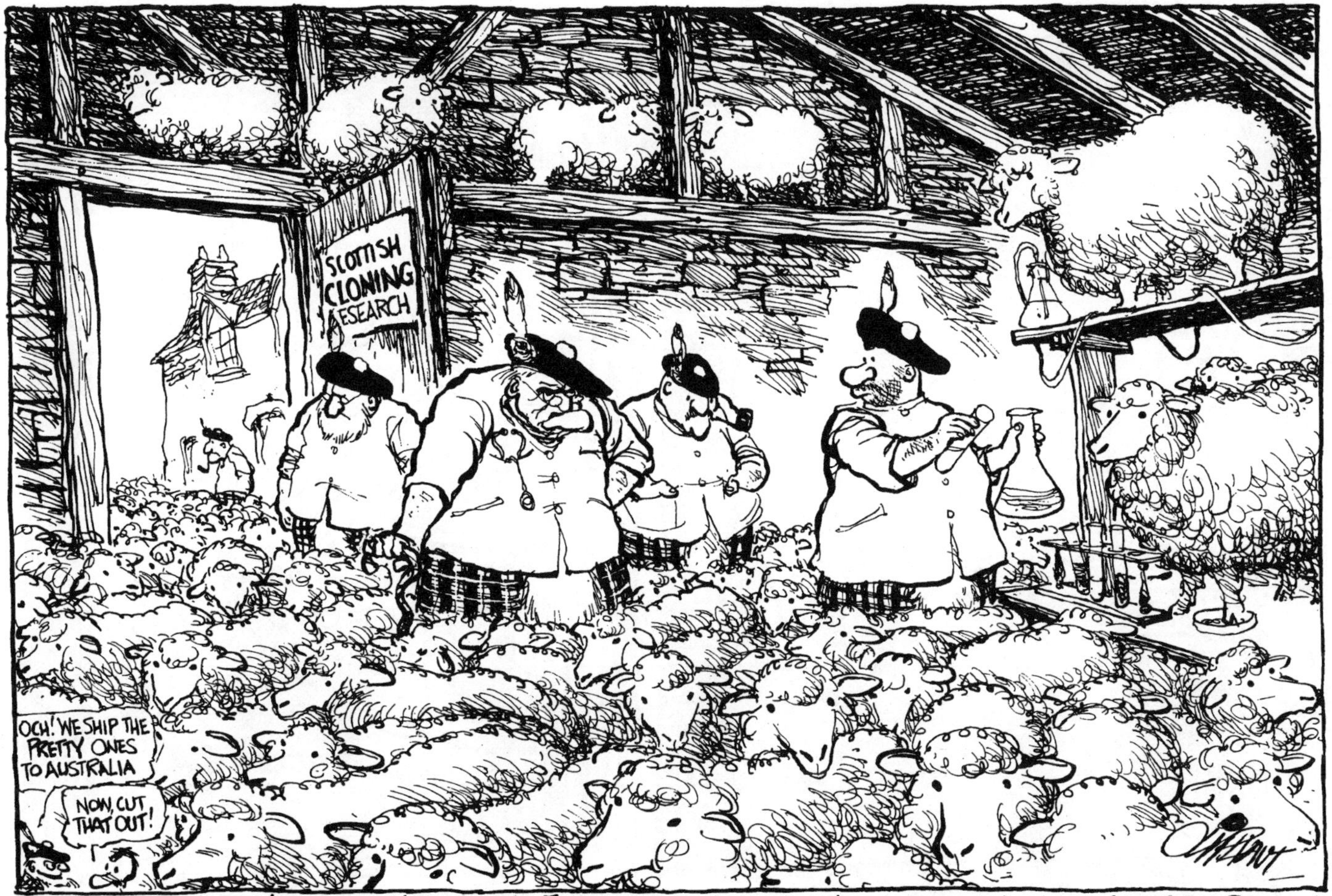
SCOTTISH
CLONING
RESEARCH
OCH! WE SHIP THE PRETTY ONES TO AUSTRALIA
NOW, CUT THAT OUT!

'MCTAVISH, WE HOPE YOU HAVE A HIGH MORAL EXPLANATION FOR WHAT YOU INTEND TO DO WITH ALL THESE SHEEP.'

February 25, 1997

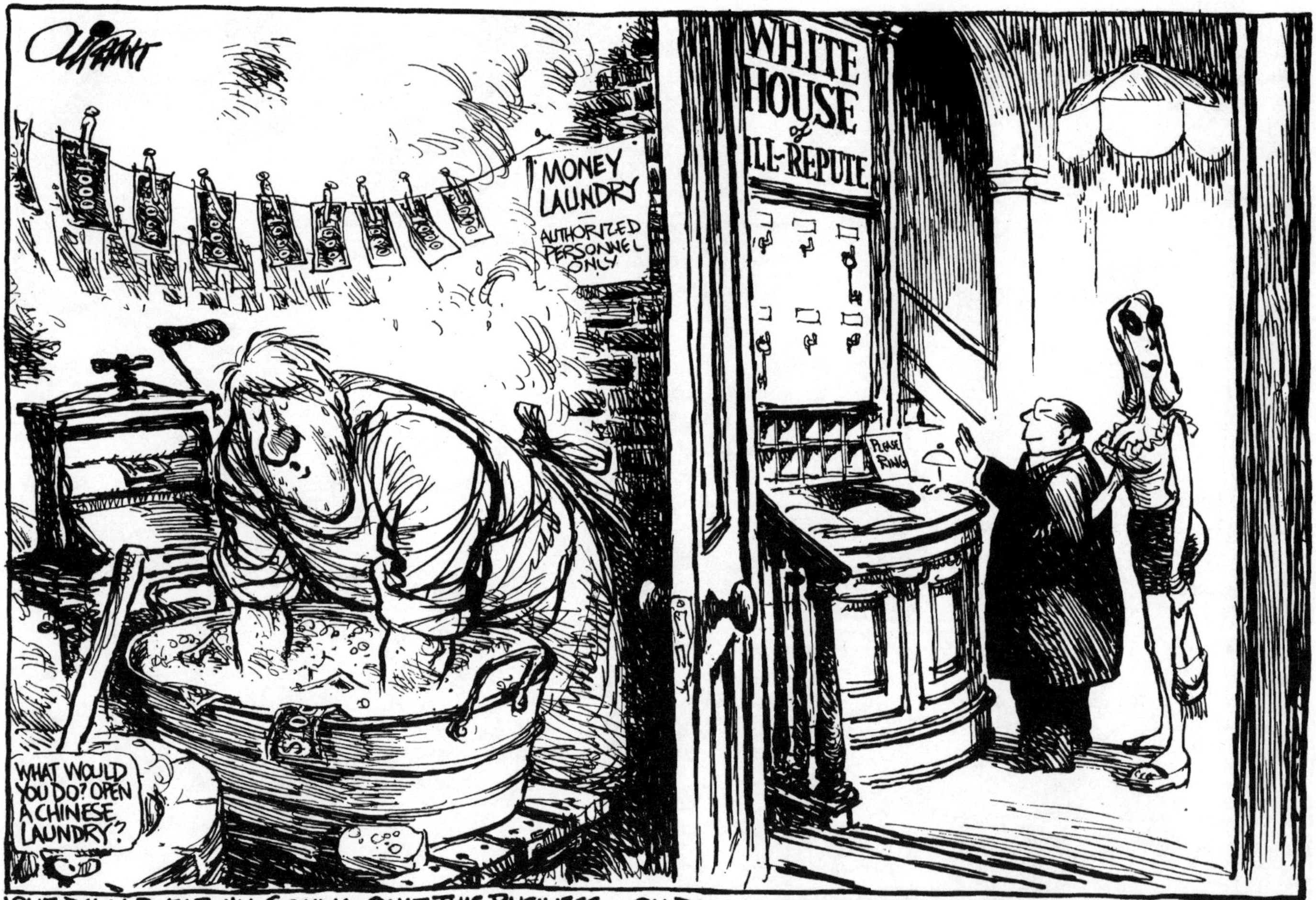
OLIPHANT
MONEY LAUNDRY
AUTHORIZED PERSONNEL ONLY
WHITE HOUSE of ILL-REPUTE
PLEASE RING
WHAT WOULD YOU DO? OPEN A CHINESE LAUNDRY?

'ONE DAY, I SWEAR, I'M GONNA QUIT THIS BUSINESS... OH, DAMNATION, ANOTHER CUSTOMER—BE RIGHT THERE!'

February 27, 1997

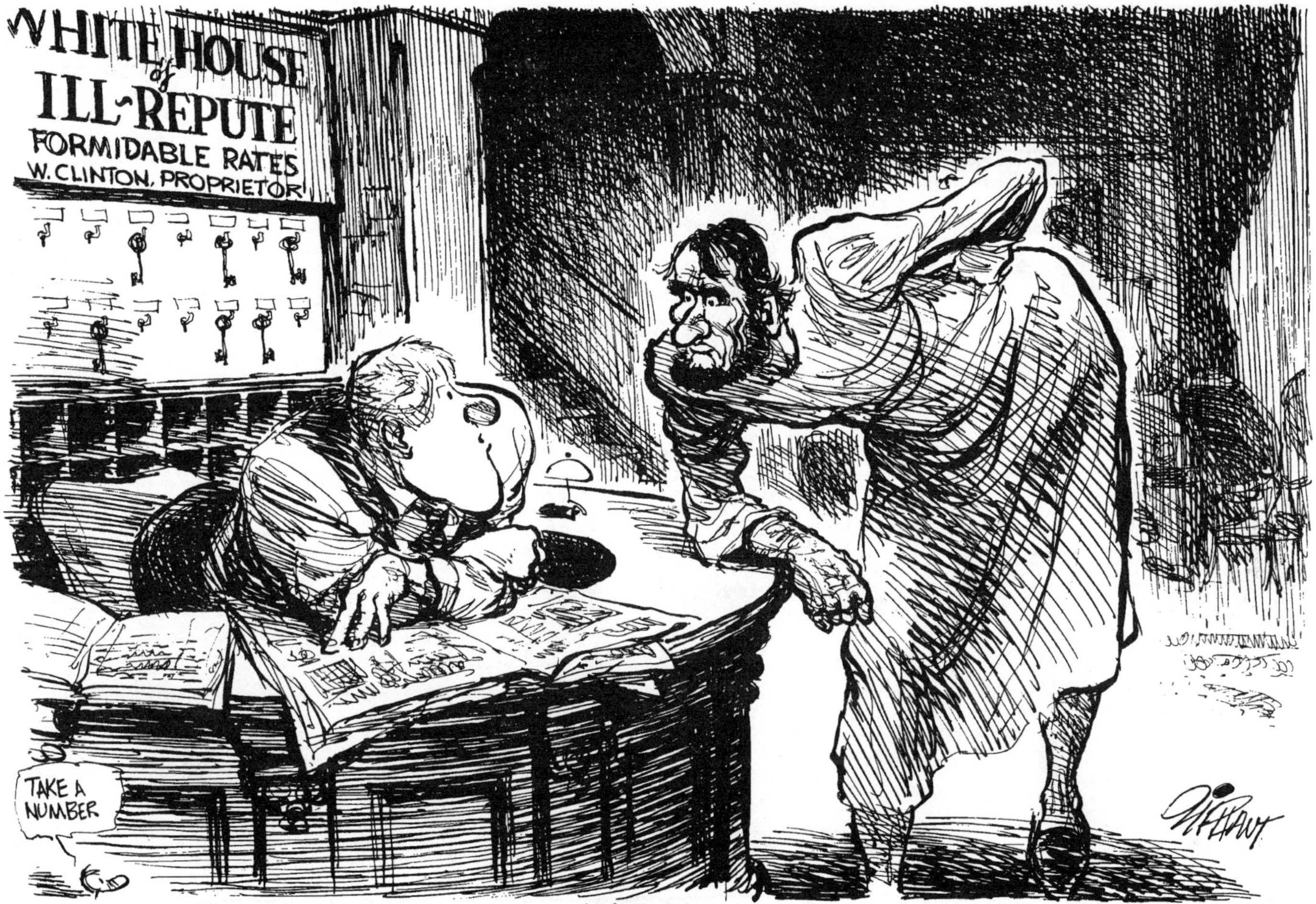
WHITE HOUSE of ILL-REPUTE
FORMIDABLE RATES
W. CLINTON, PROPRIETOR
TAKE A NUMBER

'YES?'

March 3, 1997

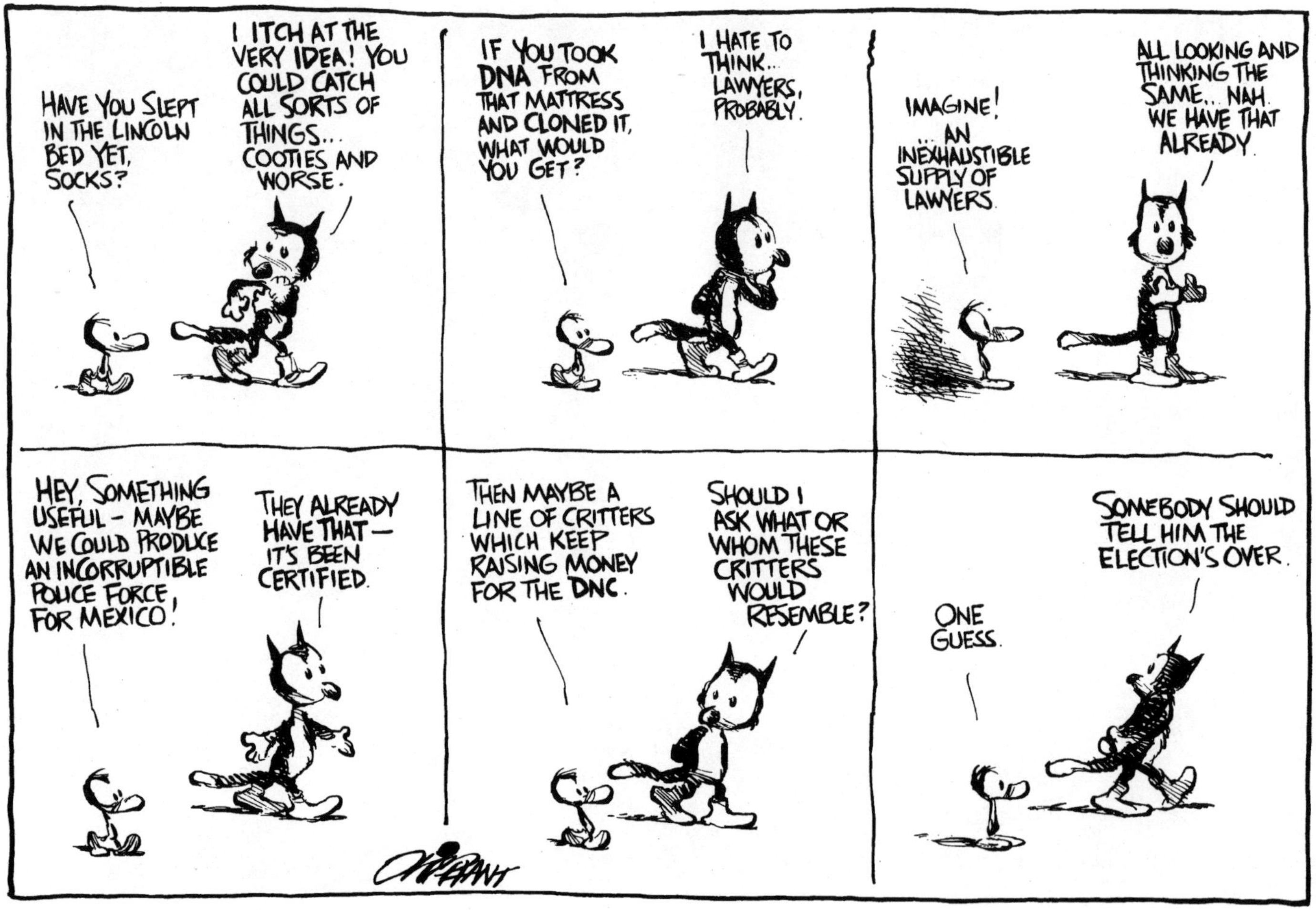
HAVE YOU SLEPT IN THE LINCOLN BED YET, SOCKS?
I ITCH AT THE VERY IDEA! YOU COULD CATCH ALL SORTS OF THINGS... COOTIES AND WORSE.
IF YOU TOOK DNA FROM THAT MATTRESS AND CLONED IT, WHAT WOULD YOU GET?
I HATE TO THINK... LAWYERS, PROBABLY.
IMAGINE! ...AN INEXHAUSTIBLE SUPPLY OF LAWYERS.
ALL LOOKING AND THINKING THE SAME... NAH. WE HAVE THAT ALREADY.
HEY, SOMETHING USEFUL - MAYBE WE COULD PRODUCE AN INCORRUPTIBLE POLICE FORCE FOR MEXICO!
THEY ALREADY HAVE THAT— IT'S BEEN CERTIFIED.
THEN MAYBE A LINE OF CRITTERS WHICH KEEP RAISING MONEY FOR THE DNC.
SHOULD I ASK WHAT OR WHOM THESE CRITTERS WOULD RESEMBLE?
ONE GUESS.
SOMEBODY SHOULD TELL HIM THE ELECTION'S OVER.
OLIPHANT

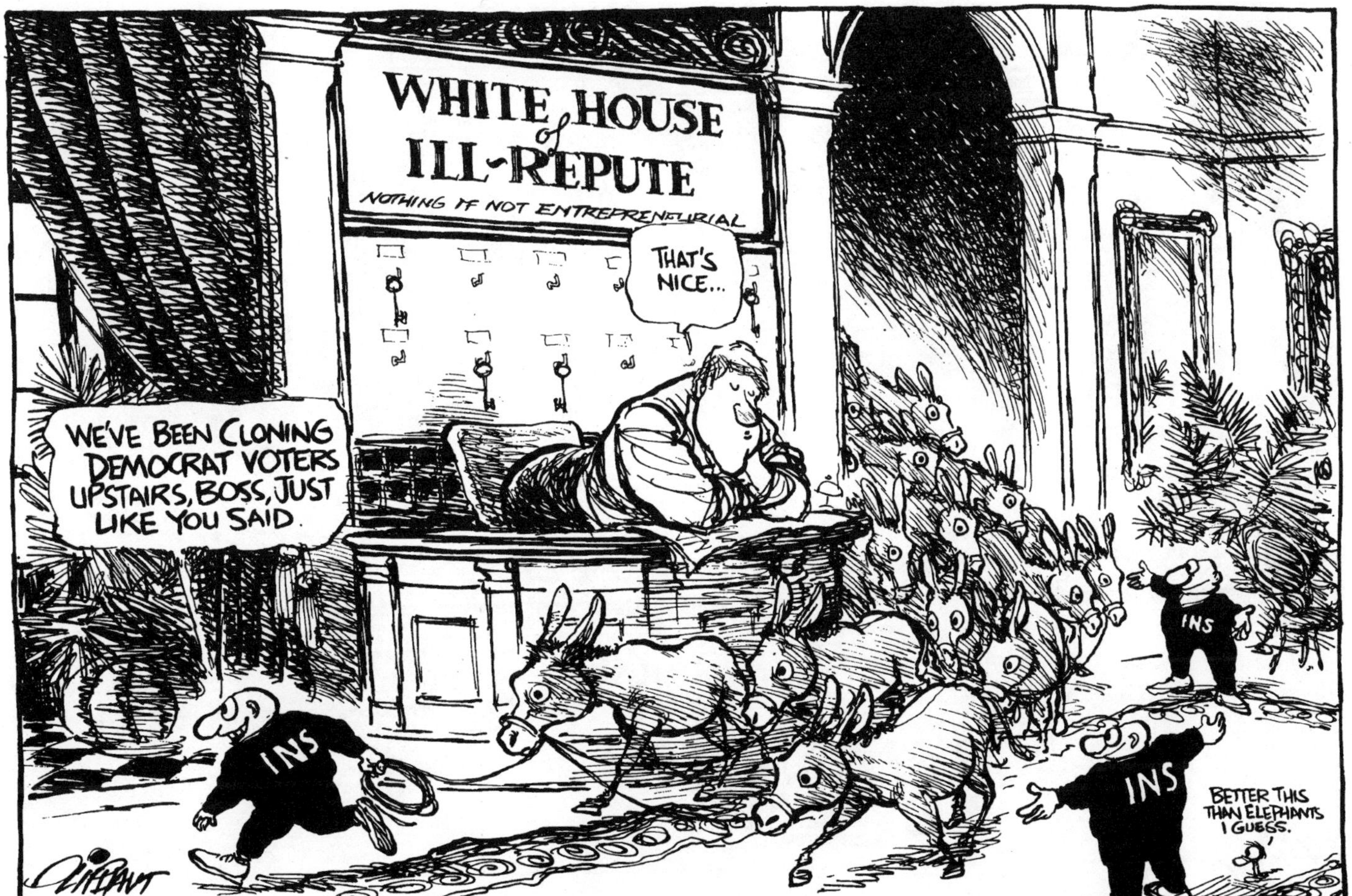
WHITE HOUSE of ILL-REPUTE
NOTHING IF NOT ENTREPRENEURIAL
THAT'S NICE...
WE'VE BEEN CLONING DEMOCRAT VOTERS UPSTAIRS, BOSS, JUST LIKE YOU SAID.
INS
INS
INS
BETTER THIS THAN ELEPHANTS I GUESS.
OLIPHANT

March 11, 1997

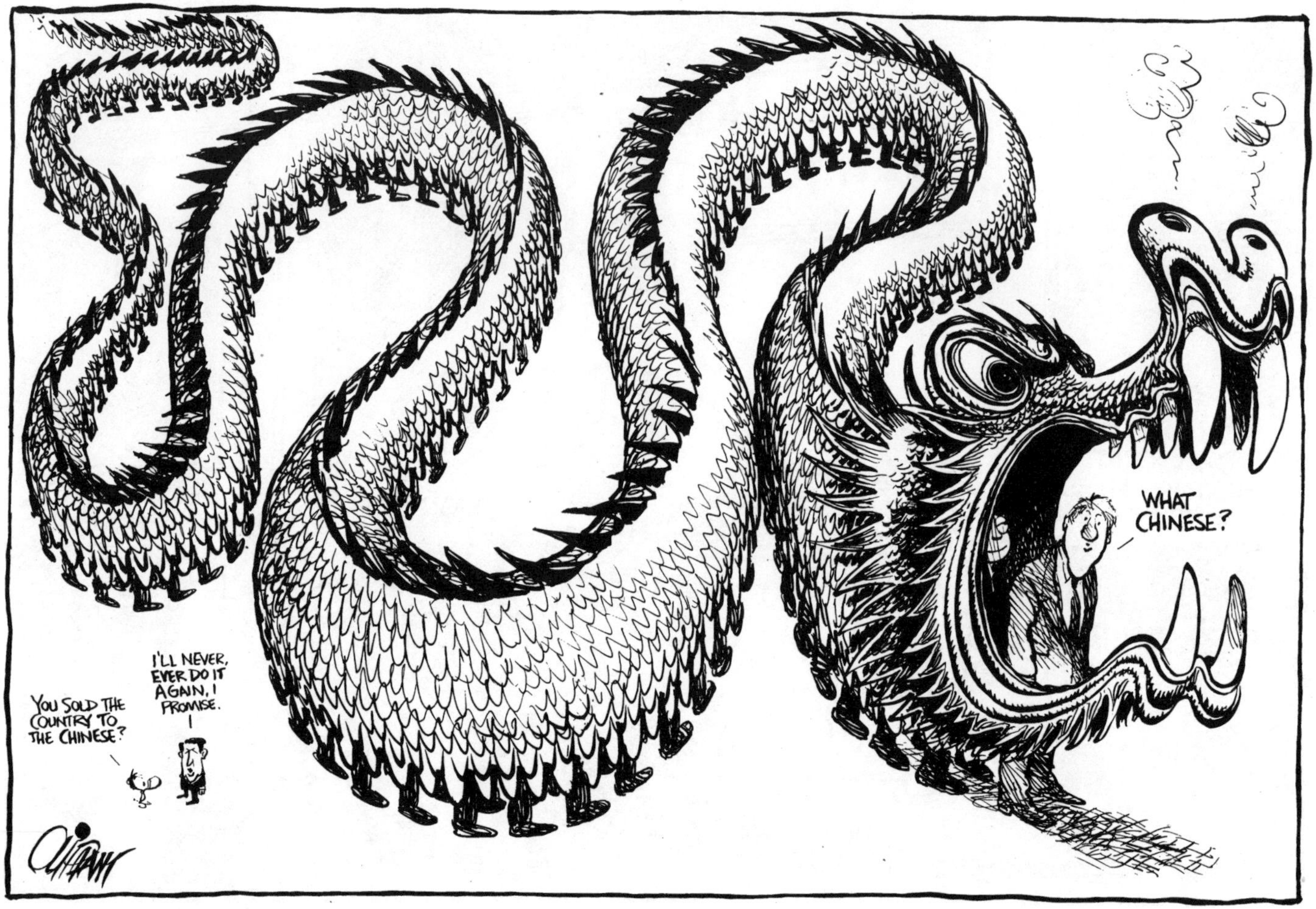
WHAT CHINESE?
YOU SOLD THE COUNTRY TO THE CHINESE?
I'LL NEVER, EVER DO IT AGAIN, I PROMISE.

March 12, 1997

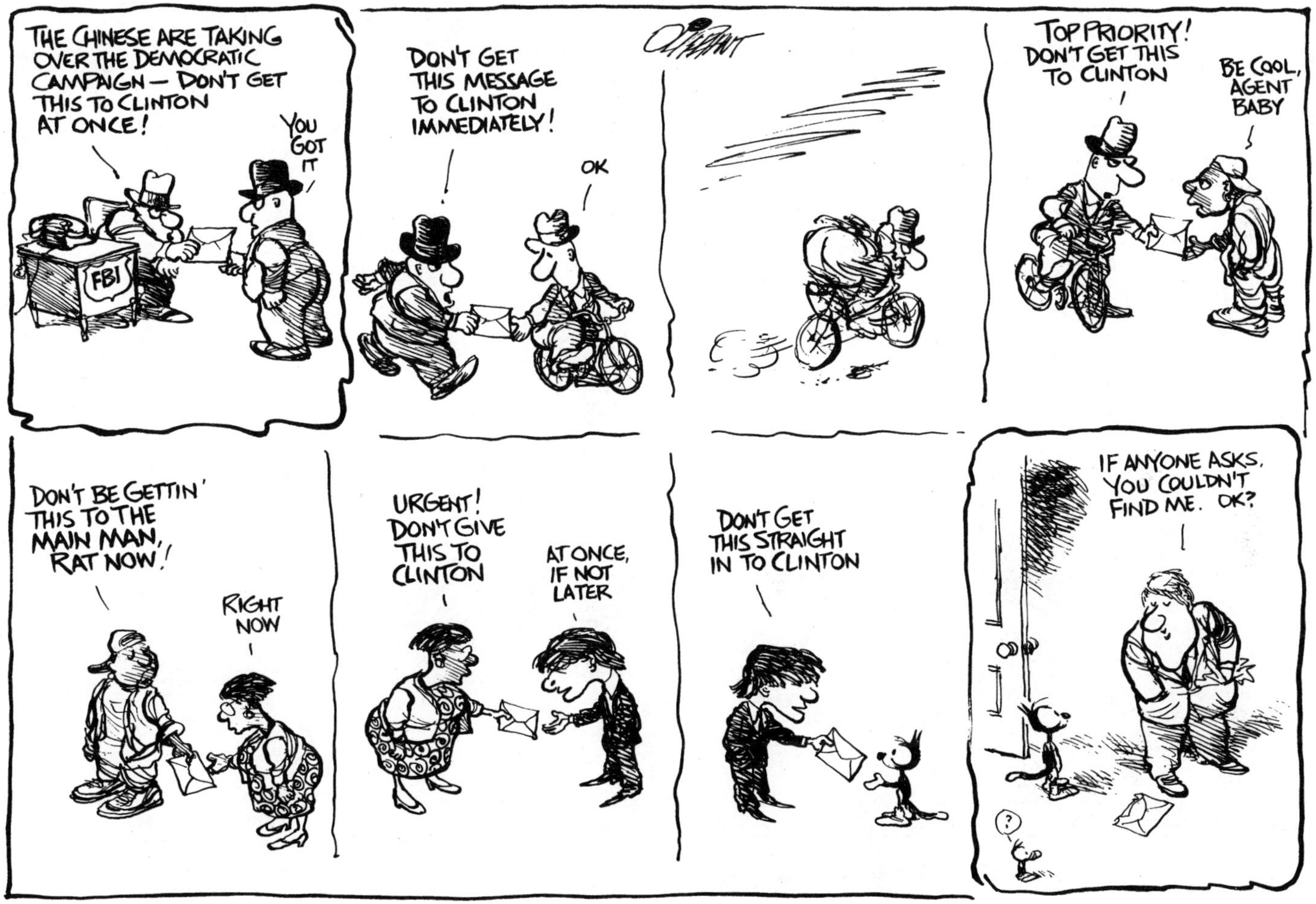
THE CHINESE ARE TAKING OVER THE DEMOCRATIC CAMPAIGN — DON'T GET THIS TO CLINTON AT ONCE!
YOU GOT IT
DON'T GET THIS MESSAGE TO CLINTON IMMEDIATELY!
OK
FBI
TOP PRIORITY! DON'T GET THIS TO CLINTON
BE COOL, AGENT BABY
DON'T BE GETTIN' THIS TO THE MAIN MAN, RAT NOW!
RIGHT NOW
URGENT! DON'T GIVE THIS TO CLINTON
AT ONCE, IF NOT LATER
DON'T GET THIS STRAIGHT IN TO CLINTON
IF ANYONE ASKS, YOU COULDN'T FIND ME. OK?
?

March 13, 1997

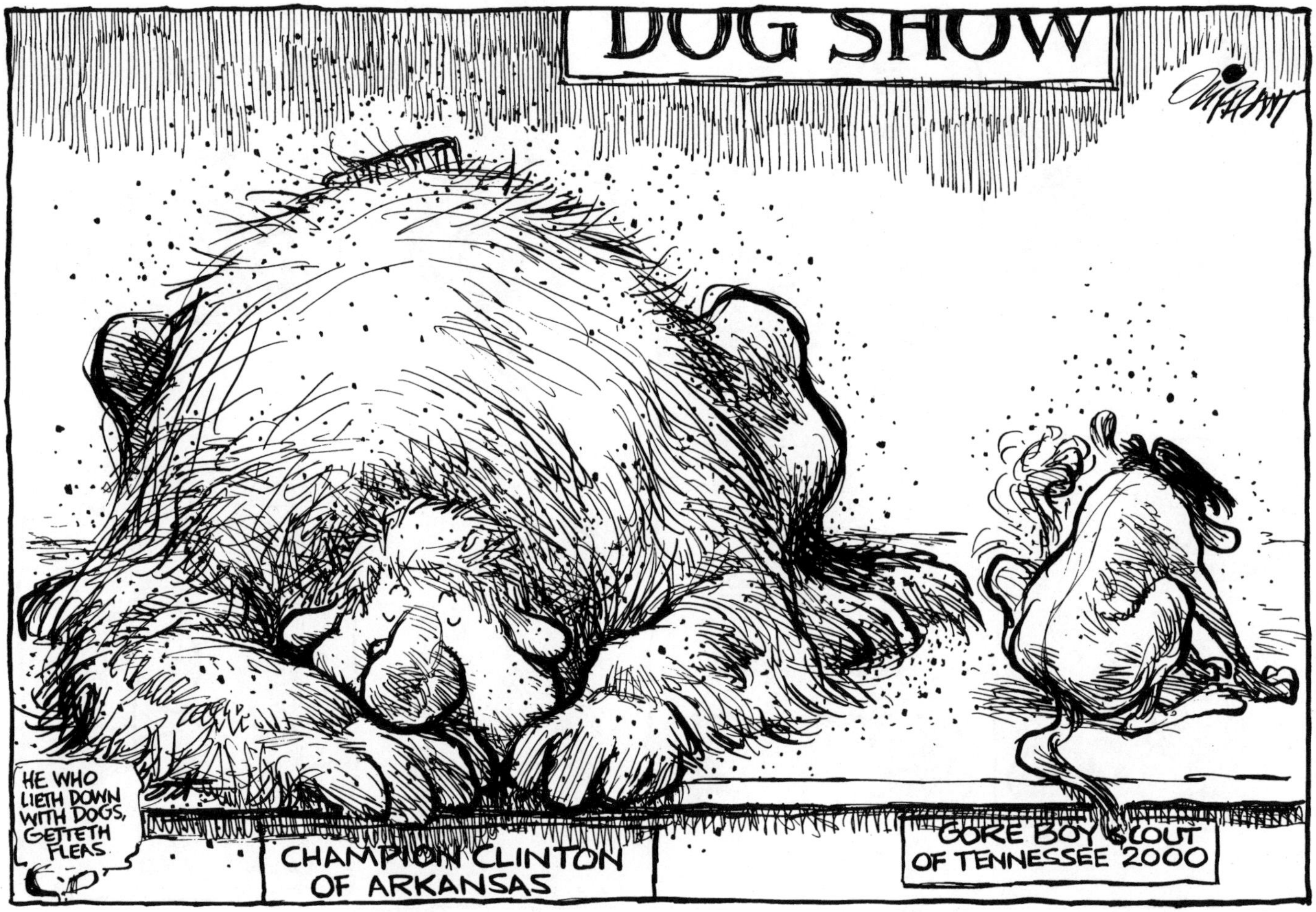
DOG SHOW
CHAMPION CLINTON OF ARKANSAS
GORE BOY SCOUT OF TENNESSEE 2000
HE WHO LIETH DOWN WITH DOGS, GETTETH FLEAS.

March 16, 1997

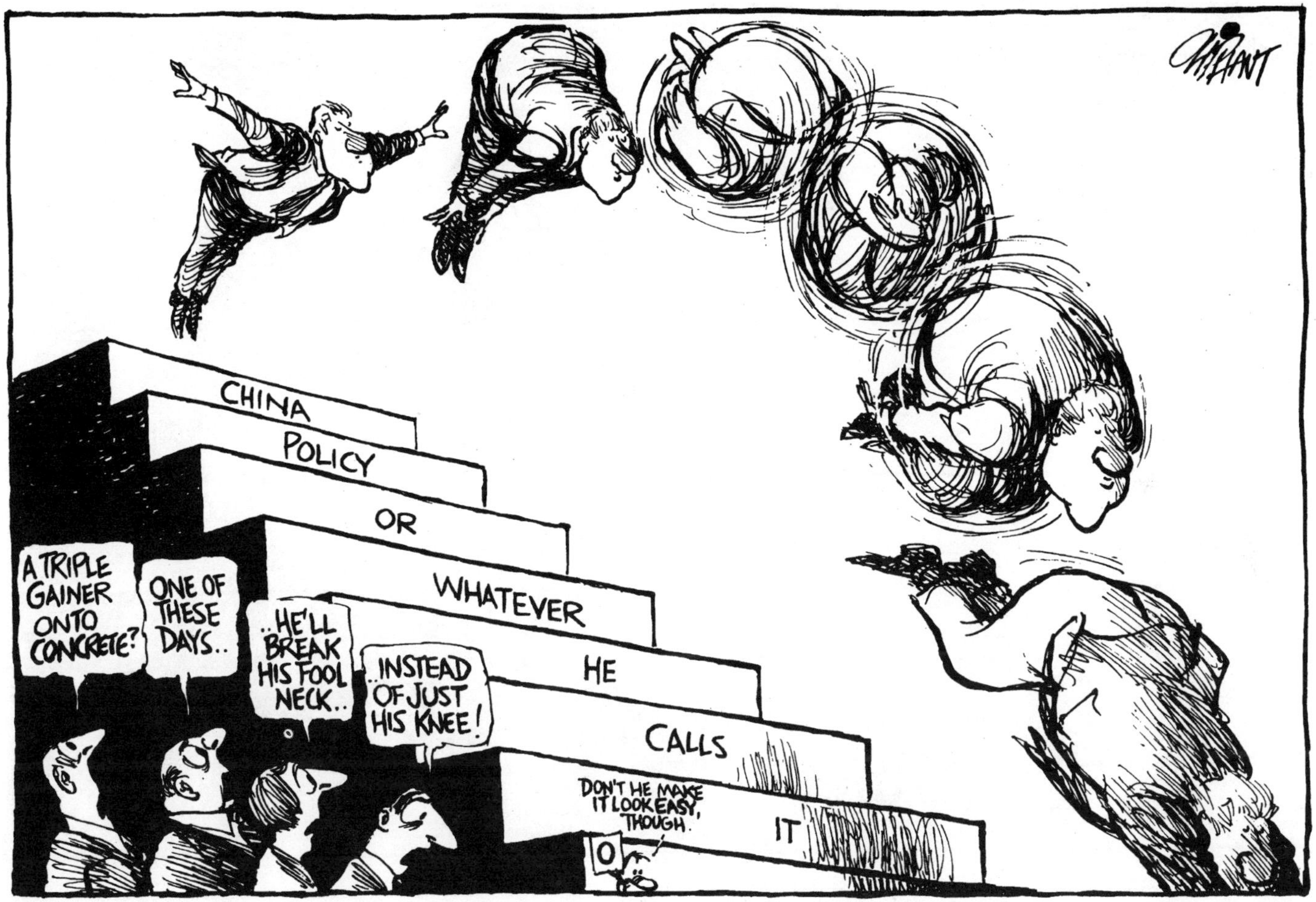
CHINA
POLICY
OR
WHATEVER
HE
CALLS
IT
A TRIPLE GAINER ONTO CONCRETE?
ONE OF THESE DAYS..
..HE'LL BREAK HIS FOOL NECK..
..INSTEAD OF JUST HIS KNEE!
DON'T HE MAKE IT LOOK EASY, THOUGH.
O

March 19, 1997

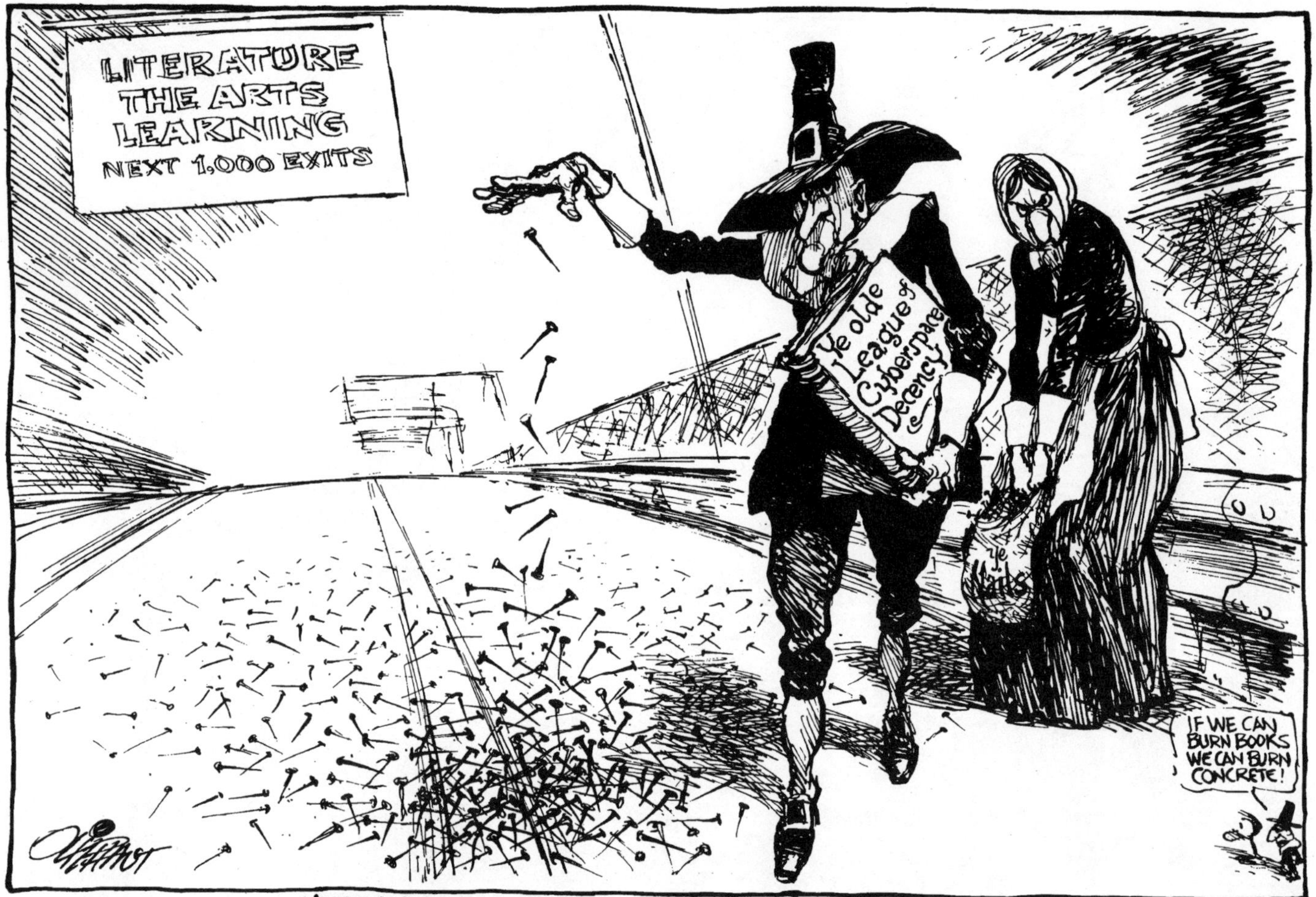
LITERATURE
THE ARTS
LEARNING
NEXT 1,000 EXITS
Ye olde League of Cyberspace Decency
Ye Nails
IF WE CAN BURN BOOKS WE CAN BURN CONCRETE!

HITCHHIKERS ON THE INFORMATION HIGHWAY.

March 26, 1997

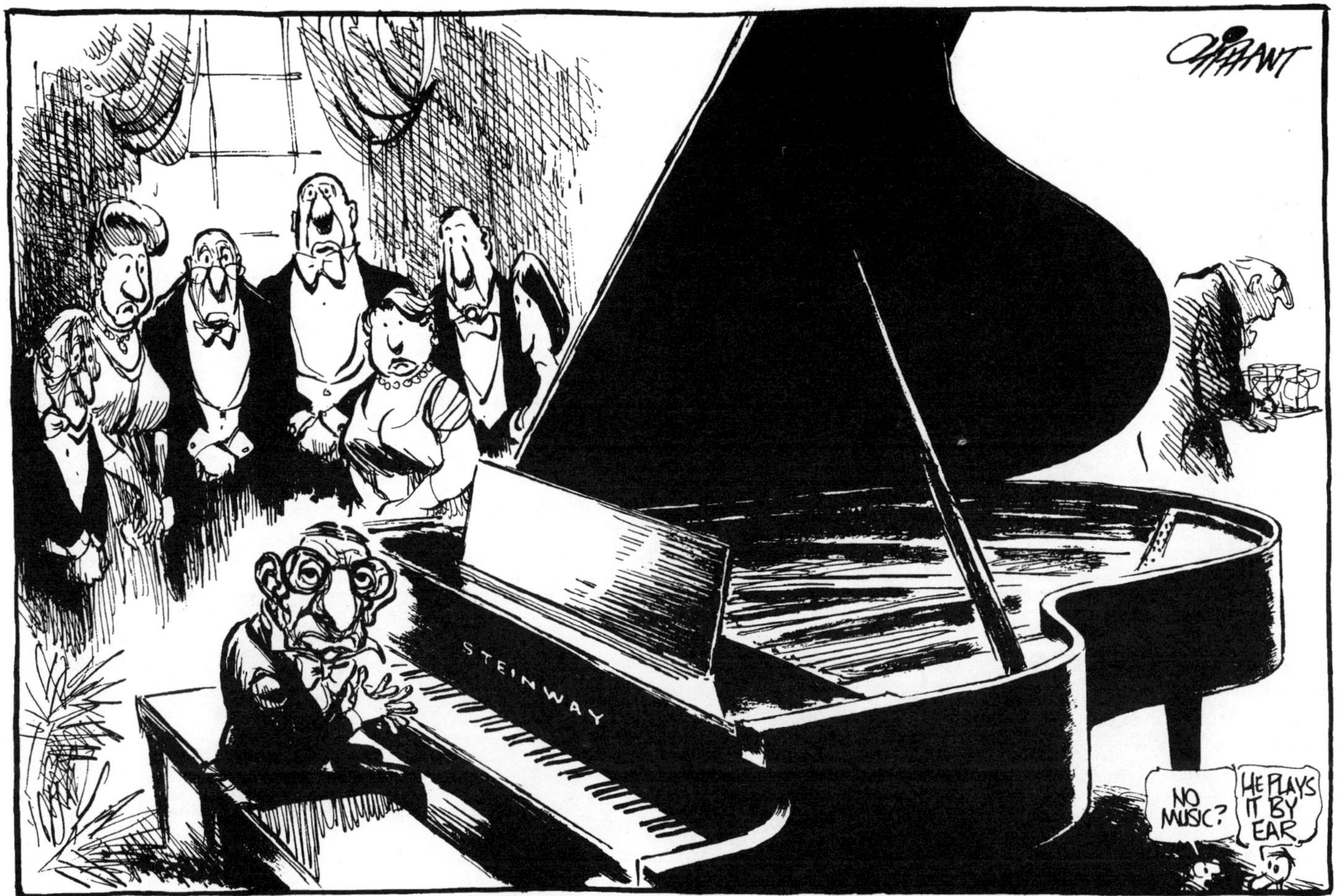
STEINWAY
NO MUSIC?
HE PLAYS IT BY EAR.

WHEN ALAN GREENSPAN SAT DOWN AT THE PIANO, ALL IRRATIONAL EXUBERANCE CEASED.

April 1, 1997

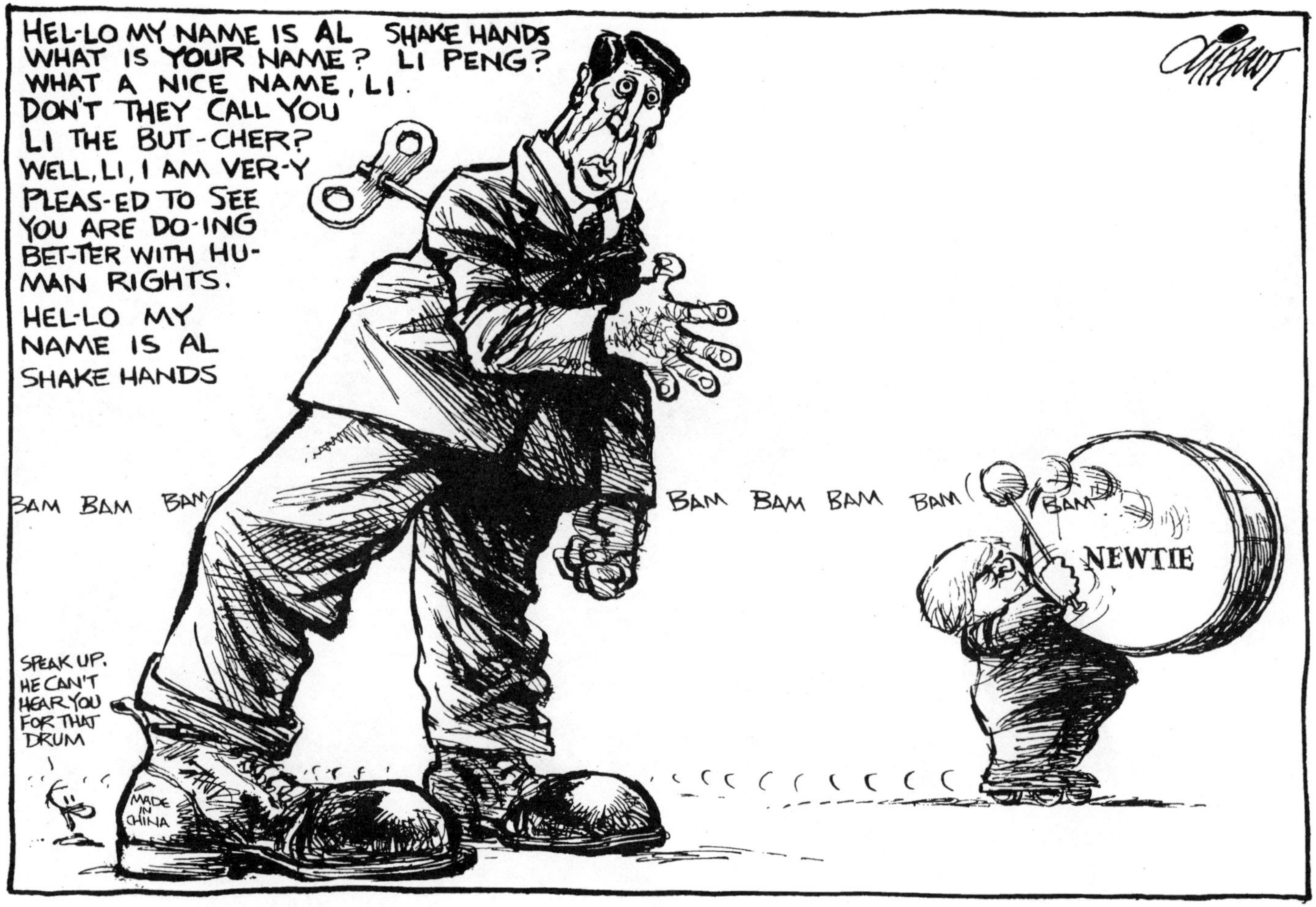
HEL-LO MY NAME IS AL SHAKE HANDS
WHAT IS YOUR NAME? LI PENG?
WHAT A NICE NAME, LI.
DON'T THEY CALL YOU
LI THE BUT-CHER?
WELL, LI, I AM VER-Y
PLEAS-ED TO SEE
YOU ARE DO-ING
BET-TER WITH HU-
MAN RIGHTS.
HEL-LO MY
NAME IS AL
SHAKE HANDS
BAM BAM BAM
BAM BAM BAM BAM BAM
NEWTIE
MADE IN CHINA
SPEAK UP. HE CAN'T HEAR YOU FOR THAT DRUM

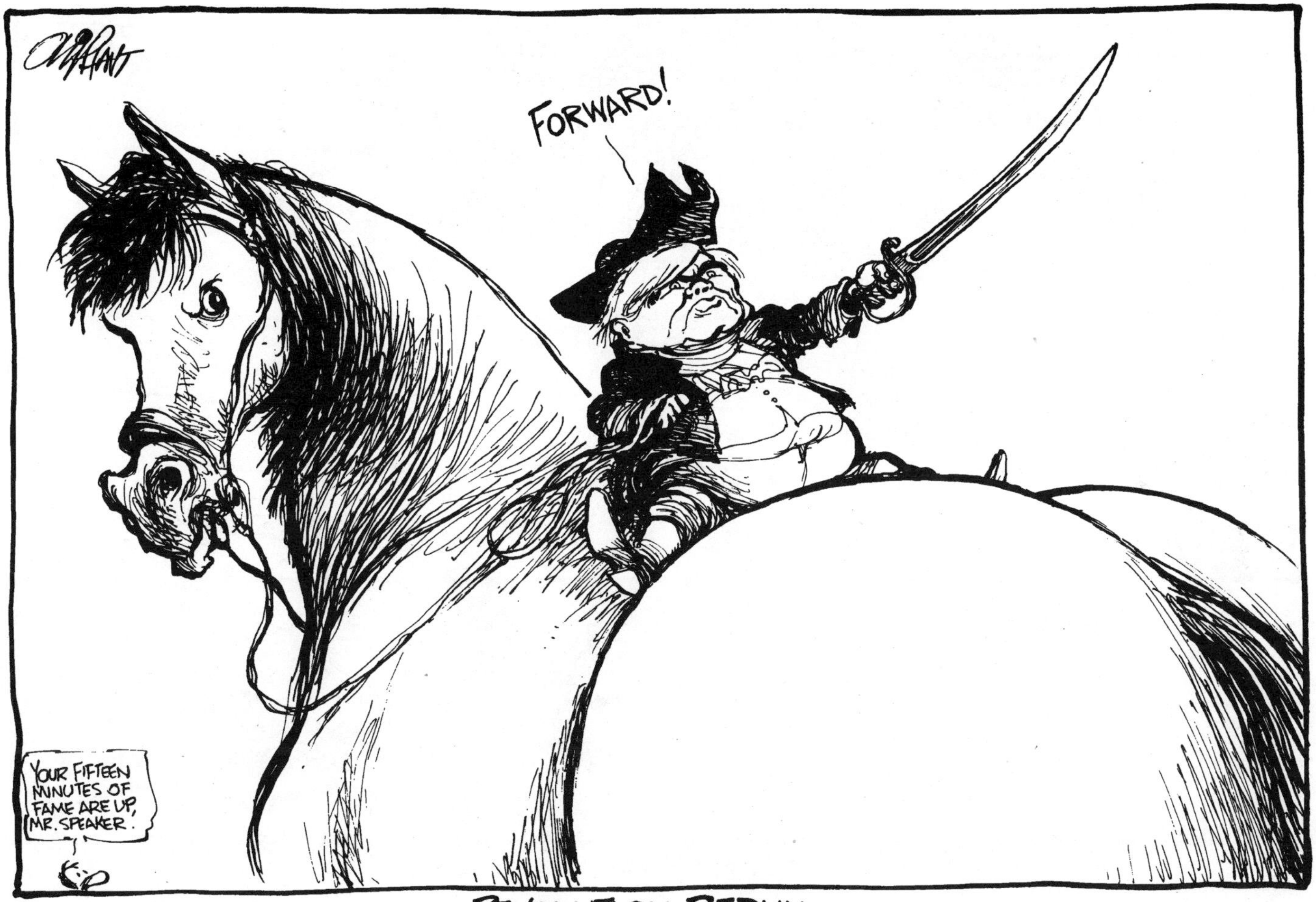
OLIPHANT
FORWARD!
YOUR FIFTEEN MINUTES OF FAME ARE UP, MR. SPEAKER.

REVOLUTION REDUX.

April 14, 1997

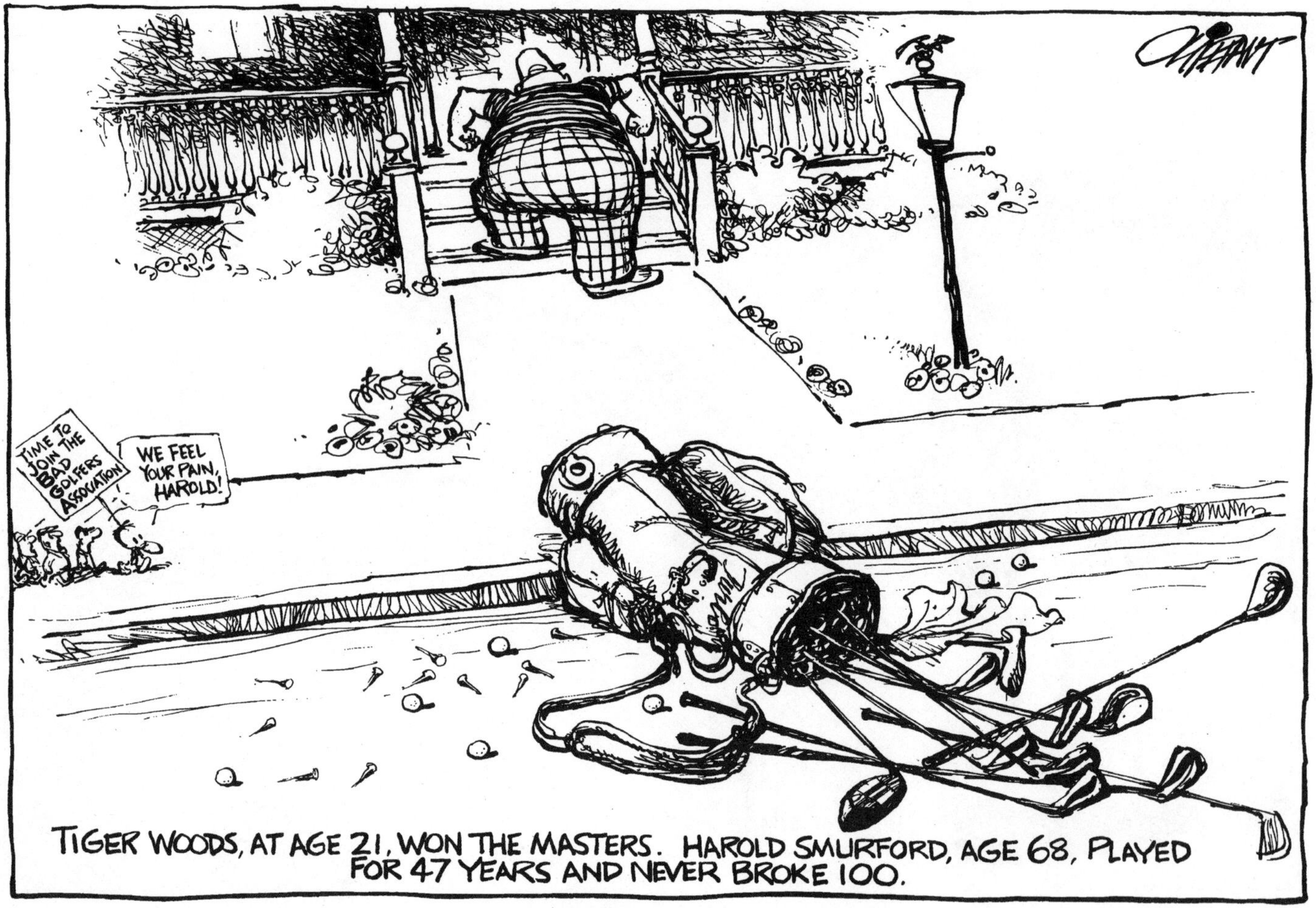
TIME TO JOIN THE BAD GOLFERS ASSOCIATION
WE FEEL YOUR PAIN, HAROLD!
TIGER WOODS, AT AGE 21, WON THE MASTERS. HAROLD SMURFORD, AGE 68, PLAYED FOR 47 YEARS AND NEVER BROKE 100.

April 15, 1997

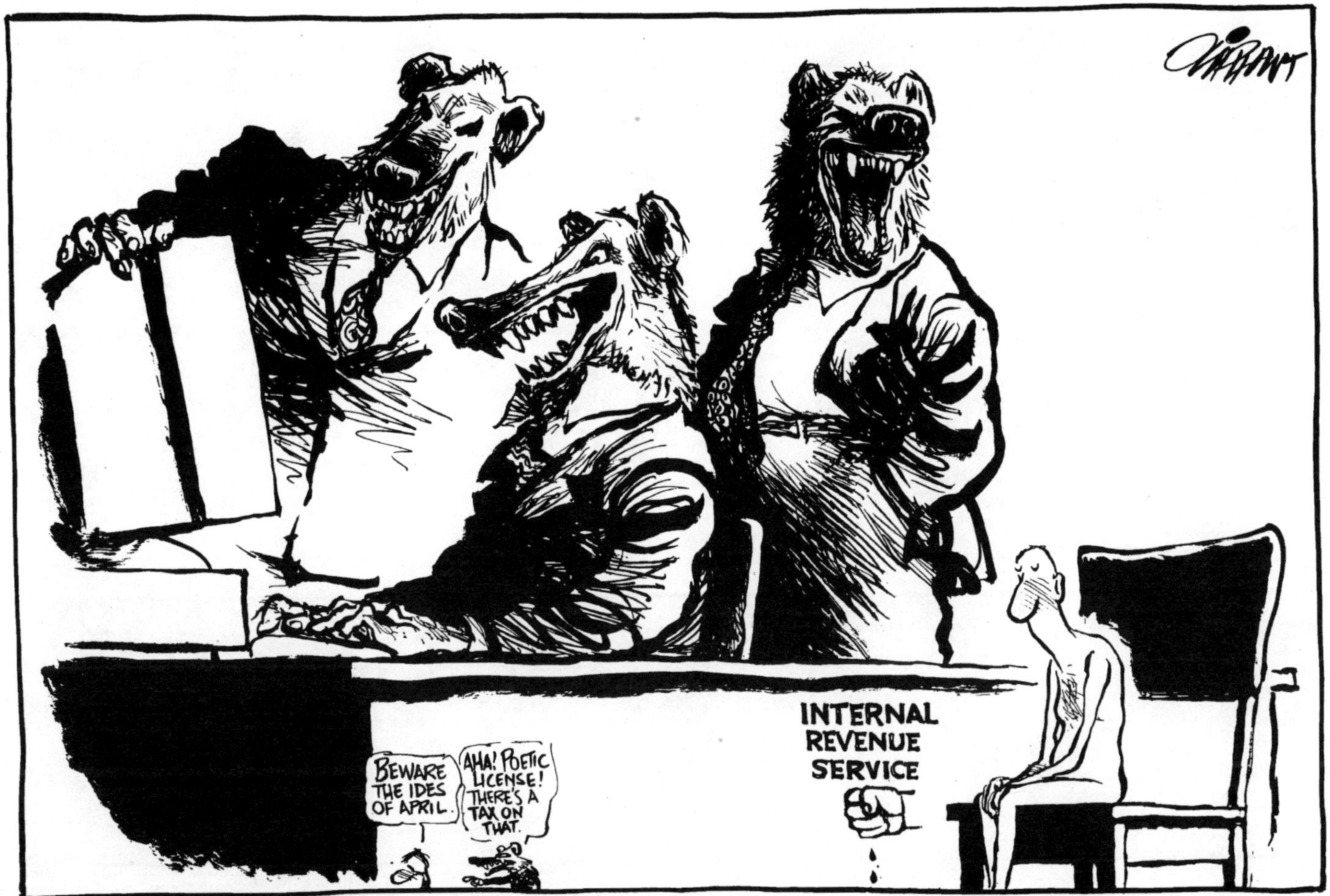
INTERNAL
REVENUE
SERVICE
BEWARE THE IDES OF APRIL.
AHA! POETIC LICENSE! THERE'S A TAX ON THAT.

'WELL, WHAT TH' HECK, WE'VE HAD ENOUGH FUN WITH YOUR RETURN... NOW WE'RE GOING TO RUIN YOU.'

April 16, 1997

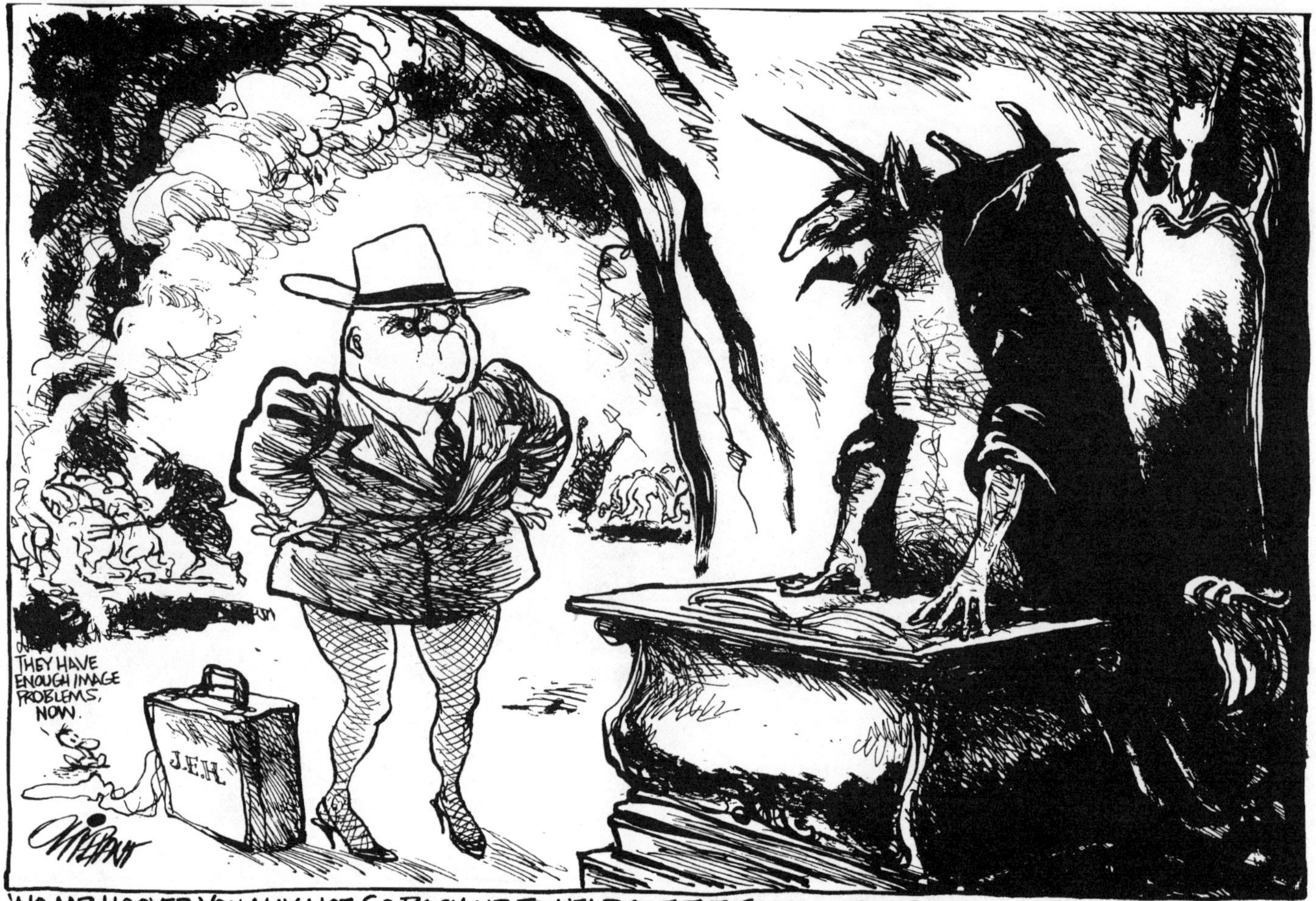
THEY HAVE ENOUGH IMAGE PROBLEMS, NOW.
J.E.H.

'NO, MR. HOOVER, YOU MAY NOT GO BACK UP TO HELP OUT THE GUYS IN THE SCIENCE LAB — THEY'LL BE DOWN TO JOIN YOU SHORTLY, ANYWAY.'

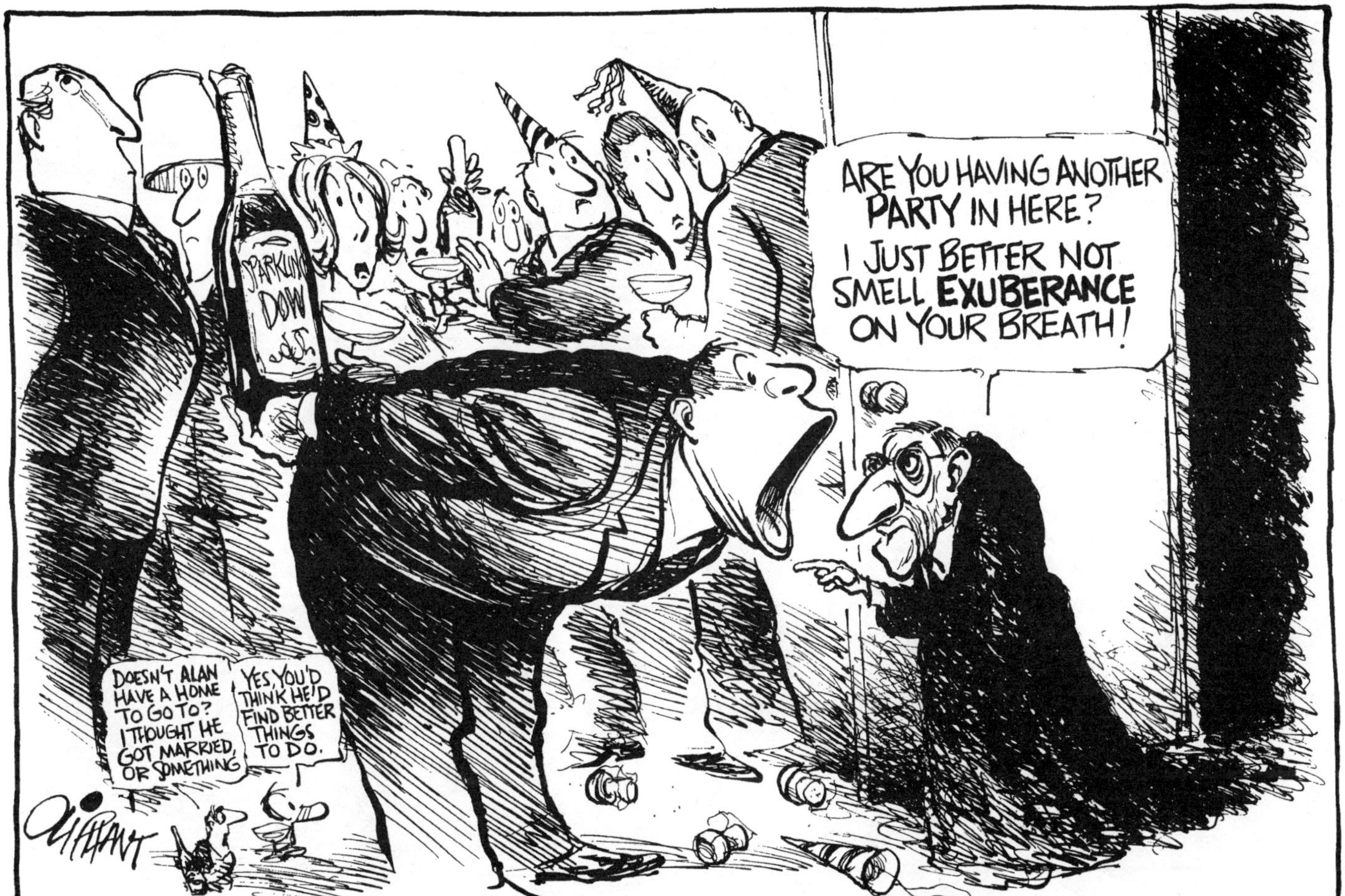
ARE YOU HAVING ANOTHER PARTY IN HERE? I JUST BETTER NOT SMELL EXUBERANCE ON YOUR BREATH!
DOESN'T ALAN HAVE A HOME TO GO TO? I THOUGHT HE GOT MARRIED, OR SOMETHING
YES, YOU'D THINK HE'D FIND BETTER THINGS TO DO.
SPARKLING DOW

THE RETURN OF THE LIFE OF THE PARTY.

April 28, 1997

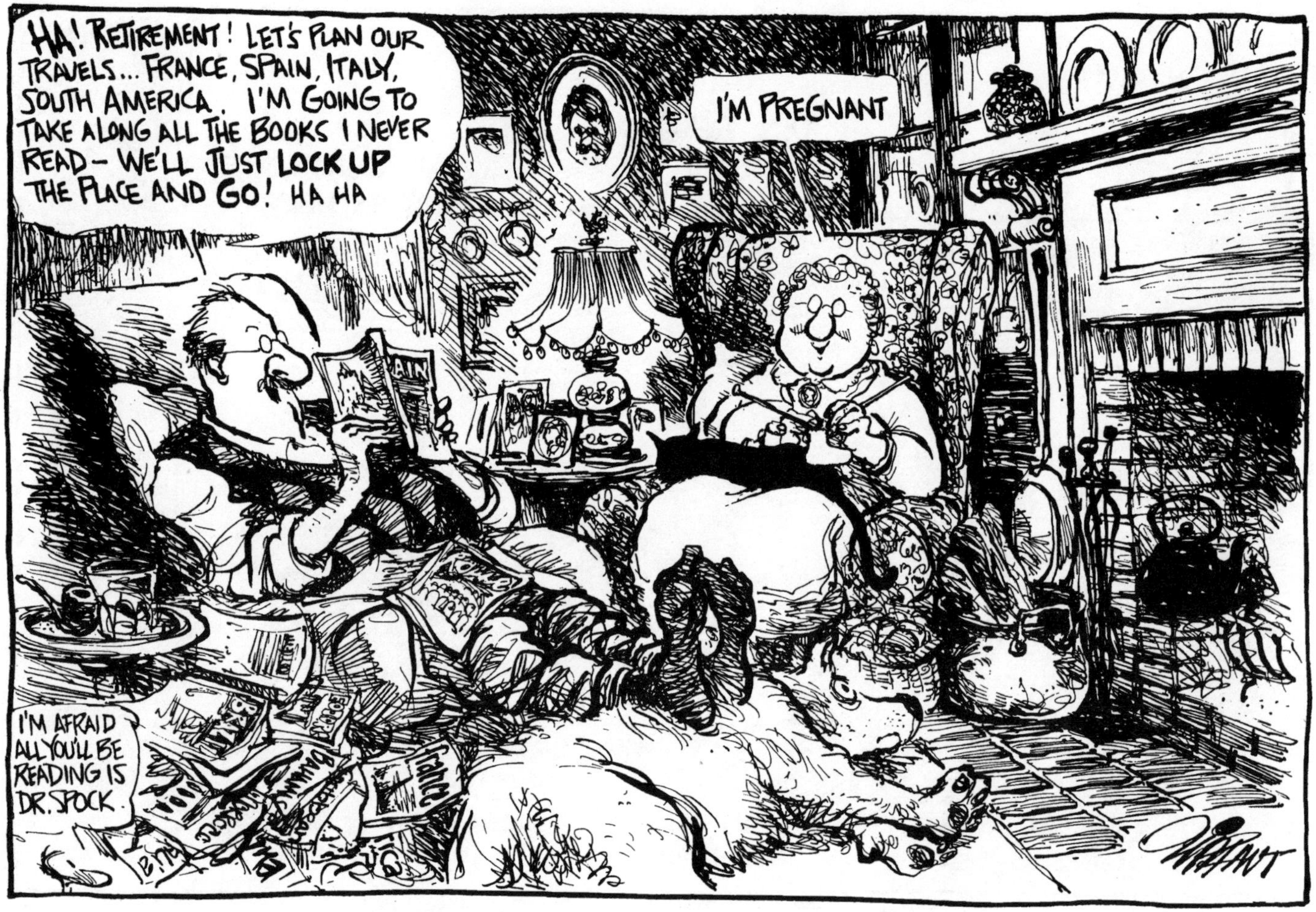
HA! RETIREMENT! LET'S PLAN OUR TRAVELS... FRANCE, SPAIN, ITALY, SOUTH AMERICA. I'M GOING TO TAKE ALONG ALL THE BOOKS I NEVER READ - WE'LL JUST LOCK UP THE PLACE AND GO! HA HA
I'M PREGNANT
I'M AFRAID ALL YOU'LL BE READING IS DR. SPOCK.

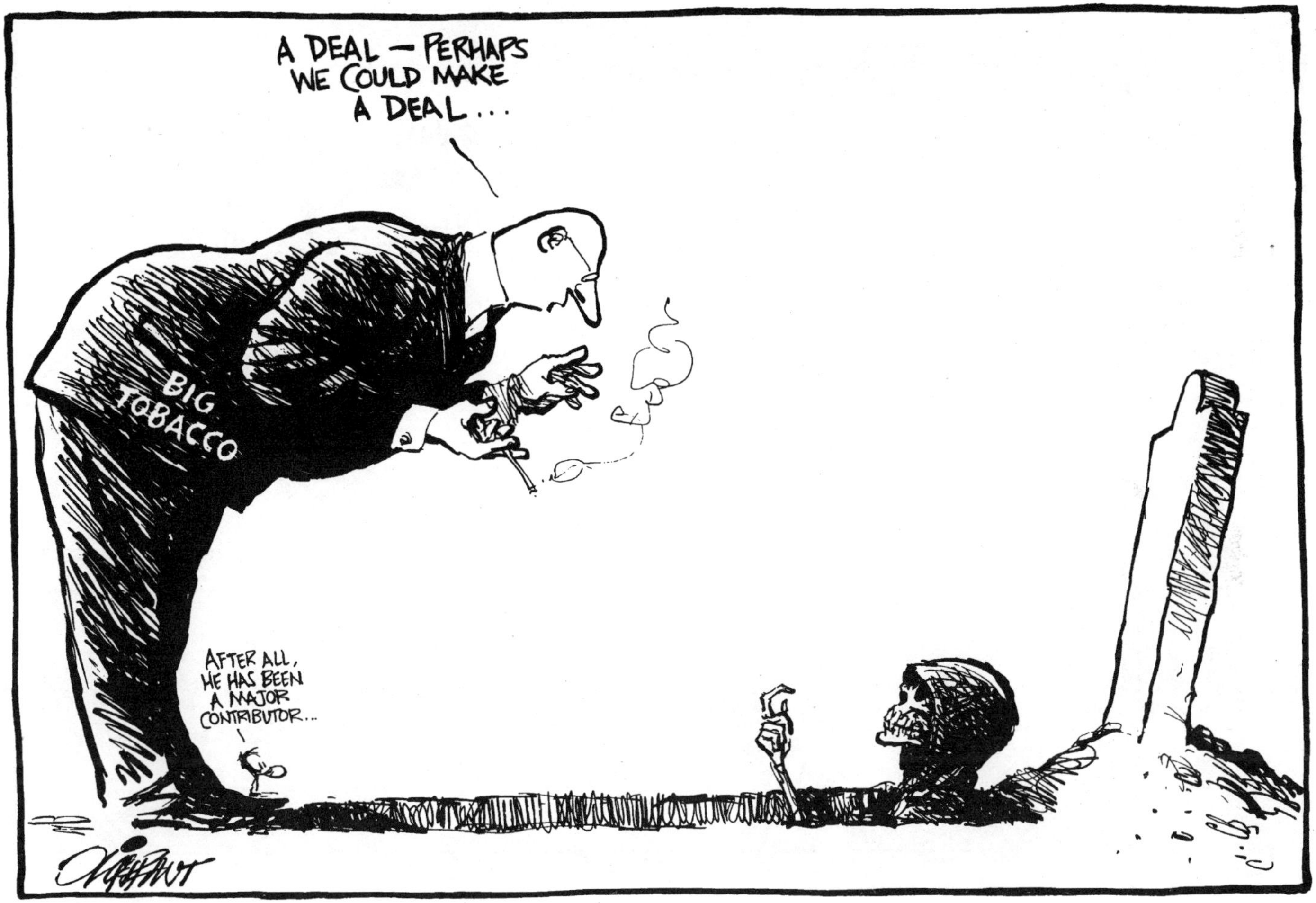
A DEAL — PERHAPS WE COULD MAKE A DEAL...
BIG TOBACCO
AFTER ALL, HE HAS BEEN A MAJOR CONTRIBUTOR...
OLIPHANT

May 8, 1997

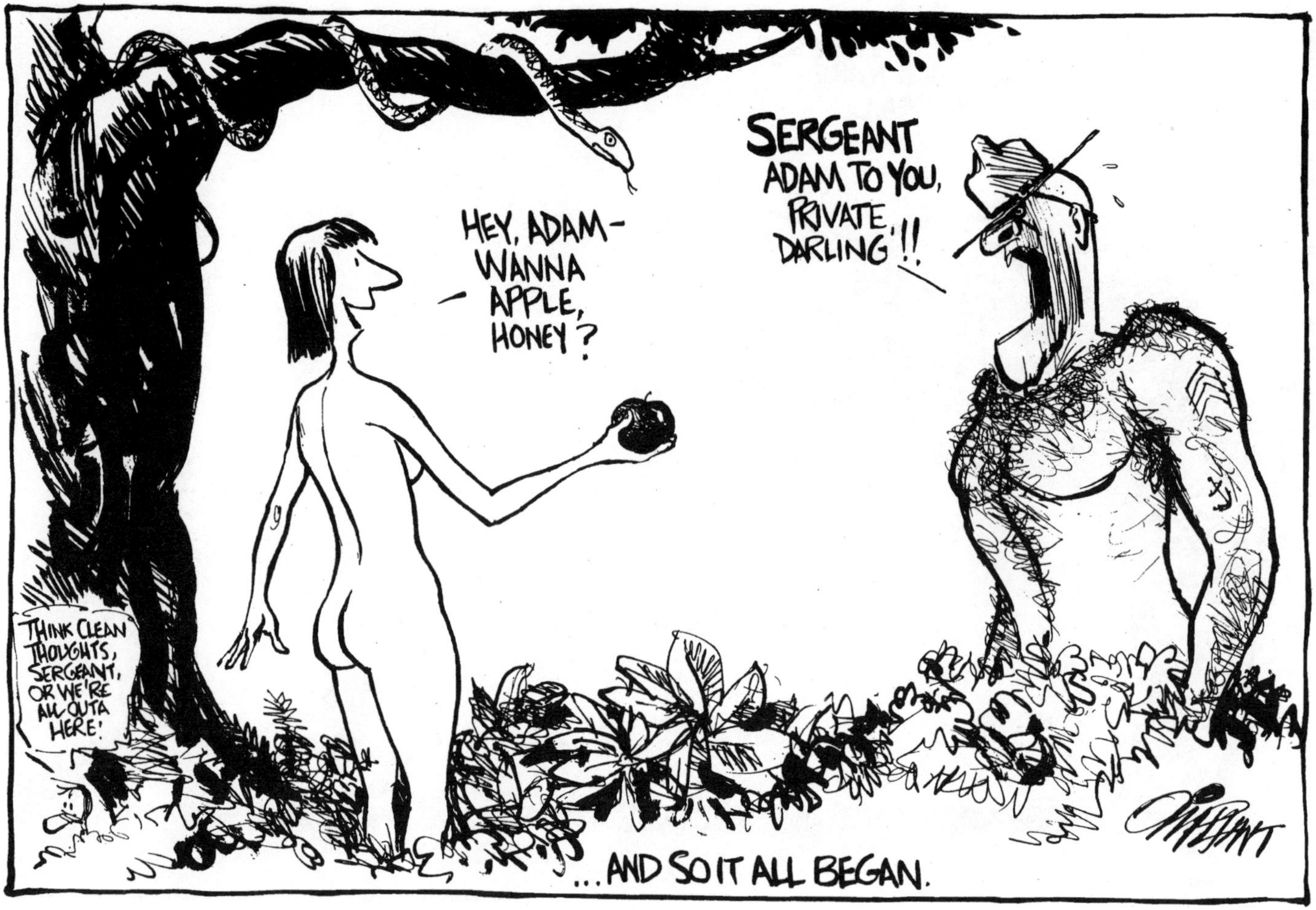
HEY, ADAM-
WANNA
APPLE,
HONEY?
SERGEANT
ADAM TO YOU,
PRIVATE,
DARLING!!
THINK CLEAN
THOUGHTS,
SERGEANT,
OR WE'RE
ALL OUTA
HERE!
...AND SO IT ALL BEGAN.

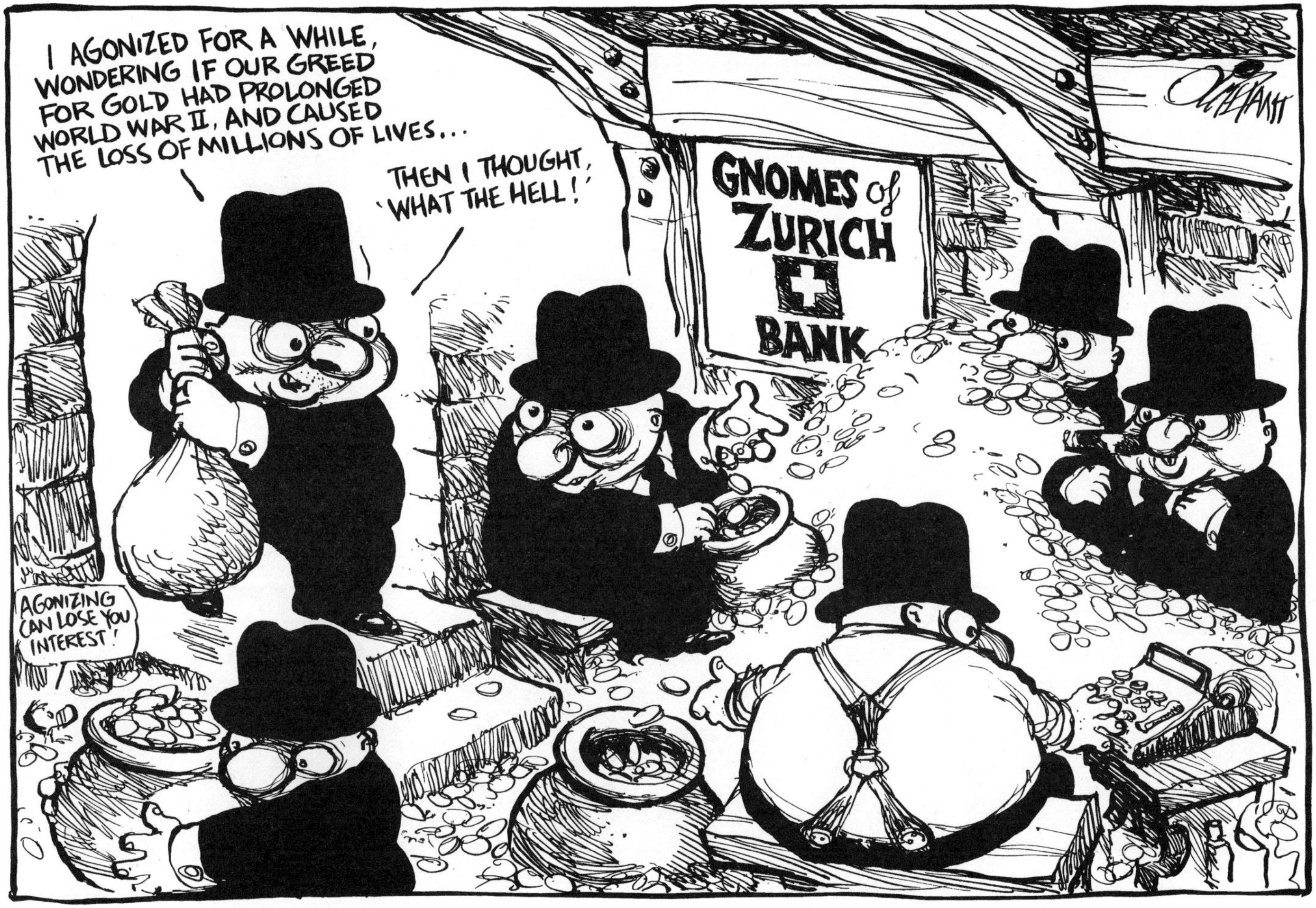
I AGONIZED FOR A WHILE, WONDERING IF OUR GREED FOR GOLD HAD PROLONGED WORLD WAR II, AND CAUSED THE LOSS OF MILLIONS OF LIVES...
THEN I THOUGHT, 'WHAT THE HELL!'
GNOMES of ZURICH BANK
AGONIZING CAN LOSE YOU INTEREST!

May 29, 1997

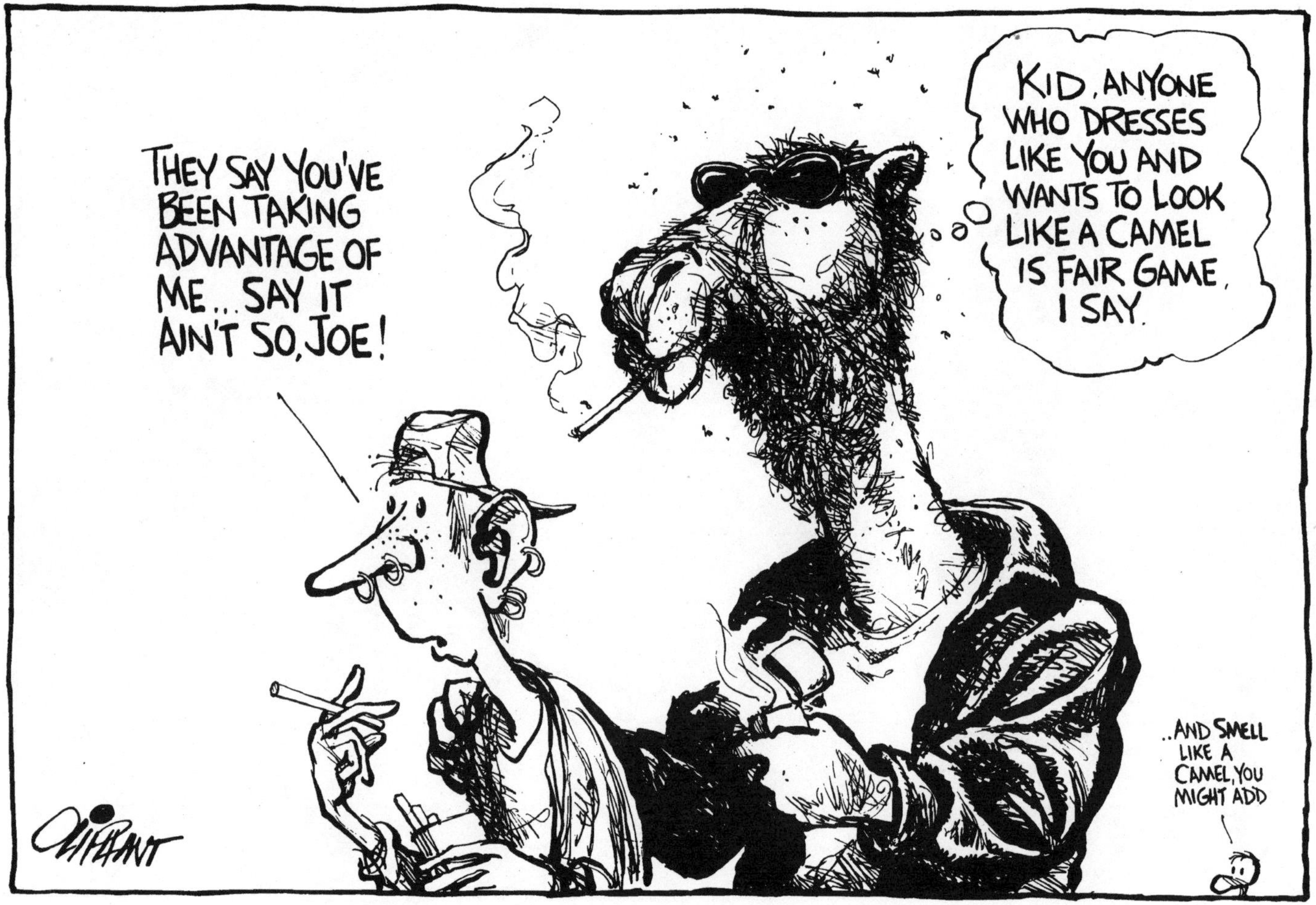
THEY SAY YOU'VE BEEN TAKING ADVANTAGE OF ME... SAY IT AIN'T SO, JOE!
KID, ANYONE WHO DRESSES LIKE YOU AND WANTS TO LOOK LIKE A CAMEL IS FAIR GAME, I SAY.
..AND SMELL LIKE A CAMEL, YOU MIGHT ADD
OLIPHANT

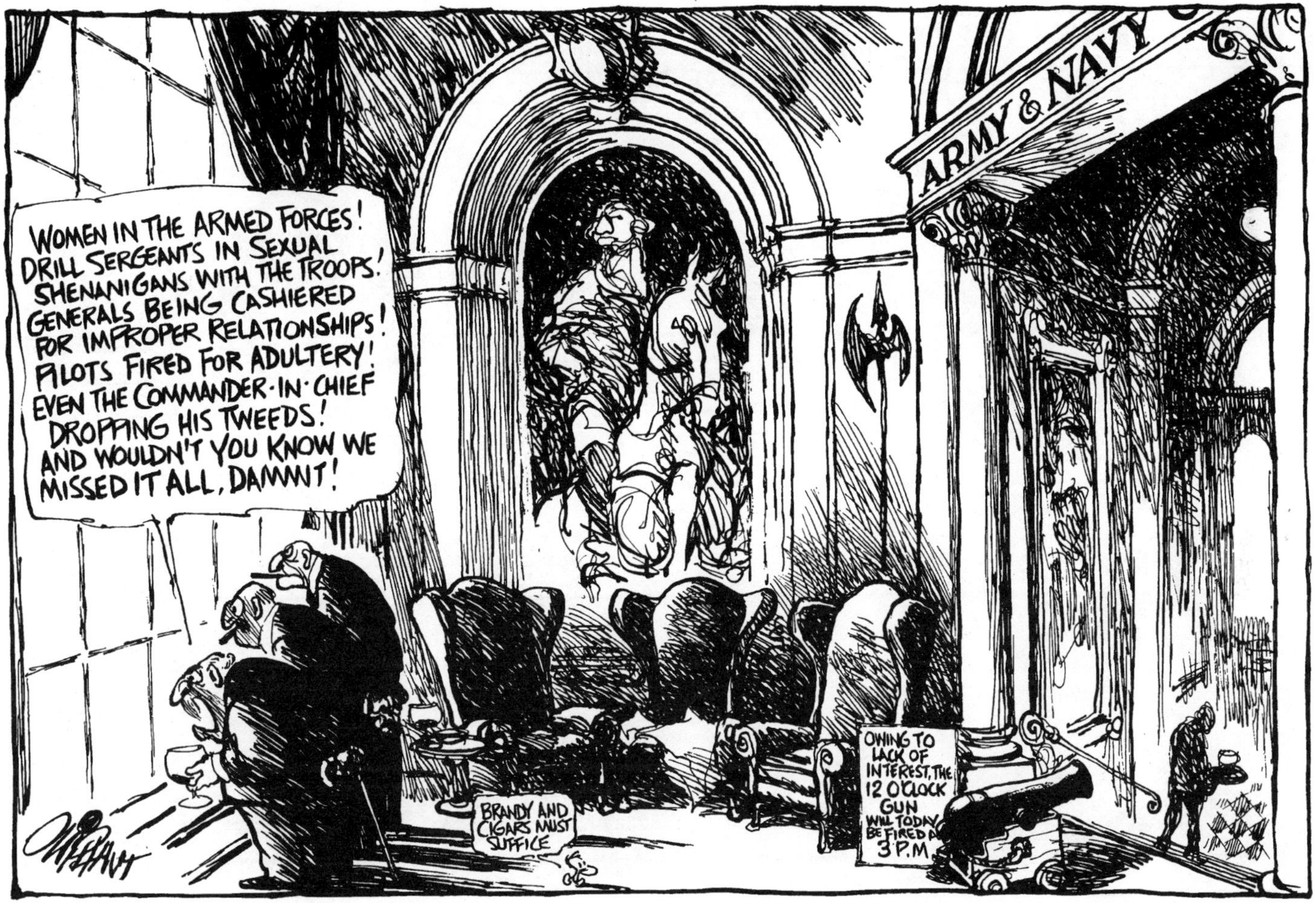
ARMY & NAVY
WOMEN IN THE ARMED FORCES! DRILL SERGEANTS IN SEXUAL SHENANIGANS WITH THE TROOPS! GENERALS BEING CASHIERED FOR IMPROPER RELATIONSHIPS! PILOTS FIRED FOR ADULTERY! EVEN THE COMMANDER-IN-CHIEF DROPPING HIS TWEEDS! AND WOULDN'T YOU KNOW WE MISSED IT ALL, DAMMIT!
BRANDY AND CIGARS MUST SUFFICE
OWING TO LACK OF INTEREST, THE 12 O'CLOCK GUN WILL TODAY BE FIRED A 3 P.M

June 2, 1997

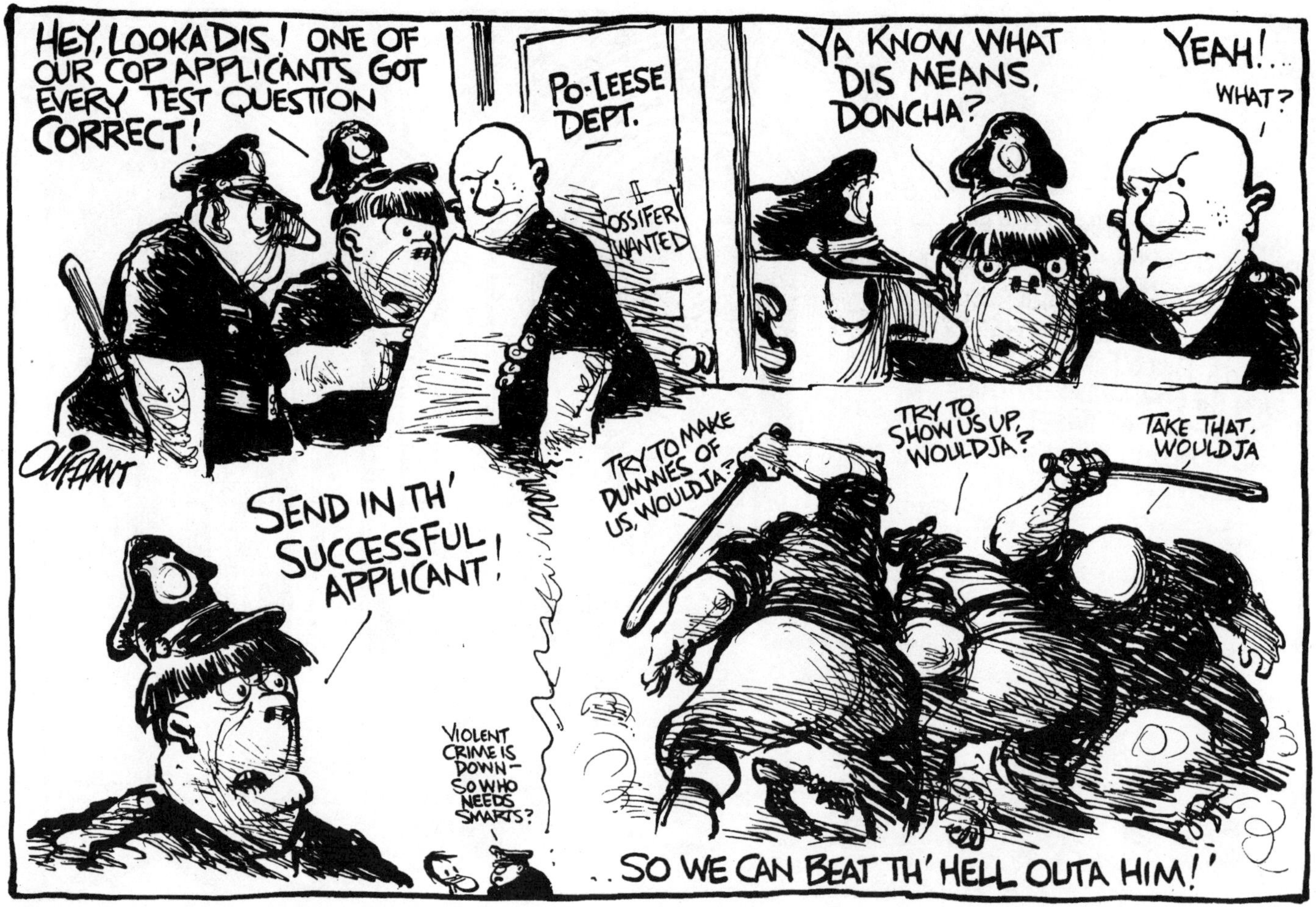
HEY, LOOKA DIS! ONE OF OUR COP APPLICANTS GOT EVERY TEST QUESTION CORRECT!
PO-LEESE DEPT.
OSSIFER WANTED
YA KNOW WHAT DIS MEANS, DONCHA?
YEAH!...
WHAT?
OLIPHANT
SEND IN TH' SUCCESSFUL APPLICANT!
TRY TO MAKE DUMMIES OF US, WOULDJA?
TRY TO SHOW US UP, WOULDJA?
TAKE THAT, WOULDJA
VIOLENT CRIME IS DOWN- SO WHO NEEDS SMARTS?
..SO WE CAN BEAT TH' HELL OUTA HIM!"

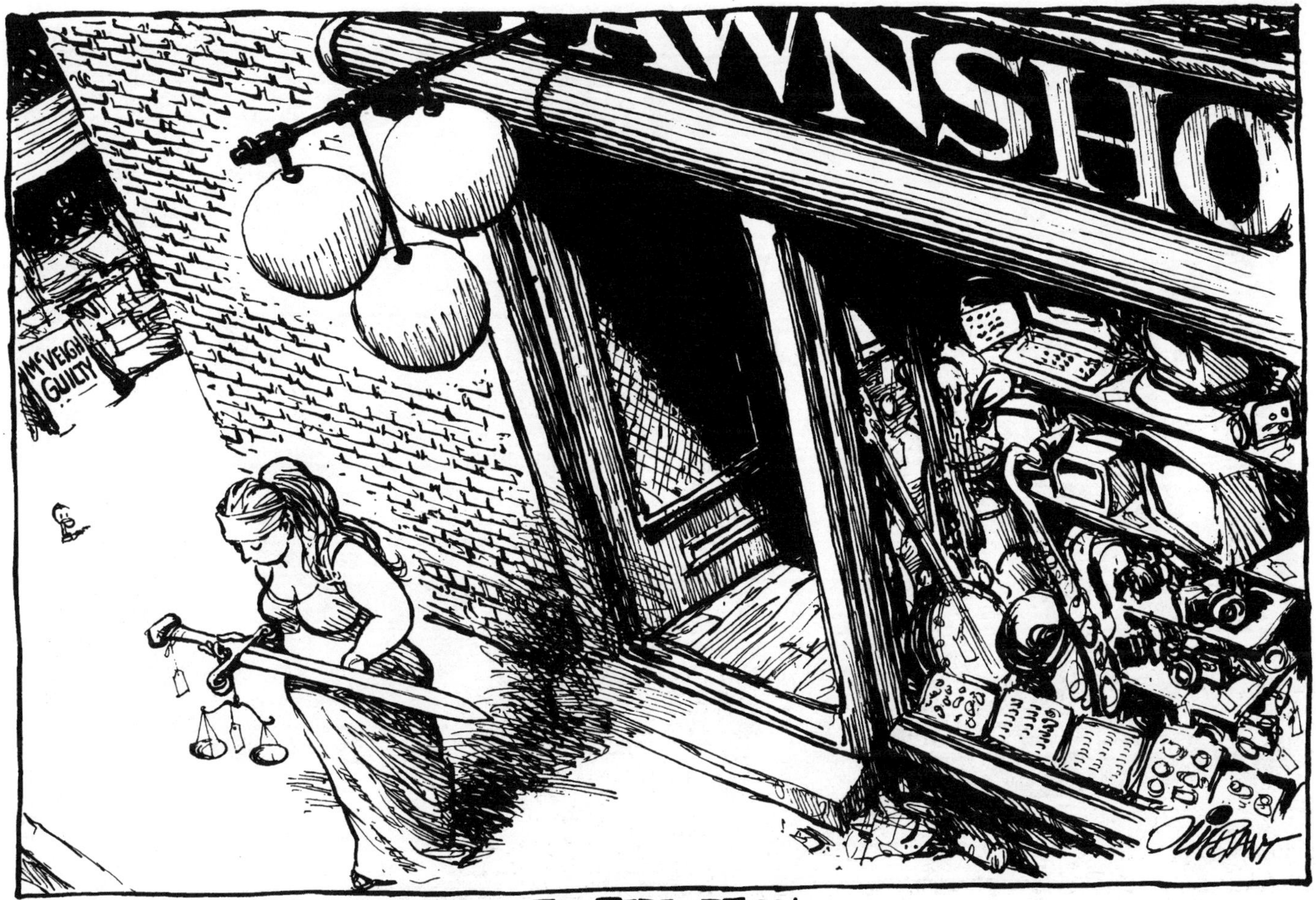
AWNSHO
McVEIGH GUILTY

THE REDEMPTION.

June 4, 1997

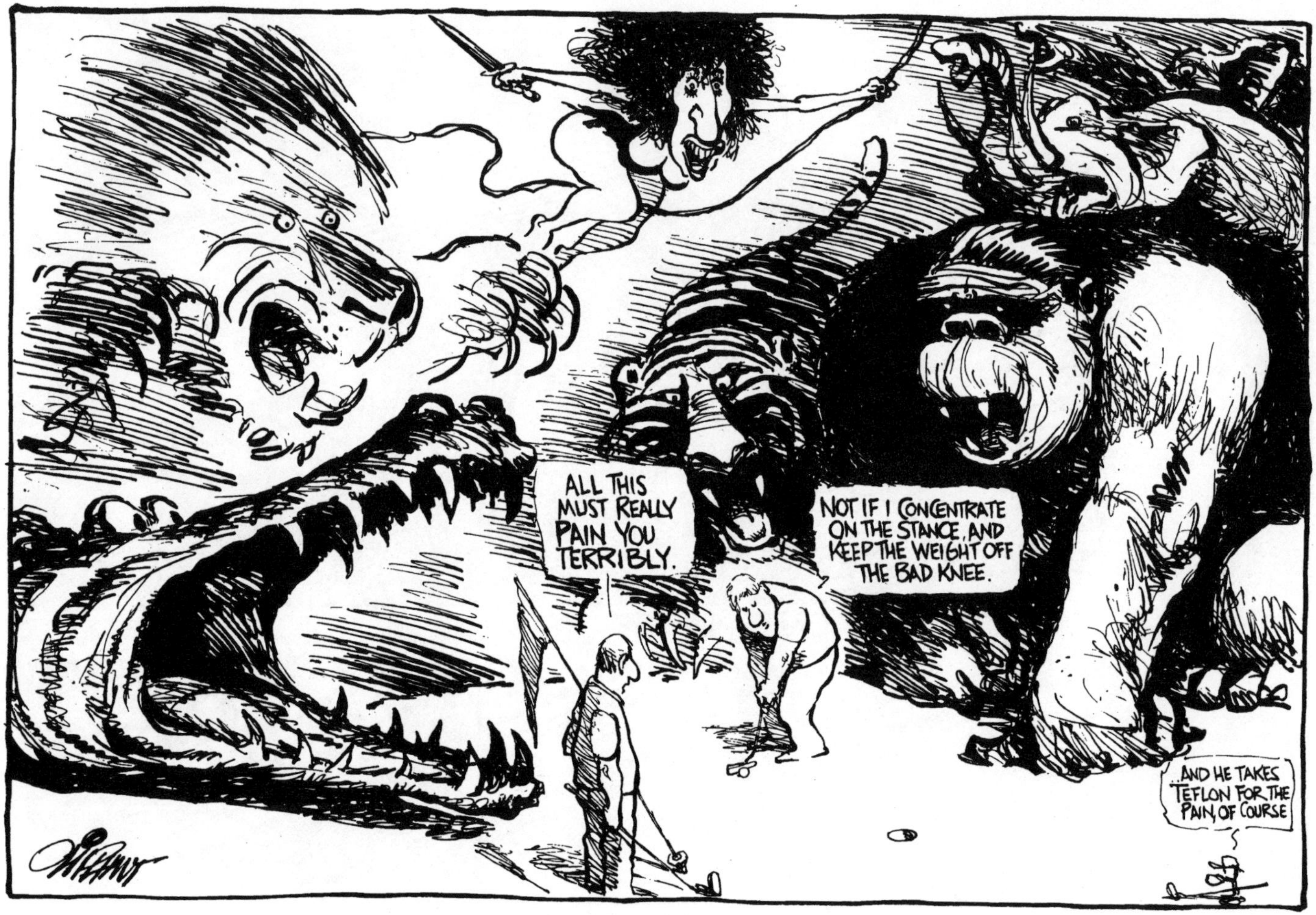

ALL THIS MUST REALLY PAIN YOU TERRIBLY.
NOT IF I CONCENTRATE ON THE STANCE, AND KEEP THE WEIGHT OFF THE BAD KNEE.
AND HE TAKES TEFLON FOR THE PAIN, OF COURSE

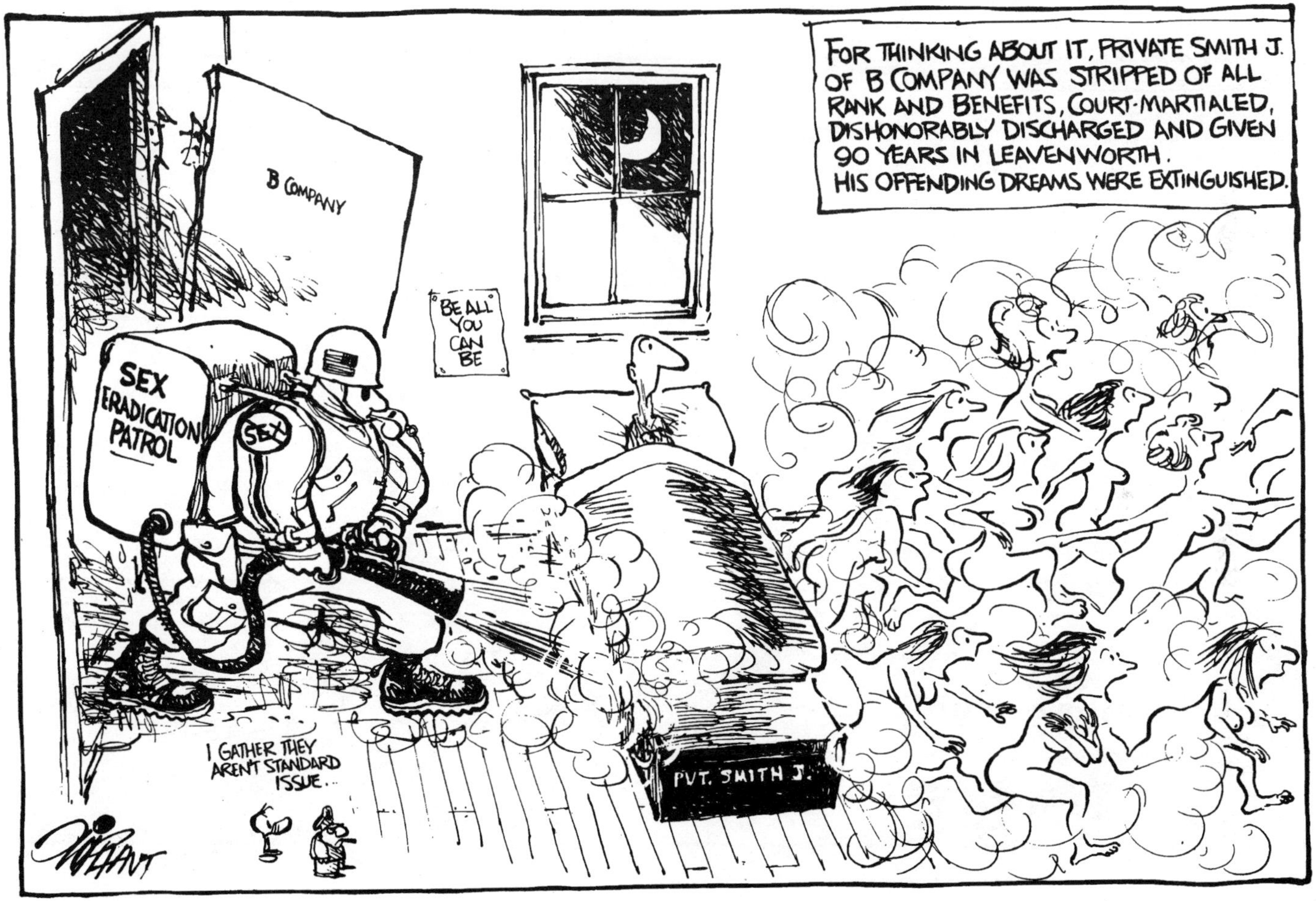
FOR THINKING ABOUT IT, PRIVATE SMITH J. OF B COMPANY WAS STRIPPED OF ALL RANK AND BENEFITS, COURT-MARTIALED, DISHONORABLY DISCHARGED AND GIVEN 90 YEARS IN LEAVENWORTH.
HIS OFFENDING DREAMS WERE EXTINGUISHED.
B COMPANY
BE ALL YOU CAN BE
SEX ERADICATION PATROL
SEX
PVT. SMITH J.
I GATHER THEY AREN'T STANDARD ISSUE...

June 12, 1997

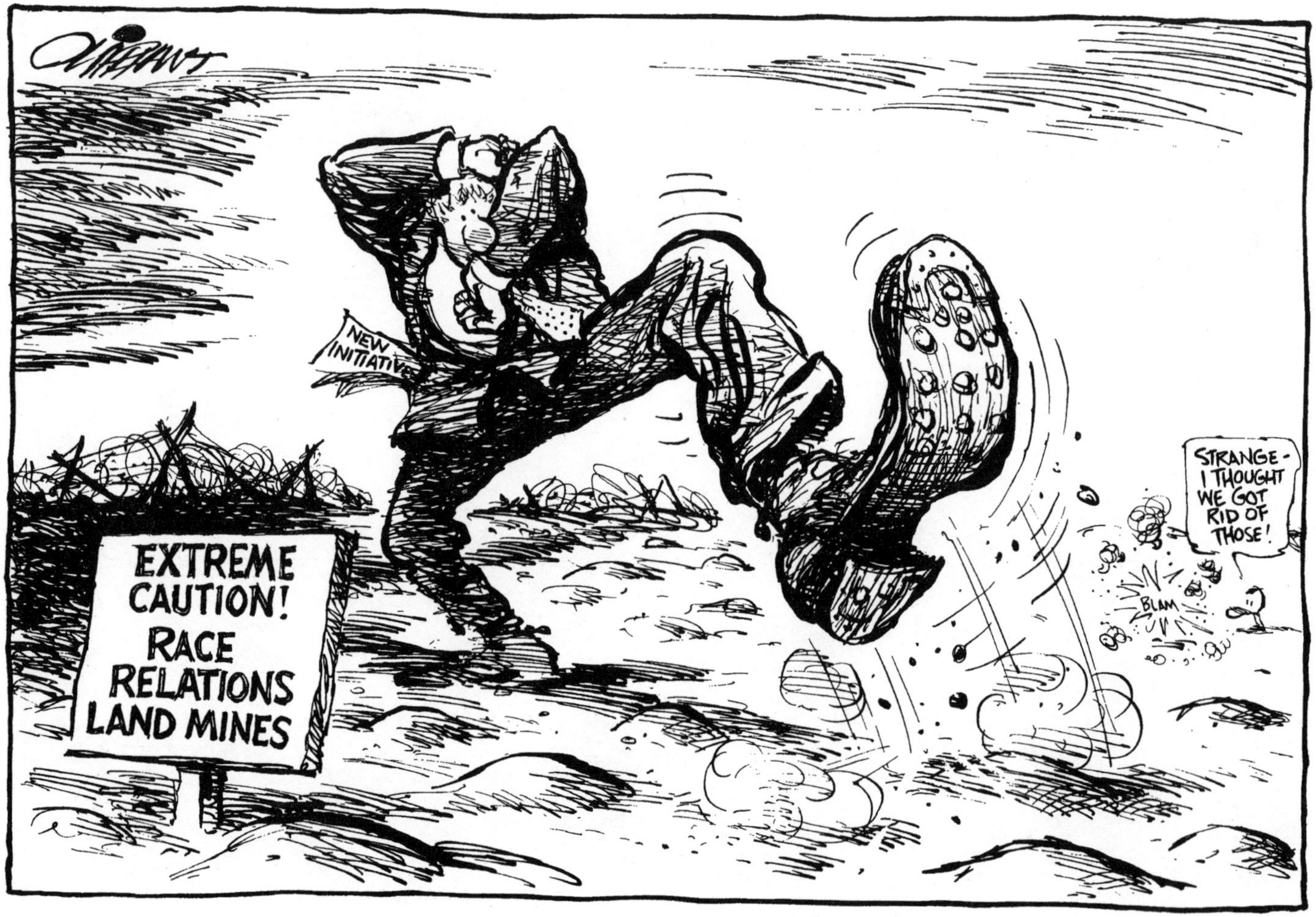
NEW INITIATIVE
EXTREME CAUTION!
RACE RELATIONS LAND MINES
STRANGE - I THOUGHT WE GOT RID OF THOSE!
BLAM

June 19, 1997

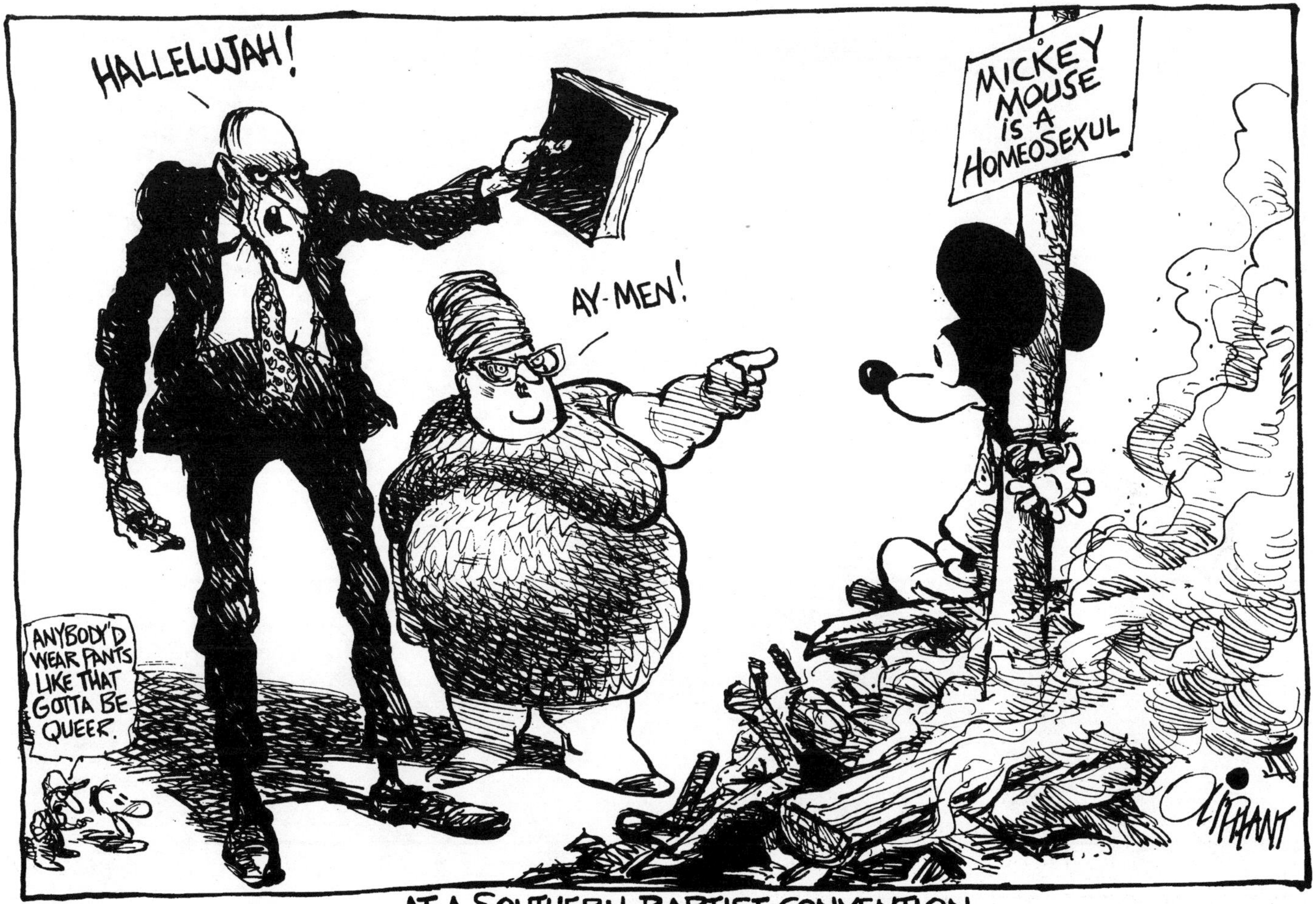
HALLELUJAH!
AY-MEN!
MICKEY MOUSE IS A HOMEOSEXUL
ANYBODY'D WEAR PANTS LIKE THAT GOTTA BE QUEER.
OLIPHANT

AT A SOUTHERN BAPTIST CONVENTION.

July 7, 1997

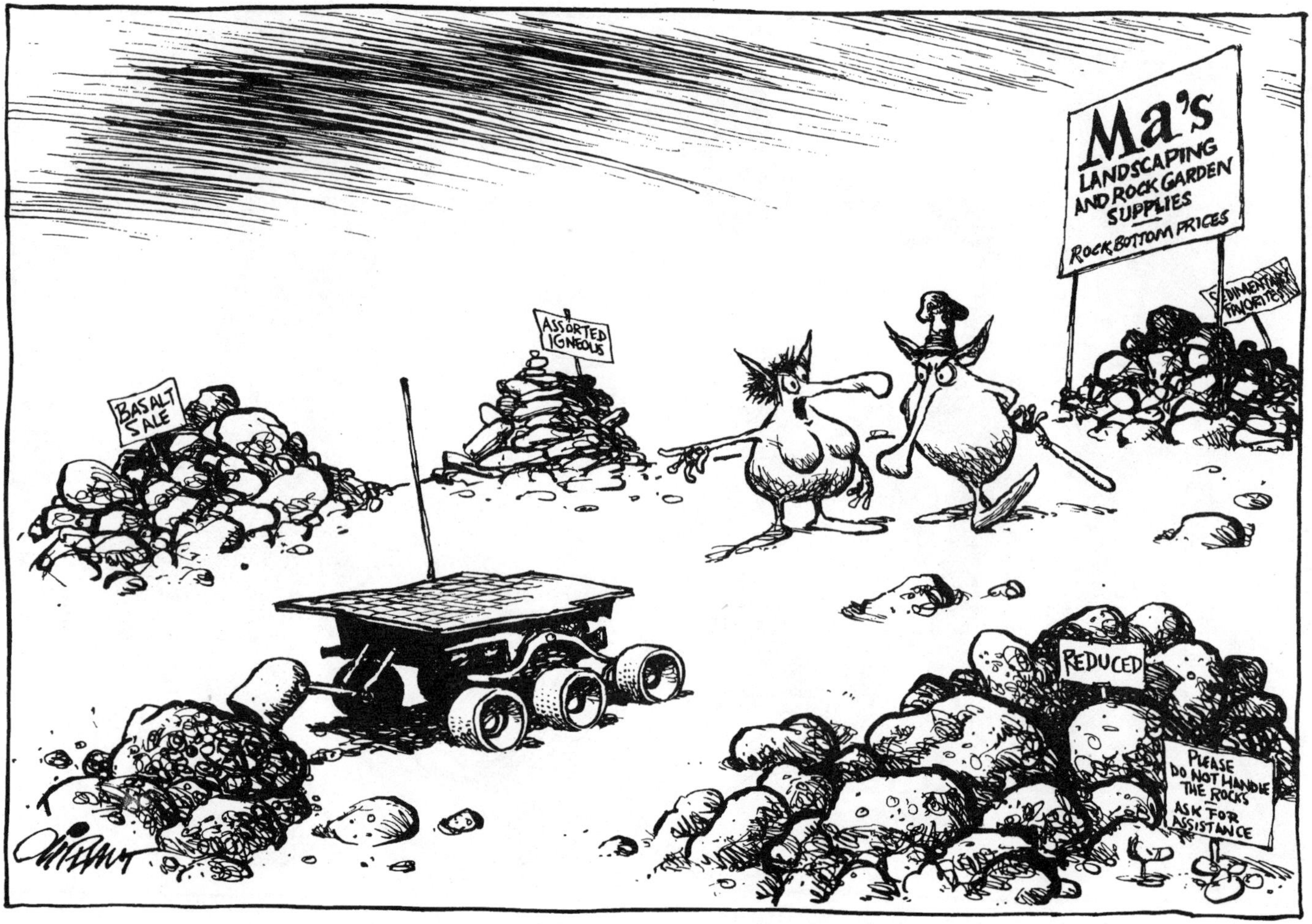
Ma's
LANDSCAPING AND ROCK GARDEN SUPPLIES
ROCK BOTTOM PRICES
SEDIMENTARY FAVORITES
ASSORTED IGNEOUS
BASALT SALE
REDUCED
PLEASE DO NOT HANDLE THE ROCKS
ASK FOR ASSISTANCE

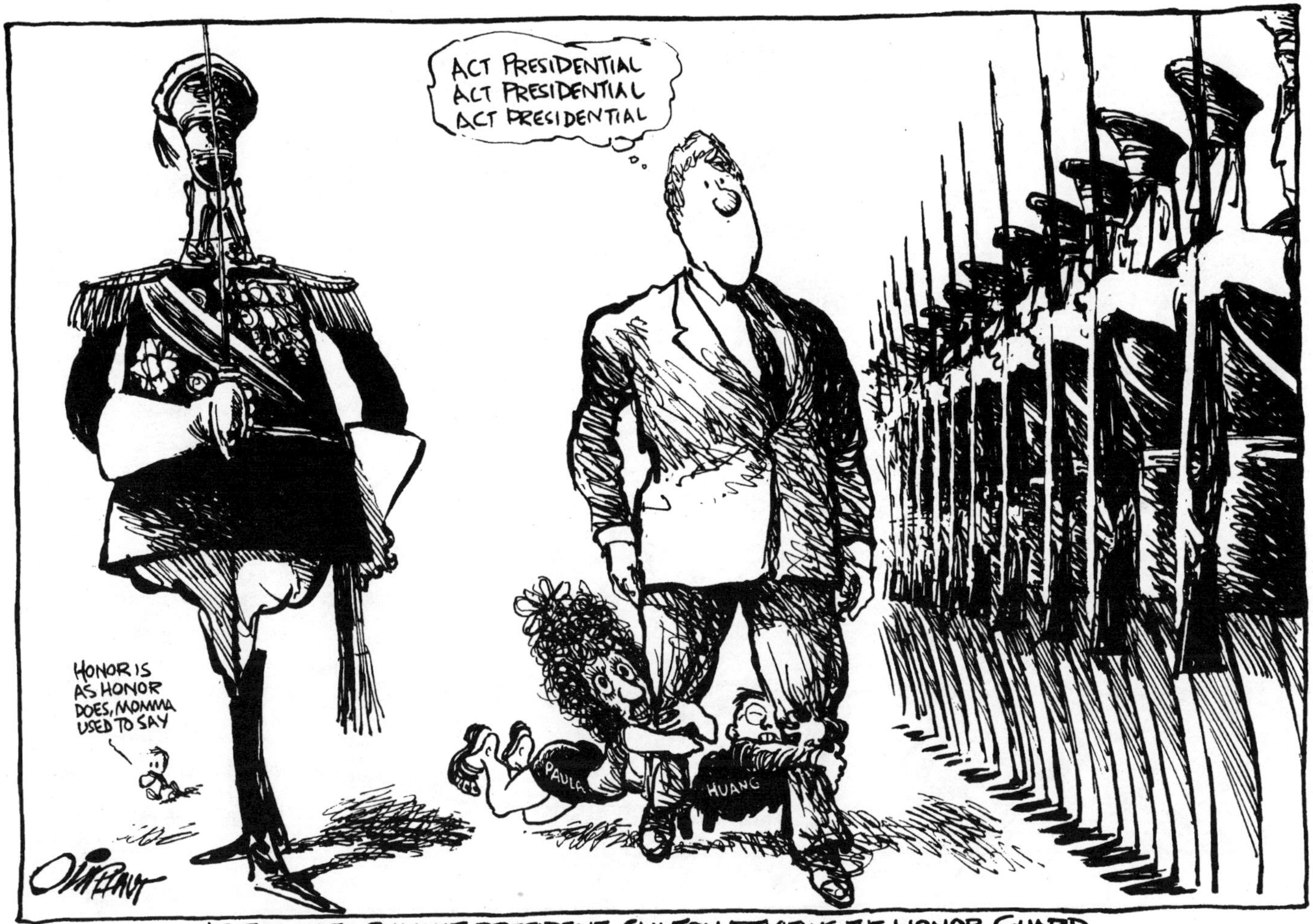
ACT PRESIDENTIAL
ACT PRESIDENTIAL
ACT PRESIDENTIAL
HONOR IS AS HONOR DOES, MOMMA USED TO SAY
PAULA
HUANG
OLIPHANT

AT THE NATO SUMMIT, PRESIDENT CLINTON REVIEWS THE HONOR GUARD...

July 16, 1997

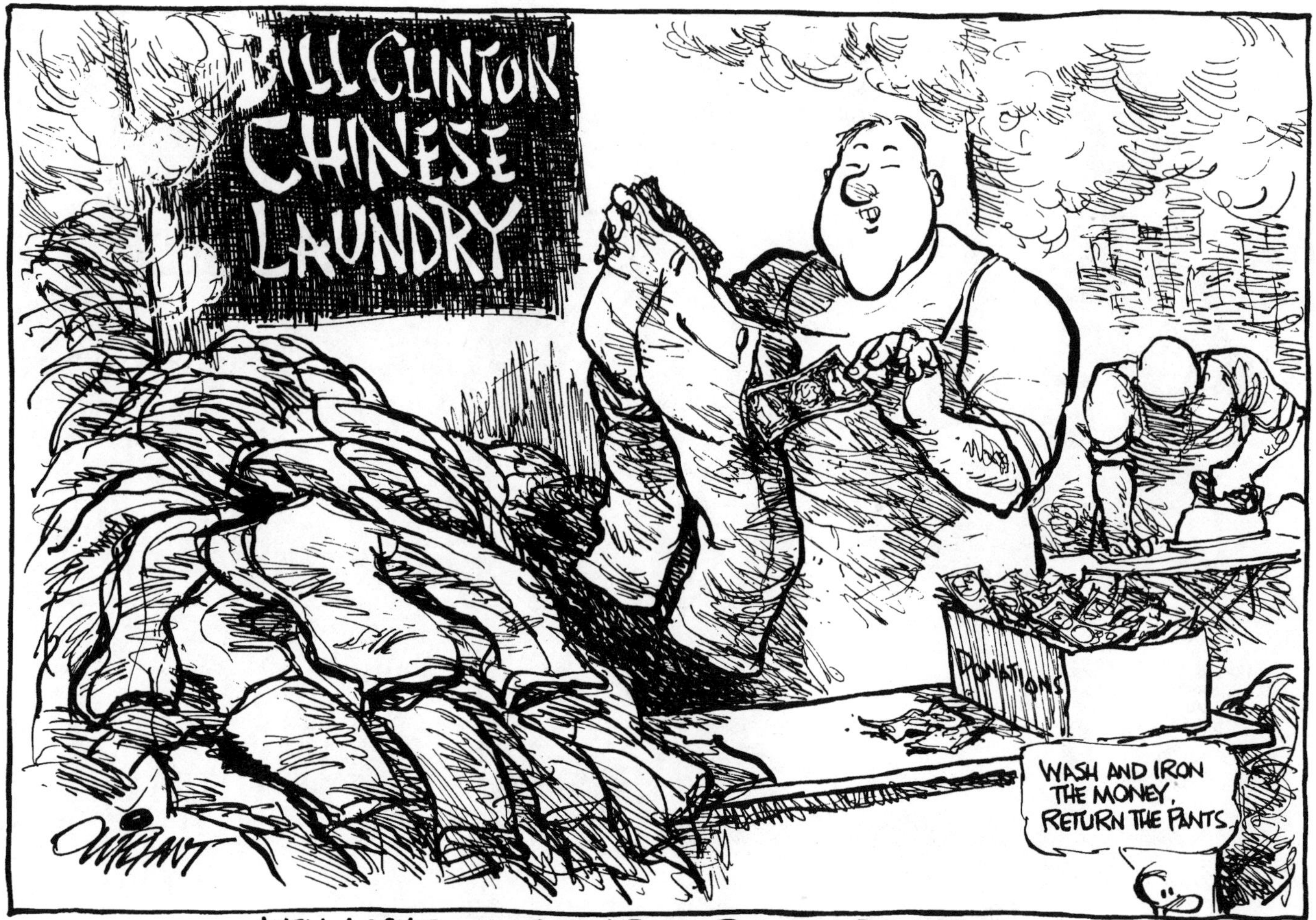
BILL CLINTON CHINESE LAUNDRY
DONATIONS
WASH AND IRON THE MONEY, RETURN THE PANTS
OLIPHANT

WELL, LOOKIE — IN EVERY PANTS POCKET, A DONATION...'

July 23, 1997

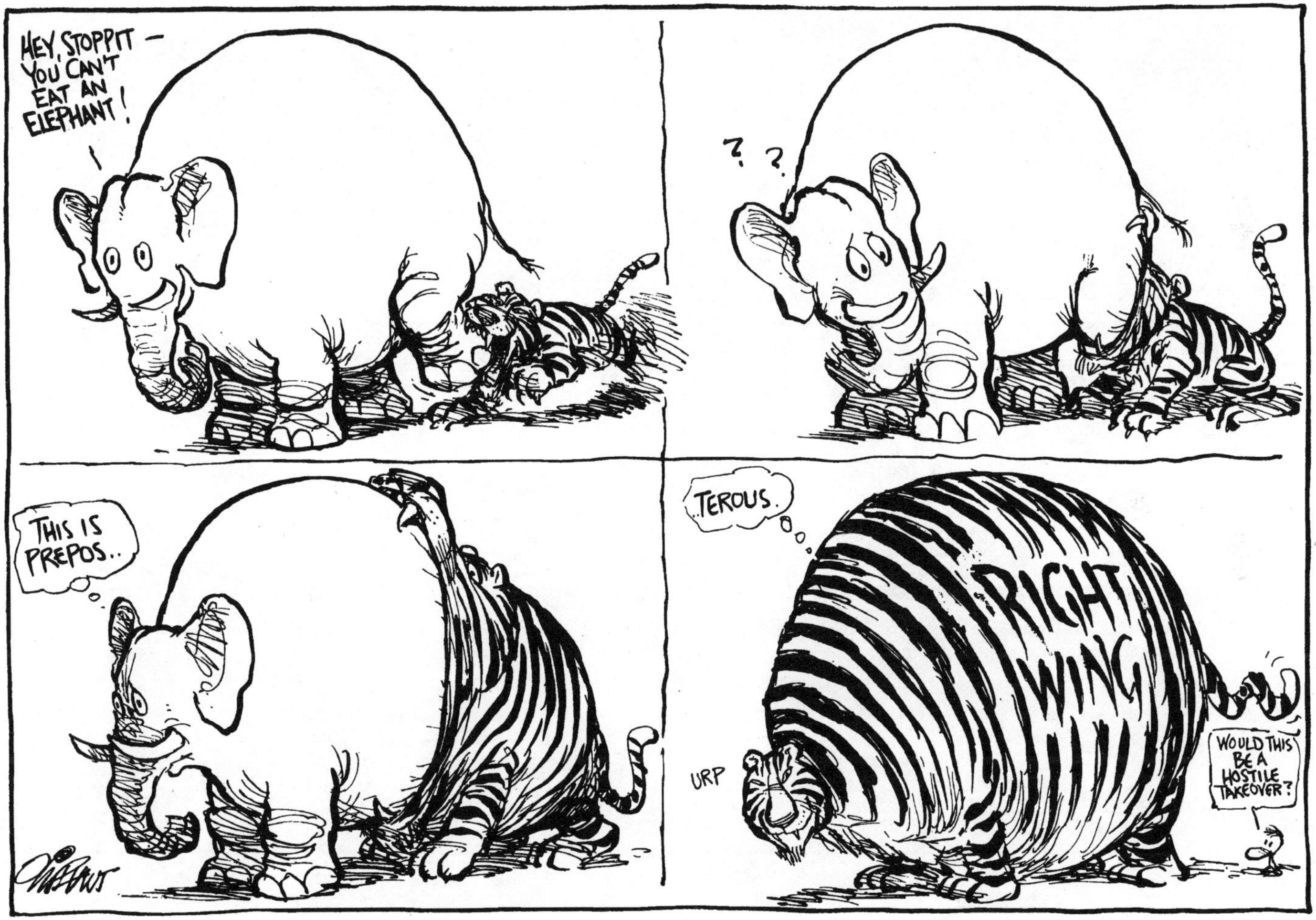
HEY, STOPPIT — YOU CAN'T EAT AN ELEPHANT!
? ?
THIS IS PREPOS..
TEROUS.
RIGHT WING
URP
WOULD THIS BE A HOSTILE TAKEOVER?

July 28, 1997

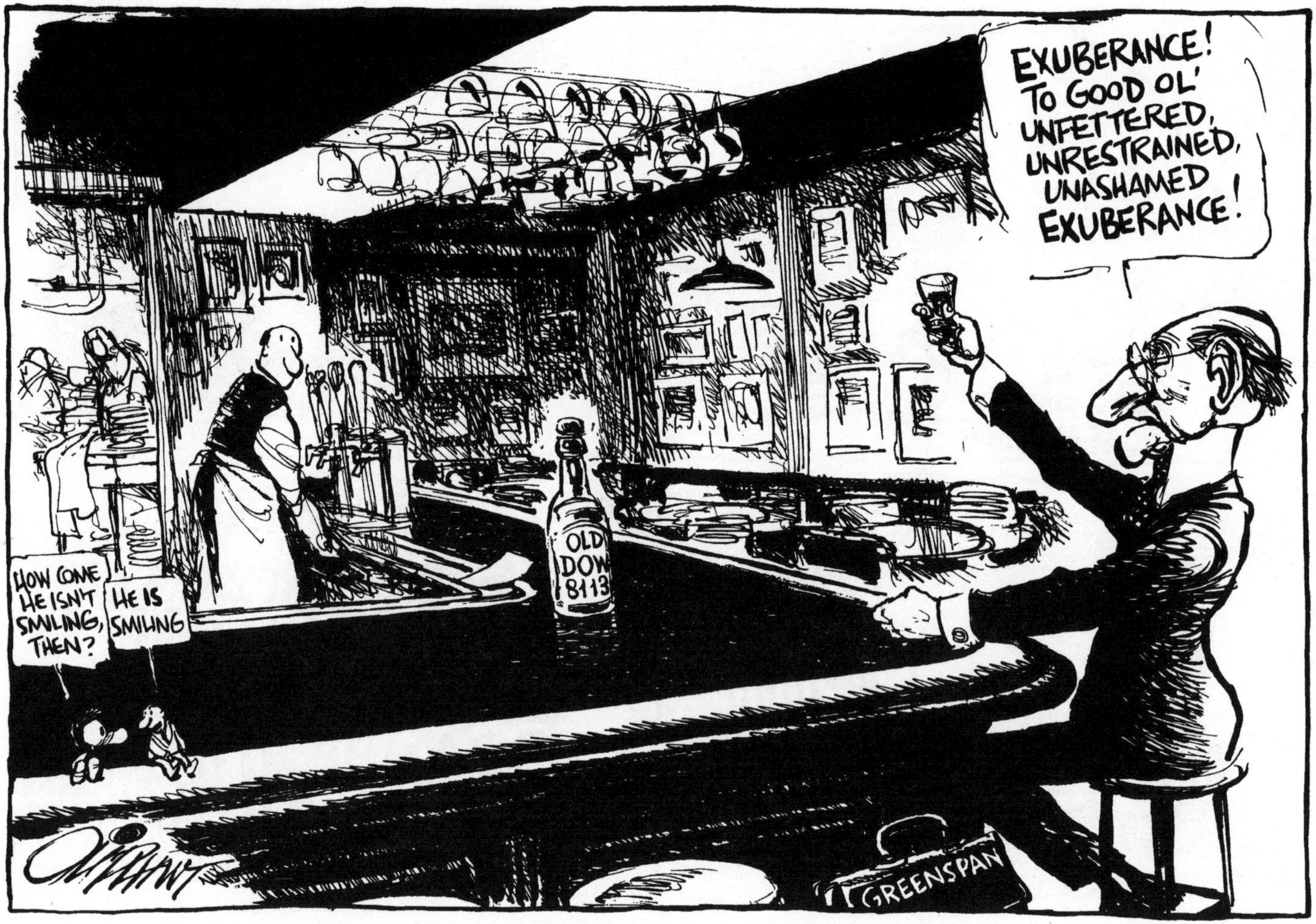
EXUBERANCE! TO GOOD OL' UNFETTERED, UNRESTRAINED, UNASHAMED EXUBERANCE!
HOW COME HE ISN'T SMILING, THEN?
HE IS SMILING
OLD DOW 8113
GREENSPAN

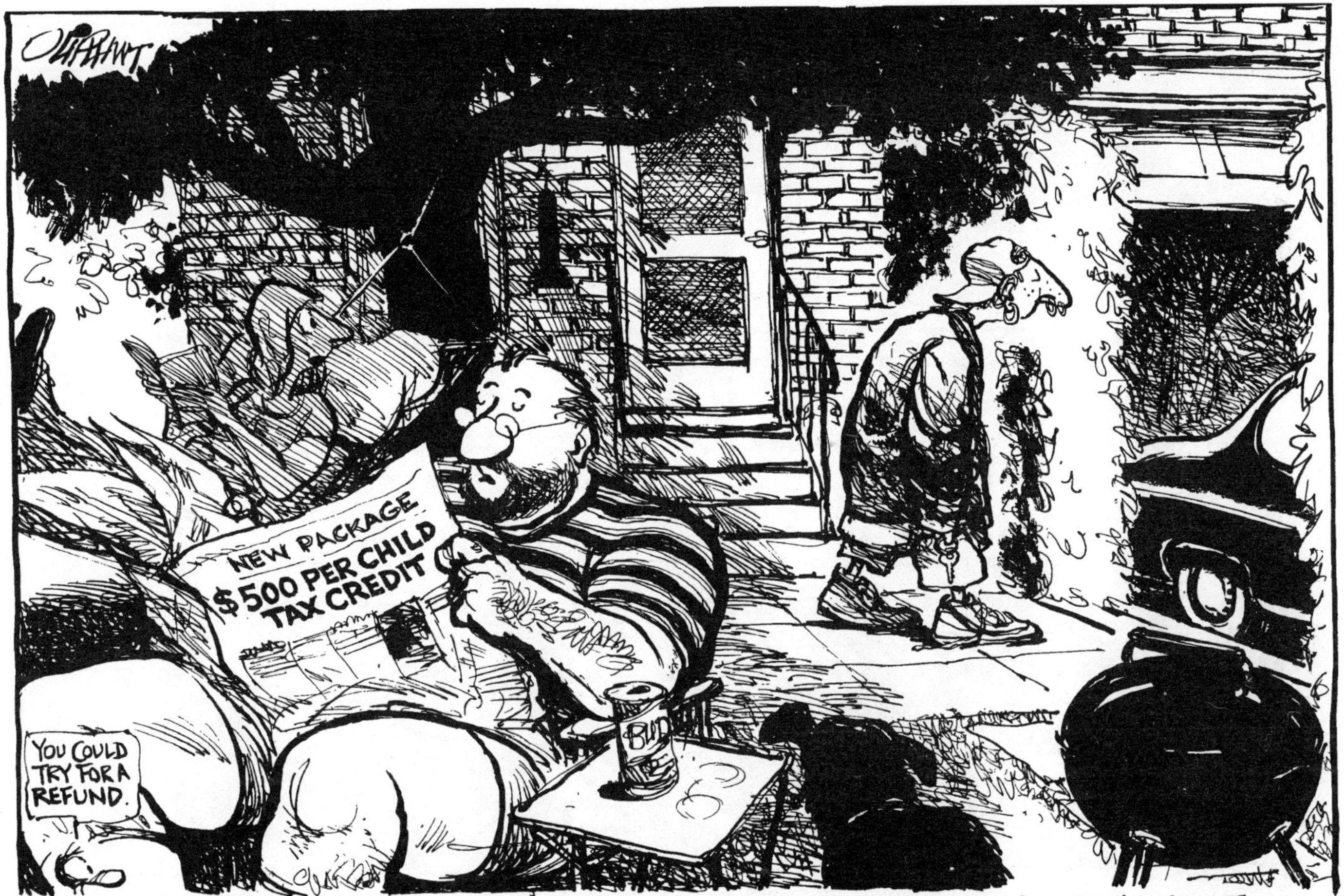
OLIPHANT
NEW PACKAGE
$500 PER CHILD TAX CREDIT
BUD
YOU COULD TRY FOR A REFUND.

'IT DOESN'T SOUND LIKE MUCH, BUT WHEN YOU THINK ABOUT IT WE COULDN'T GET FIVE BUCKS FOR HIM ON THE OPEN MARKET.'

July 31, 1997

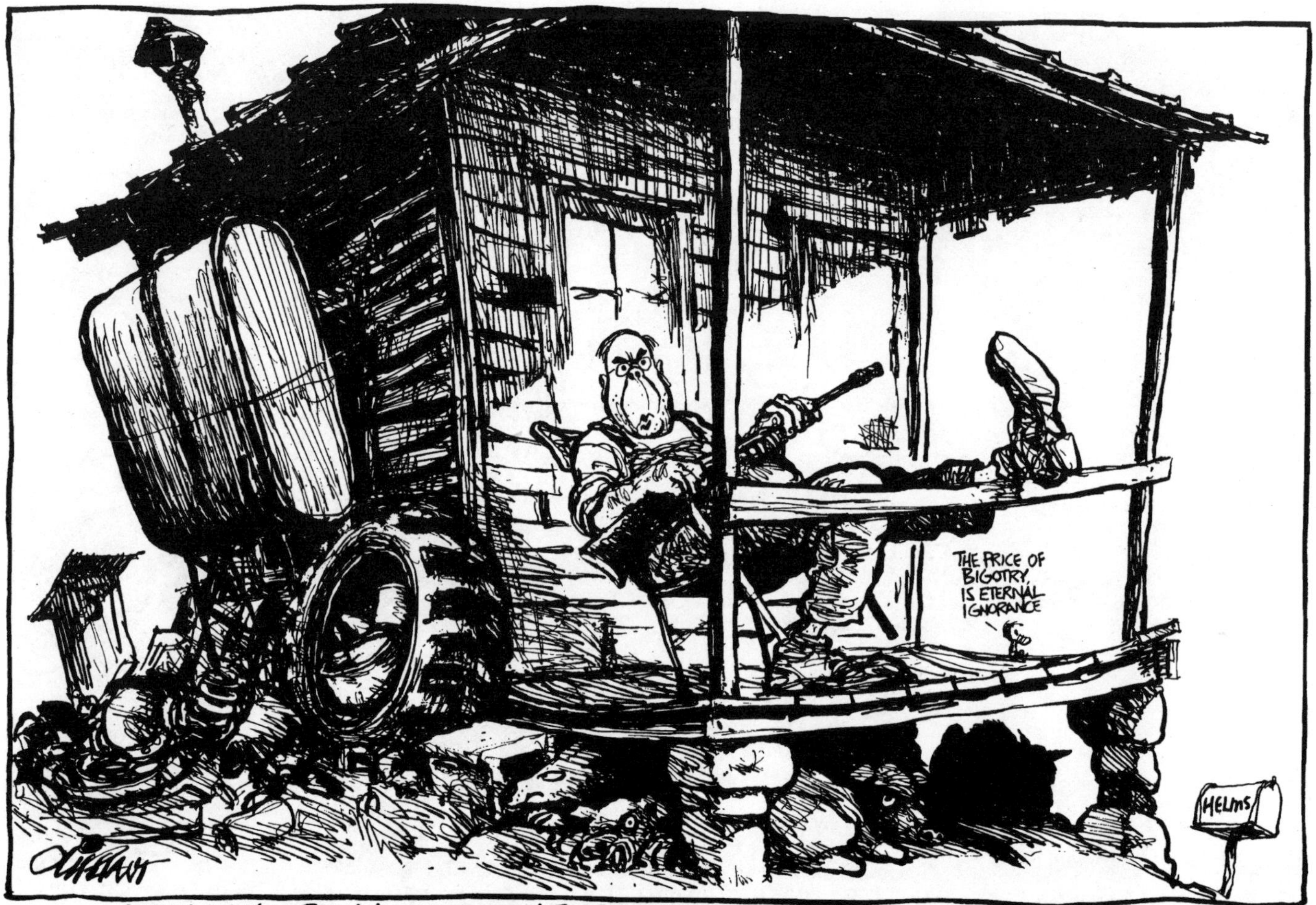
THE PRICE OF BIGOTRY IS ETERNAL IGNORANCE
HELMS

'NOW, AH KIN SEE Y'ALL WANTIN' TO SMOKE CIGARETTES FOR MEDICINAL REASONS—BUT MARRYJUANA? FERGIT IT!'

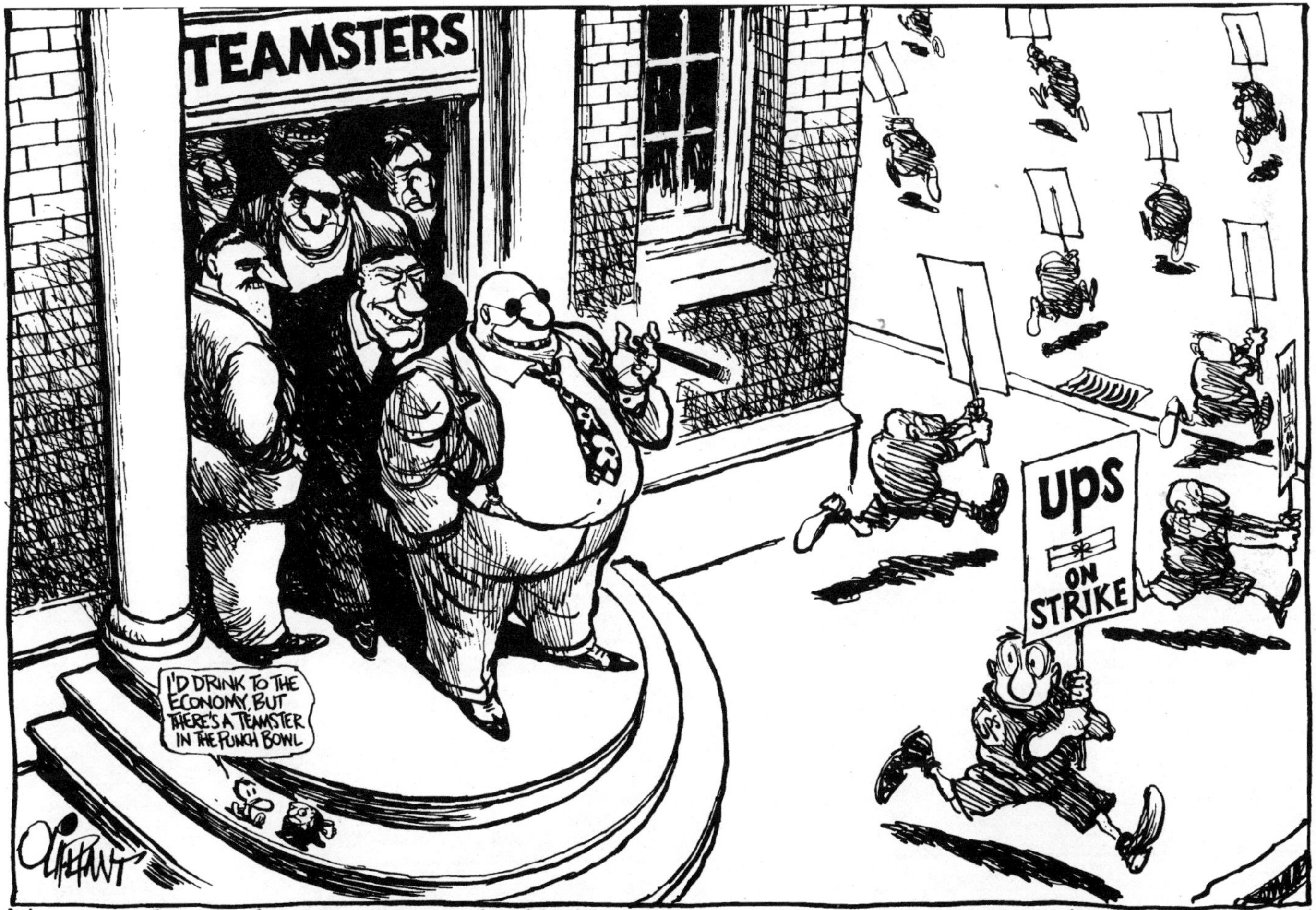
TEAMSTERS
UPS
ON STRIKE
I'D DRINK TO THE ECONOMY, BUT THERE'S A TEAMSTER IN THE PUNCH BOWL
OLIPHANT

'YOU BOOBS GET OUT THERE AND WRECK THE ECONOMIC BOOM—WE'LL BE HERE GUARDING YOUR PENSION FUND.'

August 5, 1997

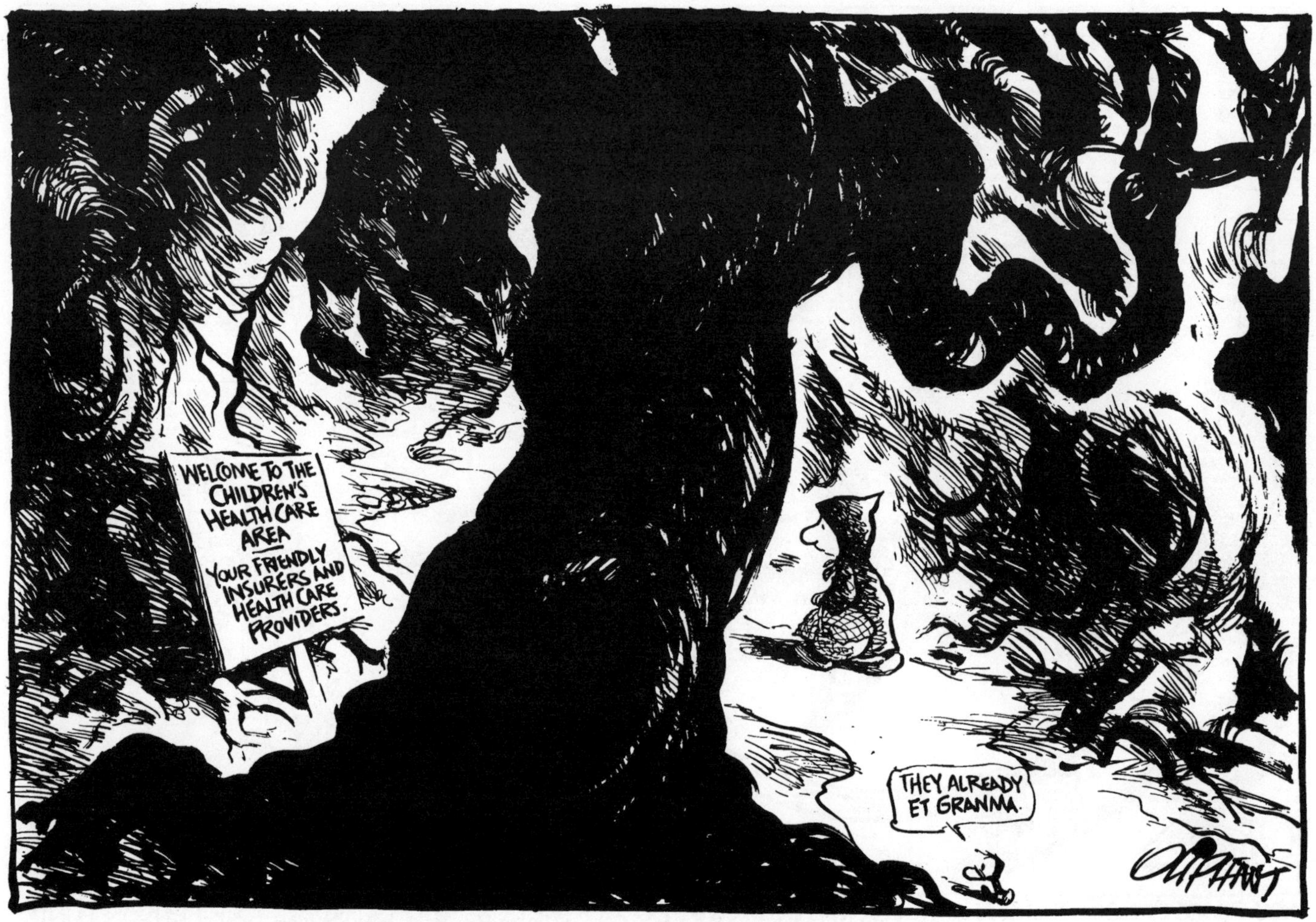
WELCOME TO THE CHILDREN'S HEALTH CARE AREA
YOUR FRIENDLY INSURERS AND HEALTH CARE PROVIDERS.
THEY ALREADY ET GRANMA.
OLIPHANT

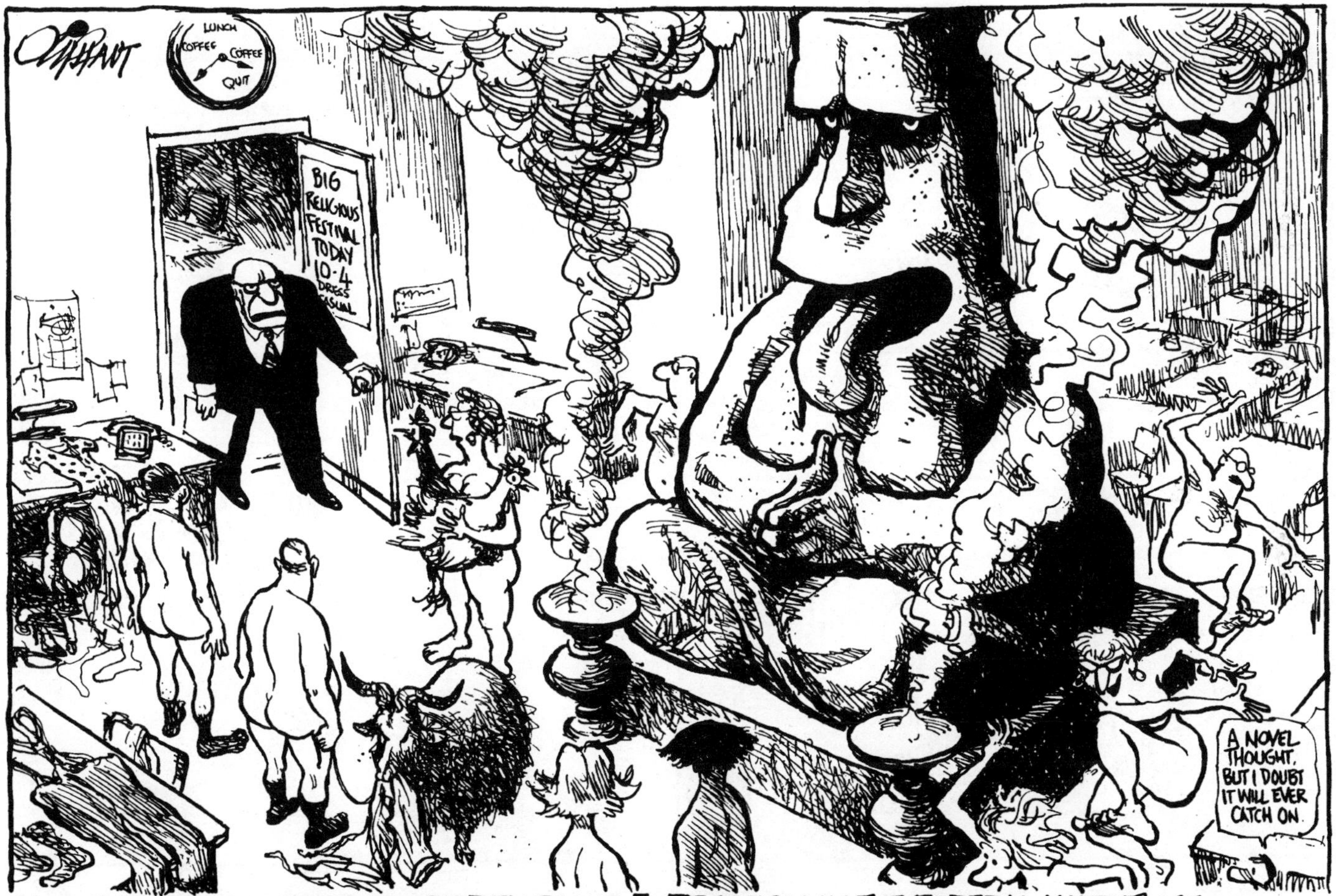
OLIPHANT
LUNCH
COFFEE
COFFEE
QUIT
BIG RELIGIOUS FESTIVAL TODAY 10-4 DRESS CASUAL
A NOVEL THOUGHT, BUT I DOUBT IT WILL EVER CATCH ON.

'NOW THAT WE HAVE FREEDOM OF RELIGIOUS EXPRESSION IN THE FEDERAL WORKPLACE, WOULD IT BE TOO MUCH TO EXPECT SOME **WORK** IN THE FEDERAL WORKPLACE?'

August 18, 1997

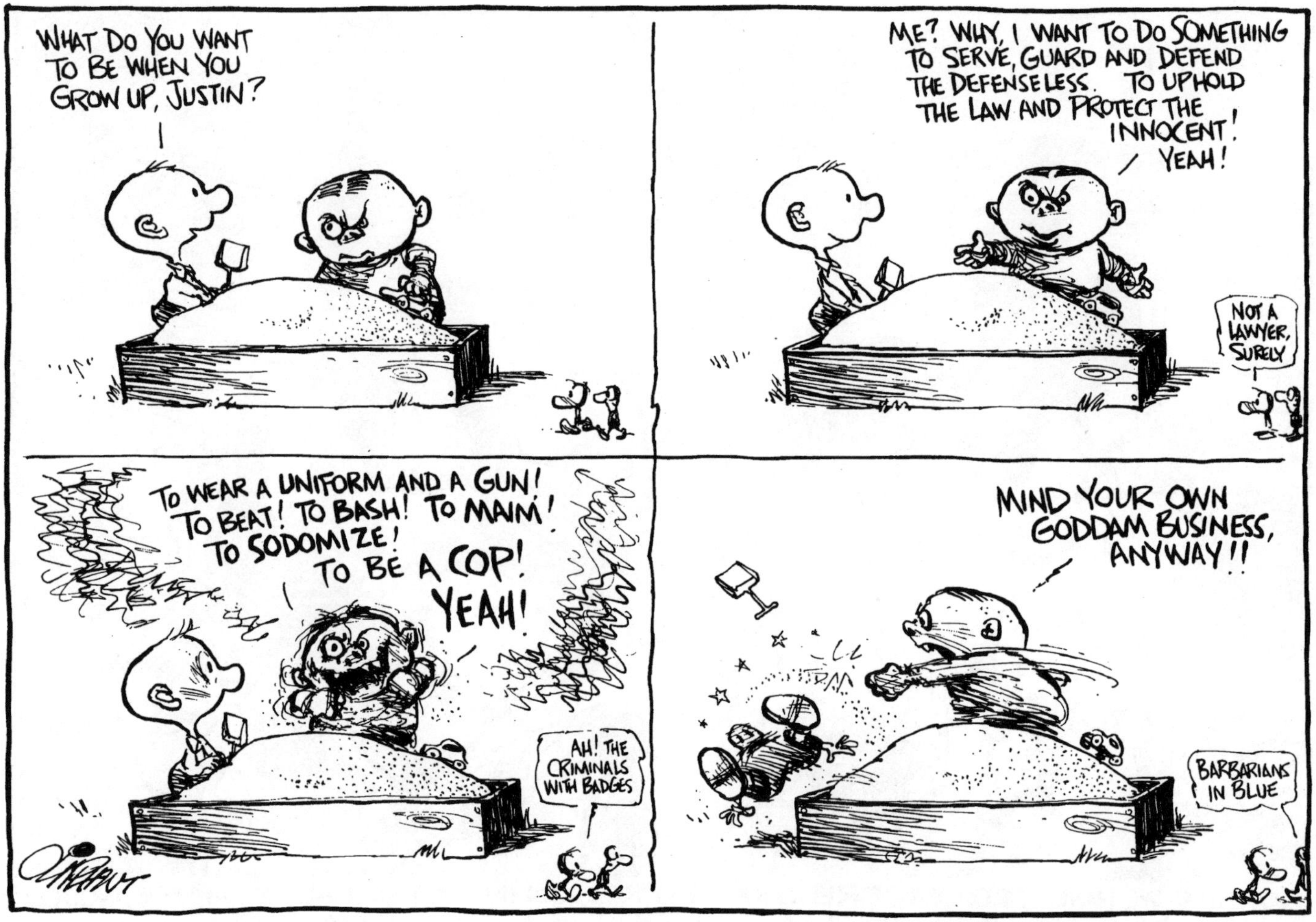
WHAT DO YOU WANT TO BE WHEN YOU GROW UP, JUSTIN?
ME? WHY, I WANT TO DO SOMETHING TO SERVE, GUARD AND DEFEND THE DEFENSELESS. TO UPHOLD THE LAW AND PROTECT THE INNOCENT! YEAH!
NOT A LAWYER, SURELY
TO WEAR A UNIFORM AND A GUN! TO BEAT! TO BASH! TO MAIM! TO SODOMIZE! TO BE A COP! YEAH!
AH! THE CRIMINALS WITH BADGES
MIND YOUR OWN GODDAM BUSINESS, ANYWAY!!
BARBARIANS IN BLUE

August 28, 1997

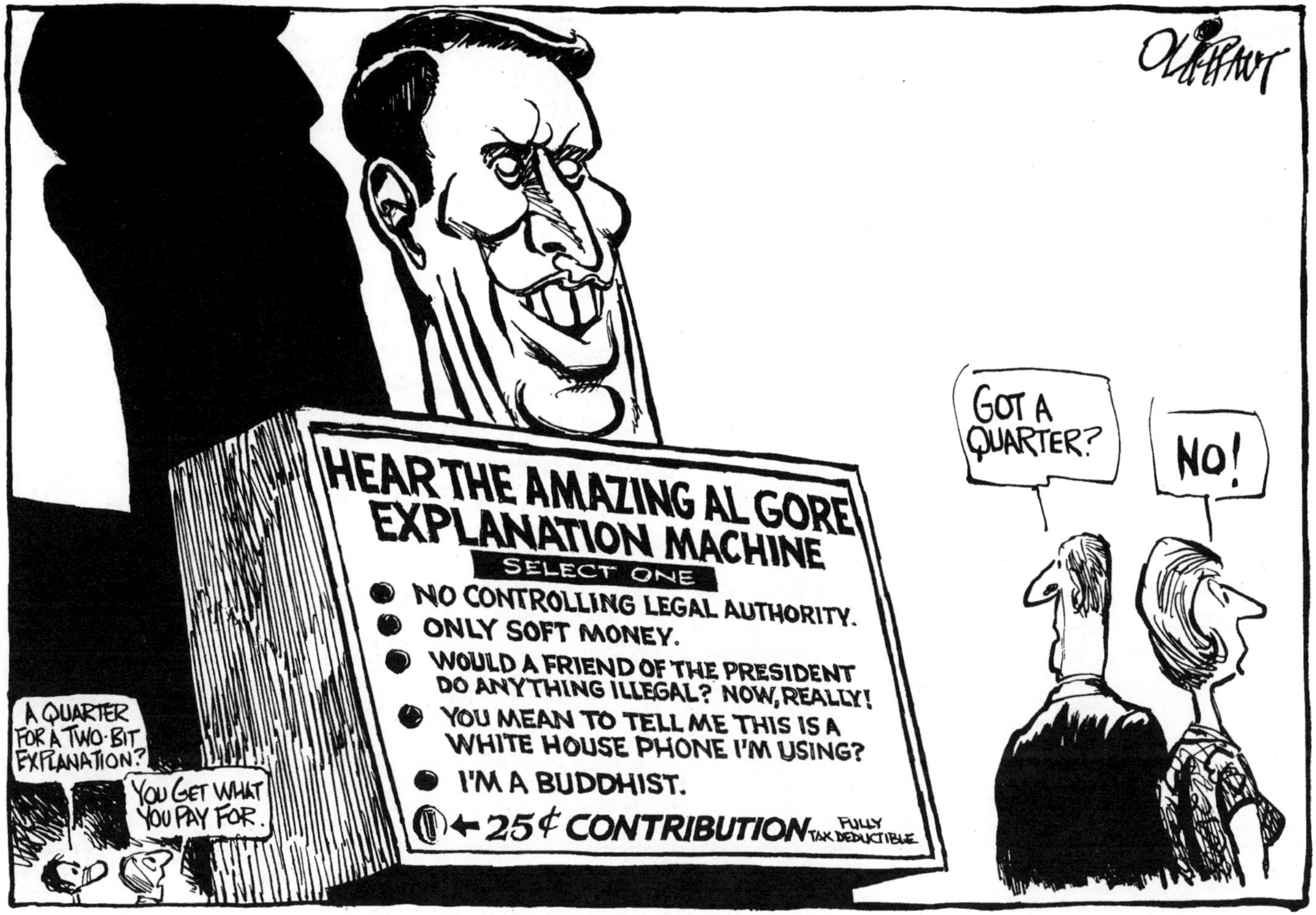
OLIPHANT
HEAR THE AMAZING AL GORE EXPLANATION MACHINE
SELECT ONE
NO CONTROLLING LEGAL AUTHORITY.
ONLY SOFT MONEY.
WOULD A FRIEND OF THE PRESIDENT DO ANYTHING ILLEGAL? NOW, REALLY!
YOU MEAN TO TELL ME THIS IS A WHITE HOUSE PHONE I'M USING?
I'M A BUDDHIST.
← 25¢ CONTRIBUTION FULLY TAX DEDUCTIBLE
GOT A QUARTER?
NO!
A QUARTER FOR A TWO-BIT EXPLANATION?
YOU GET WHAT YOU PAY FOR.

September 9, 1997

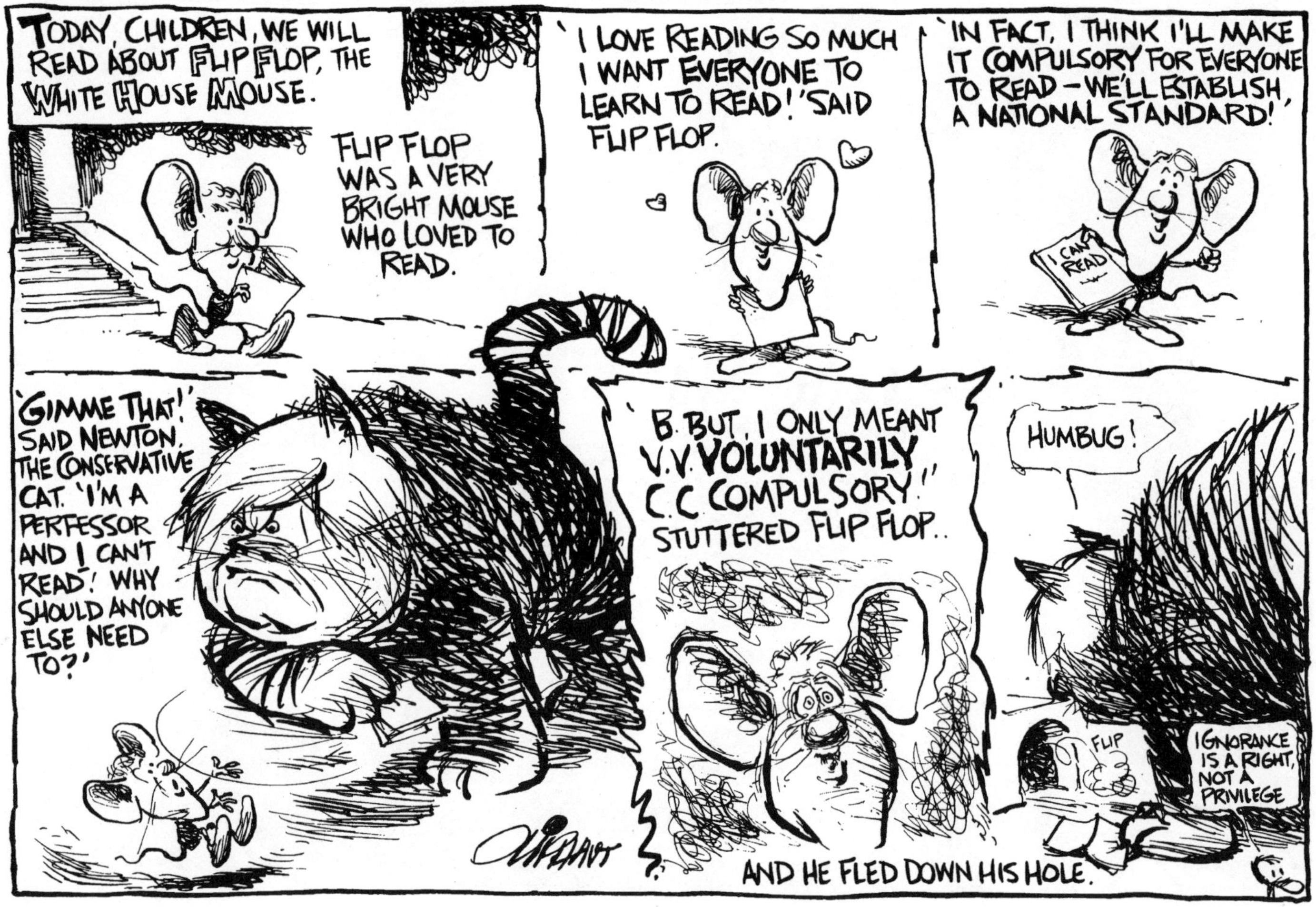
TODAY, CHILDREN, WE WILL READ ABOUT FLIP FLOP, THE WHITE HOUSE MOUSE.
FLIP FLOP WAS A VERY BRIGHT MOUSE WHO LOVED TO READ.
'I LOVE READING SO MUCH I WANT EVERYONE TO LEARN TO READ!' SAID FLIP FLOP.
'IN FACT, I THINK I'LL MAKE IT COMPULSORY FOR EVERYONE TO READ – WE'LL ESTABLISH A NATIONAL STANDARD!'
I CAN READ
'GIMME THAT!' SAID NEWTON, THE CONSERVATIVE CAT. 'I'M A PERFESSOR AND I CAN'T READ! WHY SHOULD ANYONE ELSE NEED TO?'
'B. BUT, I ONLY MEANT V. V. VOLUNTARILY C. C. COMPULSORY!' STUTTERED FLIP FLOP..
AND HE FLED DOWN HIS HOLE.
HUMBUG!
FLIP
IGNORANCE IS A RIGHT, NOT A PRIVILEGE

September 11, 1997

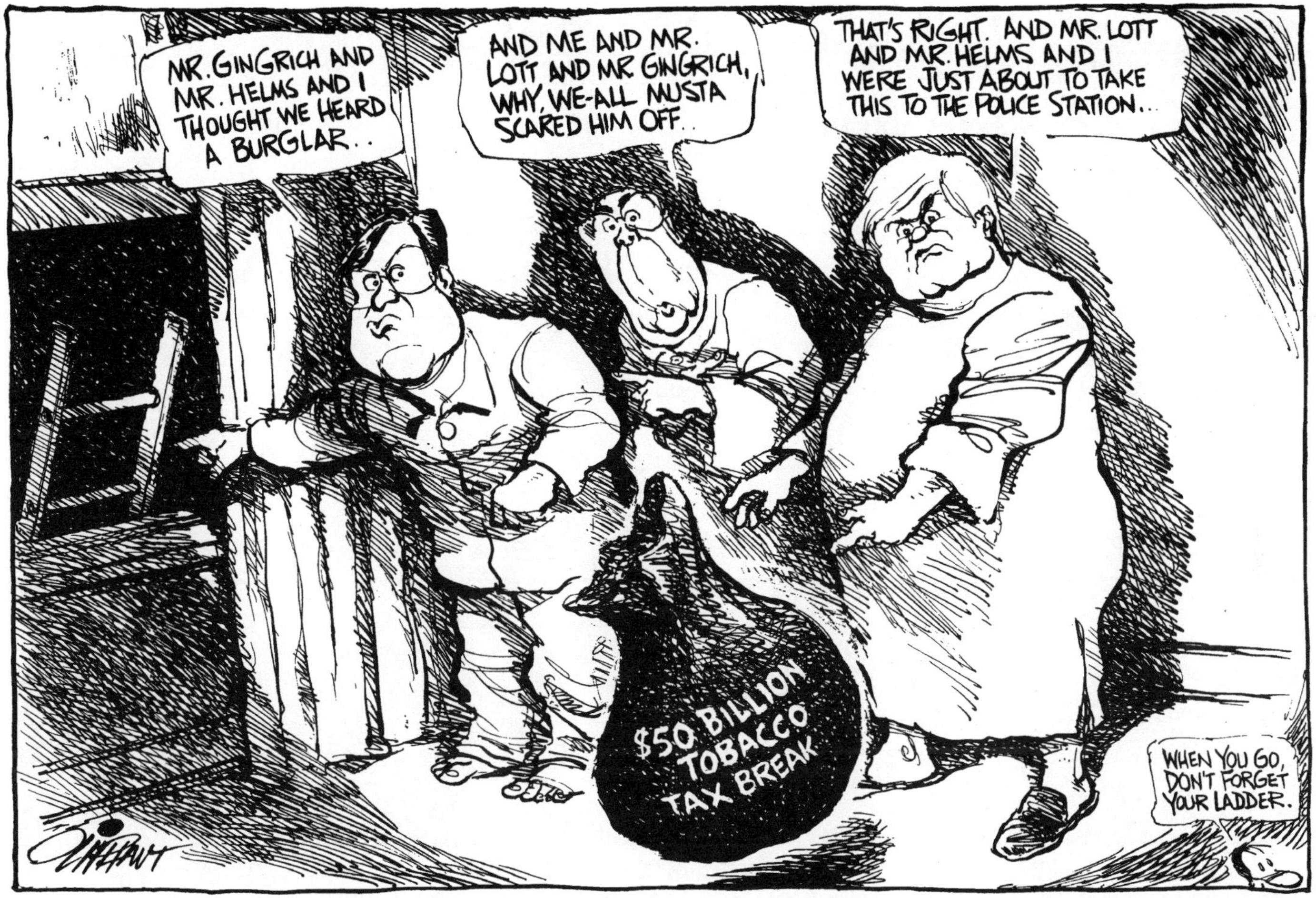
MR. GINGRICH AND MR. HELMS AND I THOUGHT WE HEARD A BURGLAR...
AND ME AND MR. LOTT AND MR. GINGRICH, WHY, WE-ALL MUSTA SCARED HIM OFF...
THAT'S RIGHT. AND MR. LOTT AND MR. HELMS AND I WERE JUST ABOUT TO TAKE THIS TO THE POLICE STATION...
$50 BILLION TOBACCO TAX BREAK
WHEN YOU GO, DON'T FORGET YOUR LADDER.

September 18, 1997

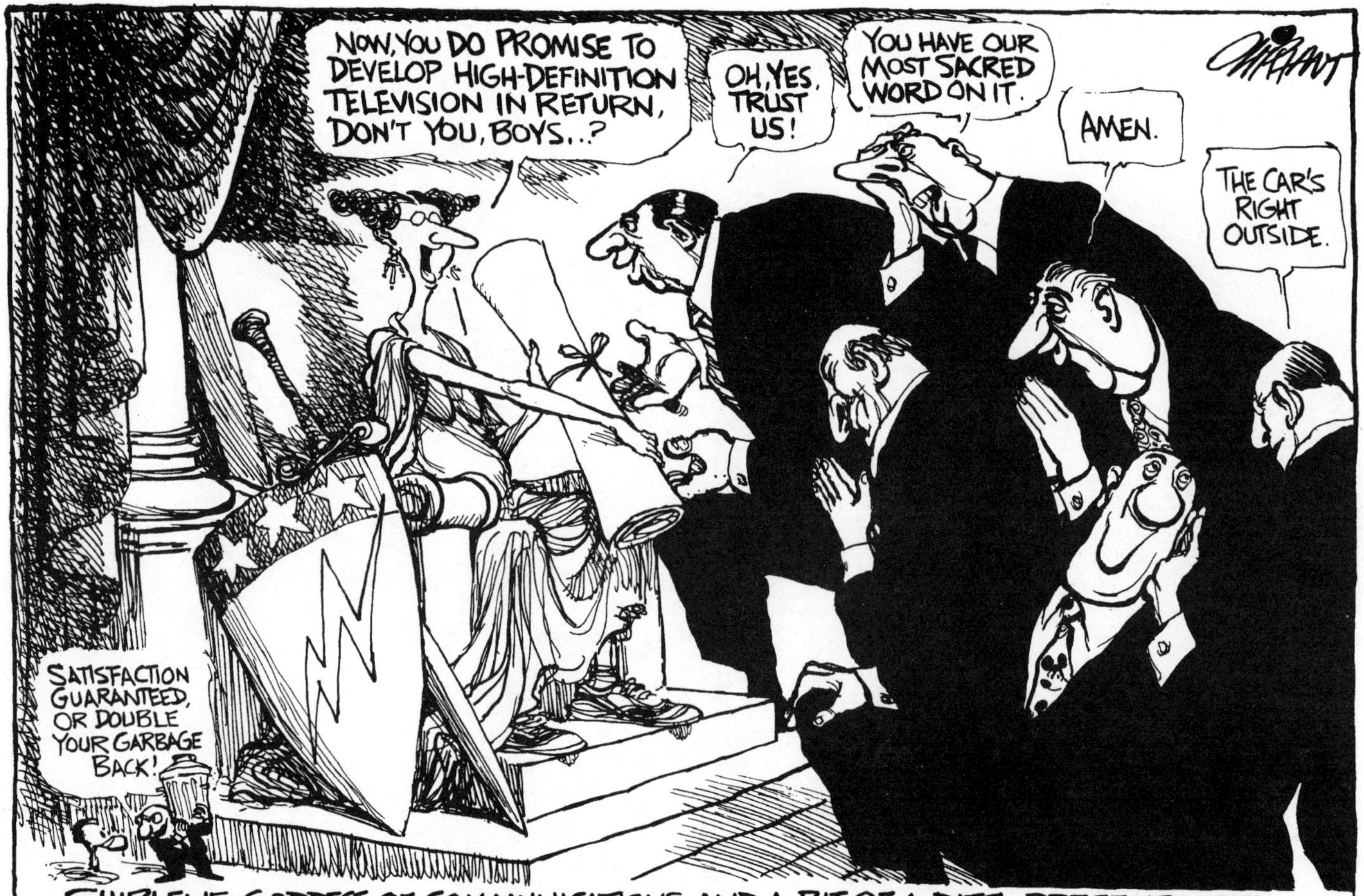
NOW, YOU DO PROMISE TO DEVELOP HIGH-DEFINITION TELEVISION IN RETURN, DON'T YOU, BOYS...?
OH, YES, TRUST US!
YOU HAVE OUR MOST SACRED WORD ON IT.
AMEN.
THE CAR'S RIGHT OUTSIDE.
SATISFACTION GUARANTEED, OR DOUBLE YOUR GARBAGE BACK!

SHIRLENE, GODDESS OF COMMUNICATIONS, AND A BIT OF A DITZ, PRESENTS THE TELEVISION BROADCASTERS THE ENTIRE CHANNEL SPECTRUM AT NO CHARGE...

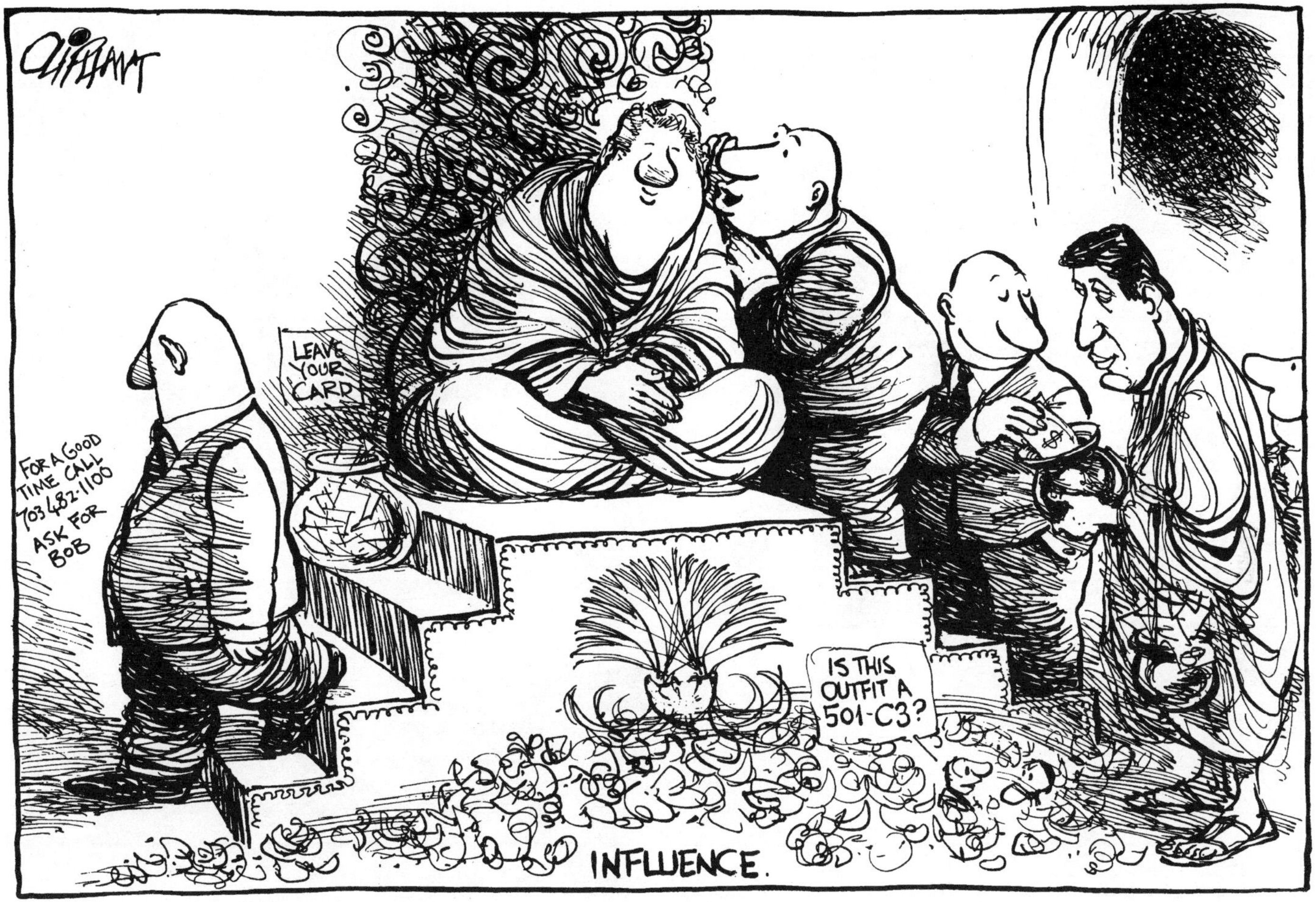
OLIPHANT
LEAVE YOUR CARD
FOR A GOOD TIME CALL 703 482-1100 ASK FOR BOB
IS THIS OUTFIT A 501-C3?
INFLUENCE.

September 22, 1997

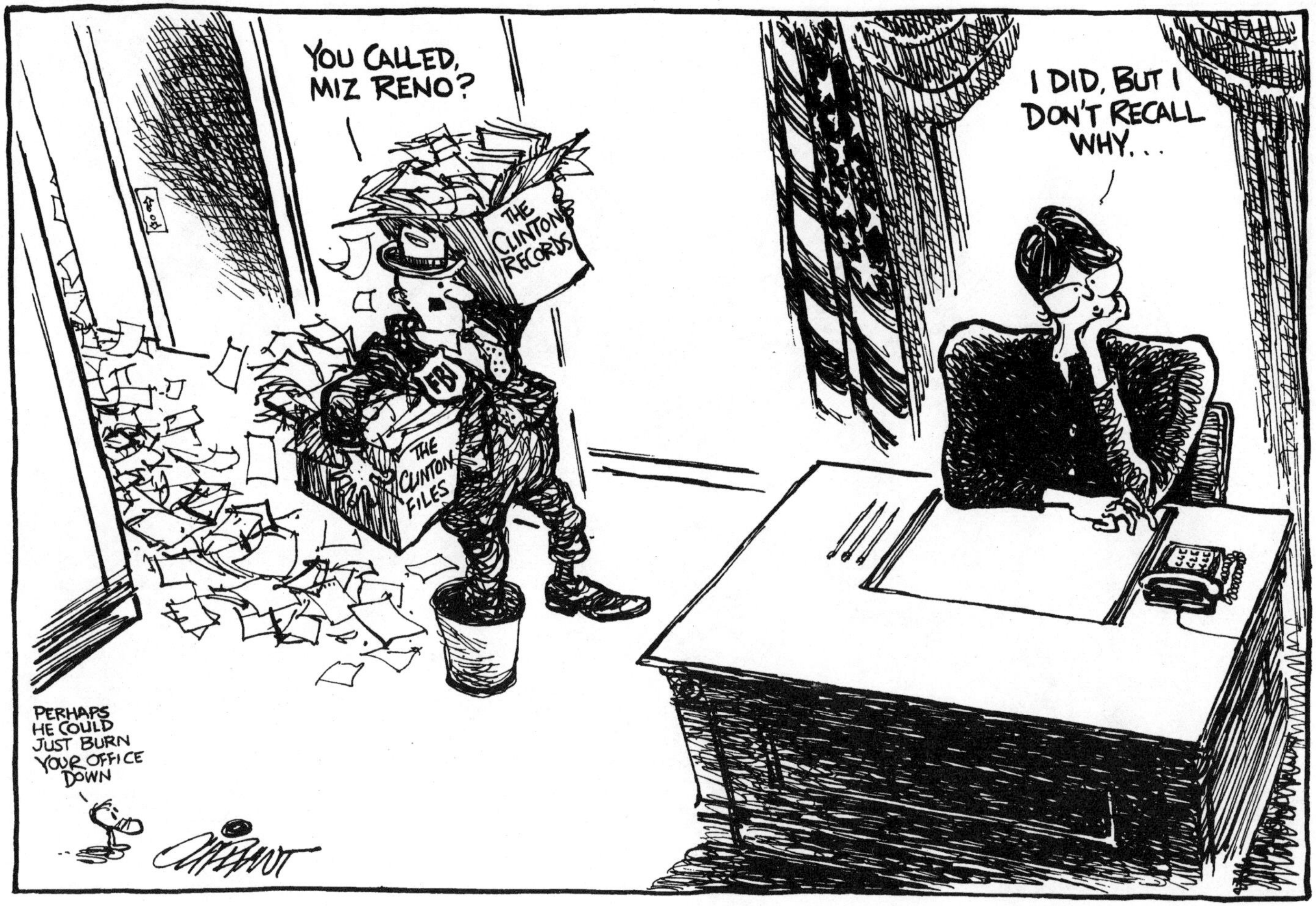
YOU CALLED, MIZ RENO?
THE CLINTON RECORDS
FBI
THE CLINTON FILES
I DID, BUT I DON'T RECALL WHY...
PERHAPS HE COULD JUST BURN YOUR OFFICE DOWN

September 23, 1997

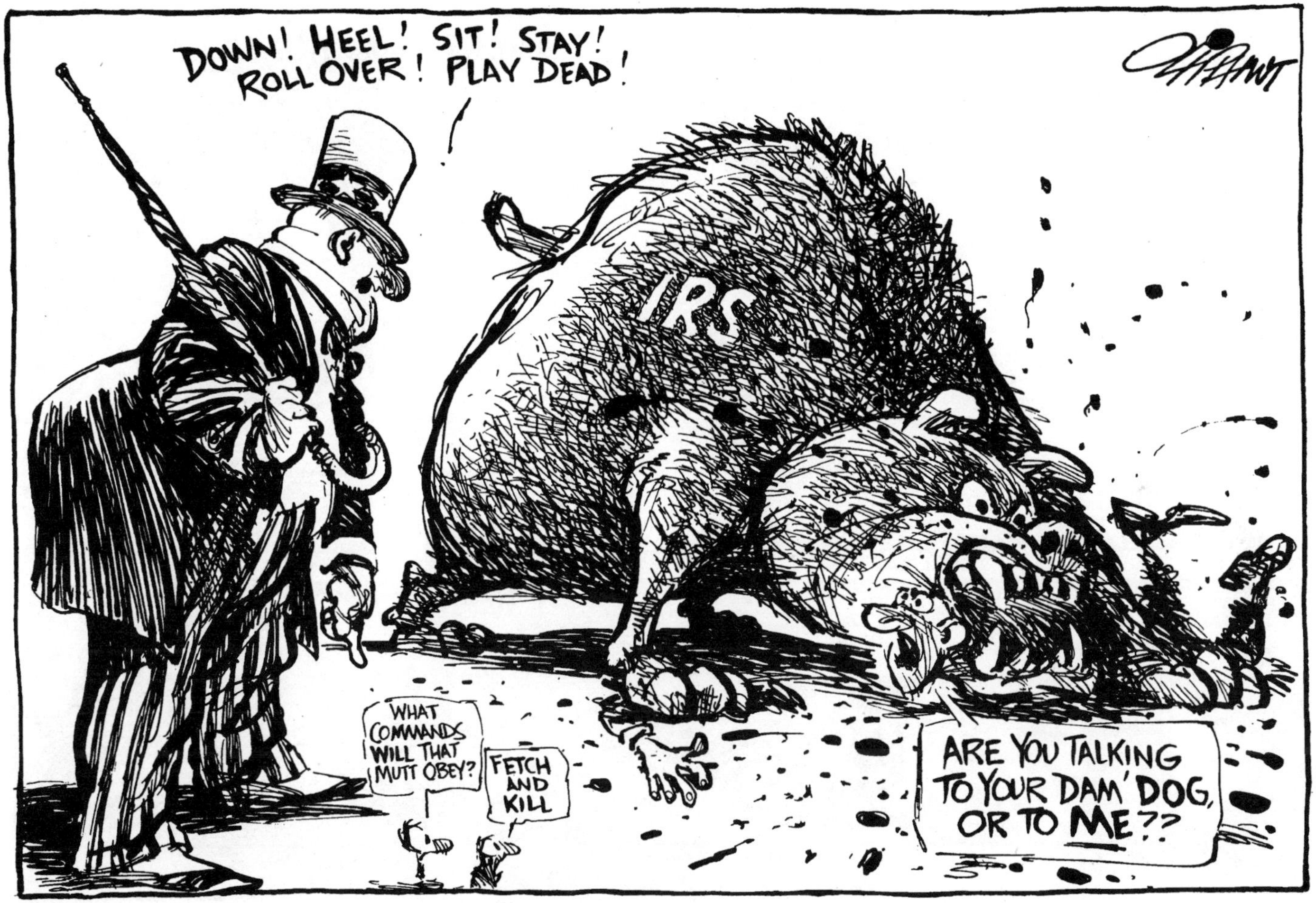
DOWN! HEEL! SIT! STAY! ROLL OVER! PLAY DEAD!
IRS
WHAT COMMANDS WILL THAT MUTT OBEY?
FETCH AND KILL
ARE YOU TALKING TO YOUR DAM' DOG, OR TO ME??

September 24, 1997

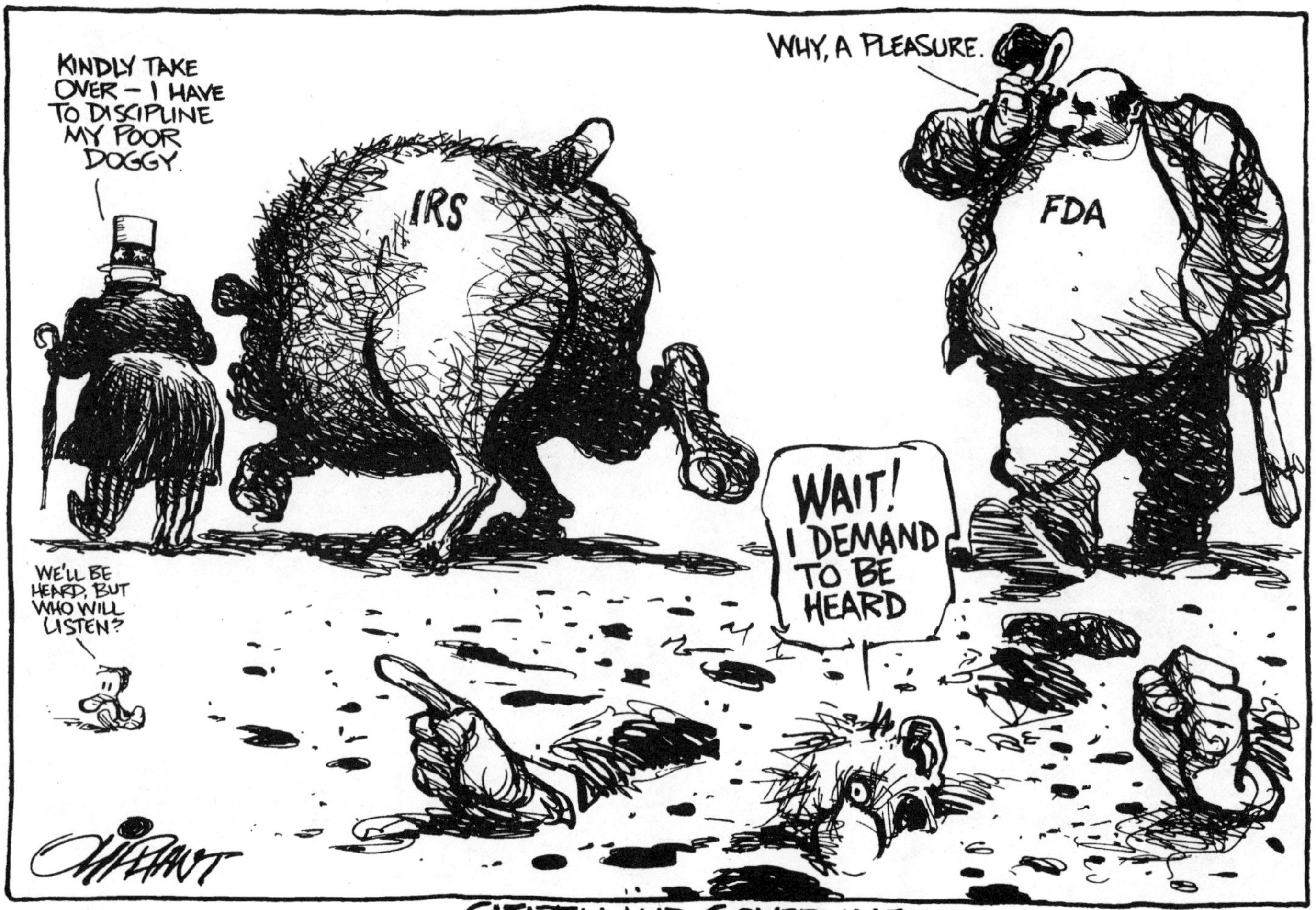
KINDLY TAKE OVER – I HAVE TO DISCIPLINE MY POOR DOGGY.
IRS
WHY, A PLEASURE.
FDA
WAIT! I DEMAND TO BE HEARD
WE'LL BE HEARD, BUT WHO WILL LISTEN?
OLIPHANT

CITIZEN AND GOVERNMENT.

October 1, 1997

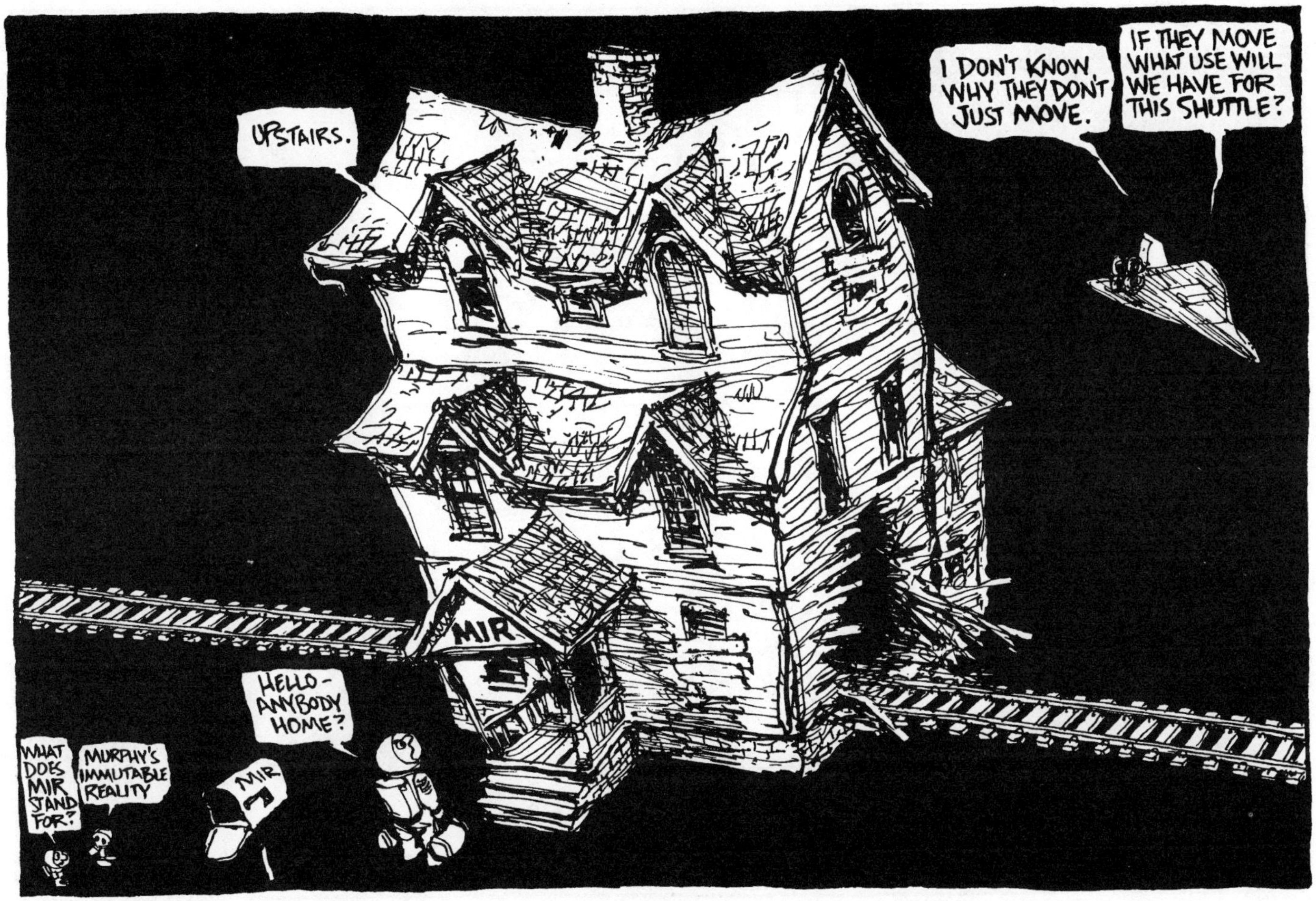
UPSTAIRS.
I DON'T KNOW WHY THEY DON'T JUST MOVE.
IF THEY MOVE WHAT USE WILL WE HAVE FOR THIS SHUTTLE?
MIR
HELLO- ANYBODY HOME?
MIR
WHAT DOES MIR STAND FOR?
MURPHY'S IMMUTABLE REALITY

October 7, 1997

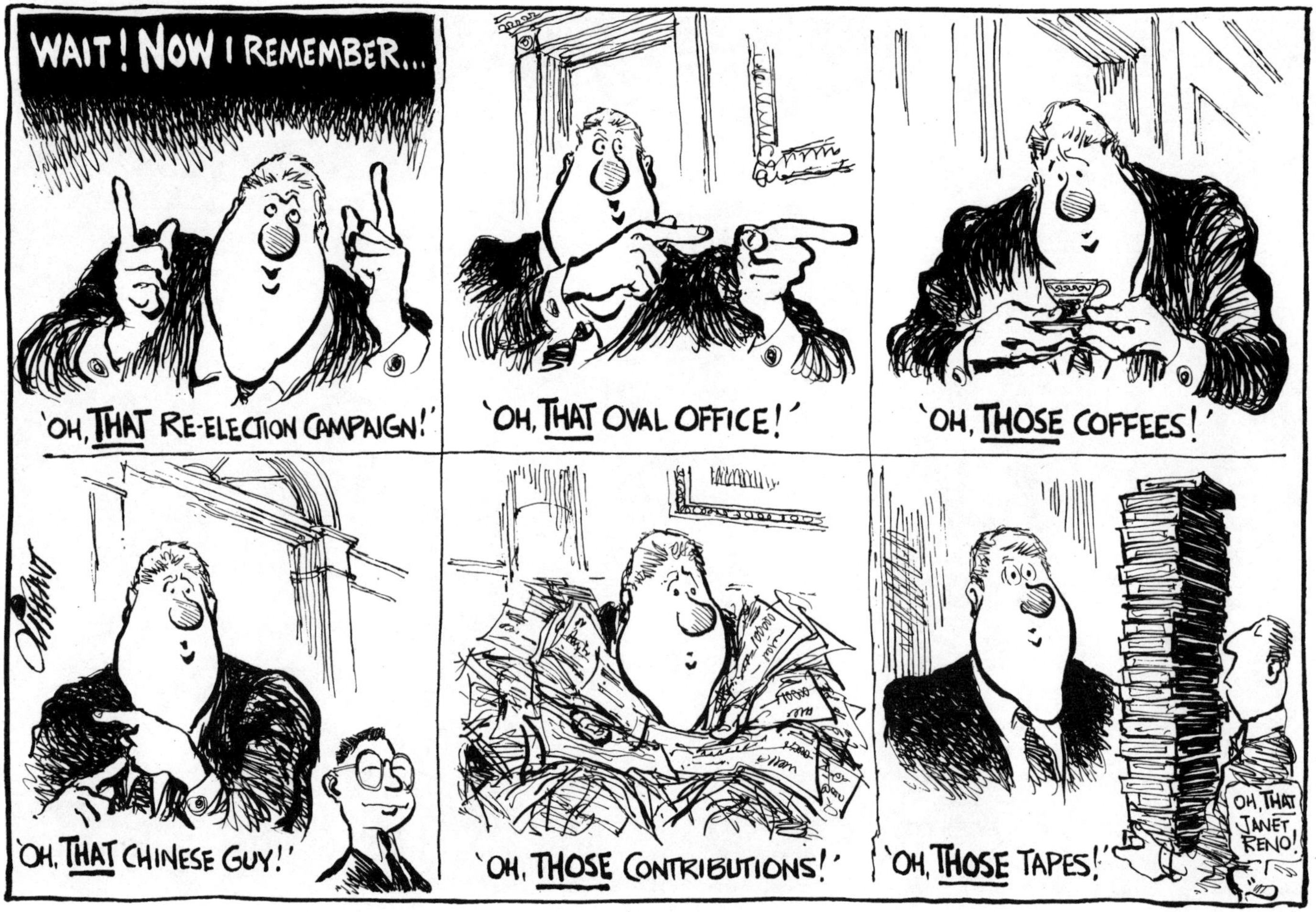
WAIT! NOW I REMEMBER...
'OH, THAT RE-ELECTION CAMPAIGN!'
'OH, THAT OVAL OFFICE!'
'OH, THOSE COFFEES!'
'OH, THAT CHINESE GUY!'
'OH, THOSE CONTRIBUTIONS!'
'OH, THOSE TAPES!'
OH, THAT JANET RENO!

October 14, 1997

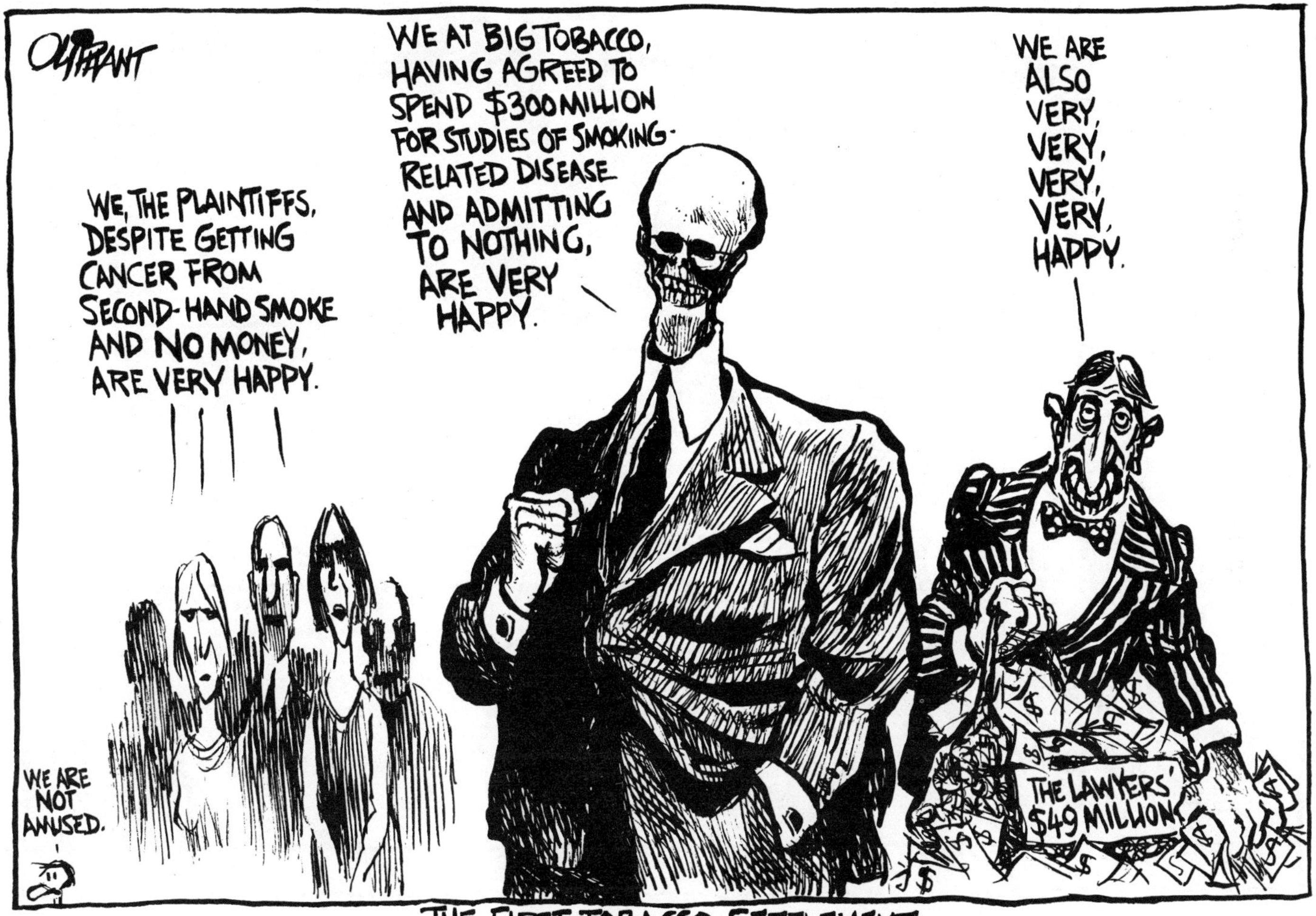
OLIPHANT
WE, THE PLAINTIFFS, DESPITE GETTING CANCER FROM SECOND-HAND SMOKE AND NO MONEY, ARE VERY HAPPY.
WE AT BIG TOBACCO, HAVING AGREED TO SPEND $300 MILLION FOR STUDIES OF SMOKING-RELATED DISEASE AND ADMITTING TO NOTHING, ARE VERY HAPPY.
WE ARE ALSO VERY, VERY, VERY, VERY, HAPPY.
THE LAWYERS' $49 MILLION
WE ARE NOT AMUSED.
THE FIRST TOBACCO SETTLEMENT.

October 15, 1997

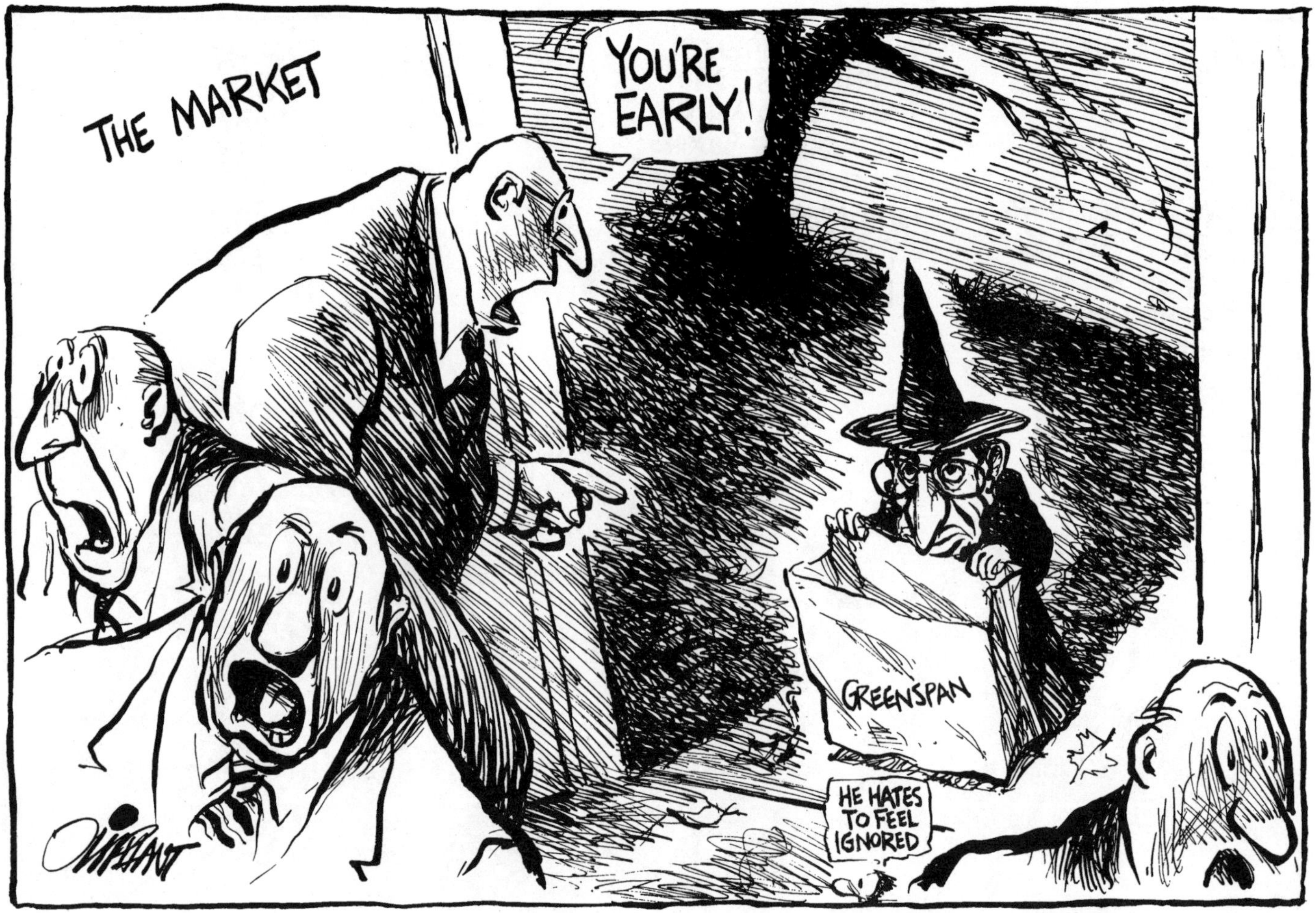
THE MARKET
YOU'RE EARLY!
GREENSPAN
HE HATES TO FEEL IGNORED
OLIPHANT

October 20, 1997

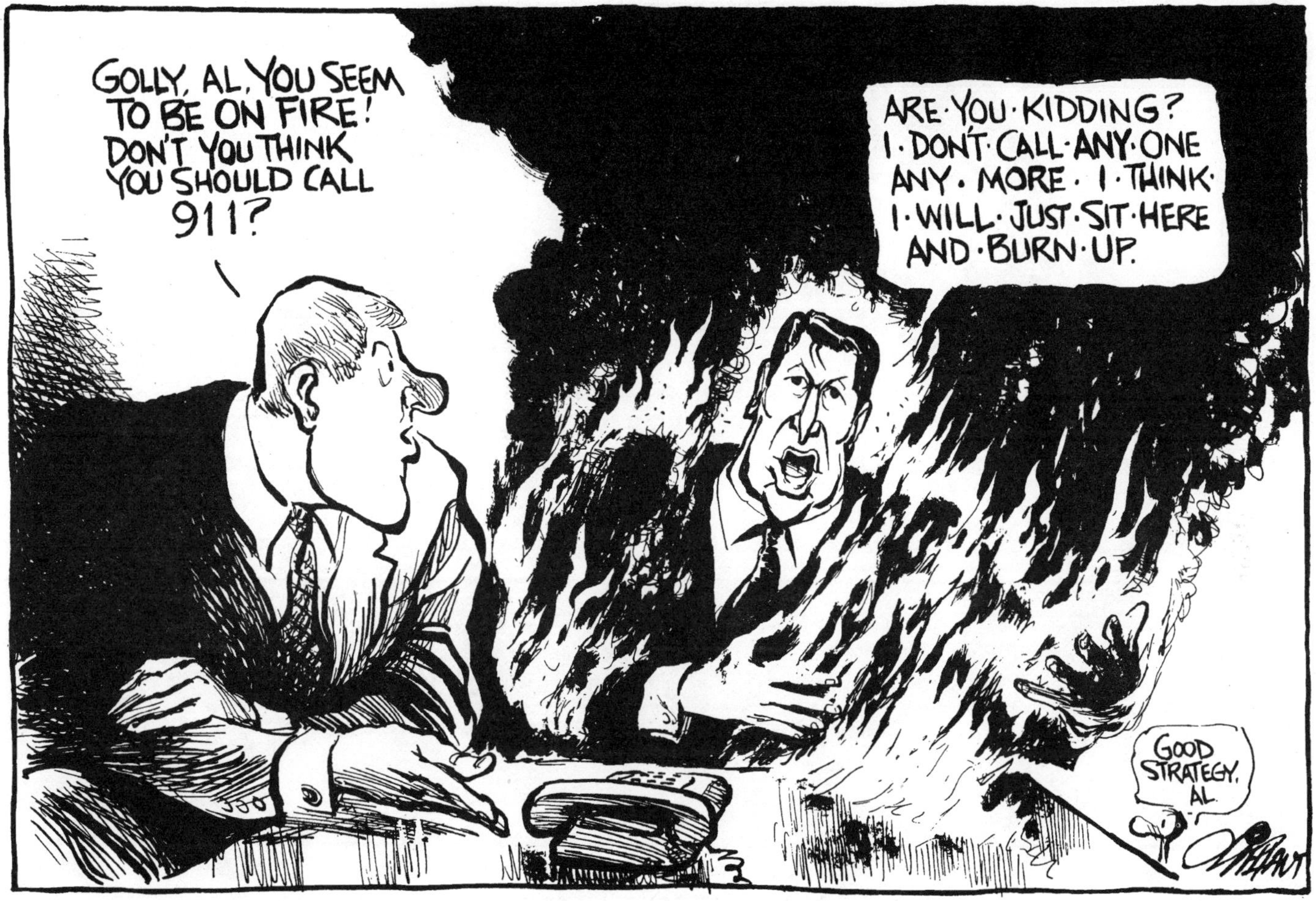
GOLLY, AL, YOU SEEM TO BE ON FIRE! DON'T YOU THINK YOU SHOULD CALL 911?
ARE·YOU·KIDDING? I·DON'T·CALL·ANY·ONE ANY·MORE. I·THINK· I·WILL·JUST·SIT·HERE AND·BURN·UP.
GOOD STRATEGY, AL.

October 22, 1997

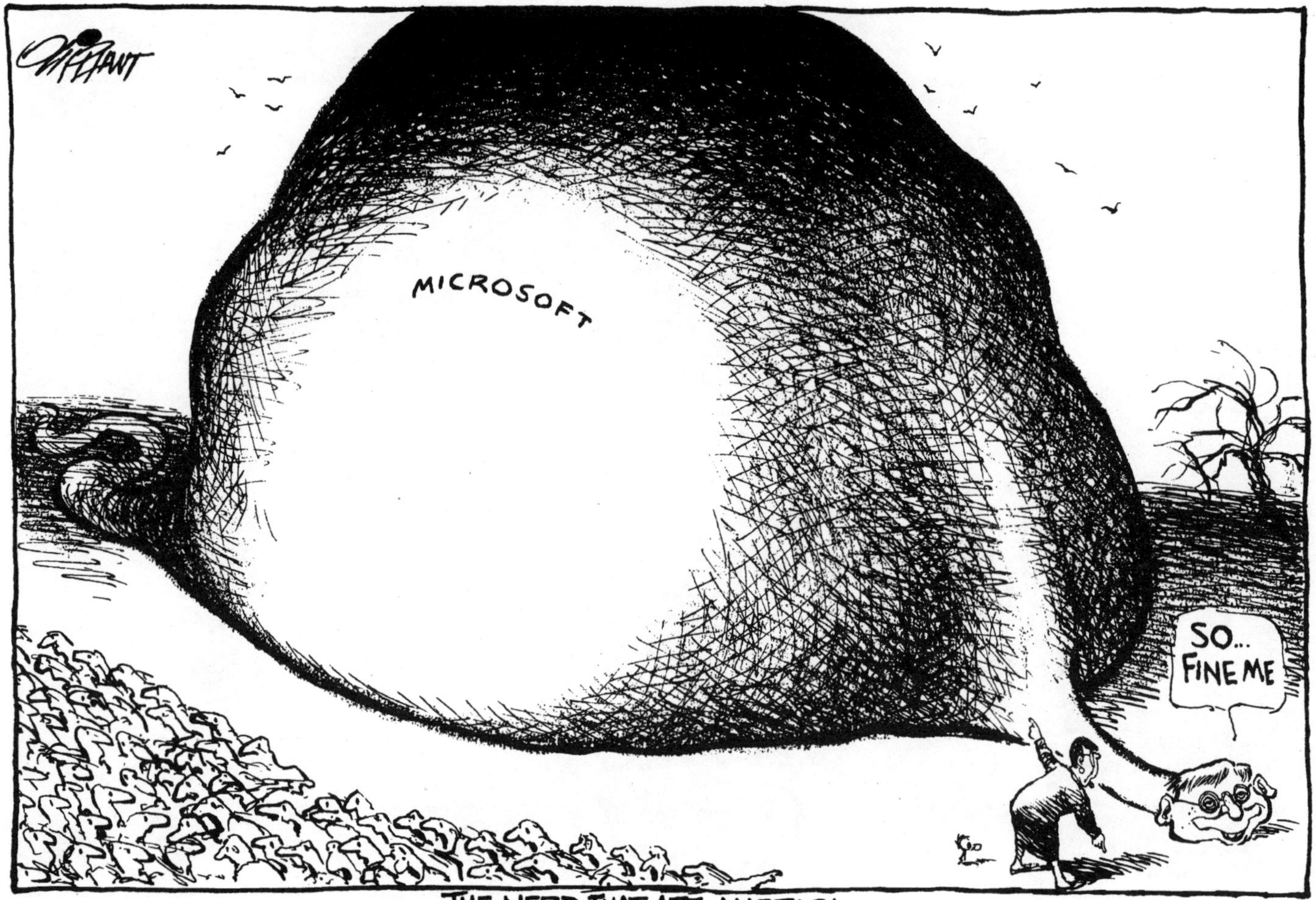
MICROSOFT
SO... FINE ME

THE NERD THAT ATE AMERICA.

October 30, 1997

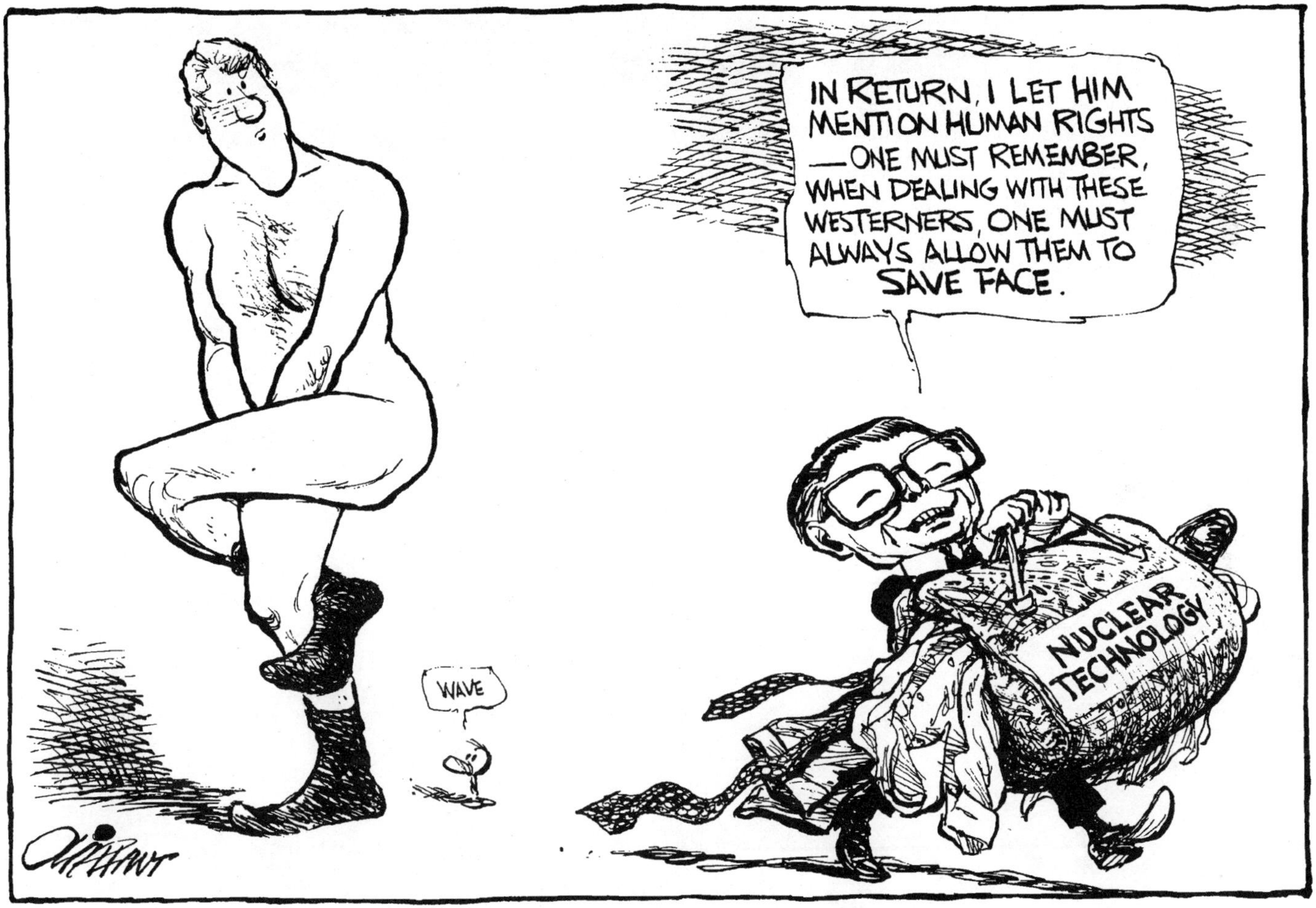
IN RETURN, I LET HIM MENTION HUMAN RIGHTS —ONE MUST REMEMBER, WHEN DEALING WITH THESE WESTERNERS, ONE MUST ALWAYS ALLOW THEM TO SAVE FACE.
WAVE
NUCLEAR TECHNOLOGY
OLIPHANT

November 3, 1997

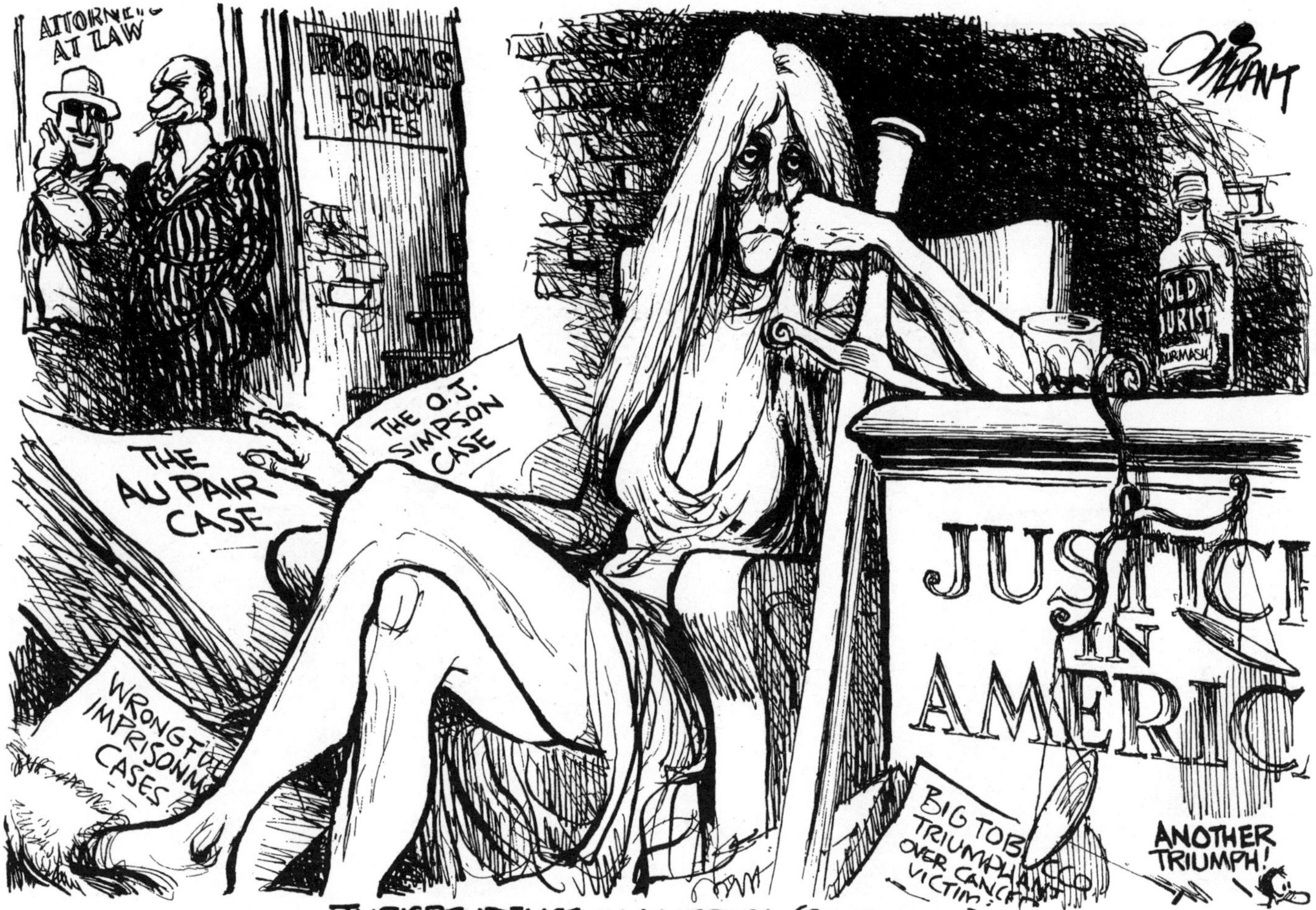

AT LAW
ROOMS
HOURLY RATES
THE O.J. SIMPSON CASE
THE AU PAIR CASE
WRONGFU
IMPRISONM
CASES
OLD JURIST
JUSTIC
IN
AMERIC
BIG TOB
TRIUMPH
OVER CANC
VICTIM
ANOTHER TRIUMPH!
OLIPHANT

JURISPRUDENCE IN AMERICA (CONTINUED).

November 6, 1997

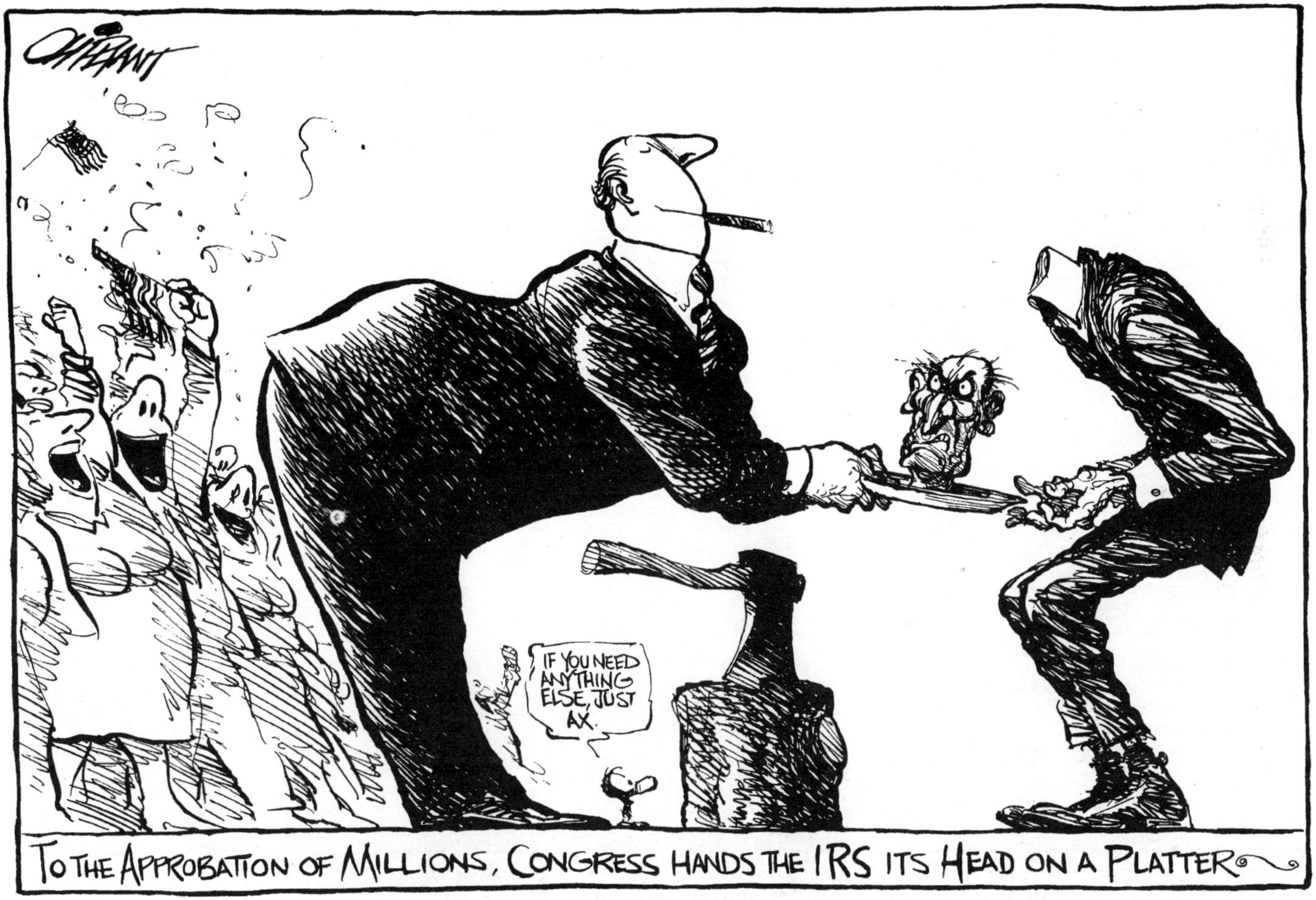
OLIPHANT
IF YOU NEED ANYTHING ELSE, JUST AX.
TO THE APPROBATION OF MILLIONS, CONGRESS HANDS THE IRS ITS HEAD ON A PLATTER

November 11, 1997

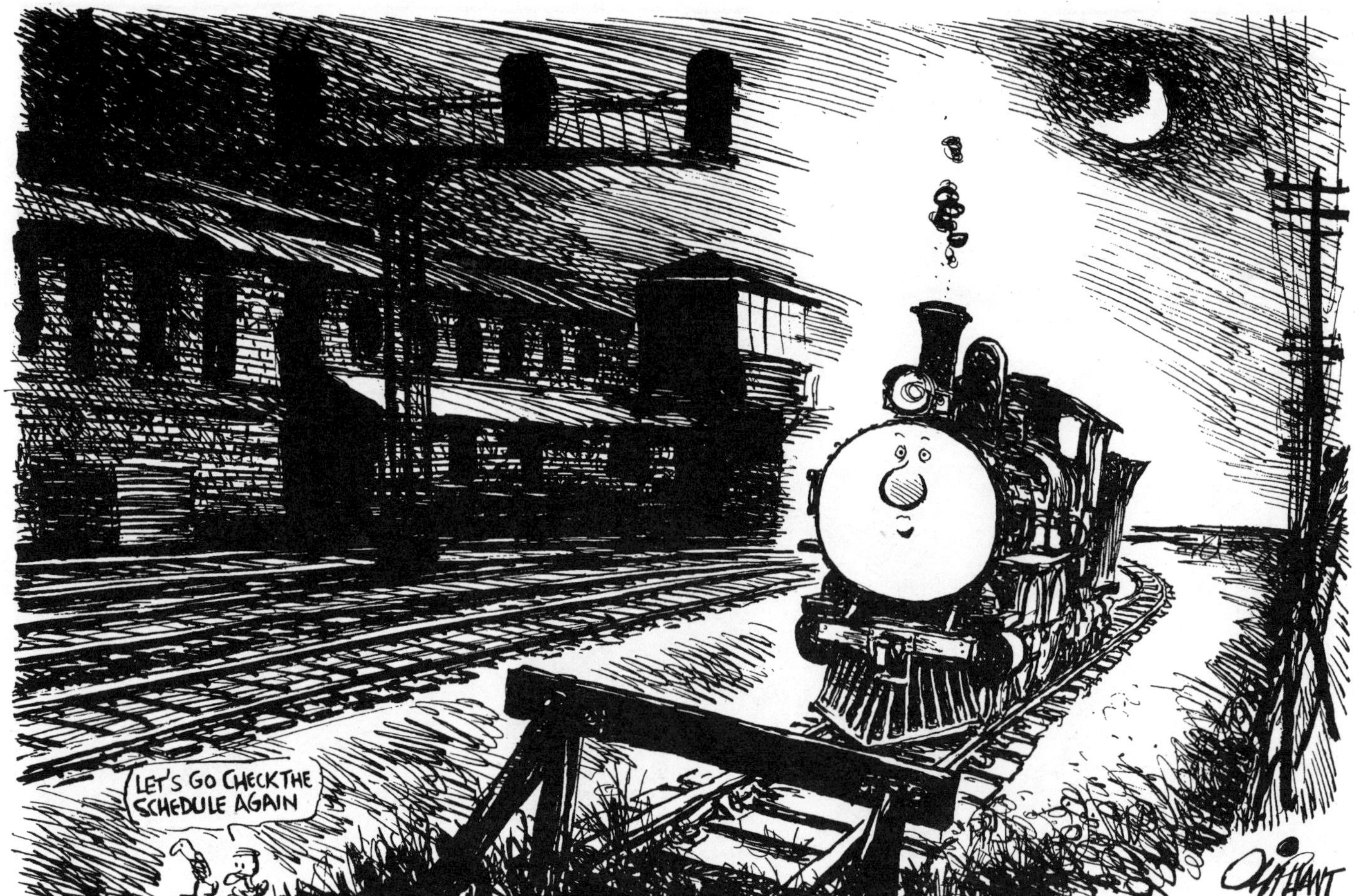
LET'S GO CHECK THE SCHEDULE AGAIN
OLIPHANT

SLOW TRACK.

November 11, 1997

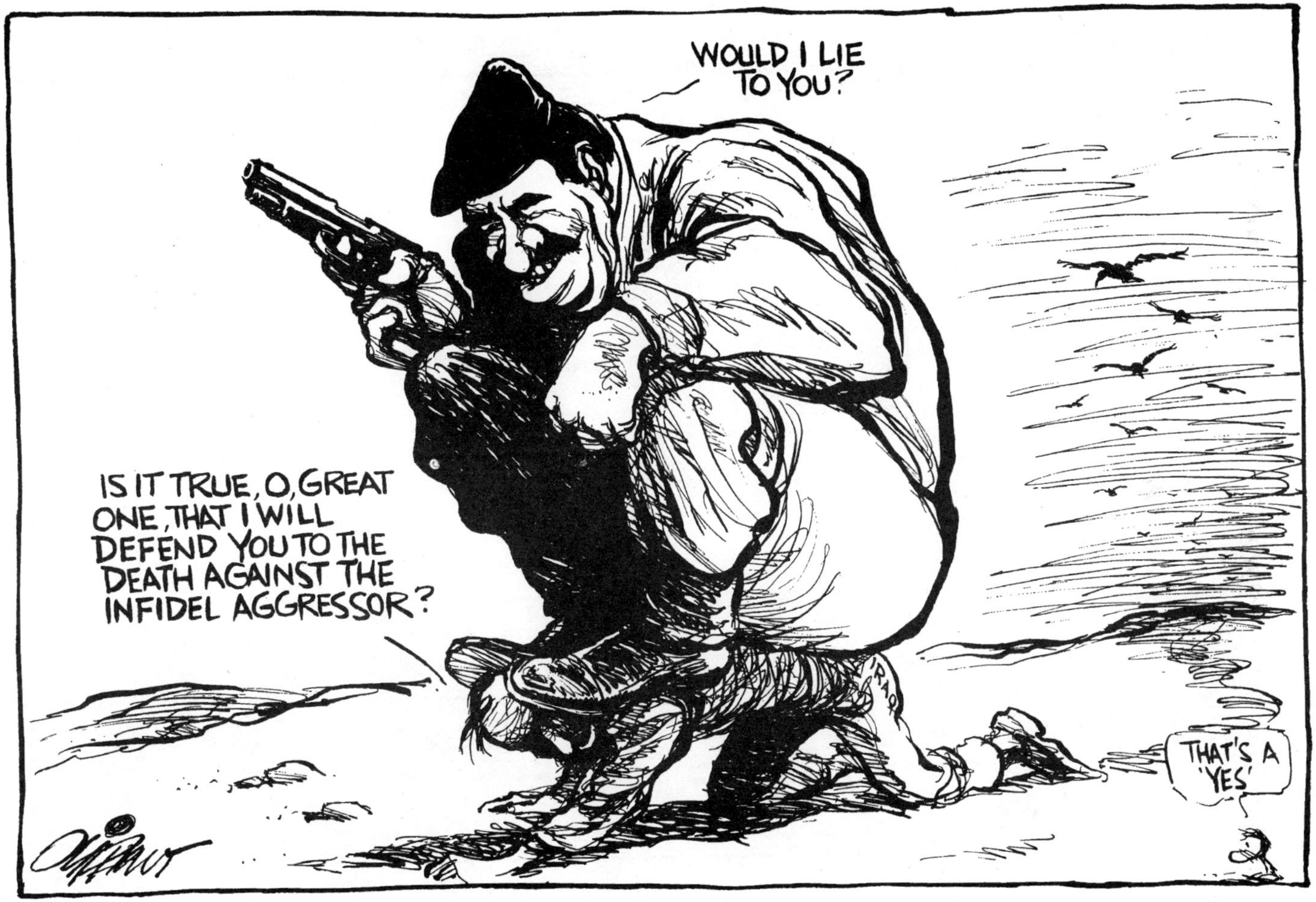
WOULD I LIE TO YOU?
IS IT TRUE, O, GREAT ONE, THAT I WILL DEFEND YOU TO THE DEATH AGAINST THE INFIDEL AGGRESSOR?
IRAQ
THAT'S A 'YES'

November 12, 1997

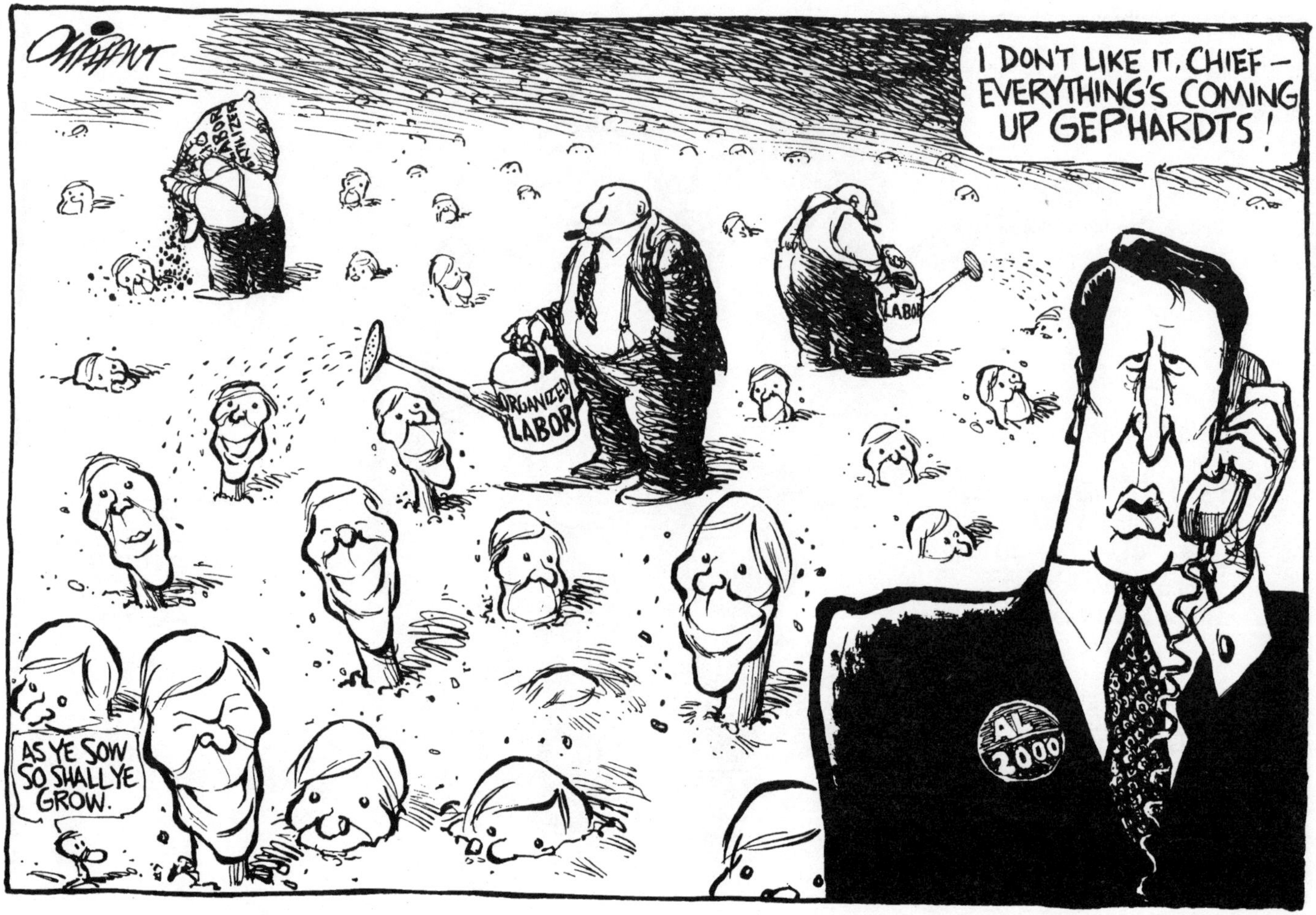
I DON'T LIKE IT, CHIEF – EVERYTHING'S COMING UP GEPHARDTS!
ORGANIZED LABOR
LABOR
AL 2000
AS YE SOW SO SHALL YE GROW.

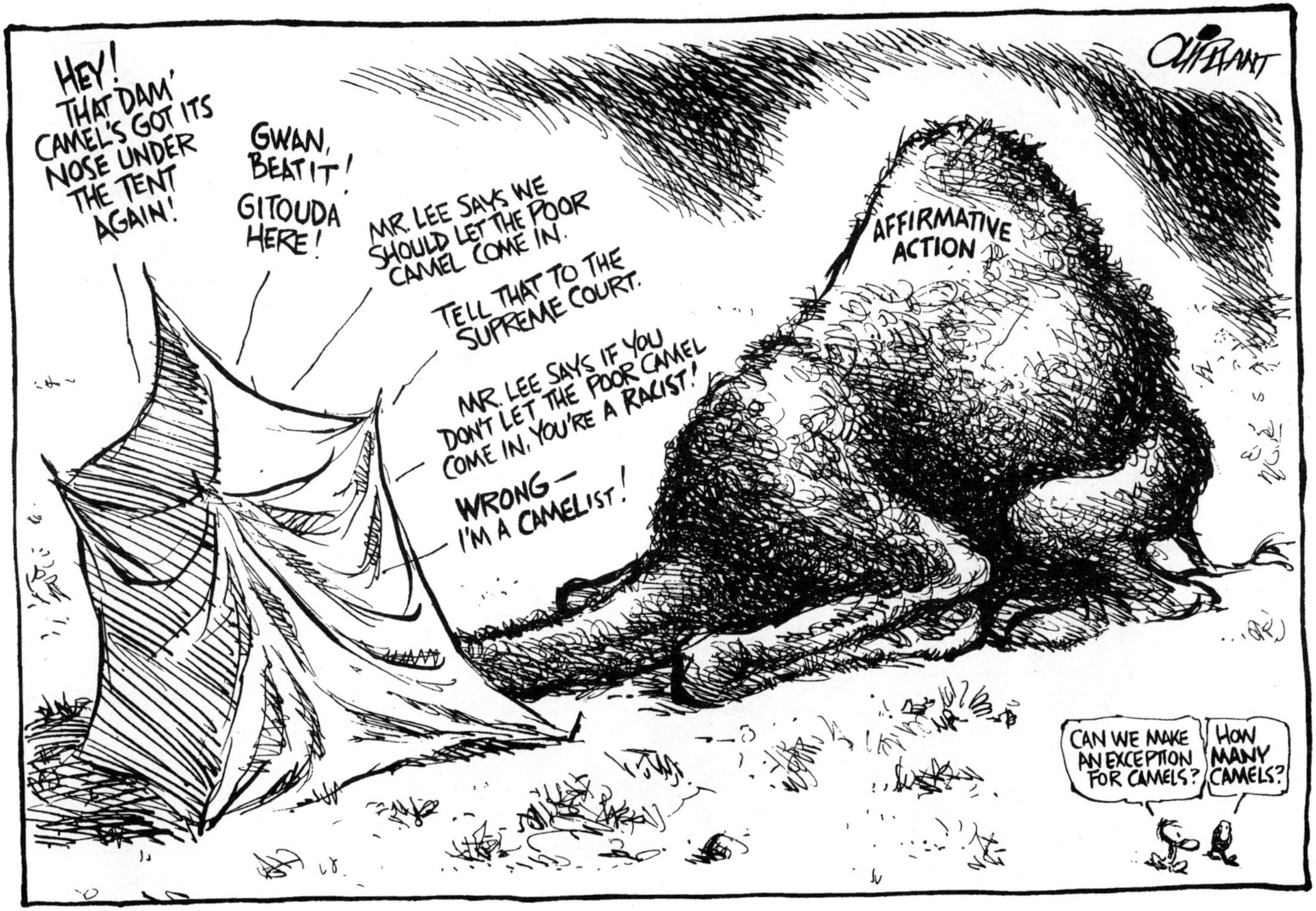
OLIPHANT
HEY! THAT DAM' CAMEL'S GOT ITS NOSE UNDER THE TENT AGAIN!
GWAN, BEAT IT! GITOUDA HERE!
MR. LEE SAYS WE SHOULD LET THE POOR CAMEL COME IN.
TELL THAT TO THE SUPREME COURT.
MR. LEE SAYS IF YOU DON'T LET THE POOR CAMEL COME IN, YOU'RE A RACIST!
WRONG— I'M A CAMELIST!
AFFIRMATIVE ACTION
CAN WE MAKE AN EXCEPTION FOR CAMELS?
HOW MANY CAMELS?

November 24, 1997

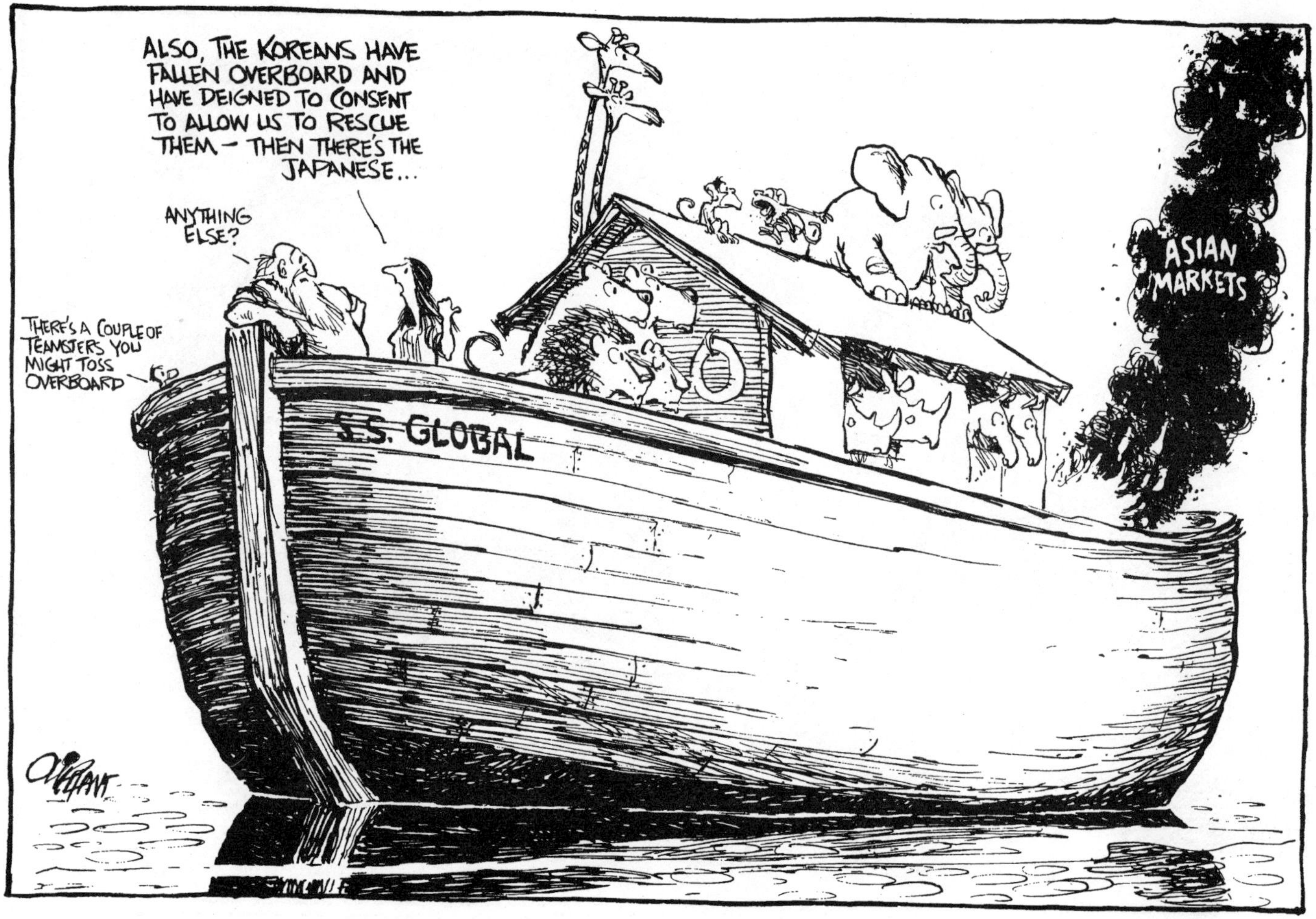
ALSO, THE KOREANS HAVE FALLEN OVERBOARD AND HAVE DEIGNED TO CONSENT TO ALLOW US TO RESCUE THEM - THEN THERE'S THE JAPANESE...
ANYTHING ELSE?
THERE'S A COUPLE OF TEAMSTERS YOU MIGHT TOSS OVERBOARD
S.S. GLOBAL
ASIAN MARKETS
OLIPHANT

December 2, 1997

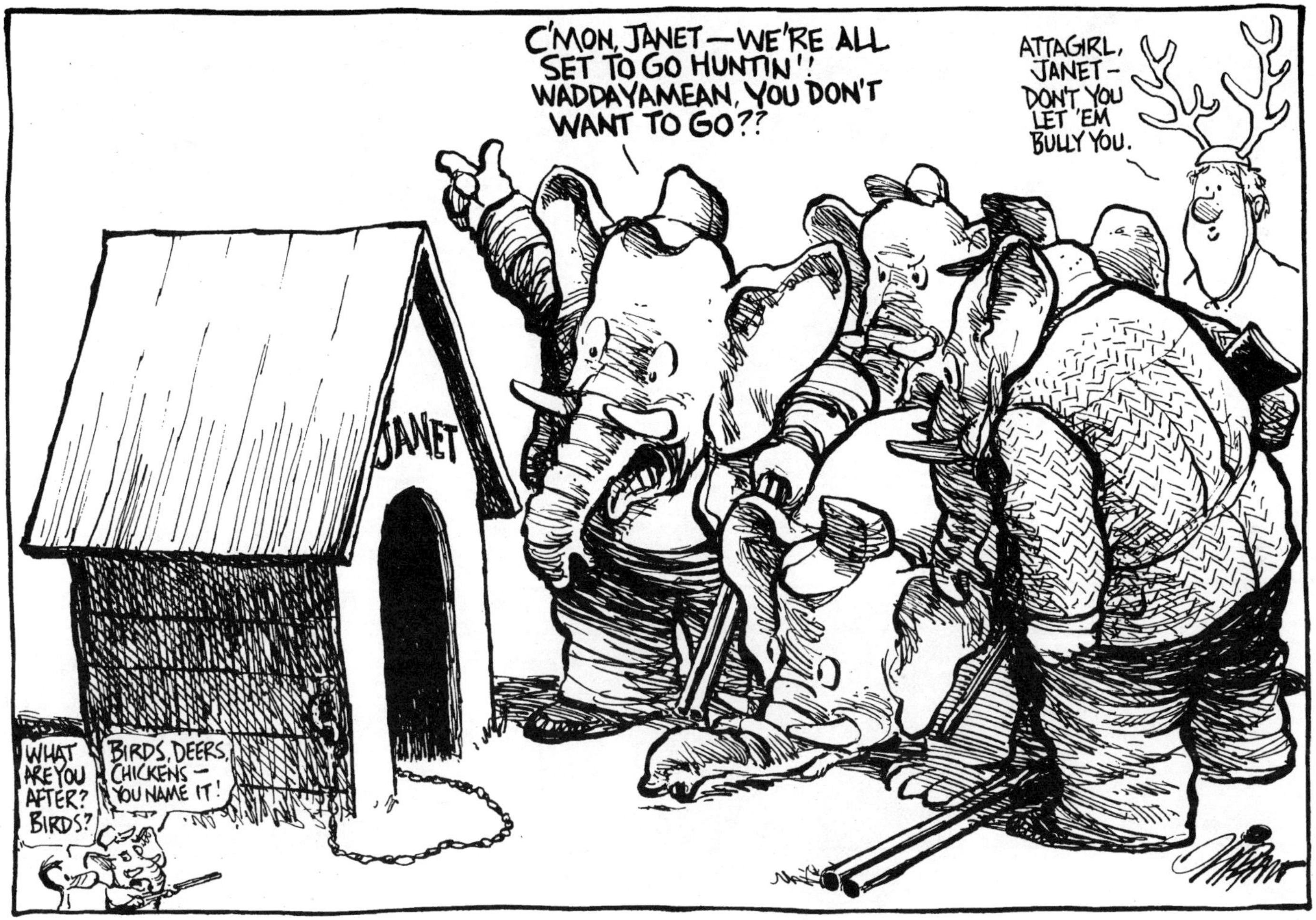
C'MON, JANET—WE'RE ALL SET TO GO HUNTIN'! WADDAYAMEAN, YOU DON'T WANT TO GO??
ATTAGIRL, JANET- DON'T YOU LET 'EM BULLY YOU.
JANET
WHAT ARE YOU AFTER? BIRDS?
BIRDS, DEERS, CHICKENS — YOU NAME IT!

December 3, 1997

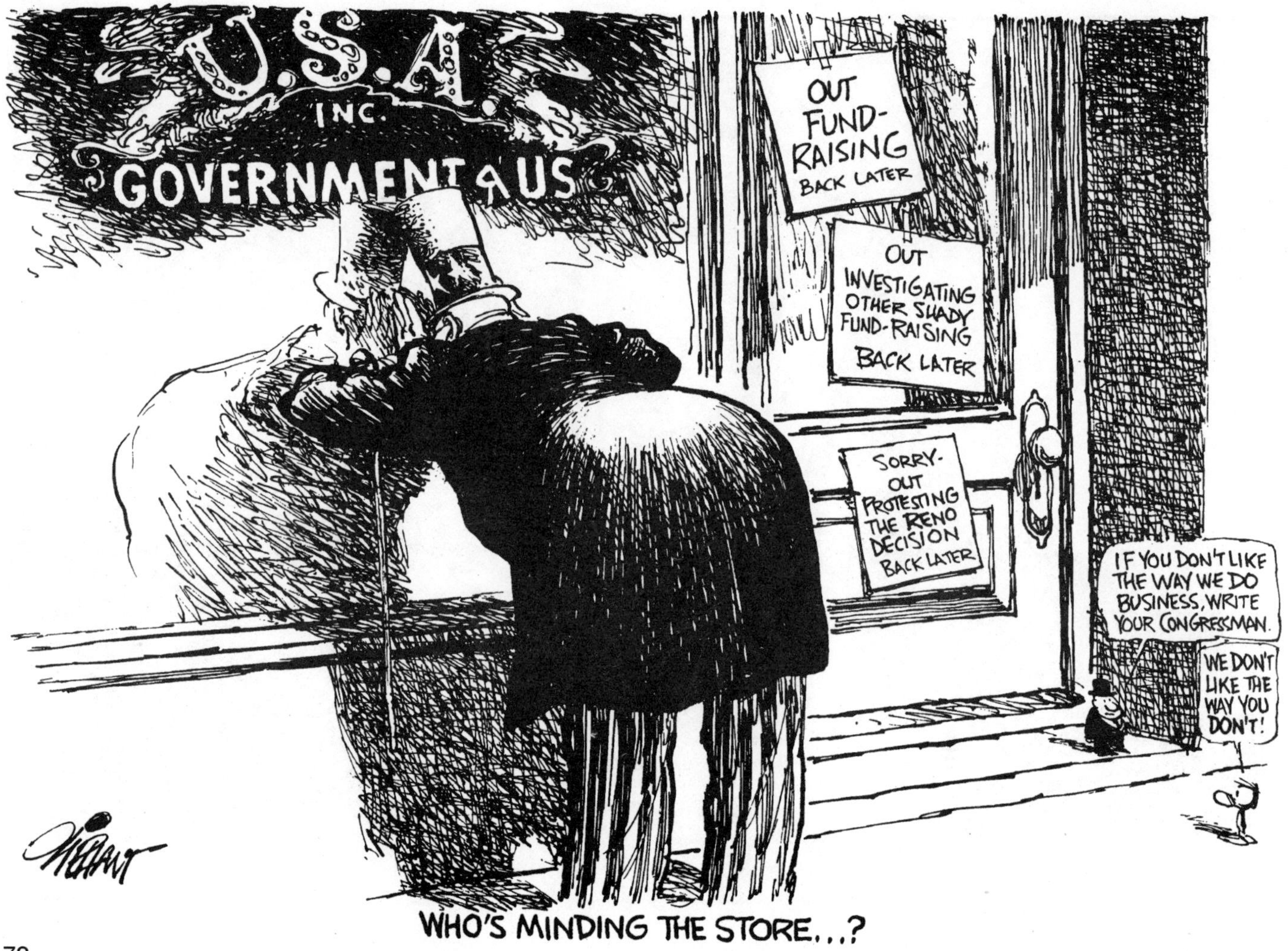
U.S.A.
INC.
GOVERNMENT ꟼ US
OUT
FUND-
RAISING
BACK LATER
OUT
INVESTIGATING
OTHER SHADY
FUND-RAISING
BACK LATER
SORRY-
OUT
PROTESTING
THE RENO
DECISION
BACK LATER
IF YOU DON'T LIKE THE WAY WE DO BUSINESS, WRITE YOUR CONGRESSMAN.
WE DON'T LIKE THE WAY YOU DON'T!
WHO'S MINDING THE STORE...?

December 9, 1997

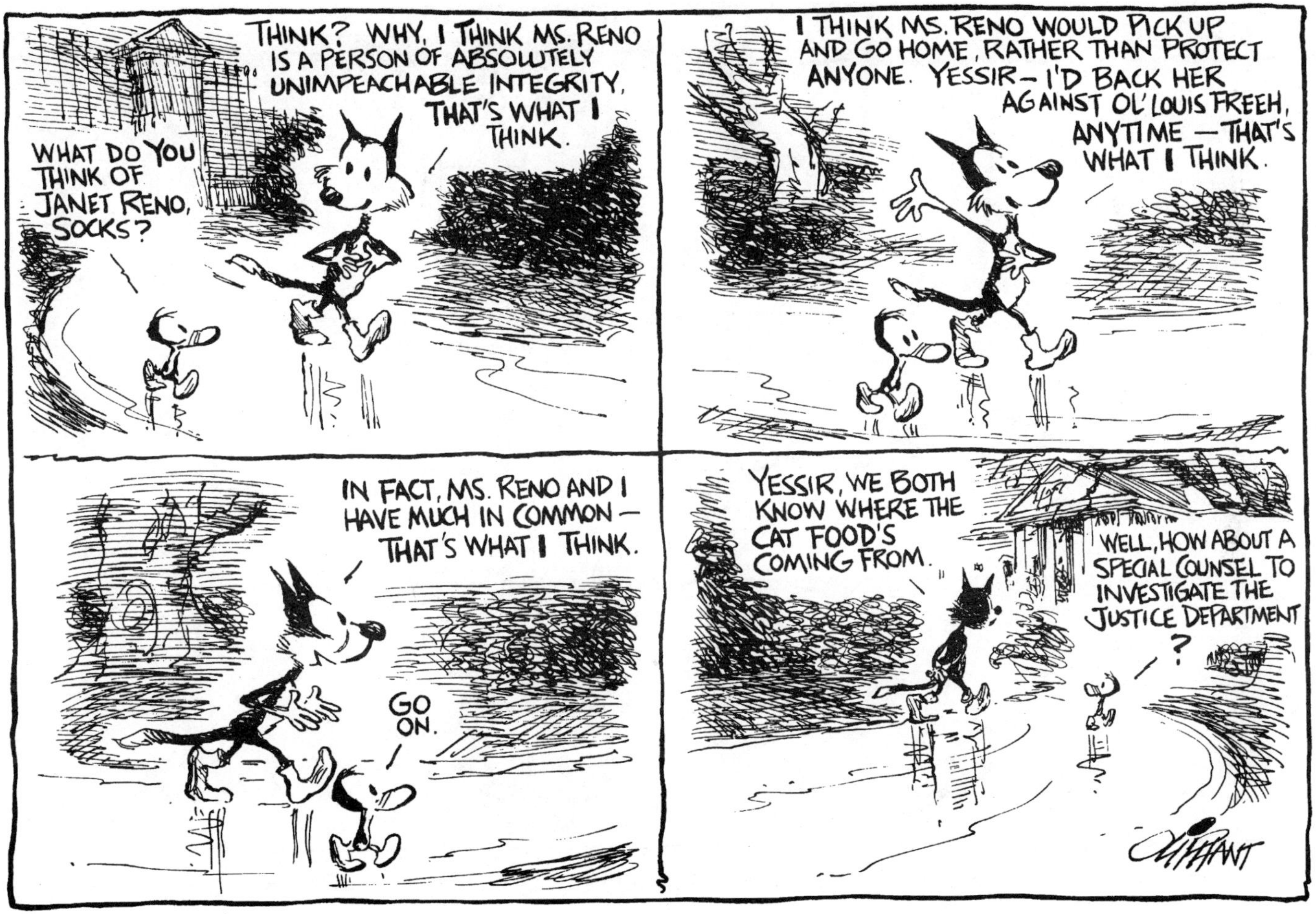
WHAT DO YOU THINK OF JANET RENO, SOCKS?
THINK? WHY, I THINK MS. RENO IS A PERSON OF ABSOLUTELY UNIMPEACHABLE INTEGRITY. THAT'S WHAT I THINK.
I THINK MS. RENO WOULD PICK UP AND GO HOME, RATHER THAN PROTECT ANYONE. YESSIR– I'D BACK HER AGAINST OL' LOUIS FREEH, ANYTIME —THAT'S WHAT I THINK.
IN FACT, MS. RENO AND I HAVE MUCH IN COMMON— THAT'S WHAT I THINK.
GO ON.
YESSIR, WE BOTH KNOW WHERE THE CAT FOOD'S COMING FROM.
WELL, HOW ABOUT A SPECIAL COUNSEL TO INVESTIGATE THE JUSTICE DEPARTMENT ?
OLIPHANT

December 11, 1997

OLIPHANT
PVC 2"
M PLUGS 3 Pin
F PLUGS 3 Pin
JUNCTN BOXES
Y's 2"
50FT
25FT
RING
WHOM SHOULD WE WORRY ABOUT? BOEING OR THE FAA OR THE FBI?
US.
15/8Y
'JOE'S PLUMBING AND ELECTRICAL . . . WHY, SURE, MR. BOEING, WE CAN REWIRE A 747 . . . HOW MANY AND WHEN? . . . NO, DON'T WORRY ABOUT THE FAA. WE WORK WITH THEM ALL THE TIME . . .'

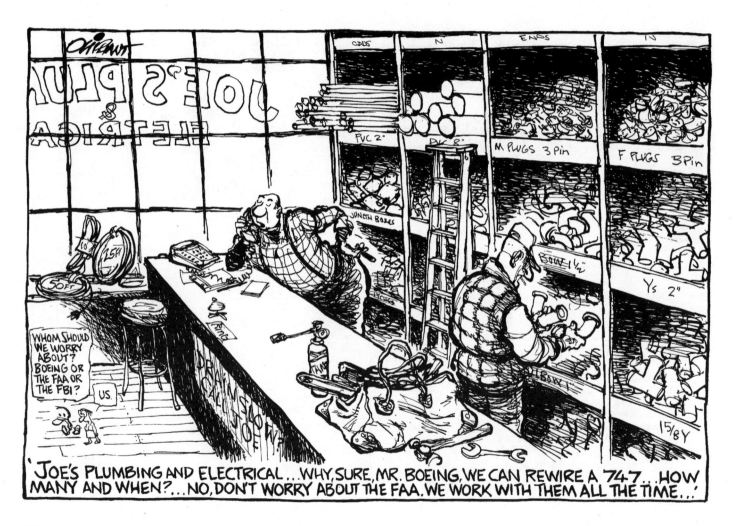

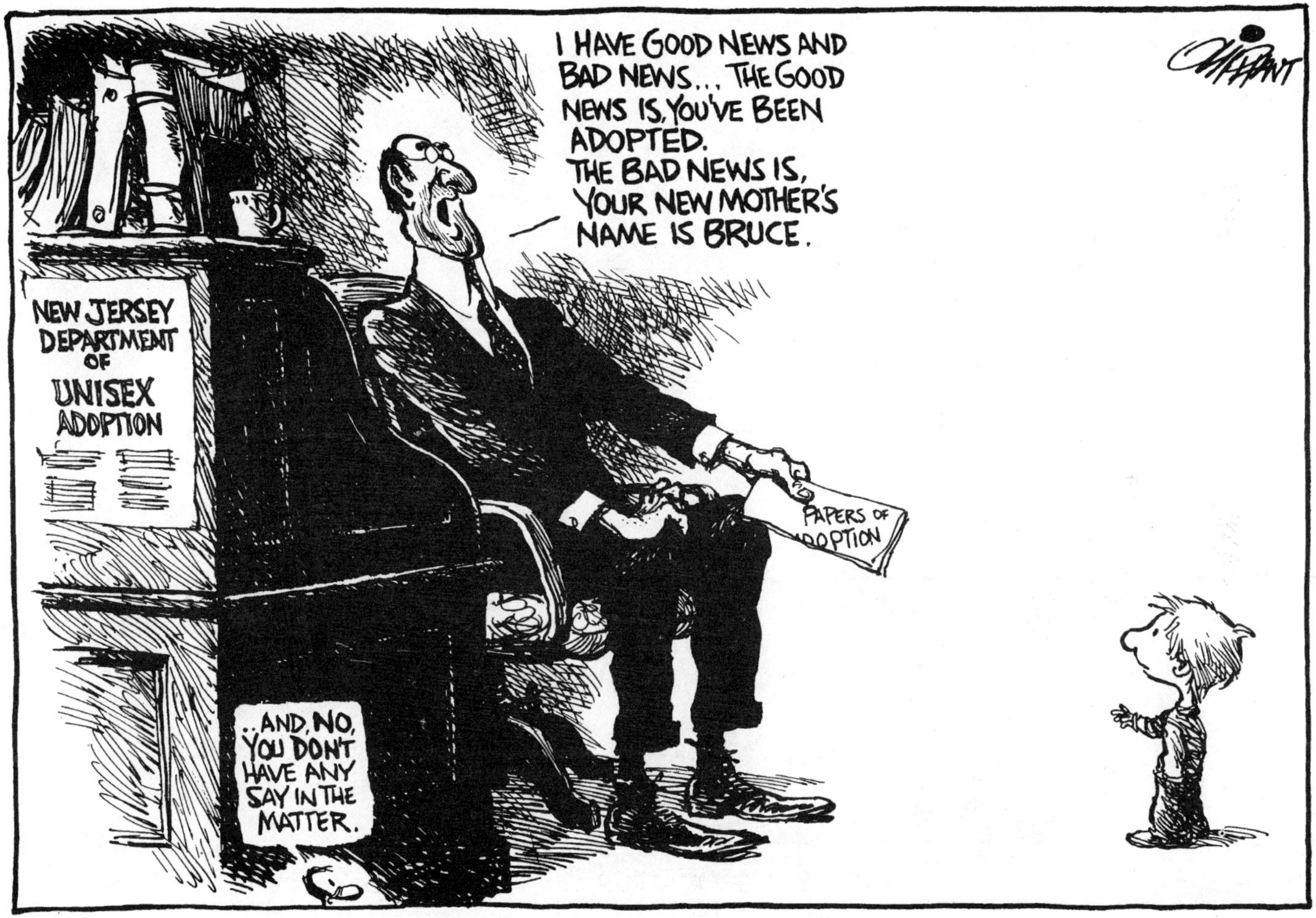
I HAVE GOOD NEWS AND BAD NEWS... THE GOOD NEWS IS, YOU'VE BEEN ADOPTED.
THE BAD NEWS IS, YOUR NEW MOTHER'S NAME IS BRUCE.
NEW JERSEY DEPARTMENT OF UNISEX ADOPTION
PAPERS OF ADOPTION
...AND, NO, YOU DON'T HAVE ANY SAY IN THE MATTER.
OLIPHANT

December 22, 1997

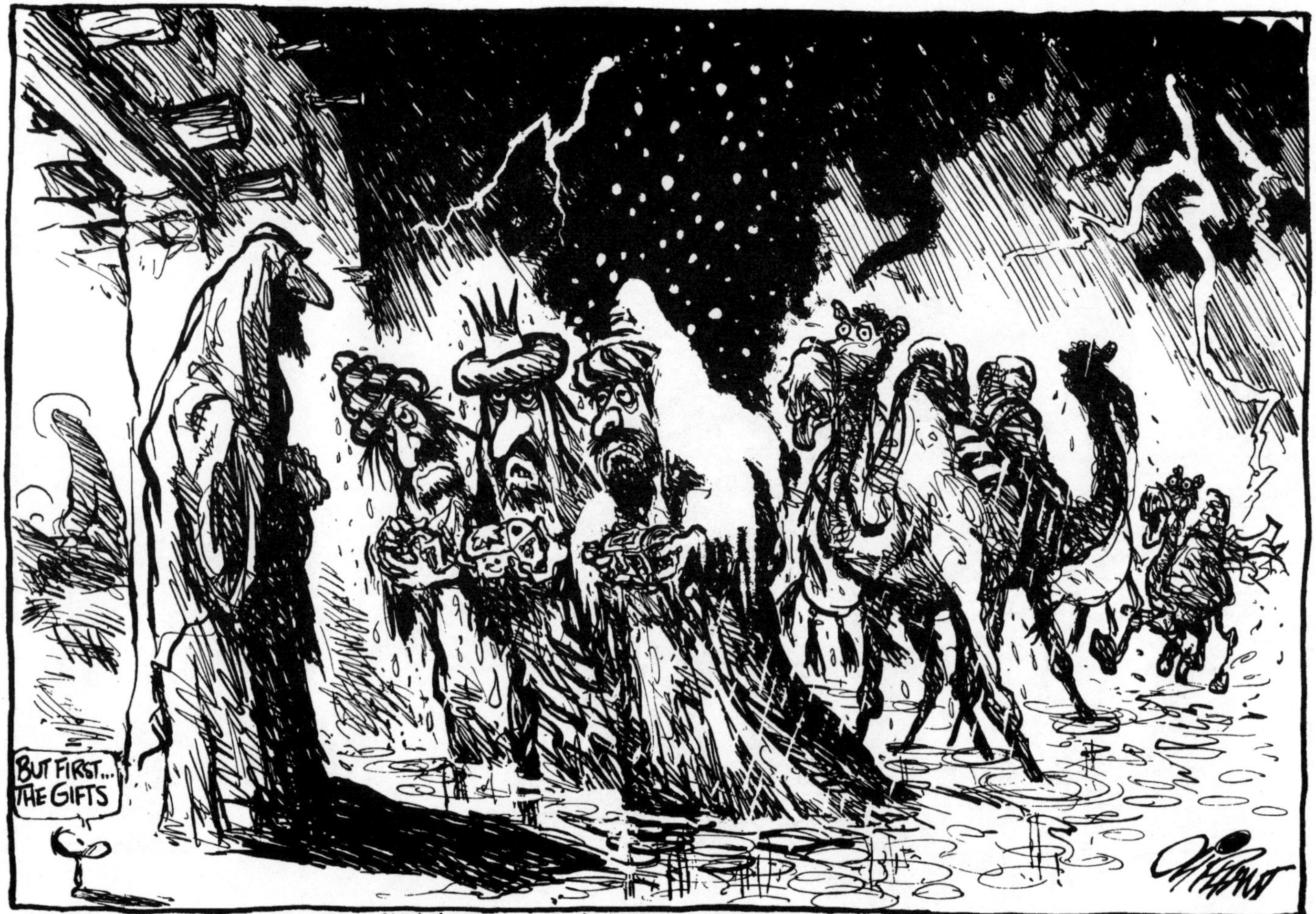
BUT FIRST...
THE GIFTS

'WE'D LIKE A WORD WITH EL NIÑO.'

December 23, 1997

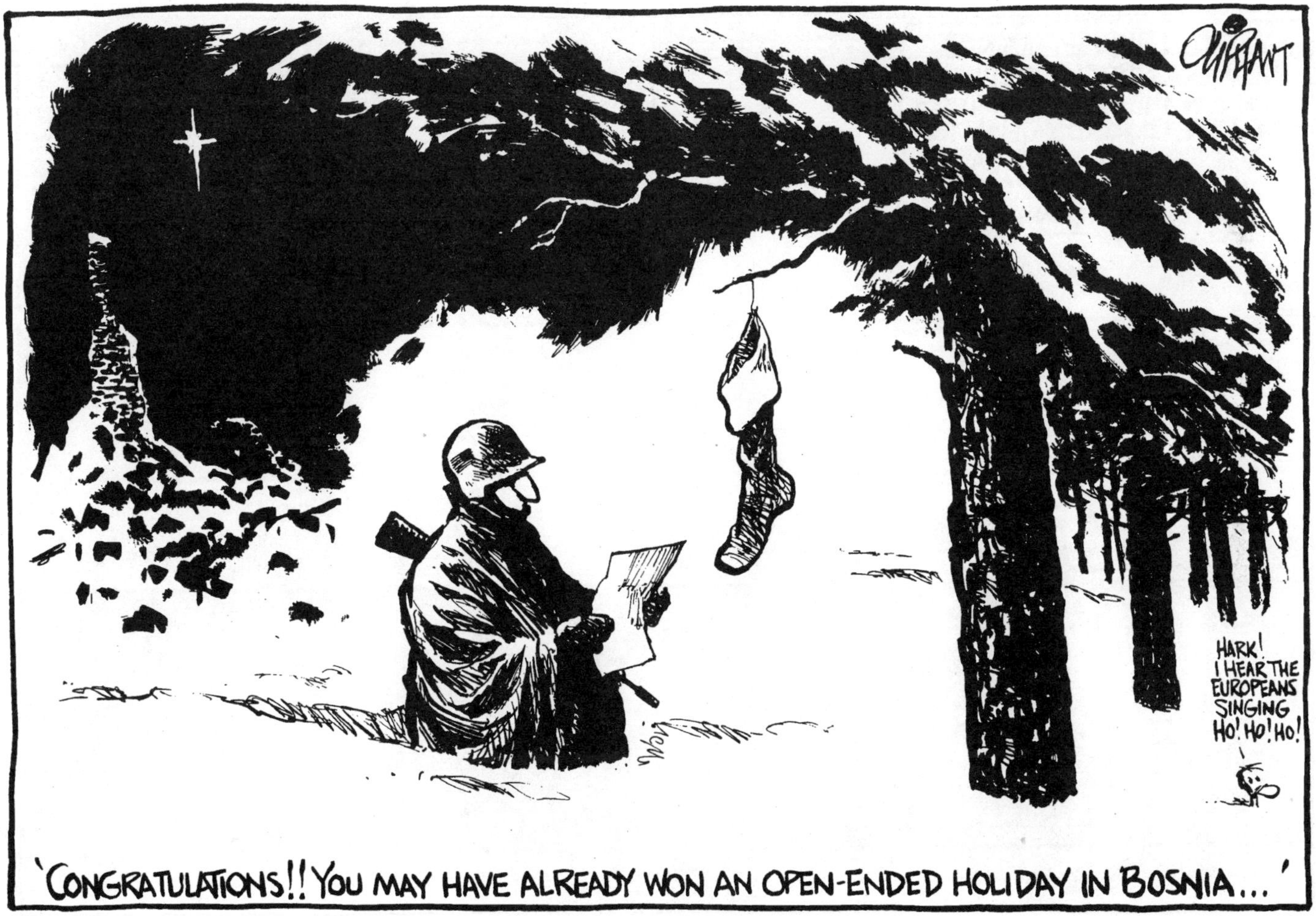
OLIPHANT
HARK! I HEAR THE EUROPEANS SINGING HO! HO! HO!
'CONGRATULATIONS!! YOU MAY HAVE ALREADY WON AN OPEN-ENDED HOLIDAY IN BOSNIA...'

January 6, 1998

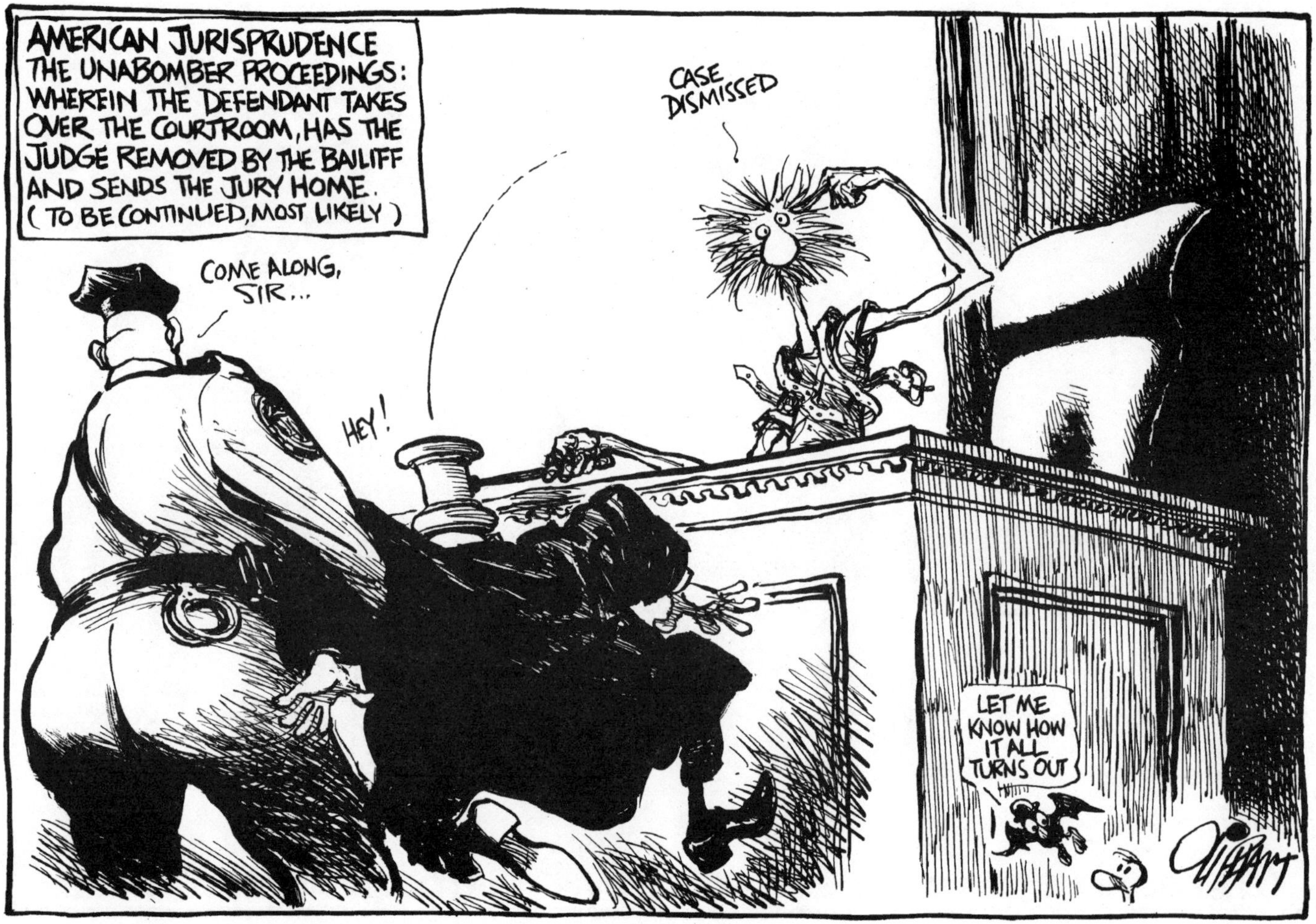
AMERICAN JURISPRUDENCE
THE UNABOMBER PROCEEDINGS:
WHEREIN THE DEFENDANT TAKES OVER THE COURTROOM, HAS THE JUDGE REMOVED BY THE BAILIFF AND SENDS THE JURY HOME.
(TO BE CONTINUED, MOST LIKELY)
COME ALONG, SIR...
HEY!
CASE DISMISSED
LET ME KNOW HOW IT ALL TURNS OUT

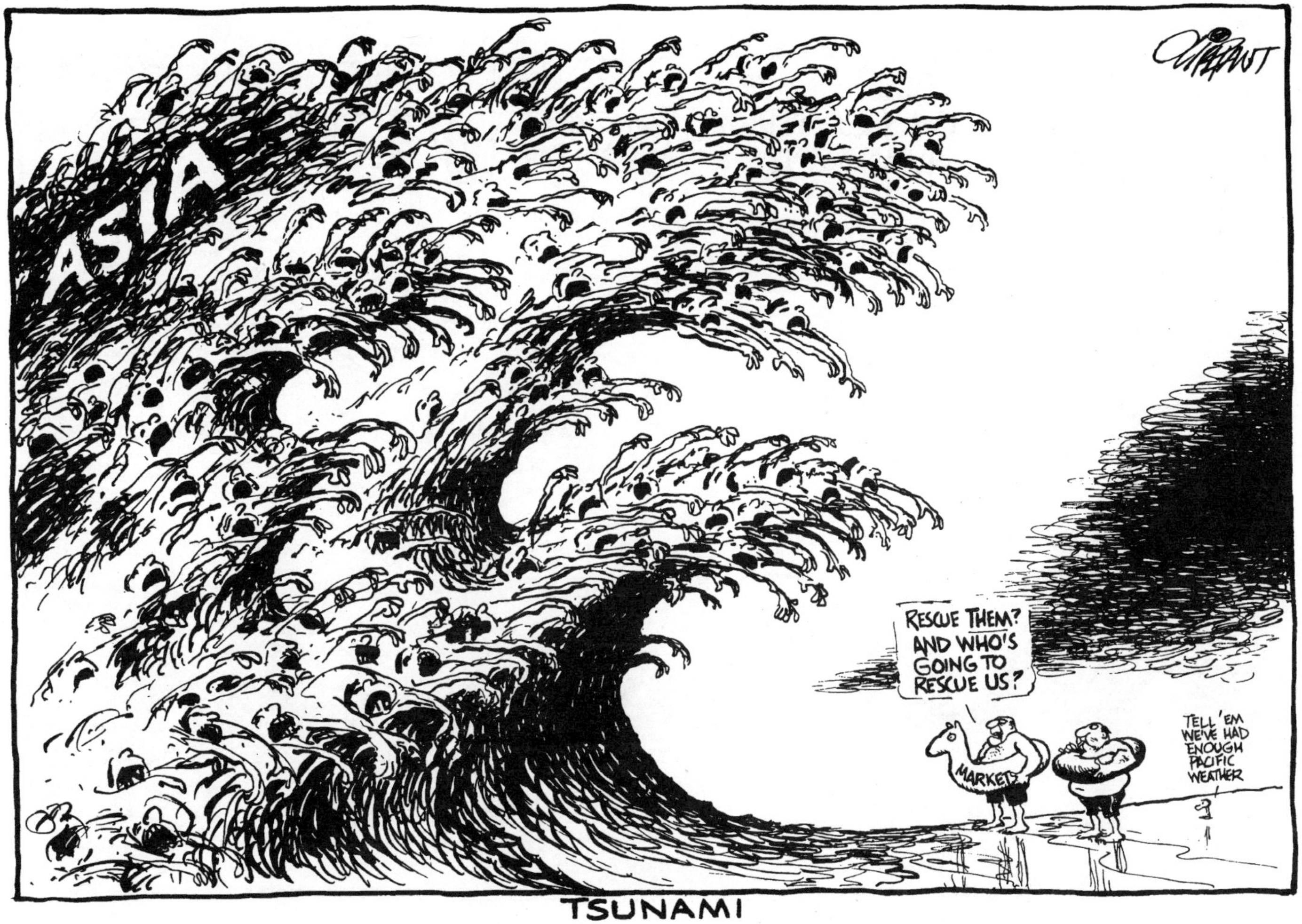
ASIA
RESCUE THEM? AND WHO'S GOING TO RESCUE US?
MARKETS
TELL 'EM WE'VE HAD ENOUGH PACIFIC WEATHER

TSUNAMI

January 14, 1998

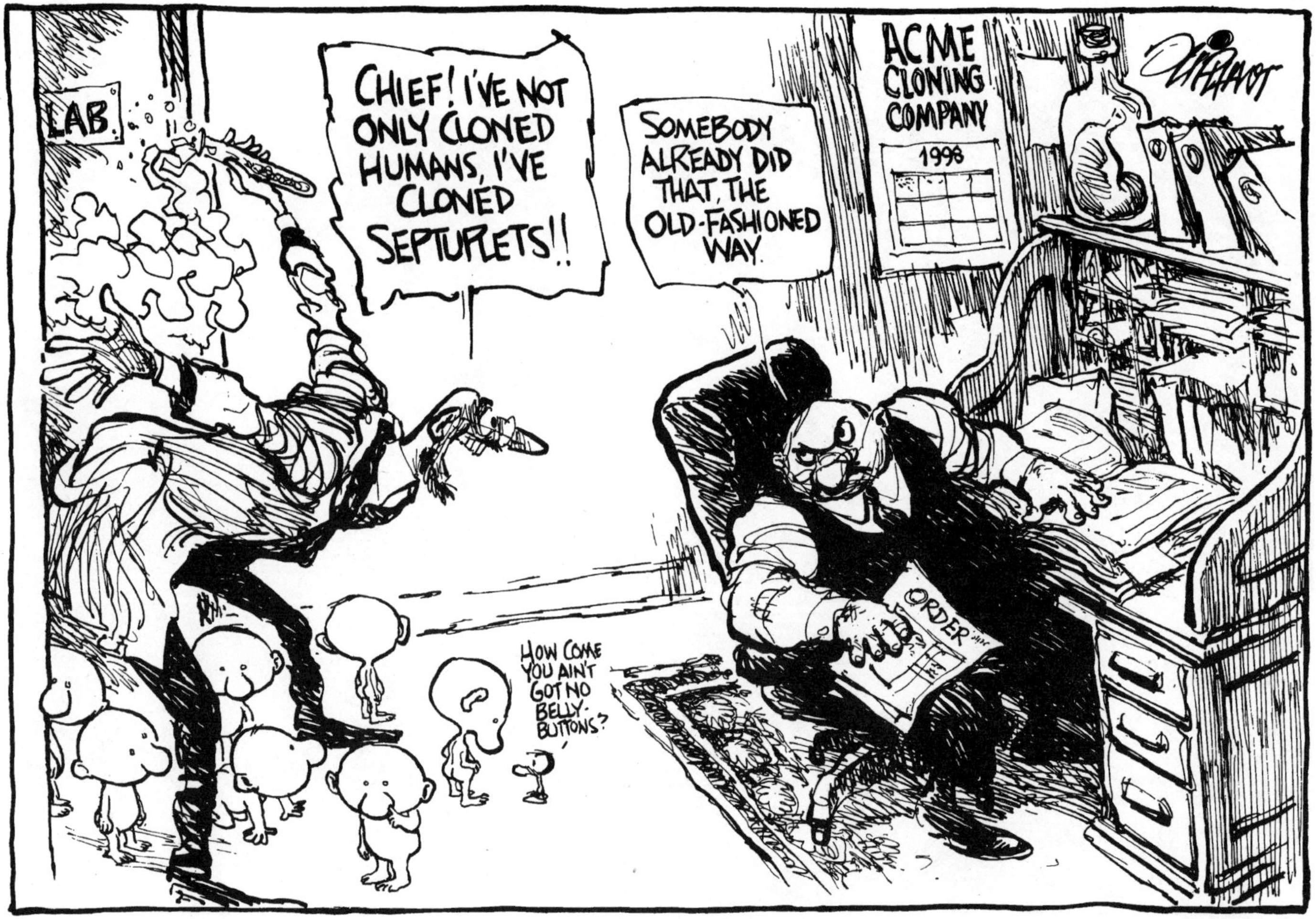
LAB
CHIEF! I'VE NOT ONLY CLONED HUMANS, I'VE CLONED SEPTUPLETS!!
SOMEBODY ALREADY DID THAT, THE OLD-FASHIONED WAY.
ACME CLONING COMPANY
1998
ORDER
HOW COME YOU AIN'T GOT NO BELLY-BUTTONS?

January 19, 1998

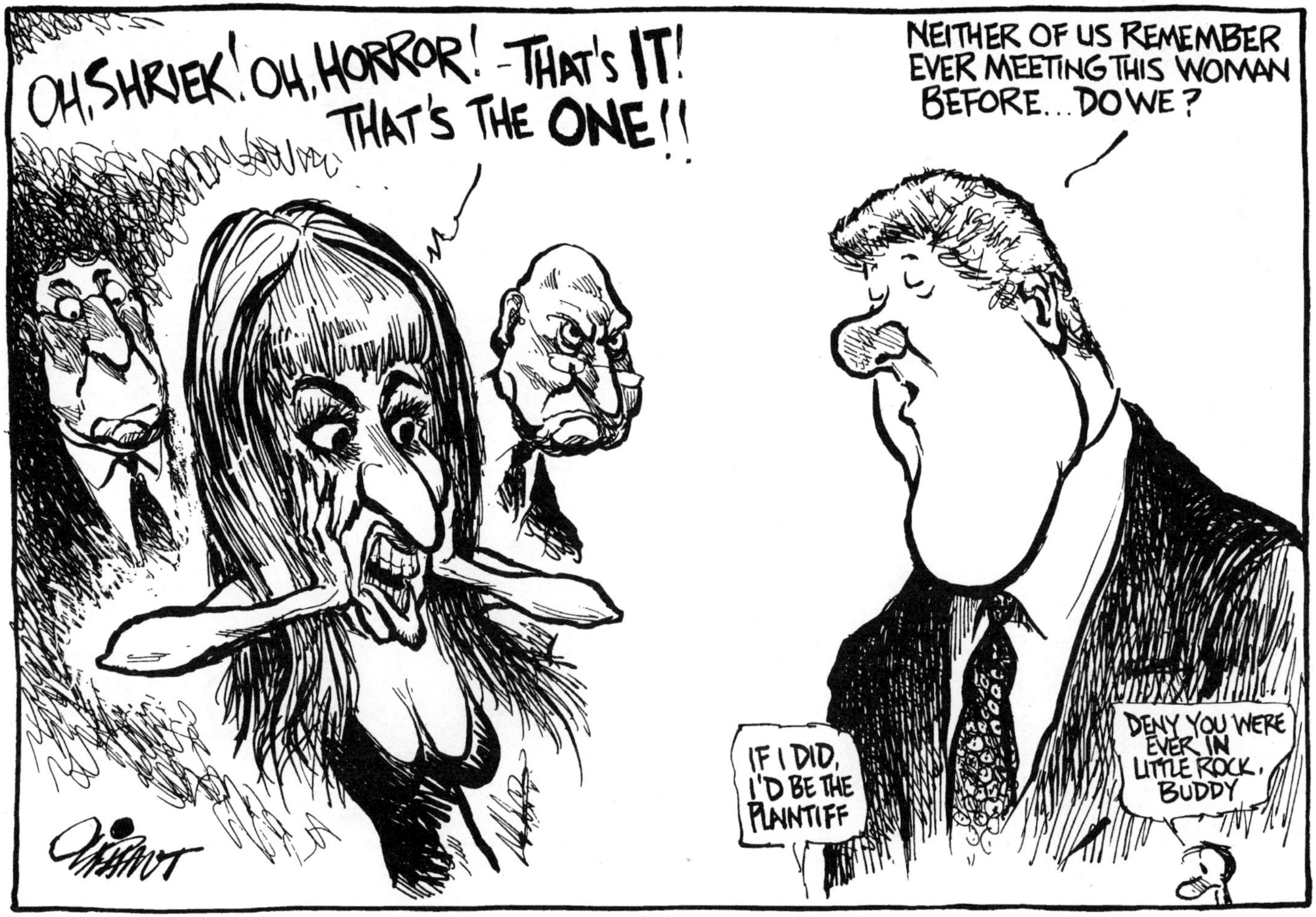
OH, SHRIEK! OH, HORROR! -THAT'S IT! THAT'S THE ONE!!
NEITHER OF US REMEMBER EVER MEETING THIS WOMAN BEFORE... DO WE?
IF I DID, I'D BE THE PLAINTIFF
DENY YOU WERE EVER IN LITTLE ROCK, BUDDY
OLIPHANT

January 21, 1998

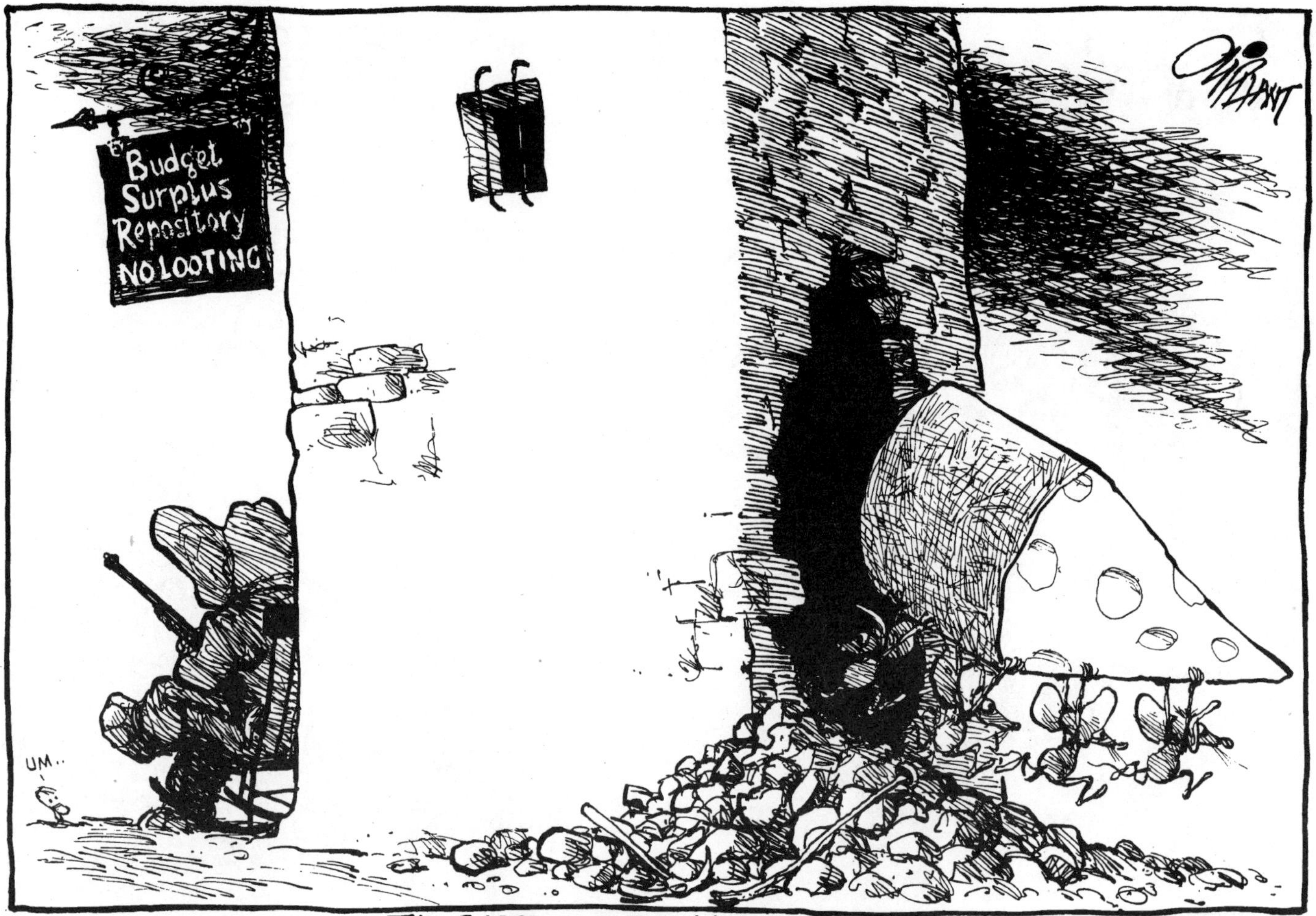
Budget Surplus Repository
NO LOOTING
UM..
OLIPHANT

THE CHEESE AND THE MOUSOCRATS.

January 22, 1998

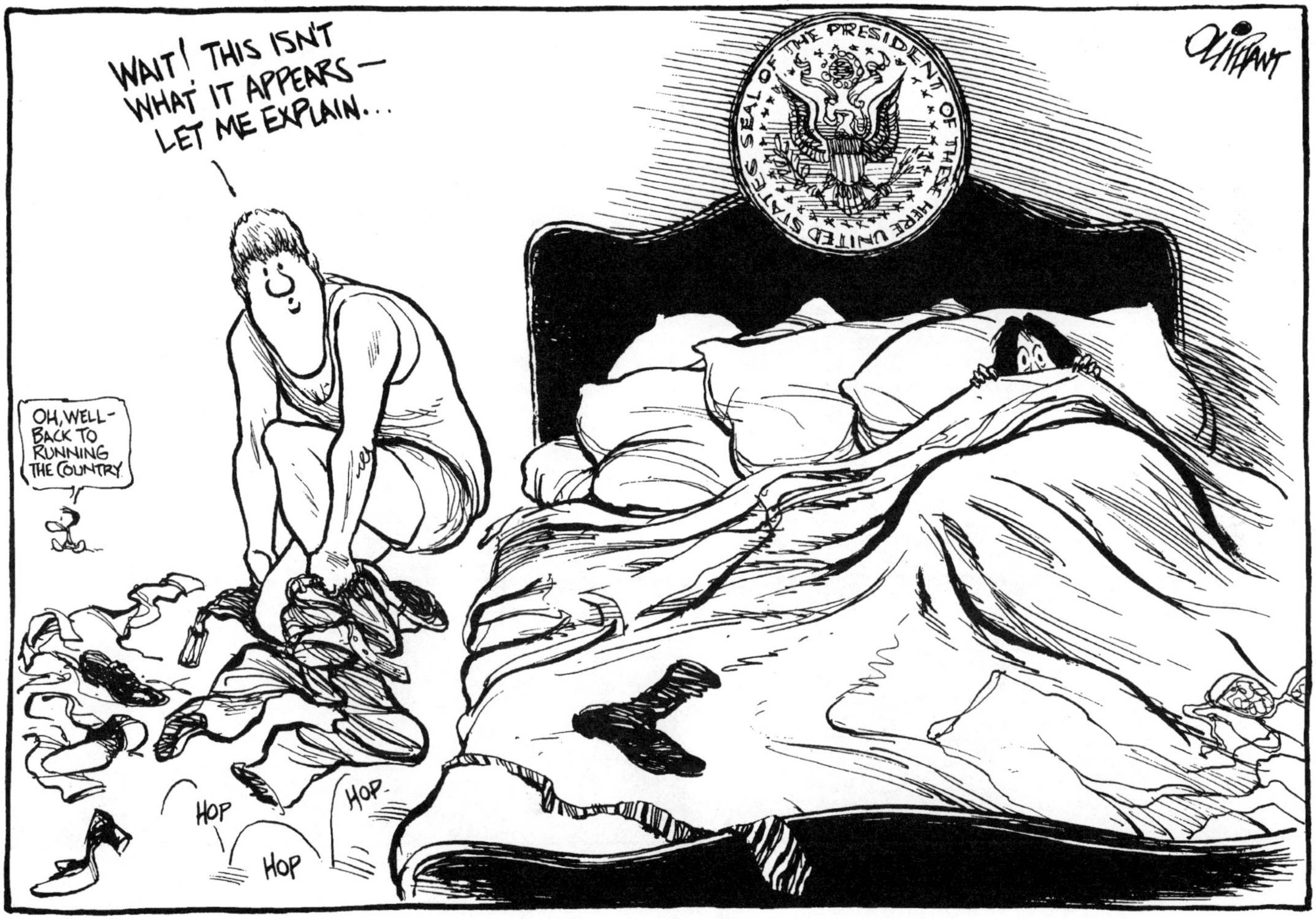
OLIPHANT
WAIT! THIS ISN'T WHAT IT APPEARS—LET ME EXPLAIN...
SEAL OF THE PRESIDENT OF THESE HERE UNITED STATES
OH, WELL- BACK TO RUNNING THE COUNTRY
HOP
HOP
HOP

January 27, 1998

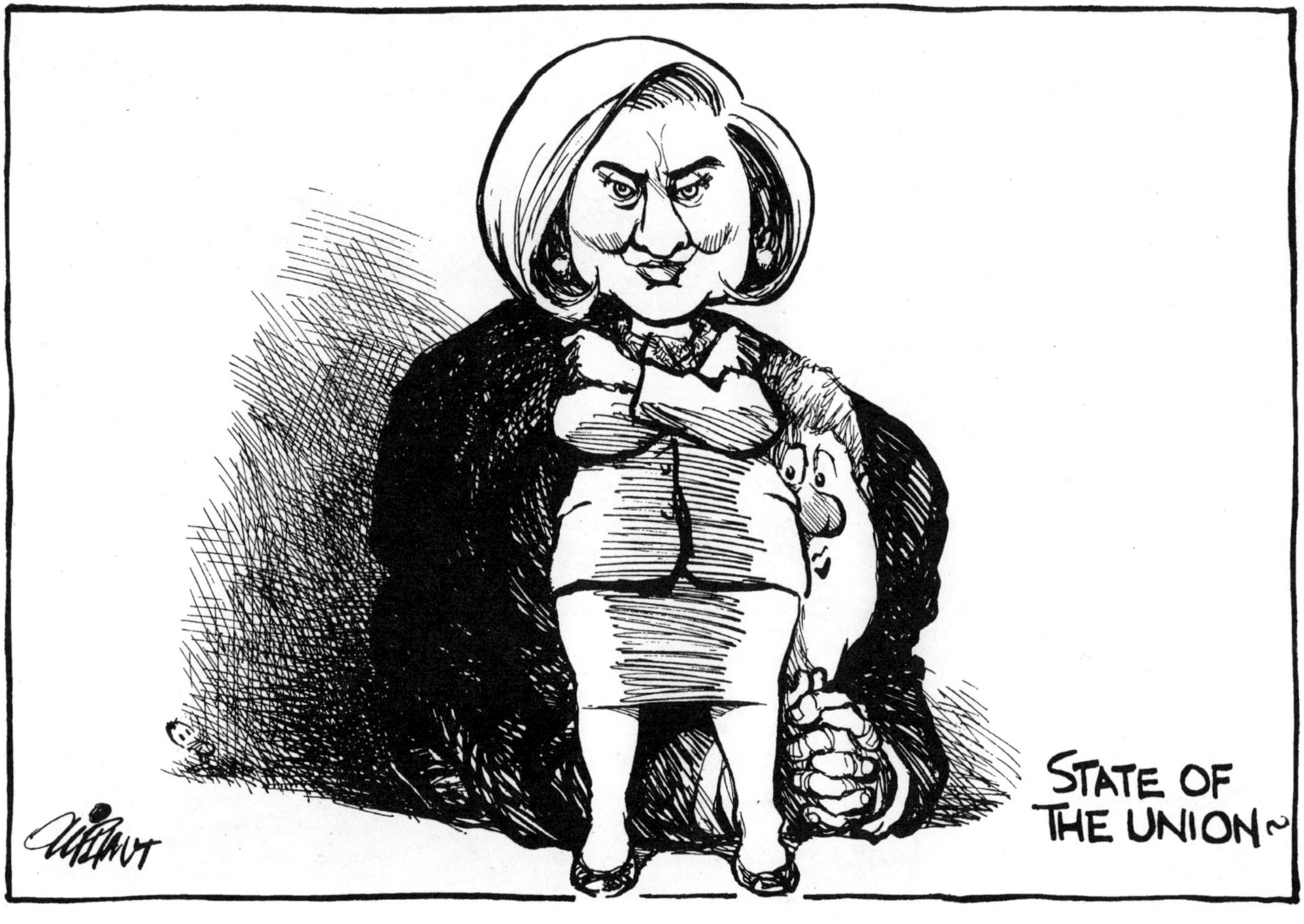
STATE OF THE UNION

January 29, 1998

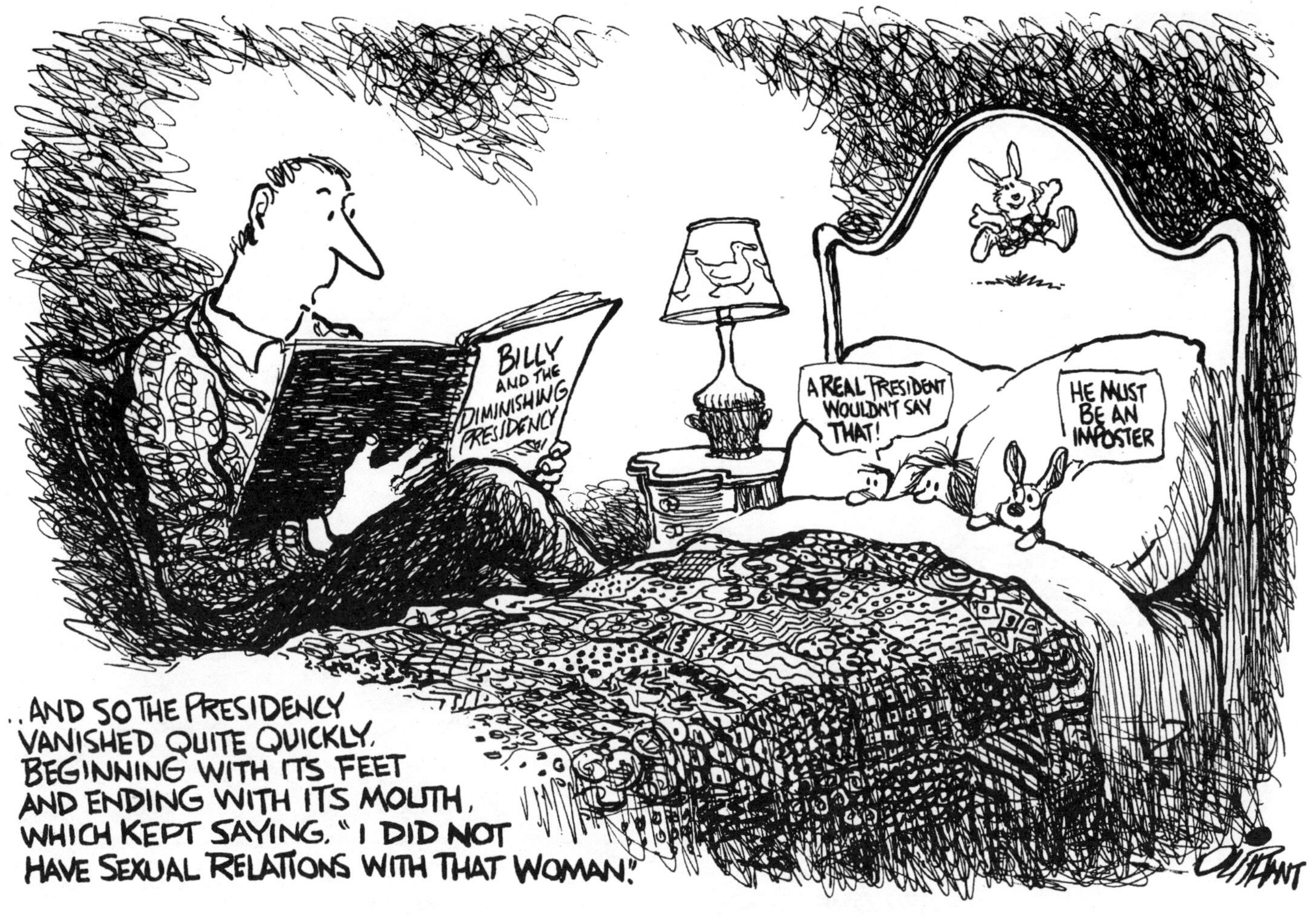
BILLY AND THE DIMINISHING PRESIDENCY
A REAL PRESIDENT WOULDN'T SAY THAT!
HE MUST BE AN IMPOSTER
..AND SO THE PRESIDENCY VANISHED QUITE QUICKLY, BEGINNING WITH ITS FEET AND ENDING WITH ITS MOUTH, WHICH KEPT SAYING, "I DID NOT HAVE SEXUAL RELATIONS WITH THAT WOMAN!"
OLIPHANT

February 4, 1998

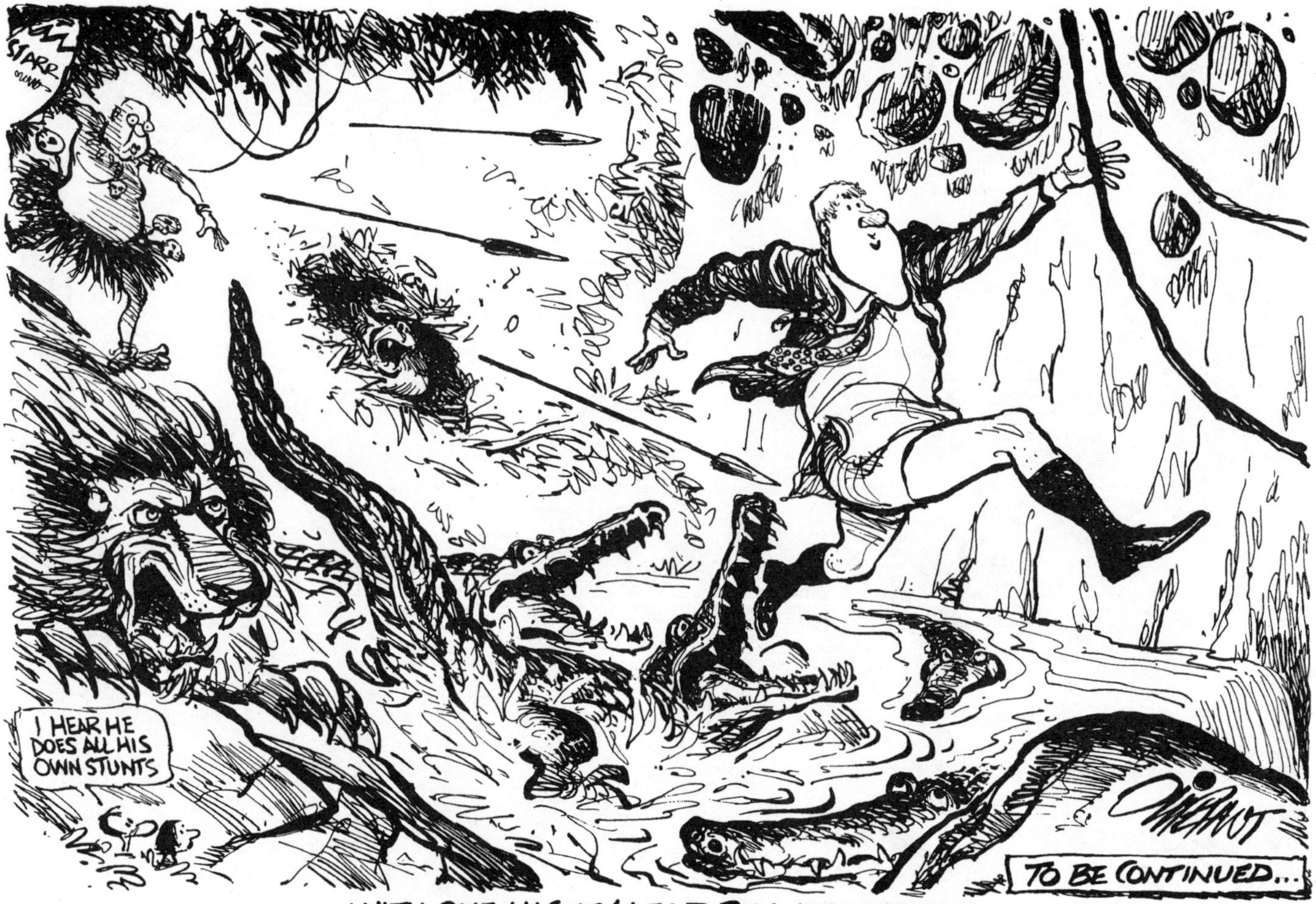
STARR
I HEAR HE DOES ALL HIS OWN STUNTS
TO BE CONTINUED...
OLIPHANT

WITH ONE MIGHTY LEAP, BILL WAS FREE.

February 10, 1998

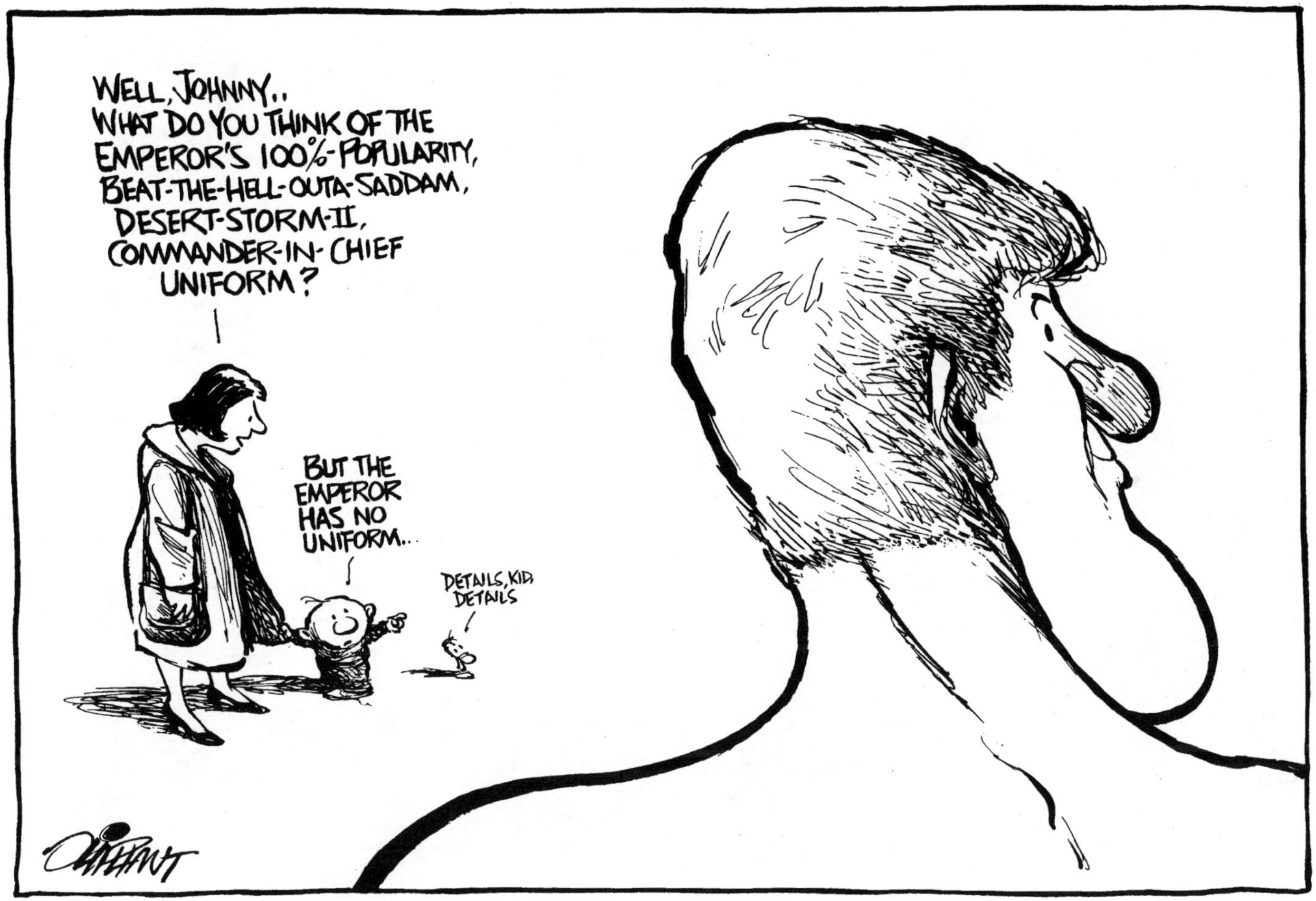
WELL, JOHNNY..
WHAT DO YOU THINK OF THE
EMPEROR'S 100%-POPULARITY,
BEAT-THE-HELL-OUTA-SADDAM,
DESERT-STORM-II,
COMMANDER-IN-CHIEF
UNIFORM?
BUT THE
EMPEROR
HAS NO
UNIFORM...
DETAILS, KID,
DETAILS
OLIPHANT

February 11, 1998

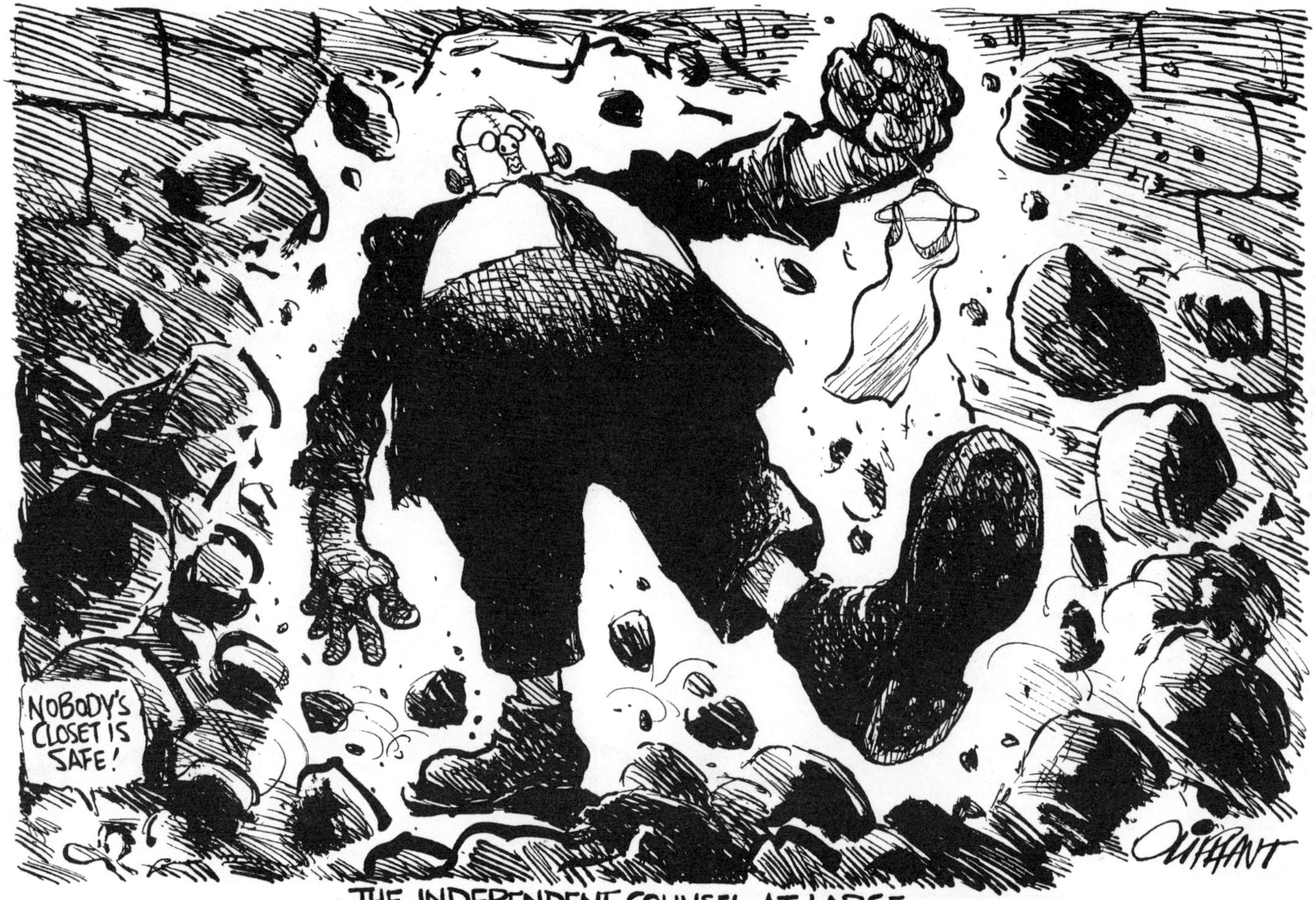
NOBODY'S CLOSET IS SAFE!
OLIPHANT

THE INDEPENDENT COUNSEL AT LARGE.

February 12, 1998

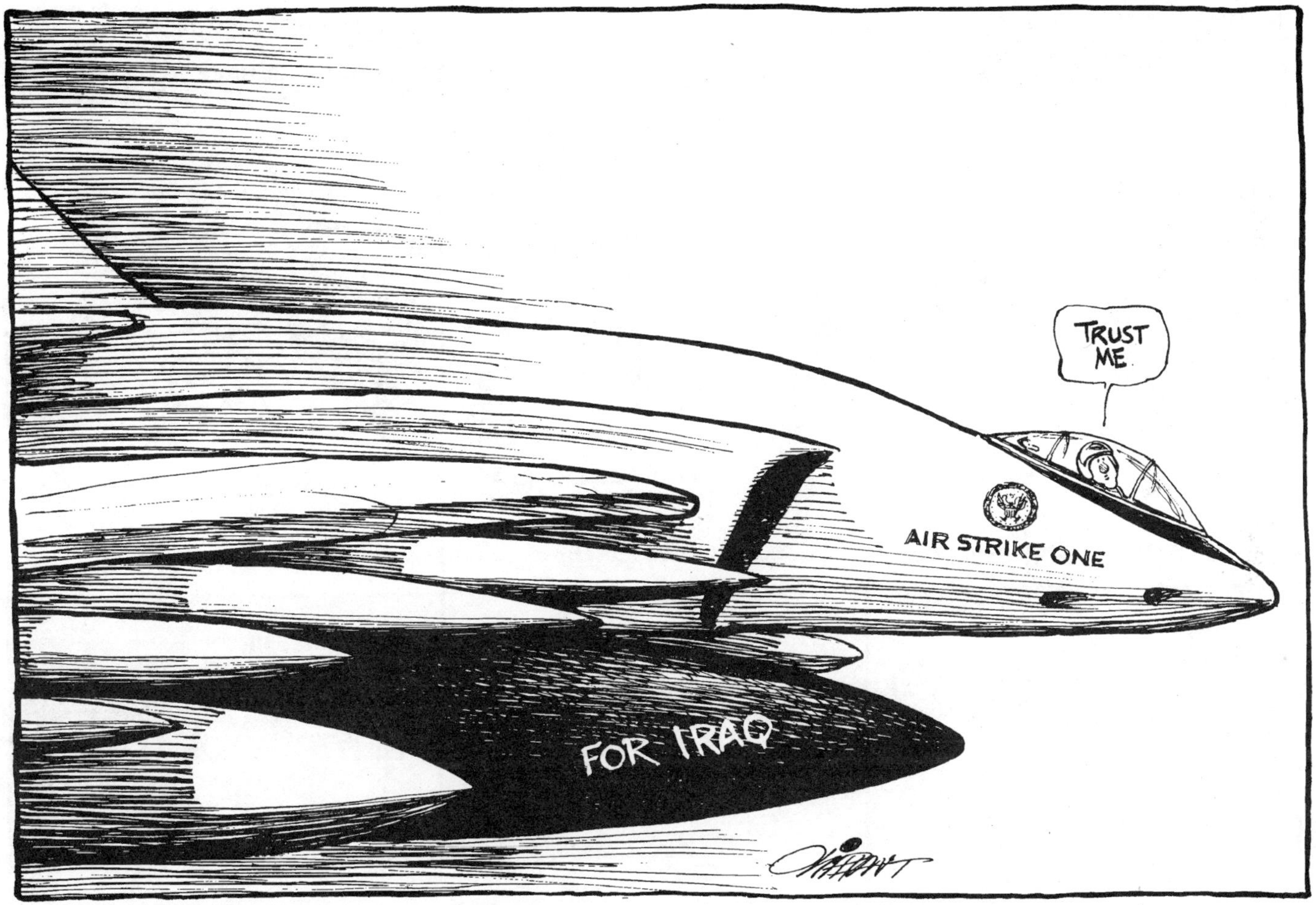
TRUST ME
AIR STRIKE ONE
FOR IRAQ
OLIPHANT

February 16, 1998

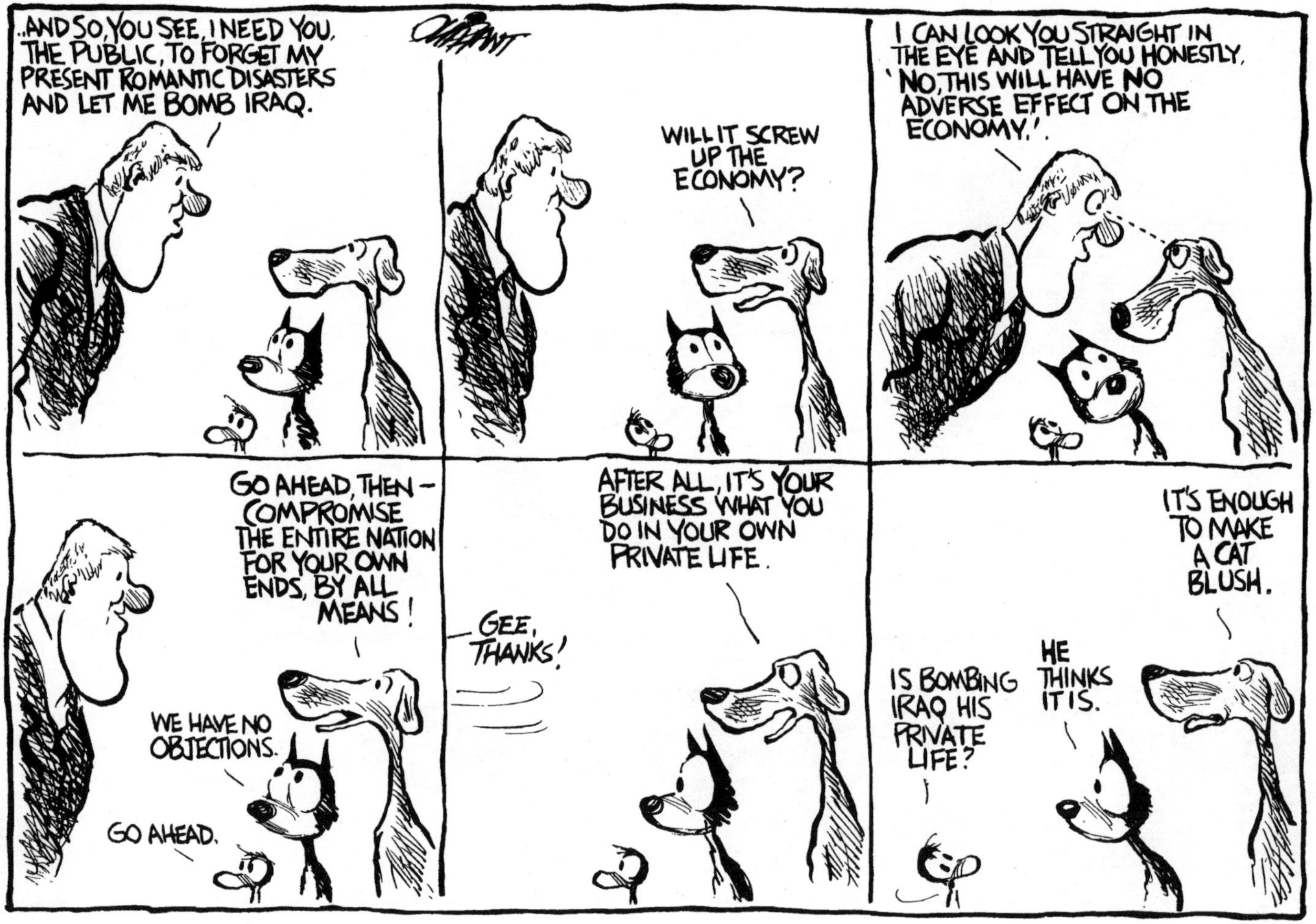
..AND SO, YOU SEE, I NEED YOU, THE PUBLIC, TO FORGET MY PRESENT ROMANTIC DISASTERS AND LET ME BOMB IRAQ.
WILL IT SCREW UP THE ECONOMY?
I CAN LOOK YOU STRAIGHT IN THE EYE AND TELL YOU HONESTLY, 'NO, THIS WILL HAVE NO ADVERSE EFFECT ON THE ECONOMY.'.
GO AHEAD, THEN - COMPROMISE THE ENTIRE NATION FOR YOUR OWN ENDS, BY ALL MEANS!
WE HAVE NO OBJECTIONS.
GO AHEAD.
GEE, THANKS!
AFTER ALL, IT'S YOUR BUSINESS WHAT YOU DO IN YOUR OWN PRIVATE LIFE.
IS BOMBING IRAQ HIS PRIVATE LIFE?
HE THINKS IT IS.
IT'S ENOUGH TO MAKE A CAT BLUSH.

February 18, 1998

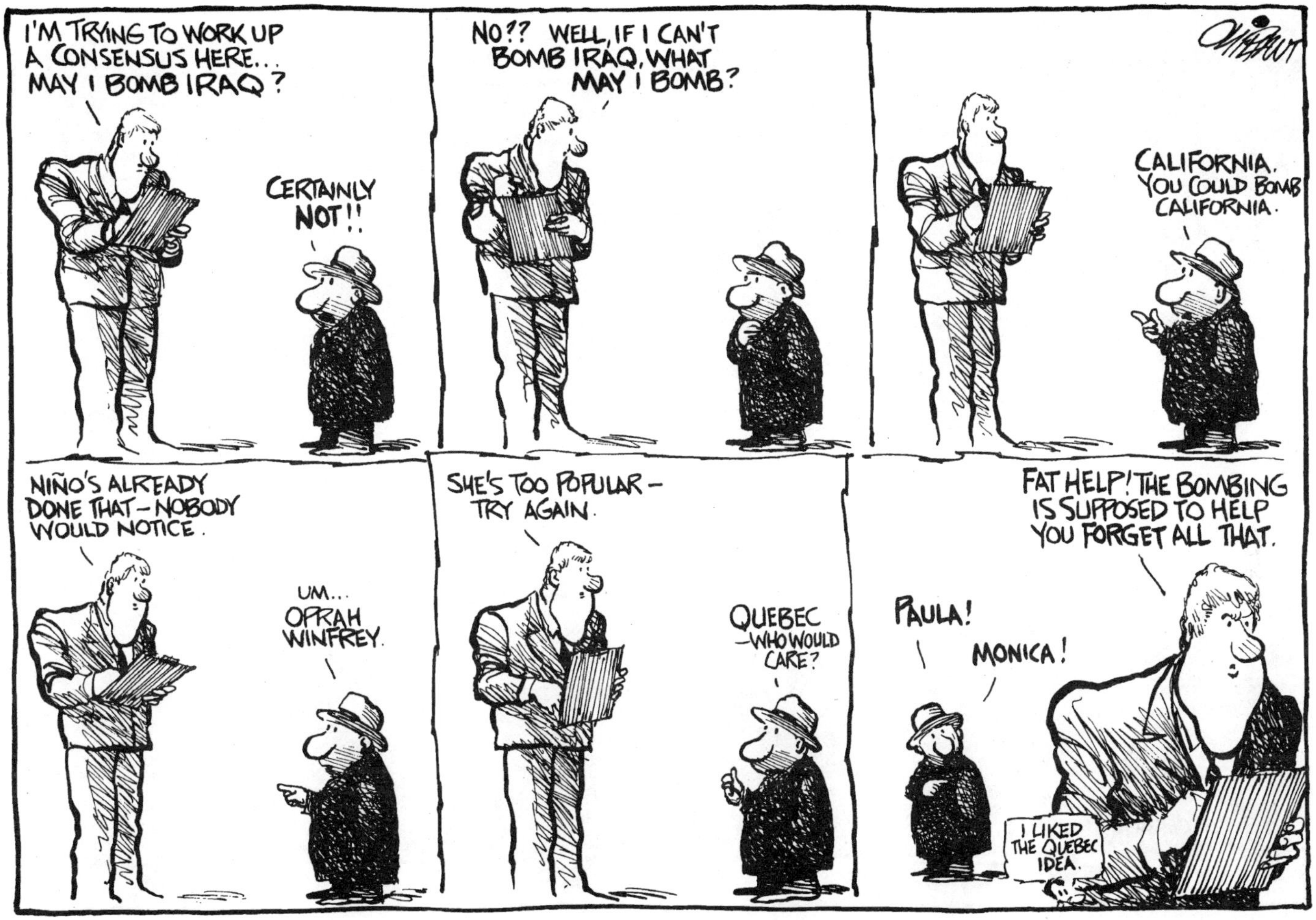
I'M TRYING TO WORK UP A CONSENSUS HERE... MAY I BOMB IRAQ?
CERTAINLY NOT!!
NO?? WELL, IF I CAN'T BOMB IRAQ, WHAT MAY I BOMB?
CALIFORNIA. YOU COULD BOMB CALIFORNIA.
NIÑO'S ALREADY DONE THAT—NOBODY WOULD NOTICE.
UM... OPRAH WINFREY.
SHE'S TOO POPULAR—TRY AGAIN.
QUEBEC —WHO WOULD CARE?
PAULA!
MONICA!
FAT HELP! THE BOMBING IS SUPPOSED TO HELP YOU FORGET ALL THAT.
I LIKED THE QUEBEC IDEA.

February 19, 1998

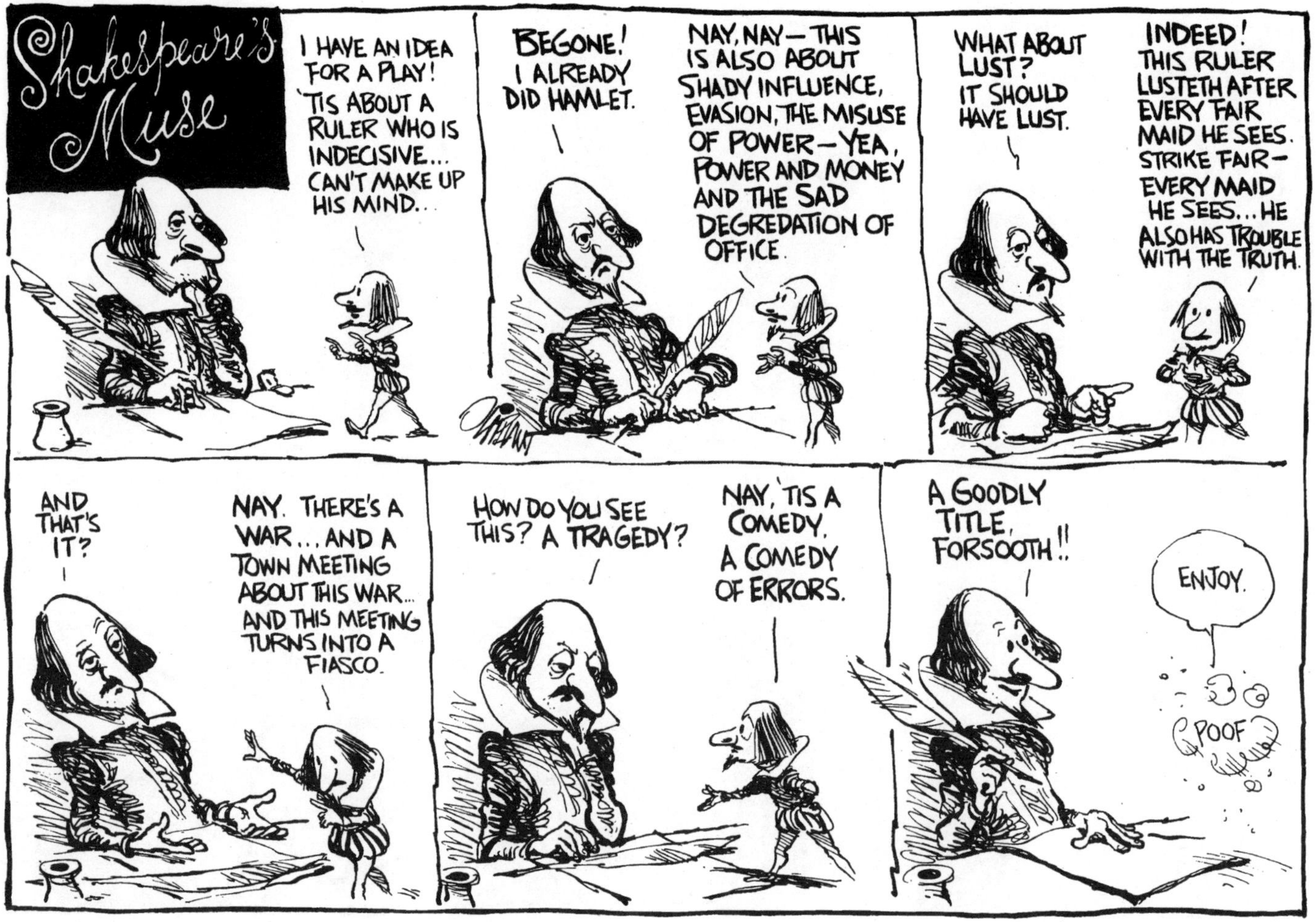
Shakespeare's Muse
I HAVE AN IDEA FOR A PLAY! 'TIS ABOUT A RULER WHO IS INDECISIVE... CAN'T MAKE UP HIS MIND...
BEGONE! I ALREADY DID HAMLET.
NAY, NAY— THIS IS ALSO ABOUT SHADY INFLUENCE, EVASION, THE MISUSE OF POWER—YEA, POWER AND MONEY AND THE SAD DEGREDATION OF OFFICE.
WHAT ABOUT LUST? IT SHOULD HAVE LUST.
INDEED! THIS RULER LUSTETH AFTER EVERY FAIR MAID HE SEES. STRIKE FAIR— EVERY MAID HE SEES... HE ALSO HAS TROUBLE WITH THE TRUTH.
AND THAT'S IT?
NAY. THERE'S A WAR... AND A TOWN MEETING ABOUT THIS WAR... AND THIS MEETING TURNS INTO A FIASCO.
HOW DO YOU SEE THIS? A TRAGEDY?
NAY, 'TIS A COMEDY, A COMEDY OF ERRORS.
A GOODLY TITLE, FORSOOTH!!
ENJOY.
POOF

March 10, 1998

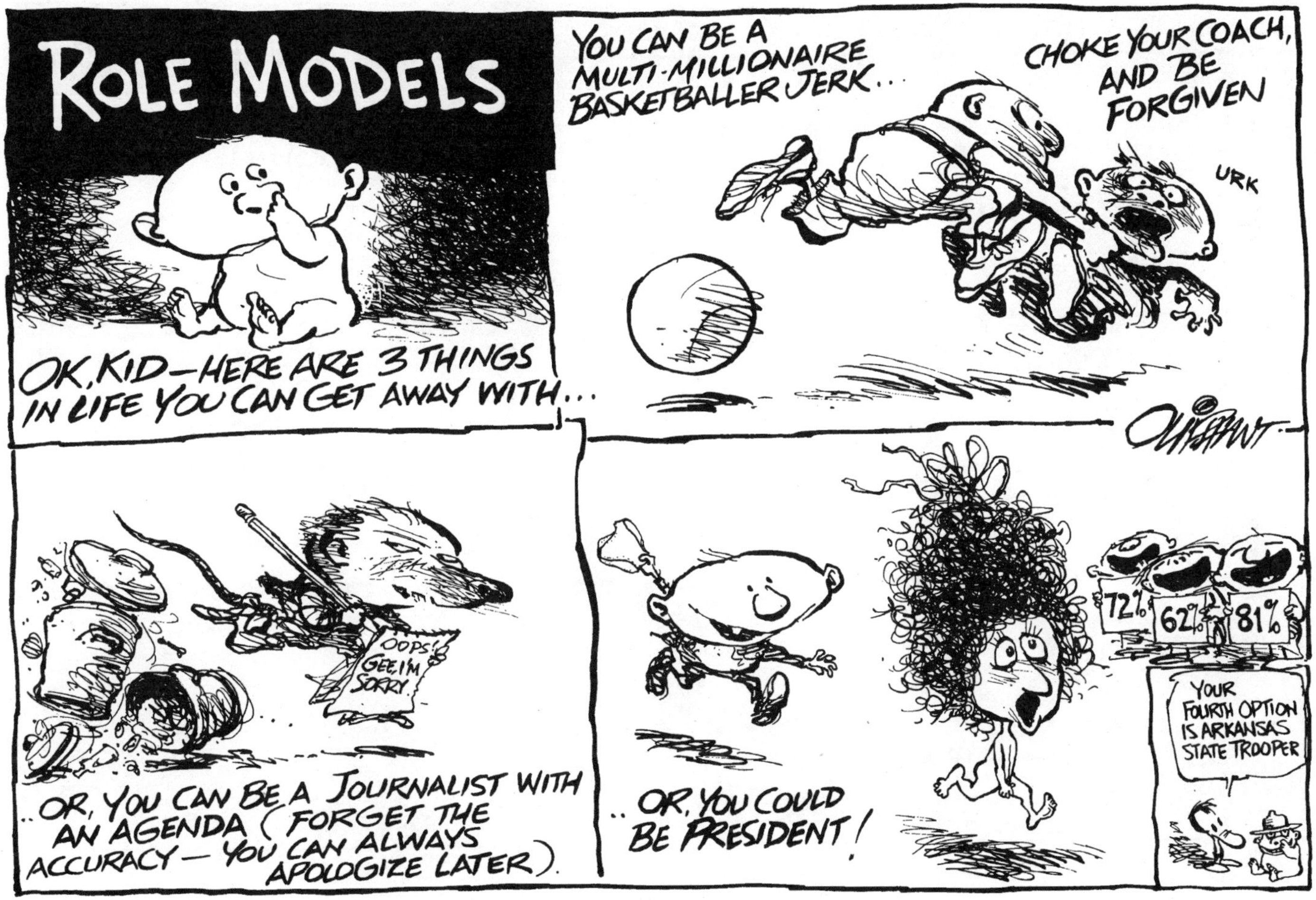
ROLE MODELS
OK, KID—HERE ARE 3 THINGS IN LIFE YOU CAN GET AWAY WITH...
YOU CAN BE A MULTI-MILLIONAIRE BASKETBALLER JERK...
CHOKE YOUR COACH, AND BE FORGIVEN
URK
OLIPHANT
OOPS! GEE, I'M SORRY
..OR, YOU CAN BE A JOURNALIST WITH AN AGENDA (FORGET THE ACCURACY—YOU CAN ALWAYS APOLOGIZE LATER).
..OR, YOU COULD BE PRESIDENT!
72%
62%
81%
YOUR FOURTH OPTION IS ARKANSAS STATE TROOPER

March 11, 1998

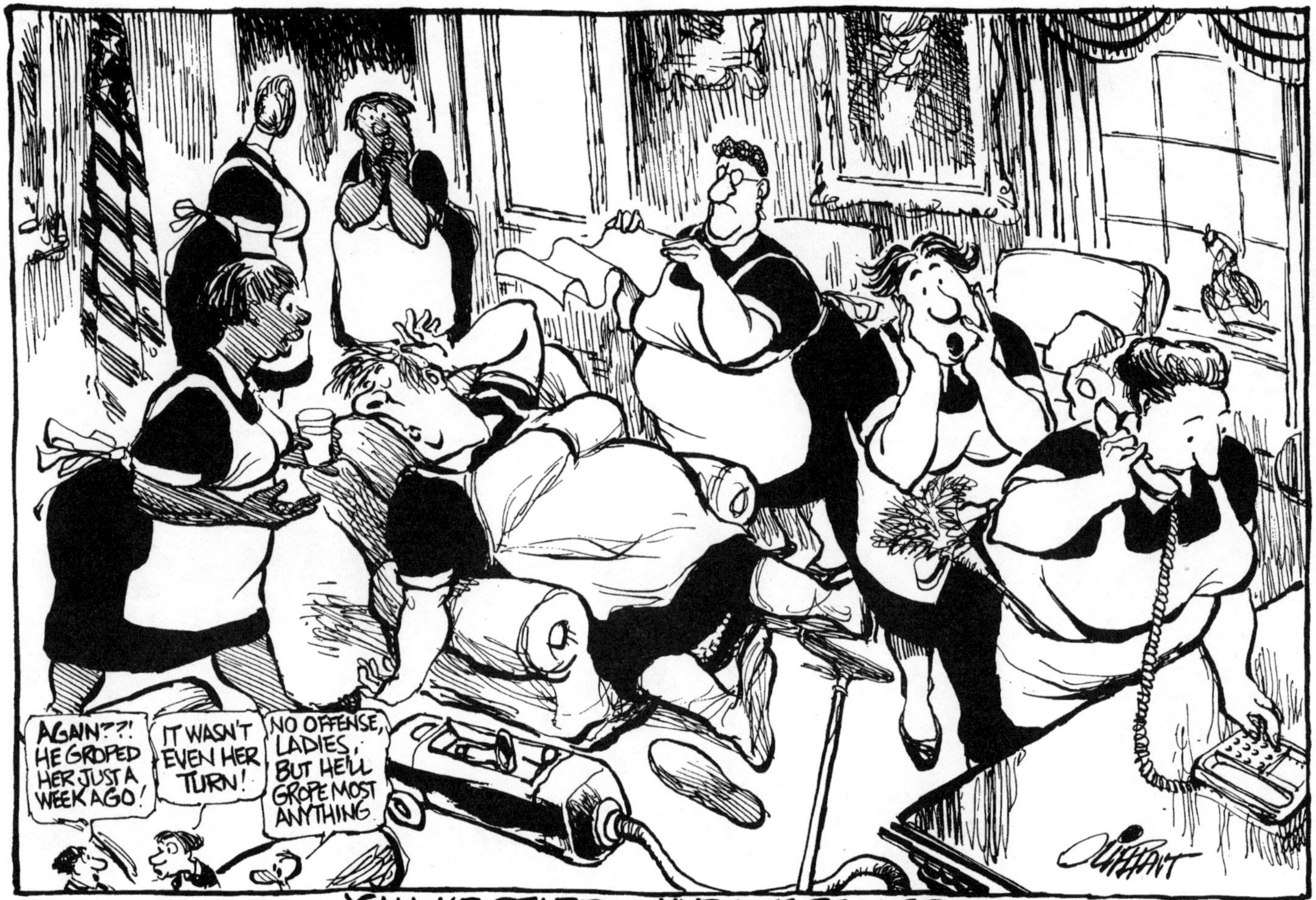
AGAIN??! HE GROPED HER JUST A WEEK AGO!
IT WASN'T EVEN HER TURN!
NO OFFENSE, LADIES, BUT HE'LL GROPE MOST ANYTHING.
OLIPHANT

'CALL MR. STARR— MYRTLE'S BEEN GROPED!'

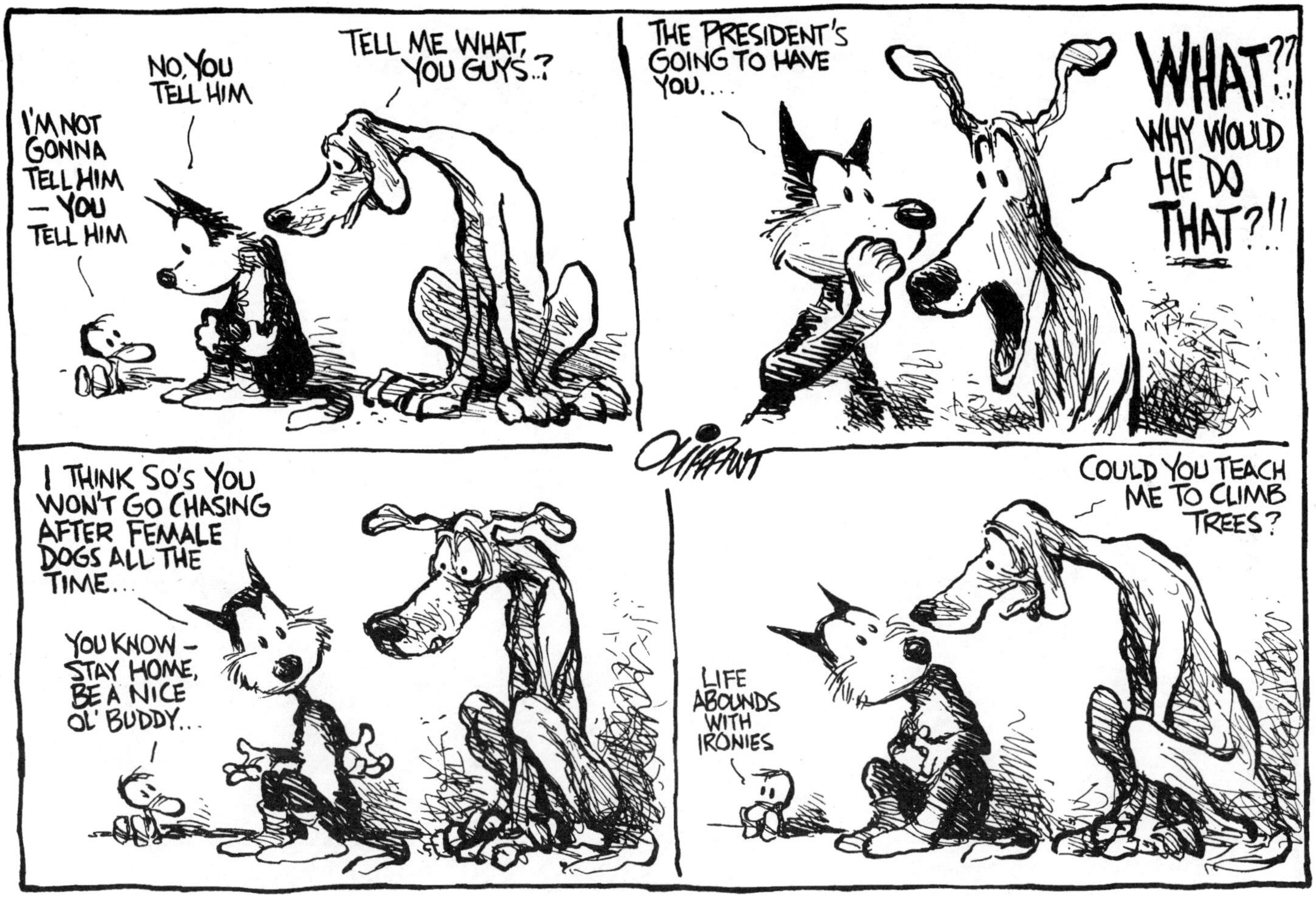
I'M NOT GONNA TELL HIM — YOU TELL HIM
NO, YOU TELL HIM
TELL ME WHAT, YOU GUYS..?
THE PRESIDENT'S GOING TO HAVE YOU...
WHAT??!! WHY WOULD HE DO THAT?!!
OLIPHANT
I THINK SO'S YOU WON'T GO CHASING AFTER FEMALE DOGS ALL THE TIME...
YOU KNOW – STAY HOME, BE A NICE OL' BUDDY...
COULD YOU TEACH ME TO CLIMB TREES?
LIFE ABOUNDS WITH IRONIES

March 16, 1998

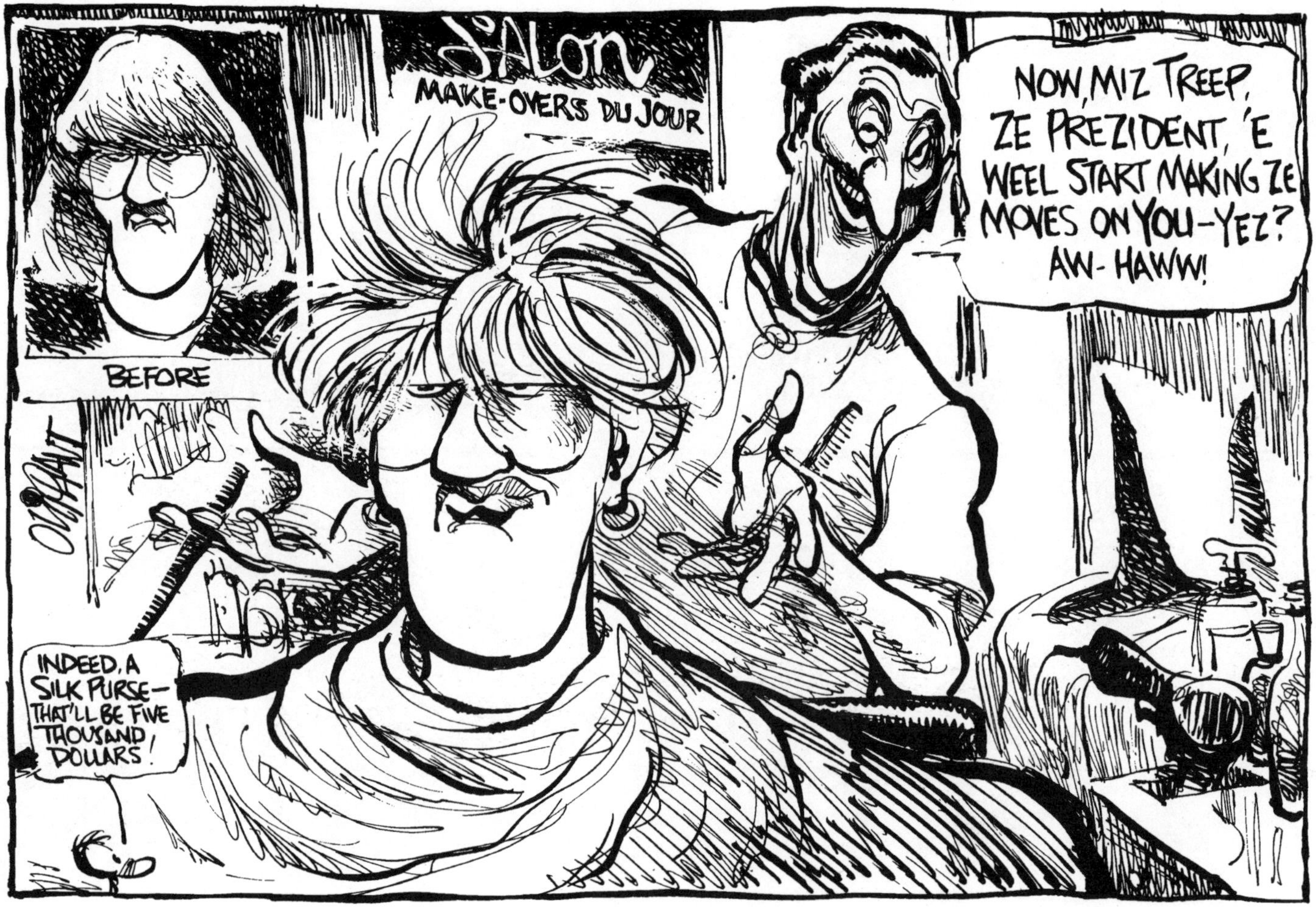
SALON
MAKE-OVERS DU JOUR
BEFORE
NOW, MIZ TREEP, ZE PREZIDENT, 'E WEEL START MAKING ZE MOVES ON YOU-YEZ? AW-HAWW!
INDEED, A SILK PURSE- THAT'LL BE FIVE THOUSAND DOLLARS!
OLIPHANT

March 25, 1998

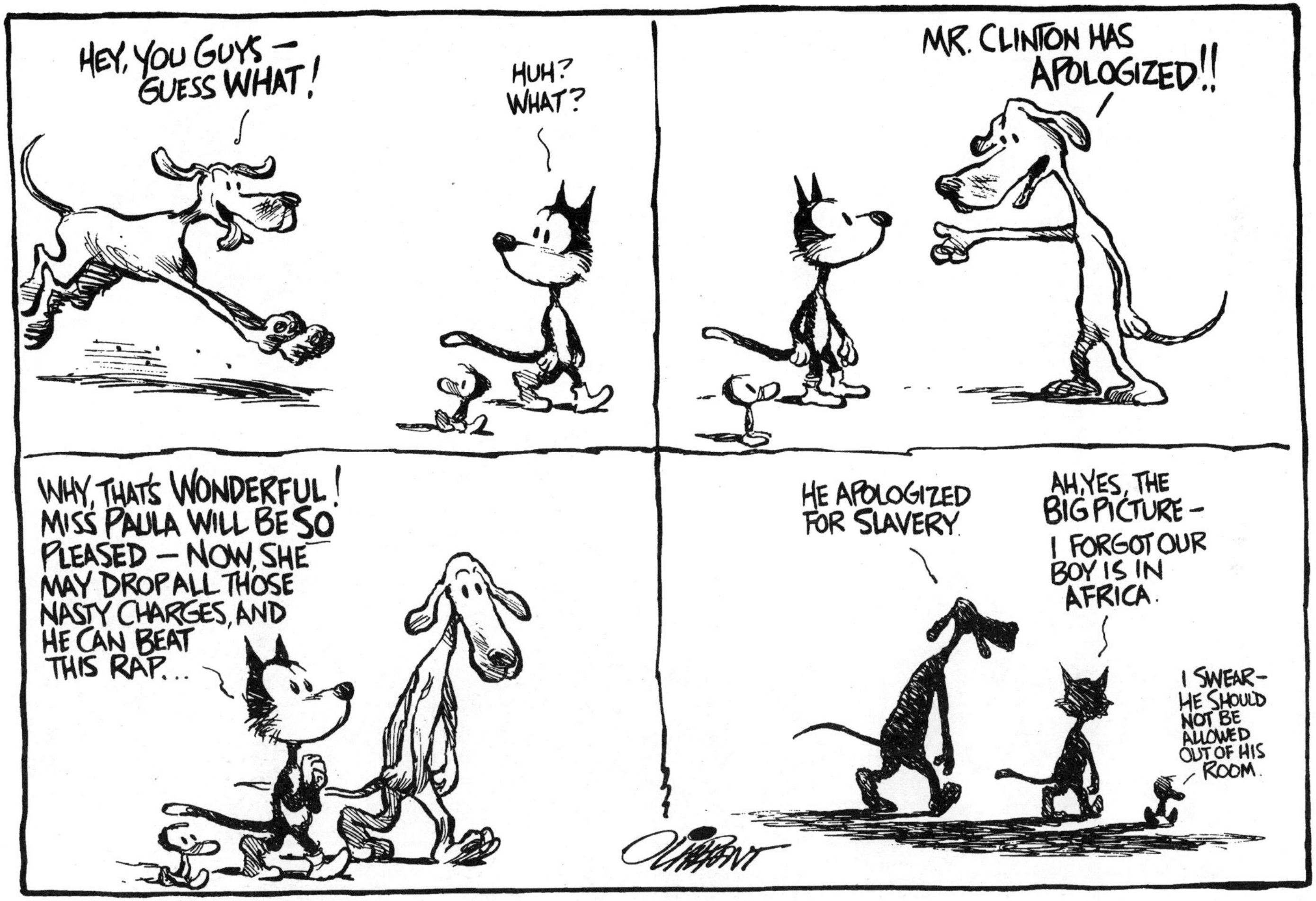
HEY, YOU GUYS – GUESS WHAT!
HUH? WHAT?
MR. CLINTON HAS APOLOGIZED!!
WHY, THAT'S WONDERFUL! MISS PAULA WILL BE SO PLEASED – NOW, SHE MAY DROP ALL THOSE NASTY CHARGES, AND HE CAN BEAT THIS RAP...
HE APOLOGIZED FOR SLAVERY.
AH, YES, THE BIG PICTURE – I FORGOT OUR BOY IS IN AFRICA.
I SWEAR – HE SHOULD NOT BE ALLOWED OUT OF HIS ROOM.
OLIPHANT

March 30, 1998

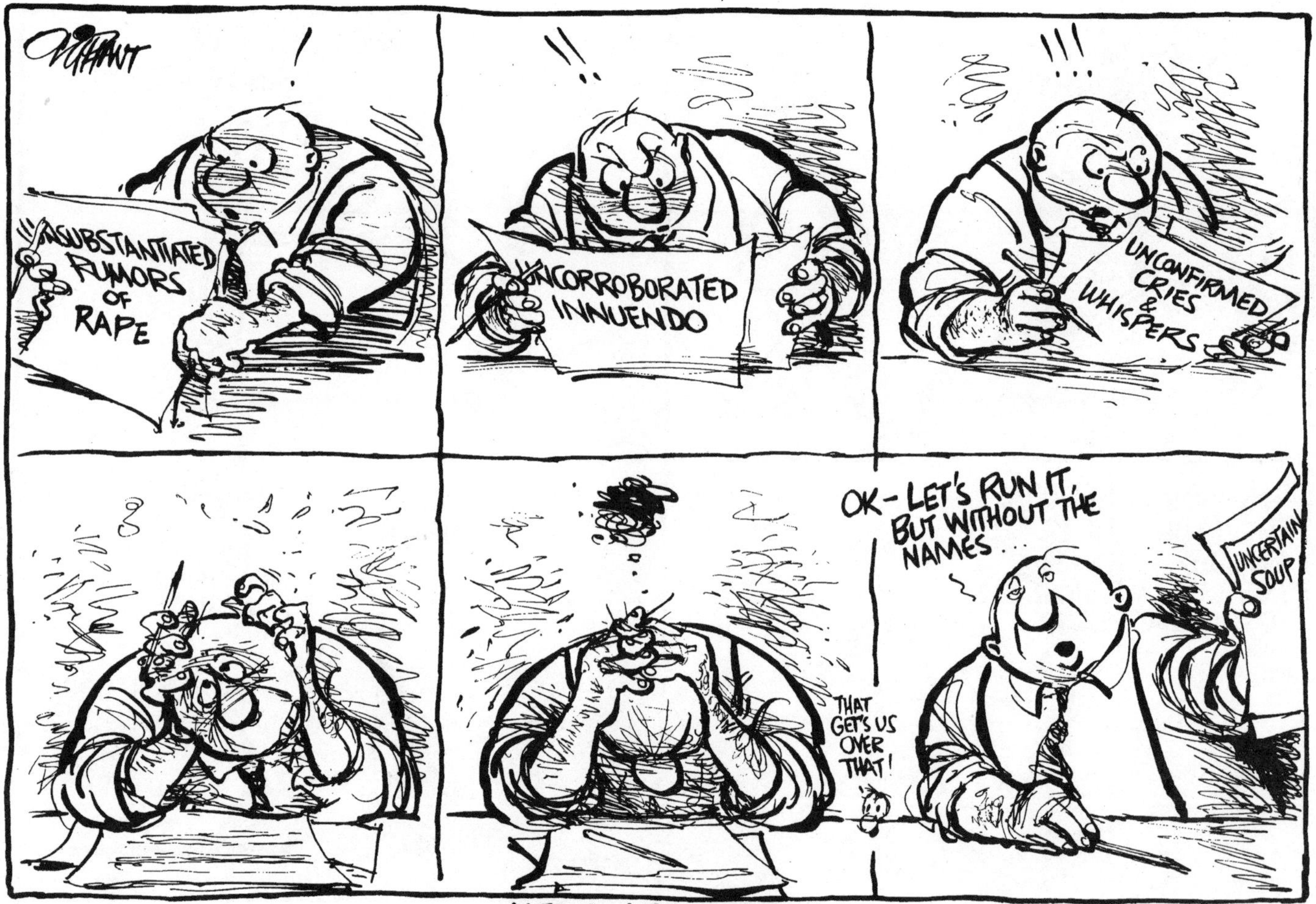

OLIPHANT
!
UNSUBSTANTIATED RUMORS OF RAPE
!!
UNCORROBORATED INNUENDO
!!!
UNCONFIRMED CRIES & WHISPERS
OK - LET'S RUN IT, BUT WITHOUT THE NAMES...
UNCERTAIN SOUP
THAT GET'S US OVER THAT!

MEDIA AGONISTES.

March 31, 1998

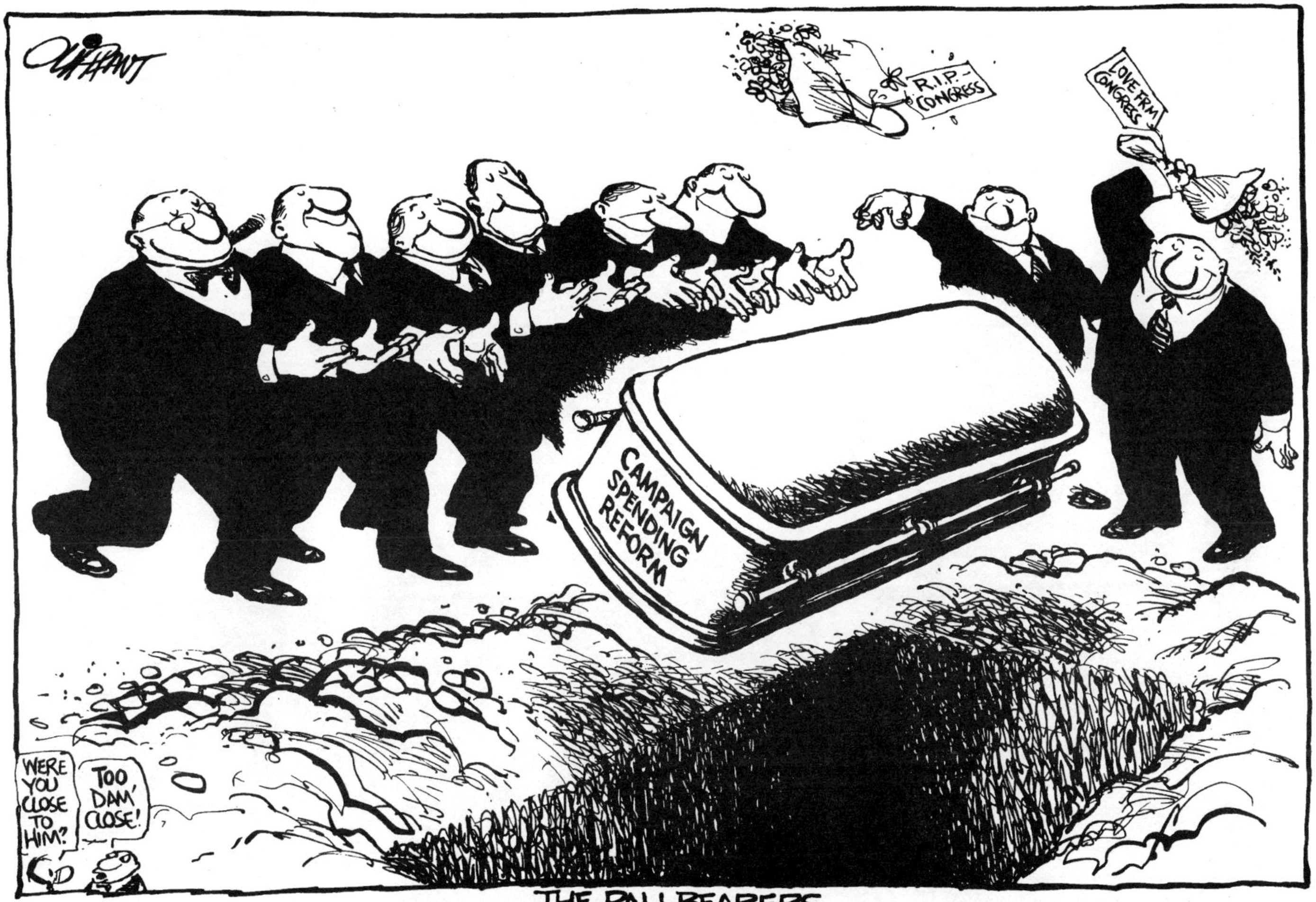
OLIPHANT
R.I.P.-CONGRESS
LOVE FRM CONGRESS
CAMPAIGN SPENDING REFORM
WERE YOU CLOSE TO HIM?
TOO DAM' CLOSE!

THE PALLBEARERS.

April 2, 1998

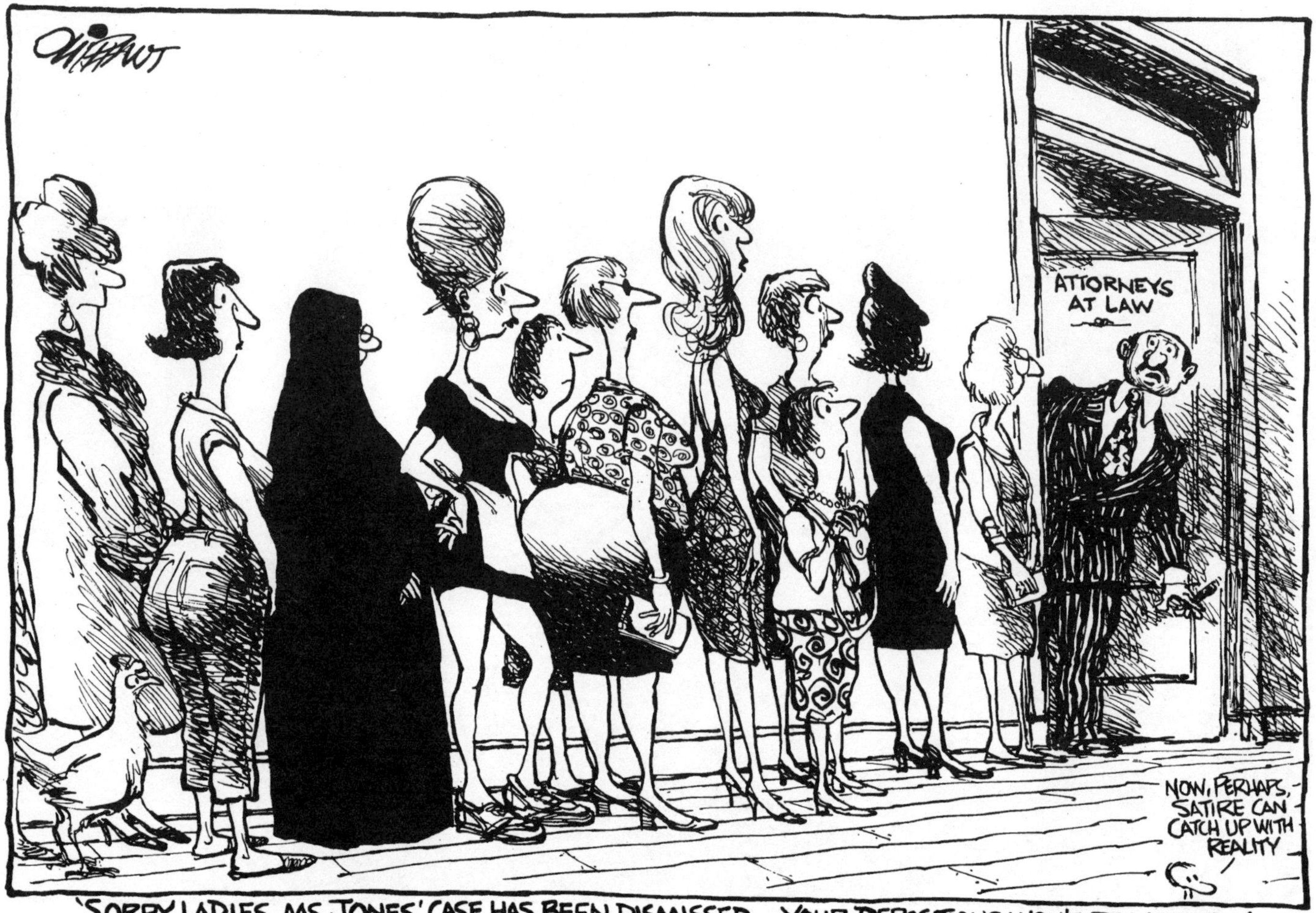
OLIPHANT
ATTORNEYS AT LAW
NOW, PERHAPS, SATIRE CAN CATCH UP WITH REALITY

'SORRY, LADIES, MS. JONES' CASE HAS BEEN DISMISSED—YOUR DEPOSITIONS WON'T BE NEEDED.'

April 6, 1998

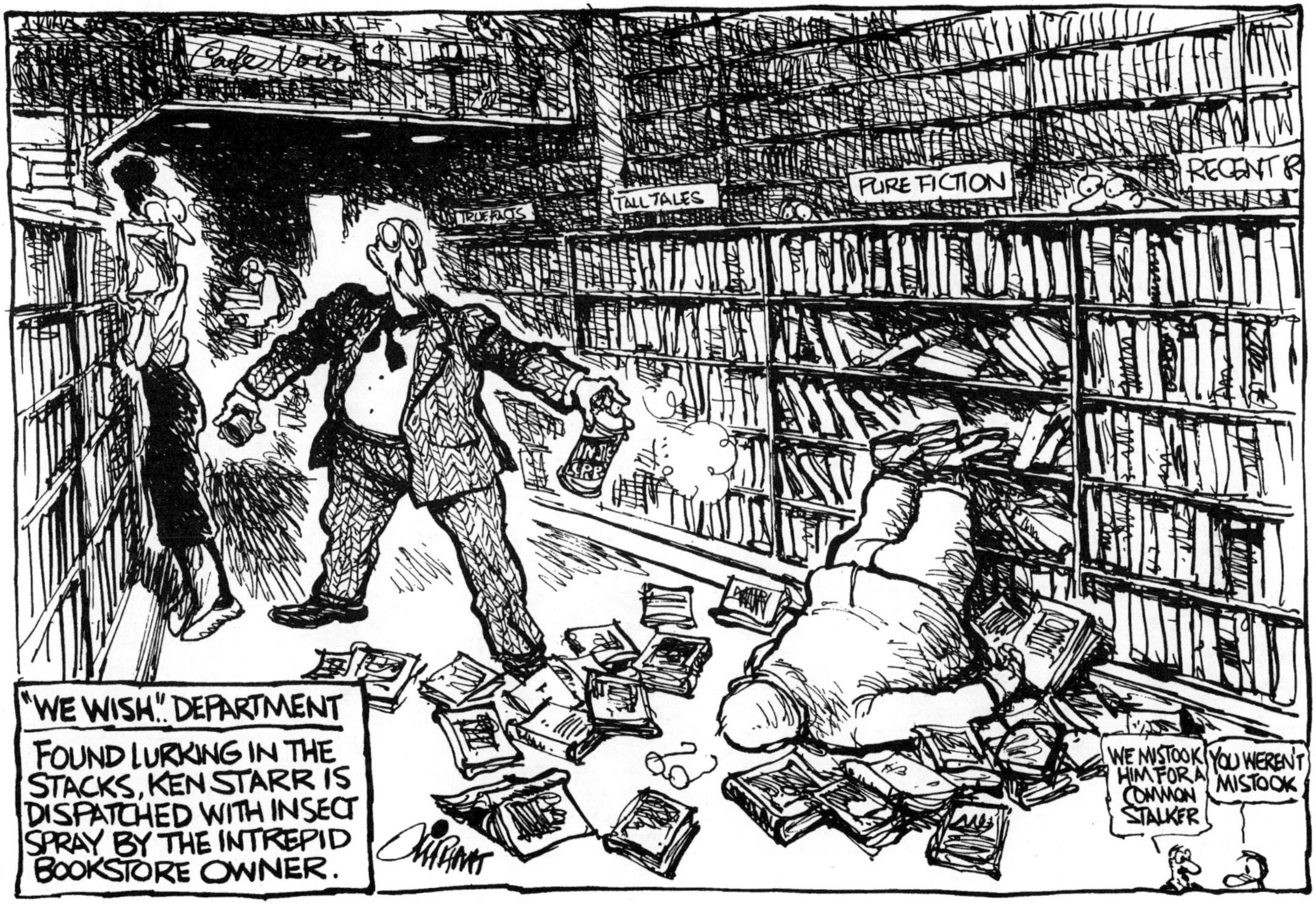
Cafe Noir
TRUE FACTS
TALL TALES
PURE FICTION
"WE WISH". DEPARTMENT
FOUND LURKING IN THE STACKS, KEN STARR IS DISPATCHED WITH INSECT SPRAY BY THE INTREPID BOOKSTORE OWNER.
WE MISTOOK HIM FOR A COMMON STALKER
YOU WEREN'T MISTOOK
OLIPHANT

April 13, 1998

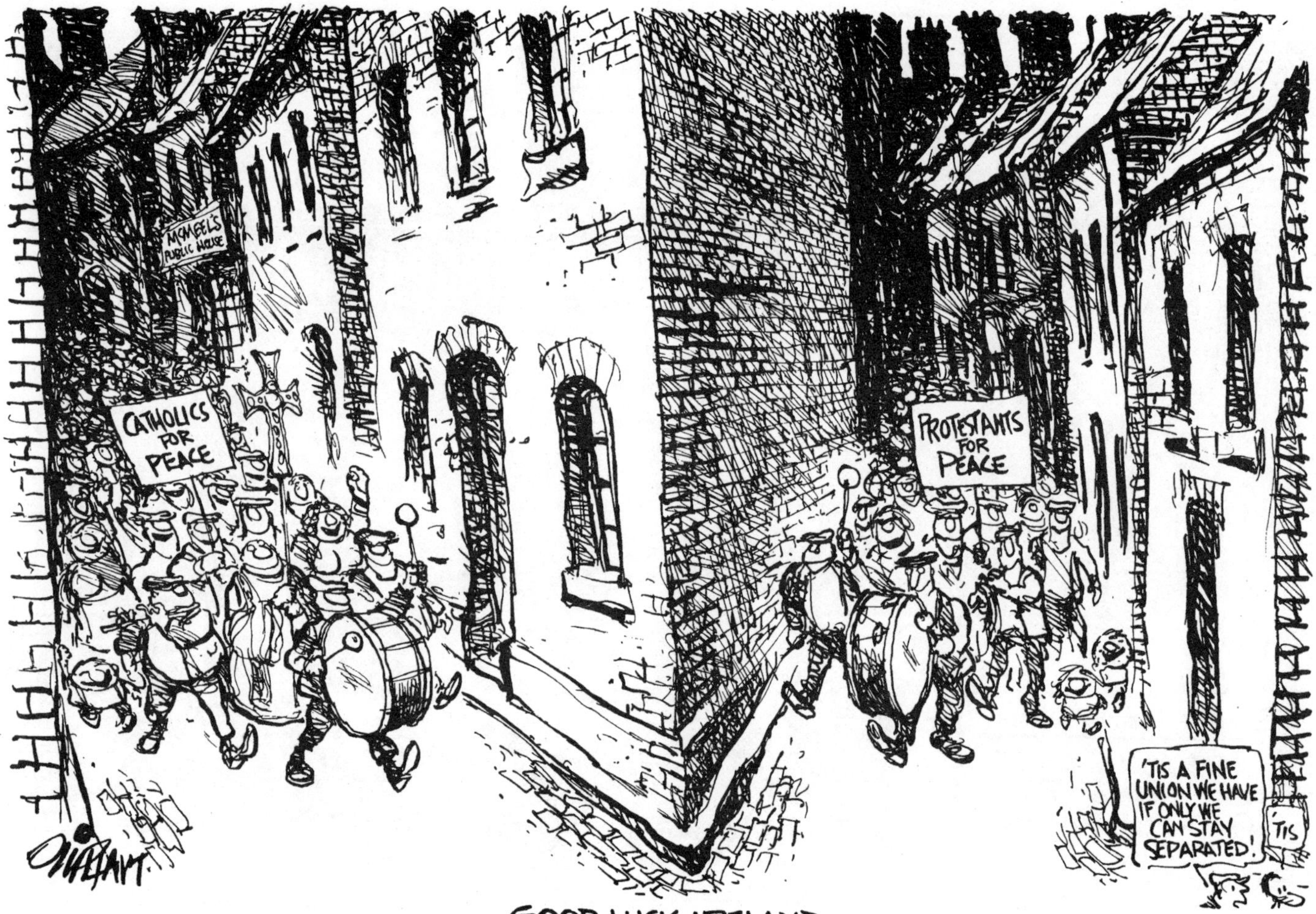
McMEEL'S
PUBLIC HOUSE
CATHOLICS FOR PEACE
PROTESTANTS FOR PEACE
'TIS A FINE UNION WE HAVE IF ONLY WE CAN STAY SEPARATED!
'TIS
OLIPHANT

GOOD LUCK, IRELAND.

April 21, 1998

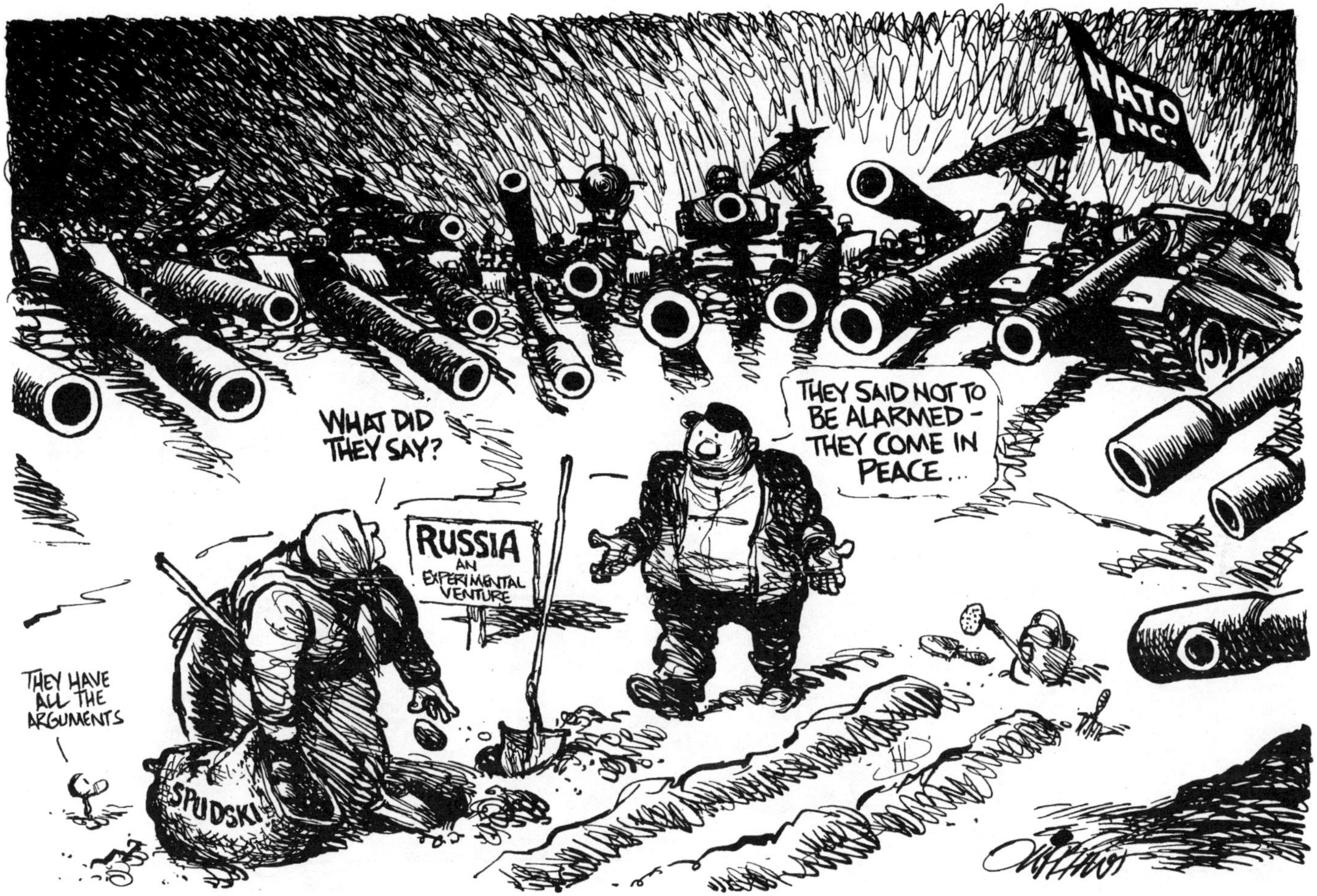
NATO INC.
WHAT DID THEY SAY?
THEY SAID NOT TO BE ALARMED - THEY COME IN PEACE...
RUSSIA AN EXPERIMENTAL VENTURE
THEY HAVE ALL THE ARGUMENTS
SPUDSKI

April 21, 1998

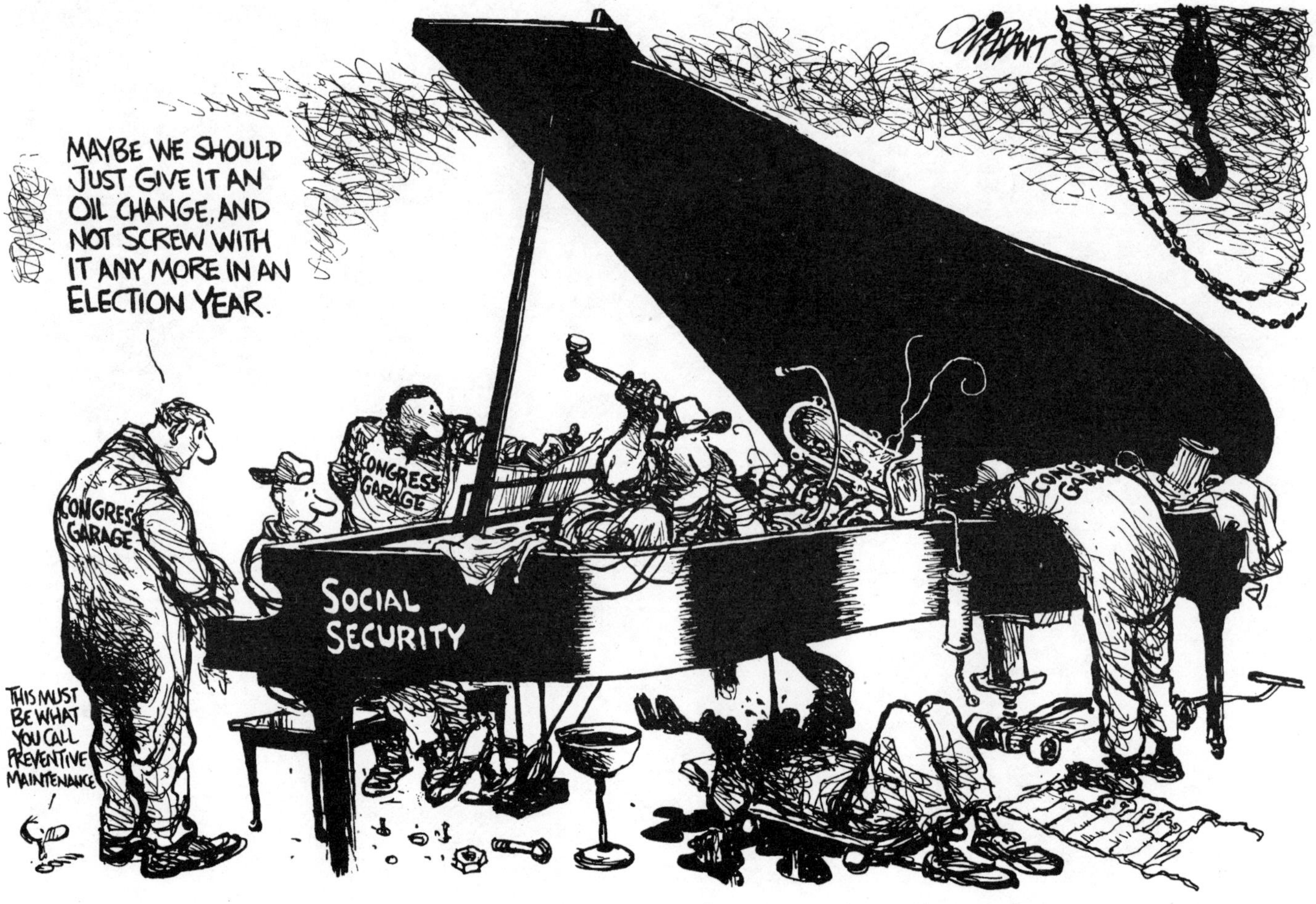
MAYBE WE SHOULD JUST GIVE IT AN OIL CHANGE, AND NOT SCREW WITH IT ANY MORE IN AN ELECTION YEAR.
CONGRESS GARAGE
CONGRESS GARAGE
SOCIAL SECURITY
THIS MUST BE WHAT YOU CALL PREVENTIVE MAINTENANCE!

May 4, 1998

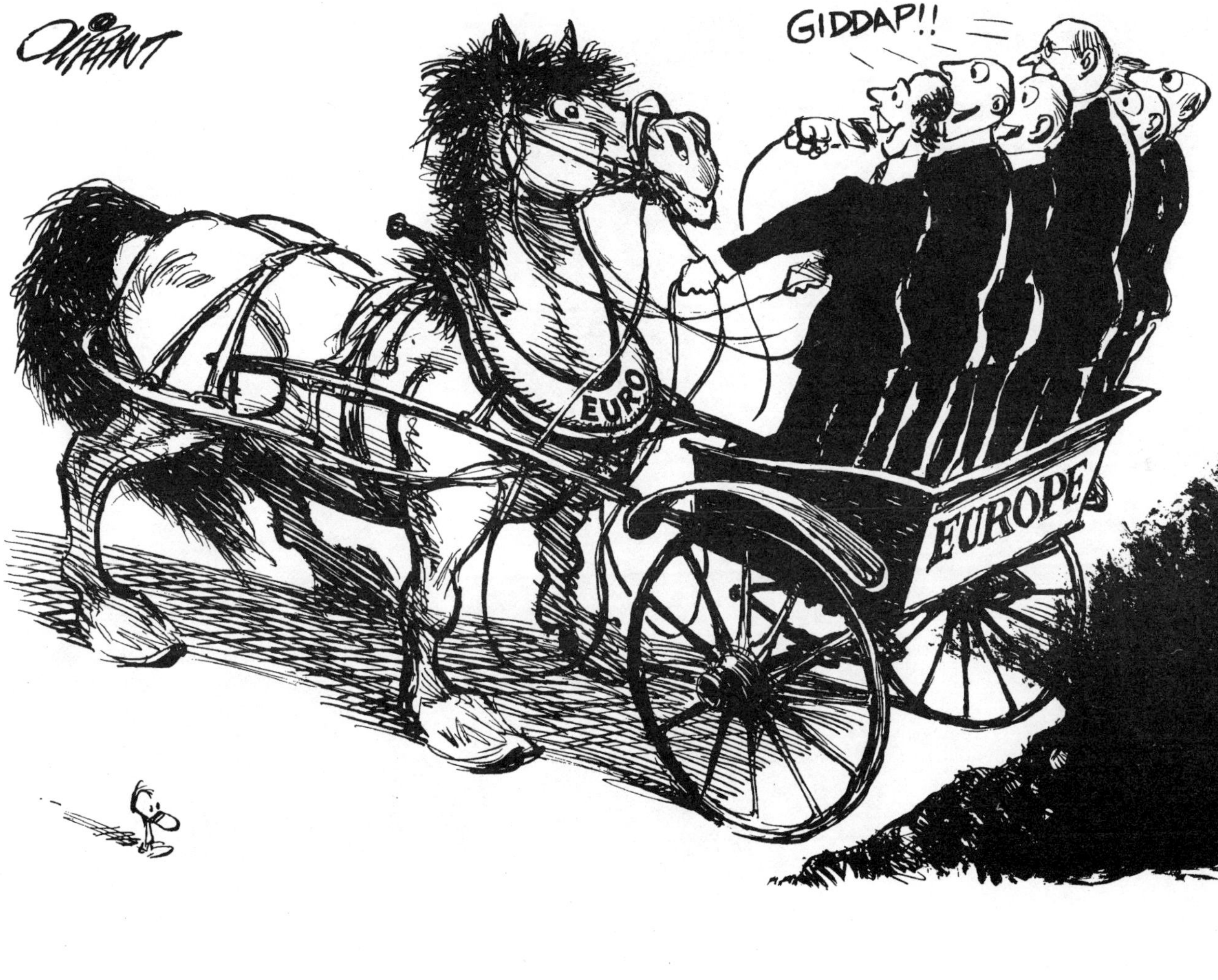
GIDDAP!!
EURO
EUROPE

May 7, 1998

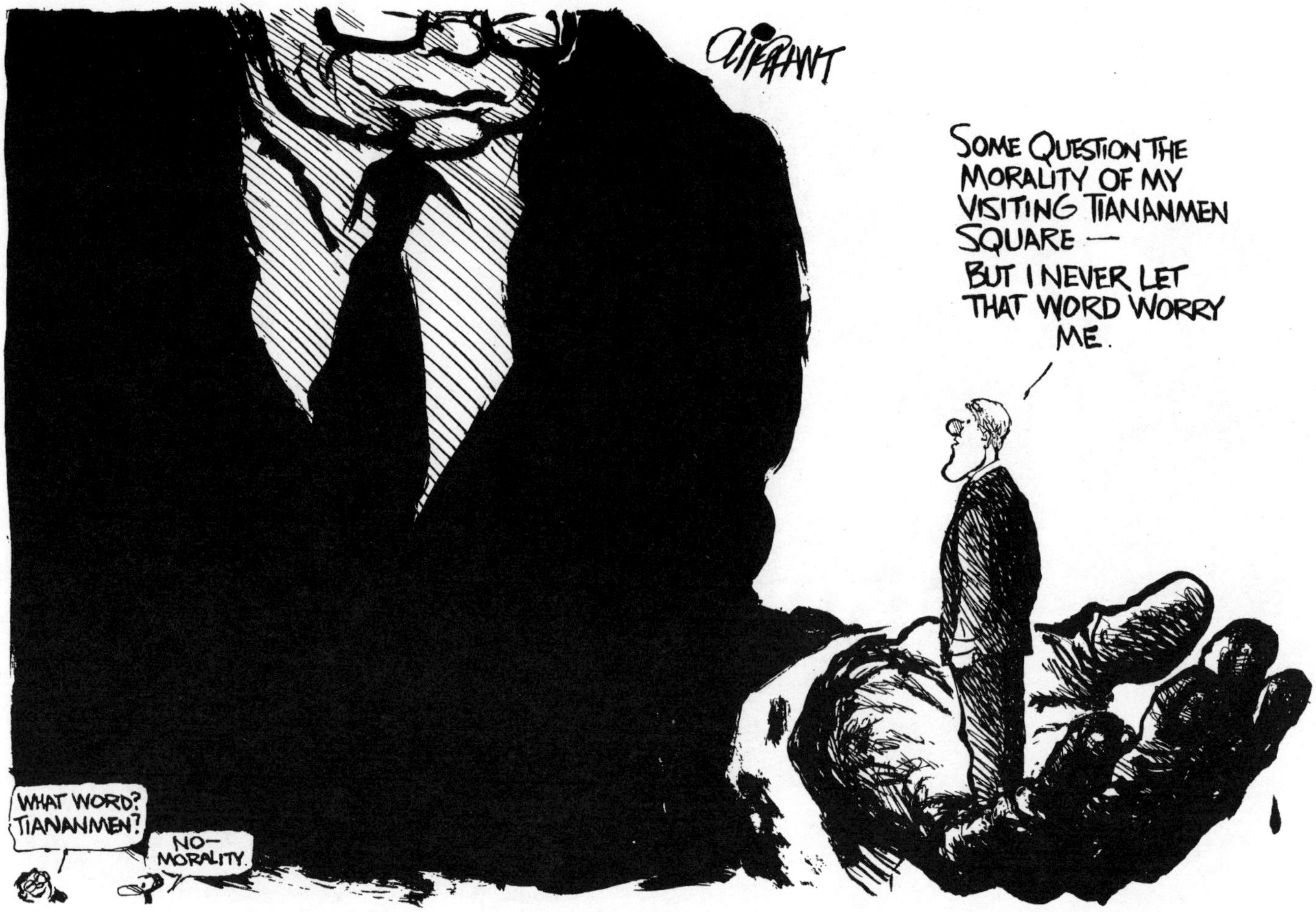
OLIPHANT
SOME QUESTION THE MORALITY OF MY VISITING TIANANMEN SQUARE — BUT I NEVER LET THAT WORD WORRY ME.
WHAT WORD? TIANANMEN?
NO— MORALITY.

May 13, 1998

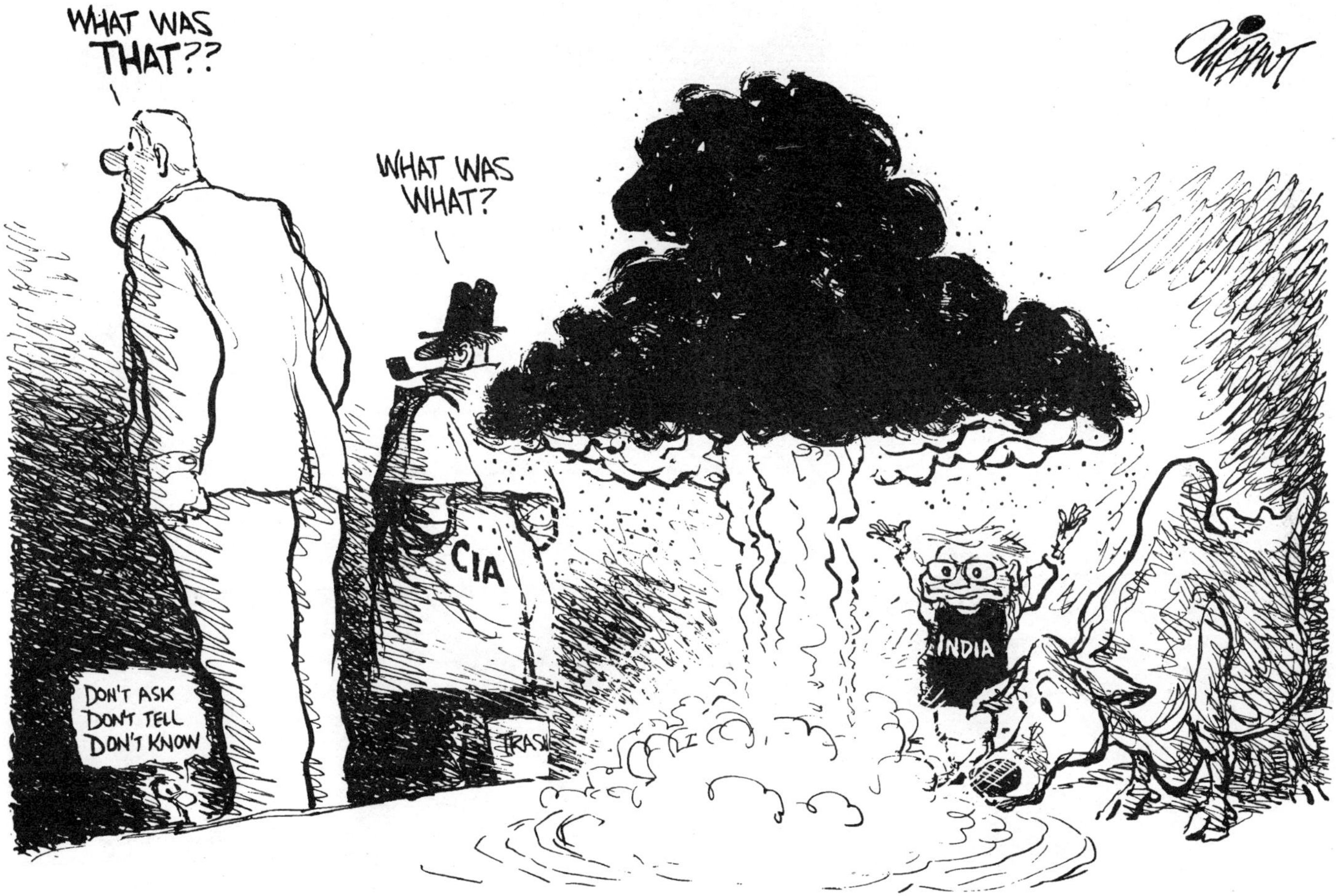
WHAT WAS THAT??
WHAT WAS WHAT?
CIA
DON'T ASK DON'T TELL DON'T KNOW
INDIA

May 14, 1998

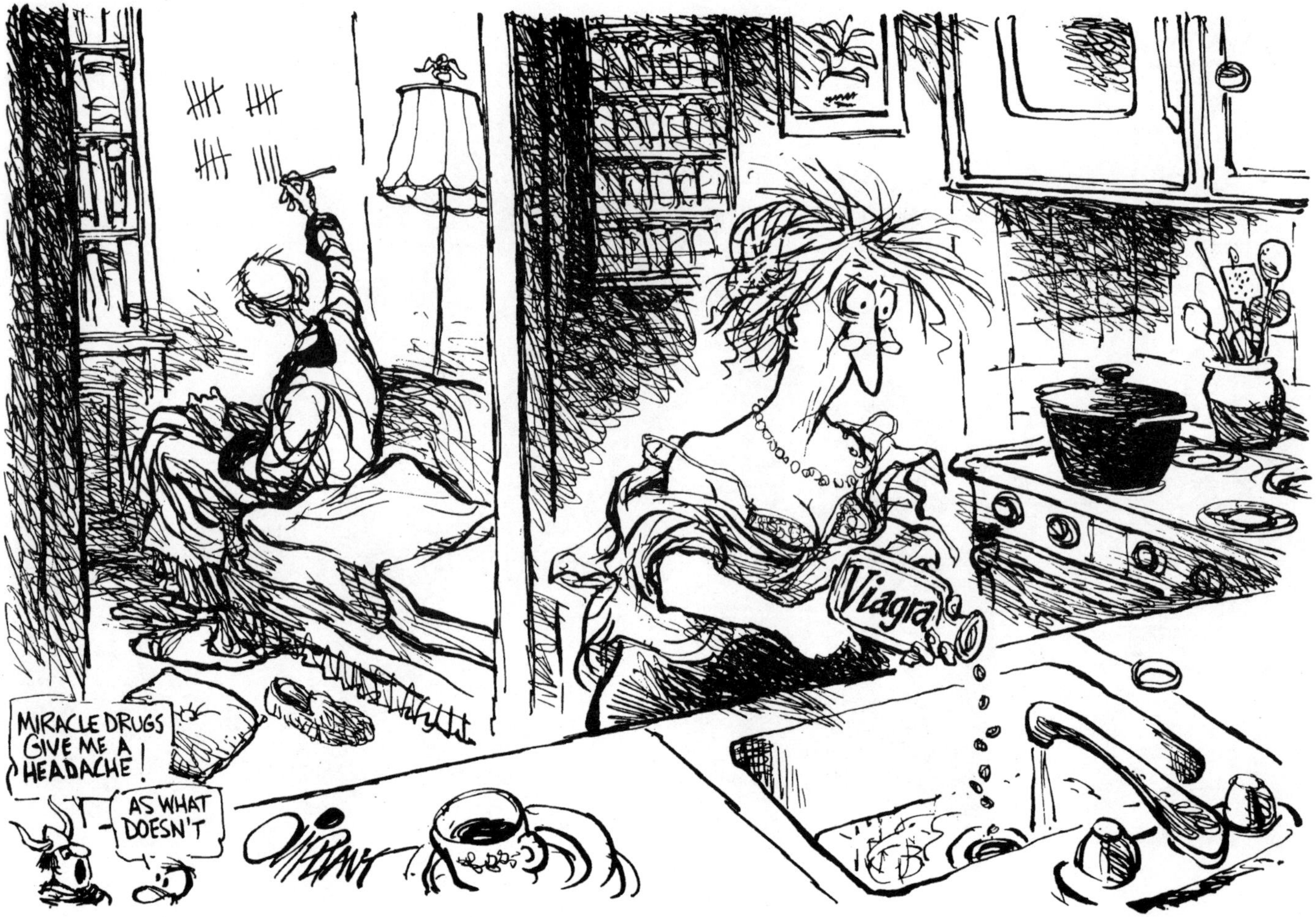
Viagra
MIRACLE DRUGS GIVE ME A HEADACHE!
AS WHAT DOESN'T
OLIPHANT

May 18, 1998

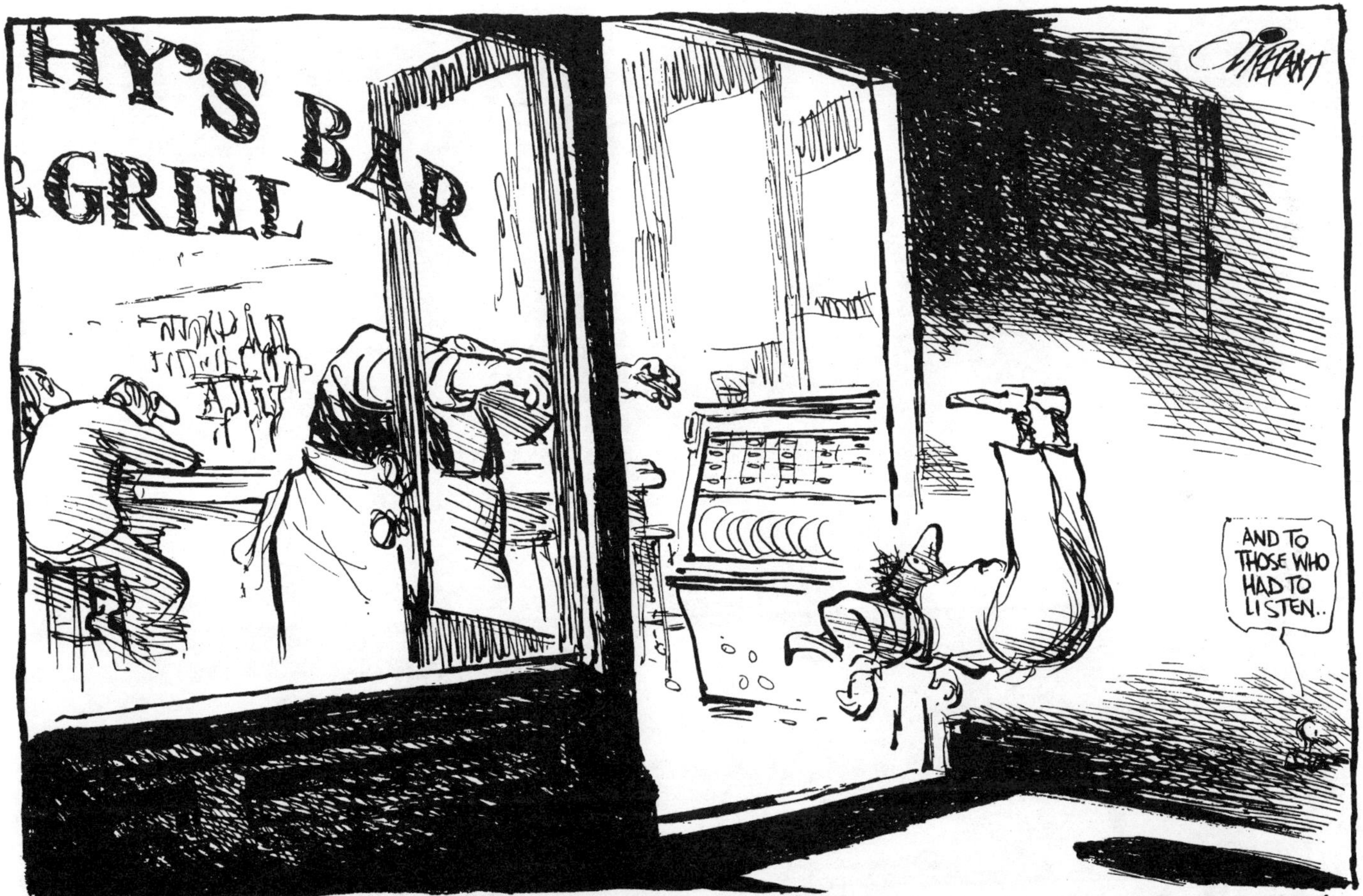
HY'S BAR
& GRILL
AND TO THOSE WHO HAD TO LISTEN..

TO EVERY WEEPY-EYED DRUNK WITH A HANDFUL OF QUARTERS WHO EVER PLAYED SINATRA'S RENDITION OF "MY WAY" NINETEEN TIMES ON THE JUKEBOX, THIS CARTOON IS DEDICATED.

May 18, 1998

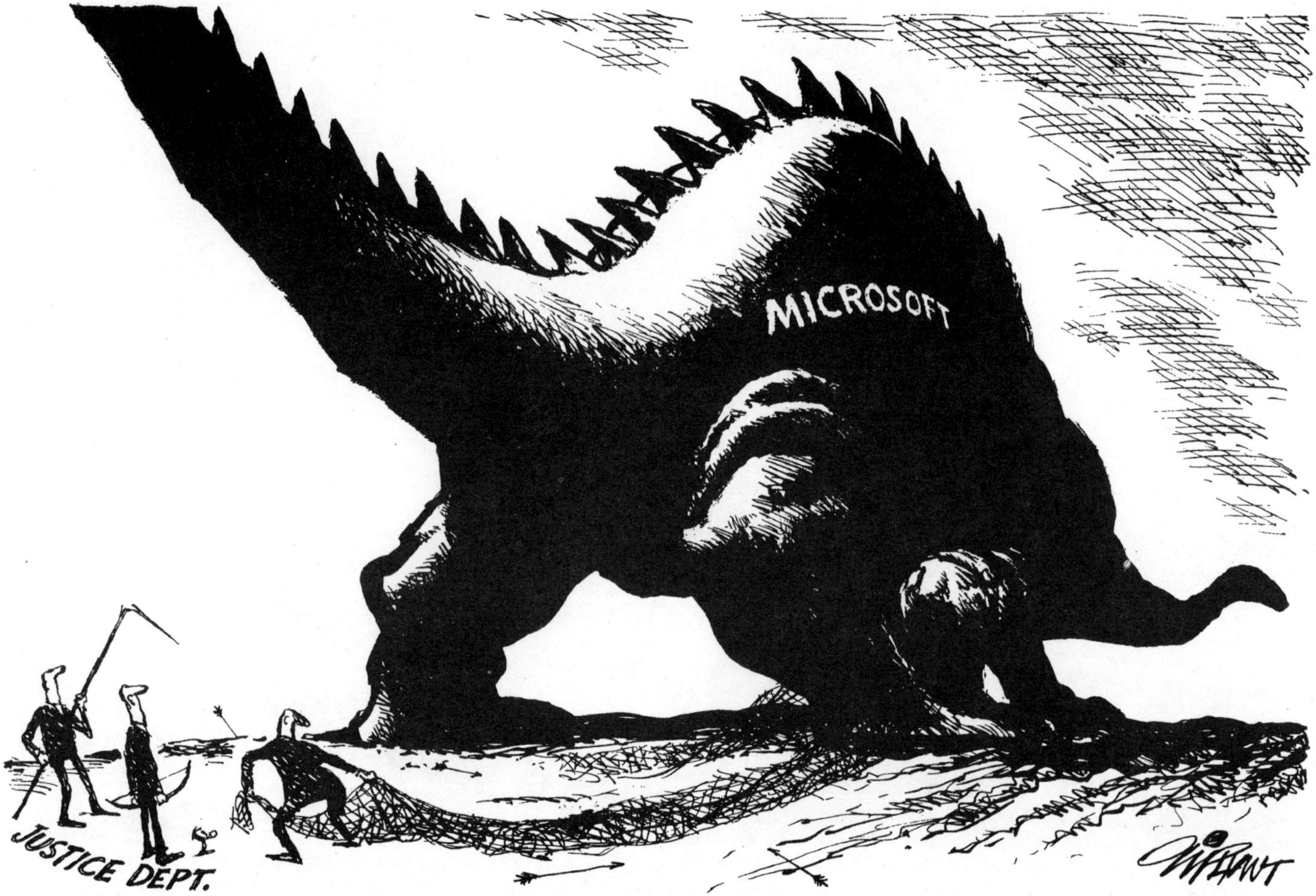
MICROSOFT
JUSTICE DEPT.

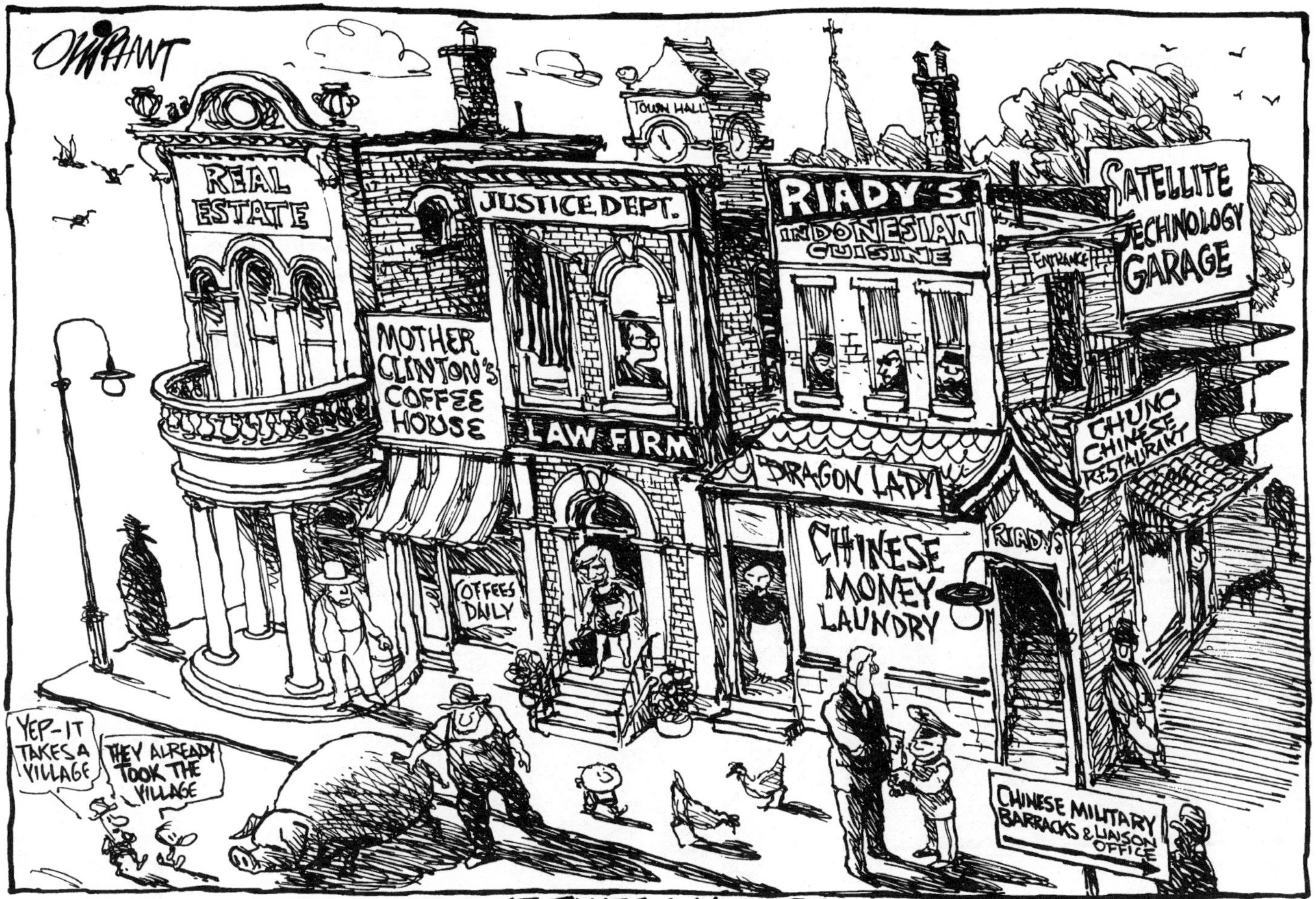
OLIPHANT
TOWN HALL
REAL ESTATE
JUSTICE DEPT.
RIADY'S INDONESIAN CUISINE
ENTRANCE
SATELLITE TECHNOLOGY GARAGE
MOTHER CLINTON'S COFFEE HOUSE
LAW FIRM
CHUNG CHINESE RESTAURANT
DRAGON LADY
COFFEES DAILY
CHINESE MONEY LAUNDRY
RIADY'S
YEP-IT TAKES A VILLAGE
THEY ALREADY TOOK THE VILLAGE
CHINESE MILITARY BARRACKS & LIAISON OFFICE

IT TAKES A VILLAGE.

June 2, 1998

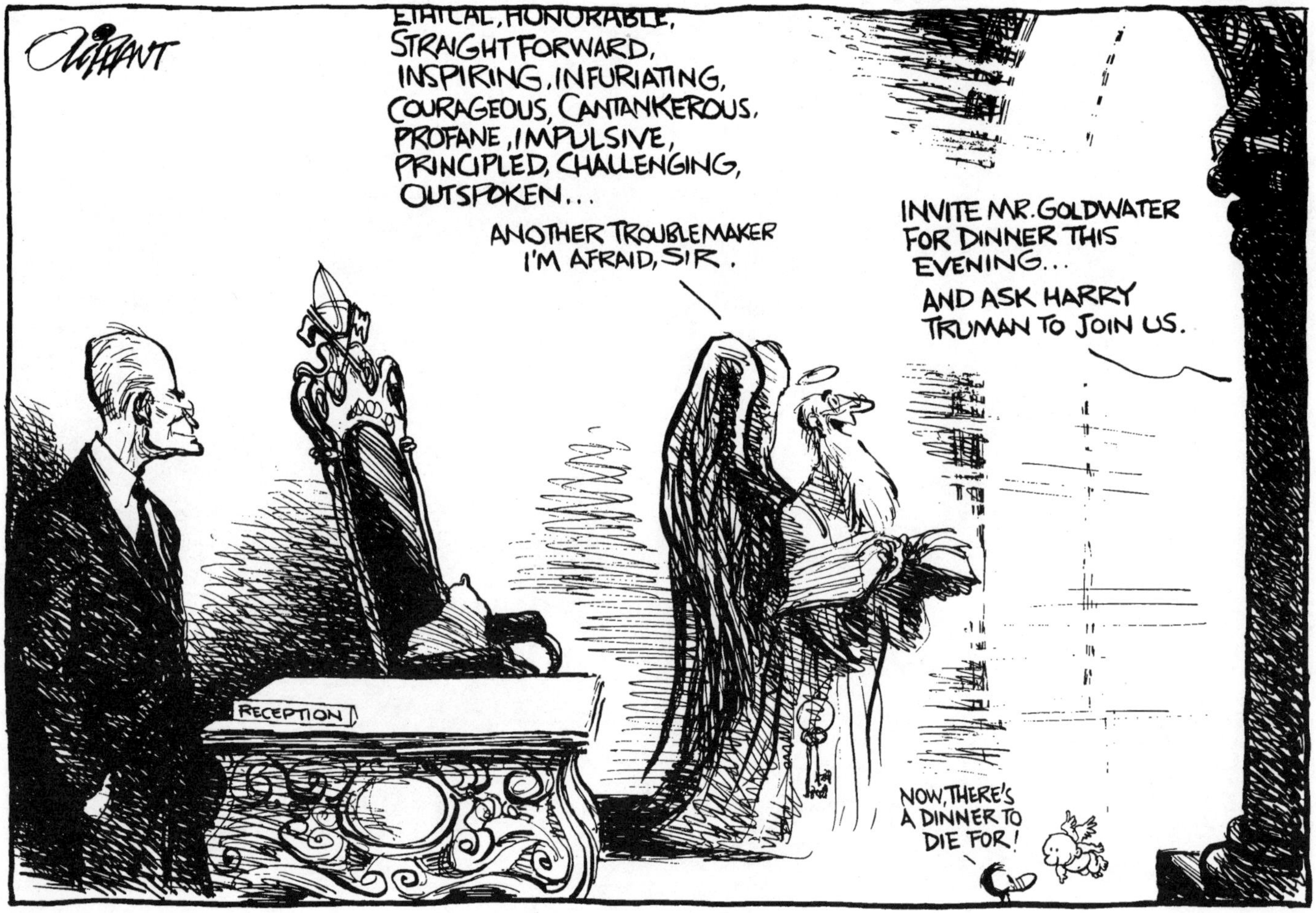
OLIPHANT
ETHICAL, HONORABLE,
STRAIGHTFORWARD,
INSPIRING, INFURIATING,
COURAGEOUS, CANTANKEROUS,
PROFANE, IMPULSIVE,
PRINCIPLED, CHALLENGING,
OUTSPOKEN...
ANOTHER TROUBLEMAKER I'M AFRAID, SIR.
INVITE MR. GOLDWATER FOR DINNER THIS EVENING...
AND ASK HARRY TRUMAN TO JOIN US.
RECEPTION
NOW, THERE'S A DINNER TO DIE FOR!

June 3, 1998

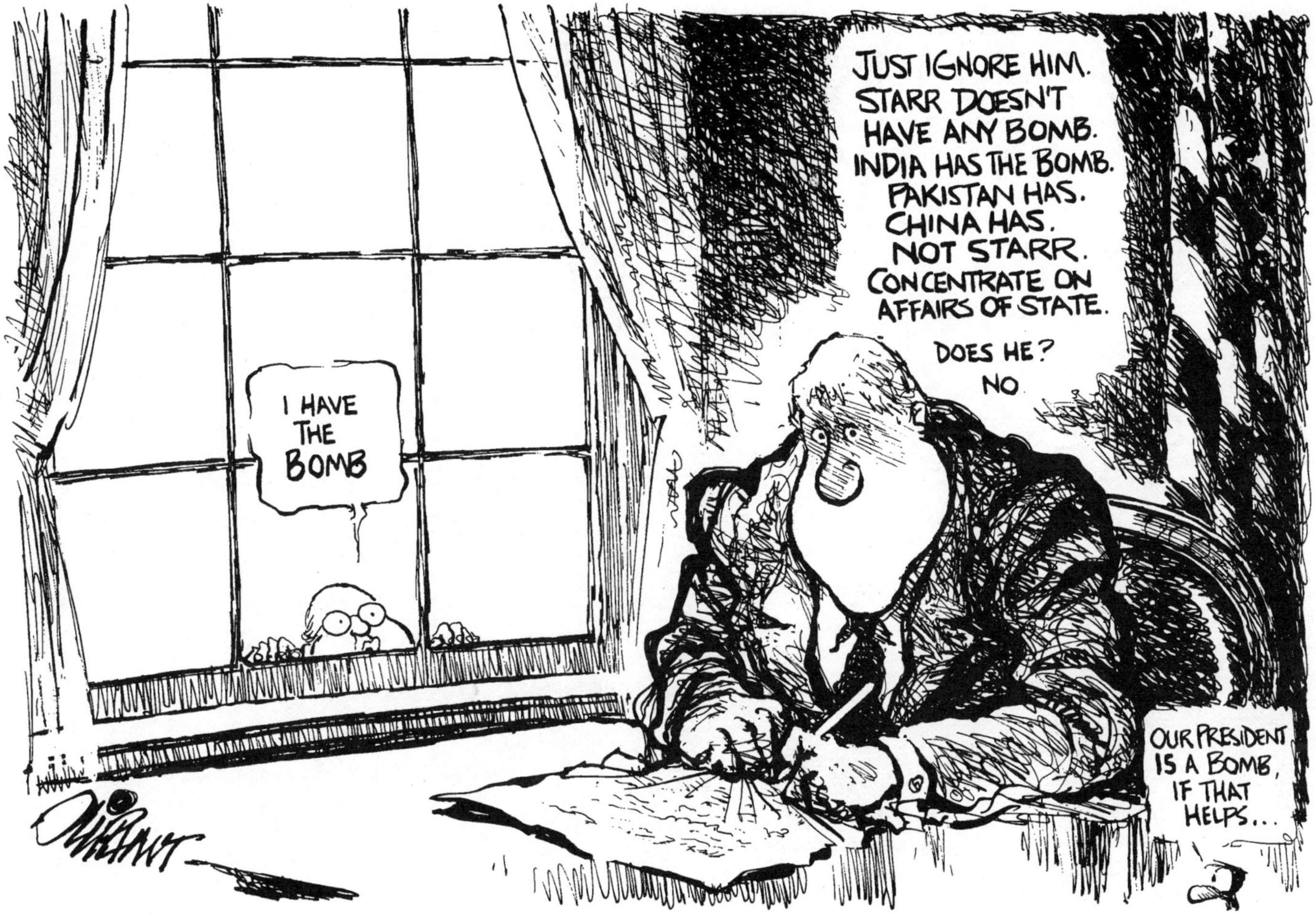
I HAVE THE BOMB
JUST IGNORE HIM. STARR DOESN'T HAVE ANY BOMB. INDIA HAS THE BOMB. PAKISTAN HAS. CHINA HAS. NOT STARR. CONCENTRATE ON AFFAIRS OF STATE.
DOES HE?
NO
OUR PRESIDENT IS A BOMB, IF THAT HELPS...
OLIPHANT

June 4, 1998

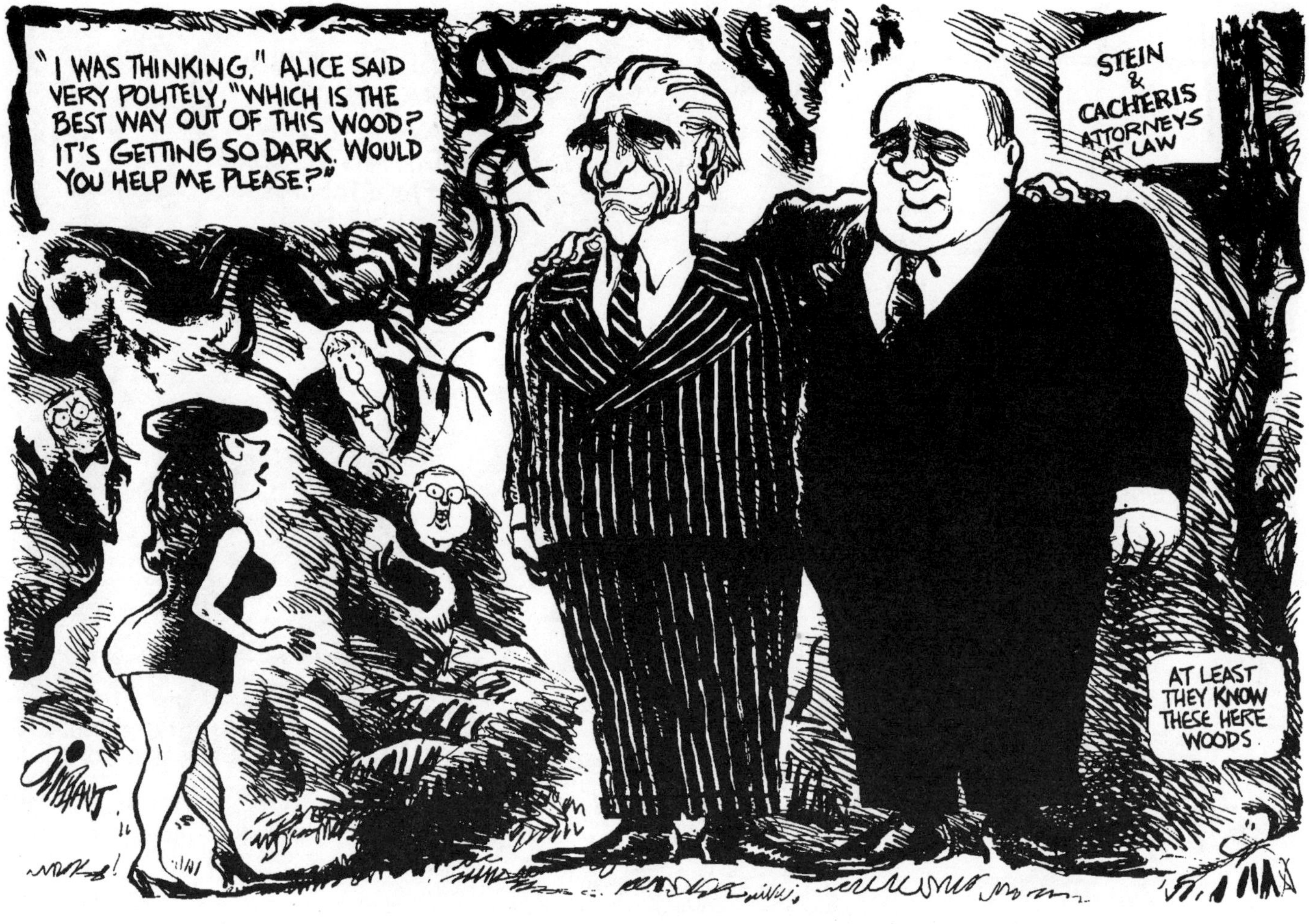
"I WAS THINKING," ALICE SAID VERY POLITELY, "WHICH IS THE BEST WAY OUT OF THIS WOOD? IT'S GETTING SO DARK. WOULD YOU HELP ME PLEASE?"
STEIN & CACHERIS ATTORNEYS AT LAW
AT LEAST THEY KNOW THESE HERE WOODS

June 10, 1998

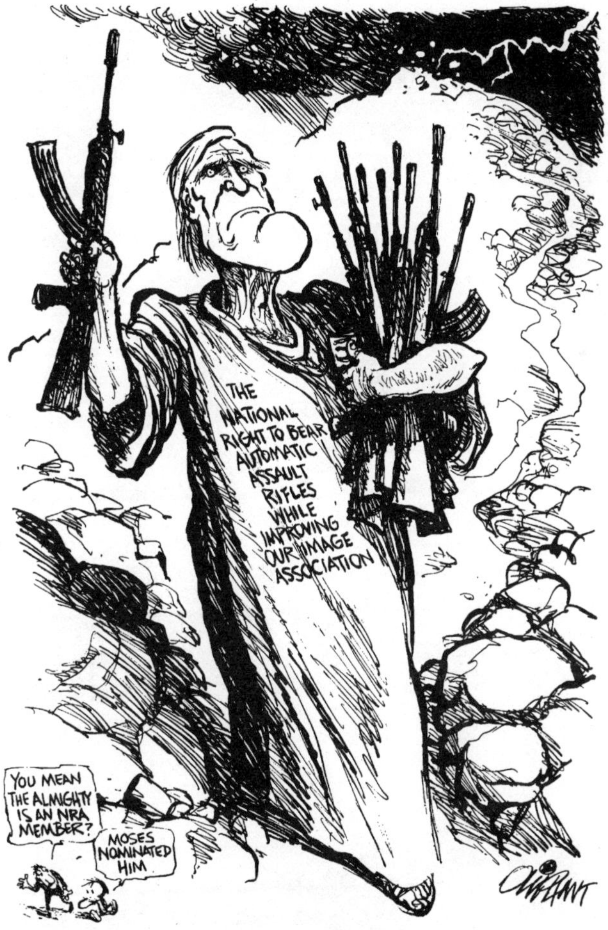
THE NATIONAL RIGHT TO BEAR AUTOMATIC ASSAULT RIFLES WHILE IMPROVING OUR IMAGE ASSOCIATION
YOU MEAN THE ALMIGHTY IS AN NRA MEMBER?
MOSES NOMINATED HIM

STARRING MOSES HESTON

June 11, 1998

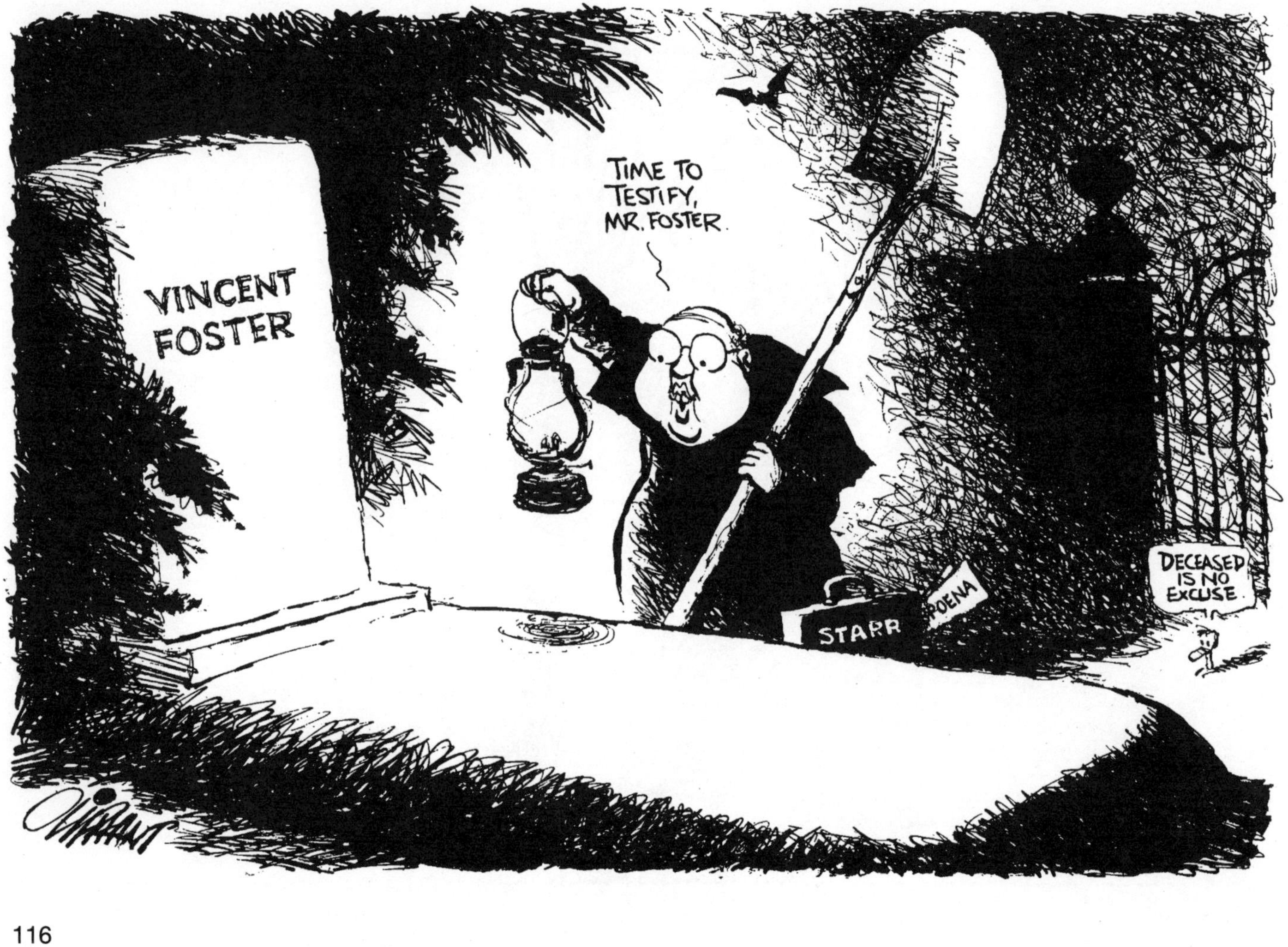

VINCENT
FOSTER
TIME TO
TESTIFY,
MR. FOSTER.
STARR
POENA
DECEASED
IS NO
EXCUSE.

June 12, 1998

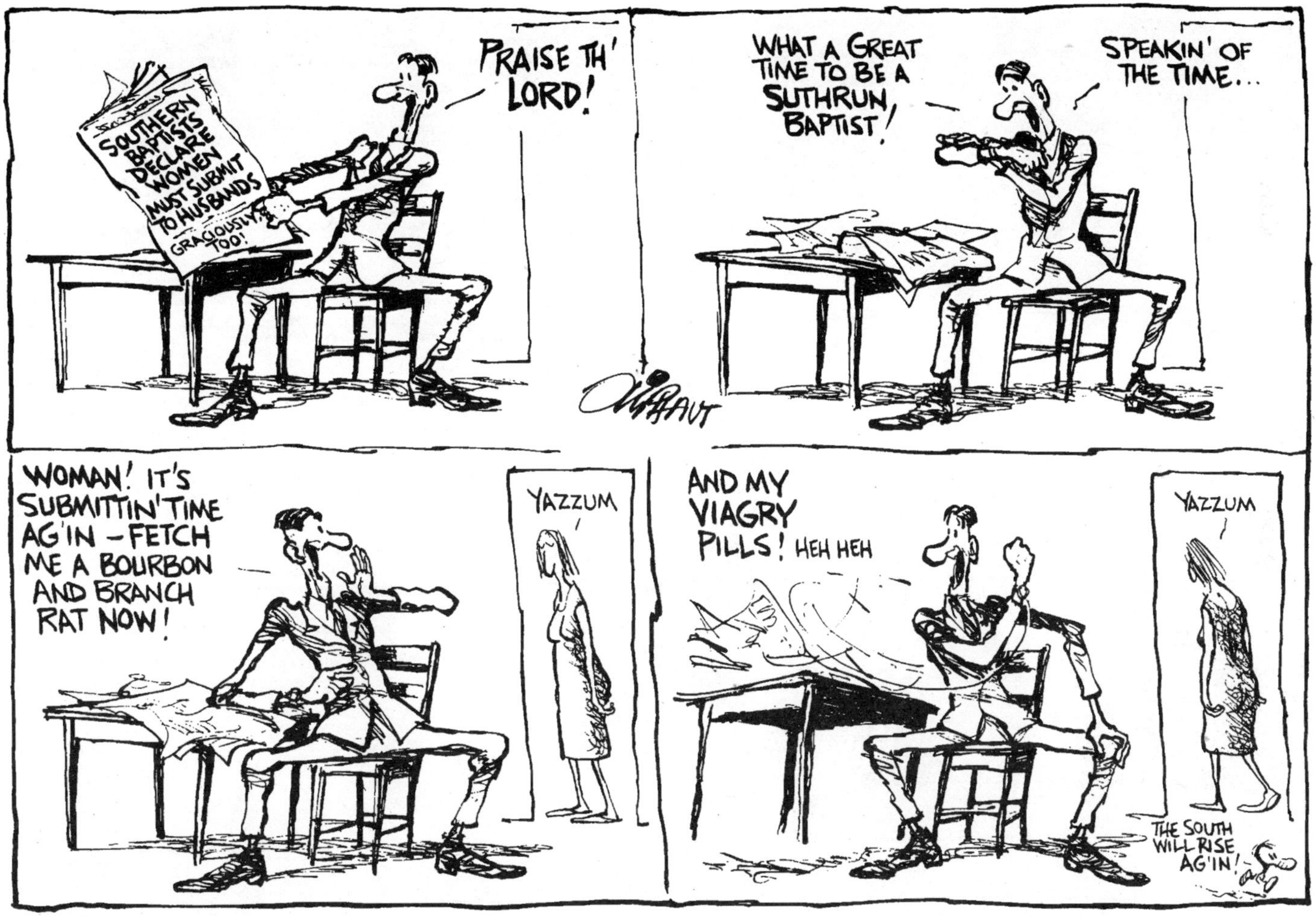
SOUTHERN BAPTISTS DECLARE WOMEN MUST SUBMIT TO HUSBANDS
GRACIOUSLY, TOO!
PRAISE TH' LORD!
WHAT A GREAT TIME TO BE A SUTHRUN BAPTIST!
SPEAKIN' OF THE TIME...
WOMAN! IT'S SUBMITTIN' TIME AG'IN – FETCH ME A BOURBON AND BRANCH RAT NOW!
YAZZUM
AND MY VIAGRY PILLS! HEH HEH
YAZZUM
THE SOUTH WILL RISE AG'IN!

June 24, 1998

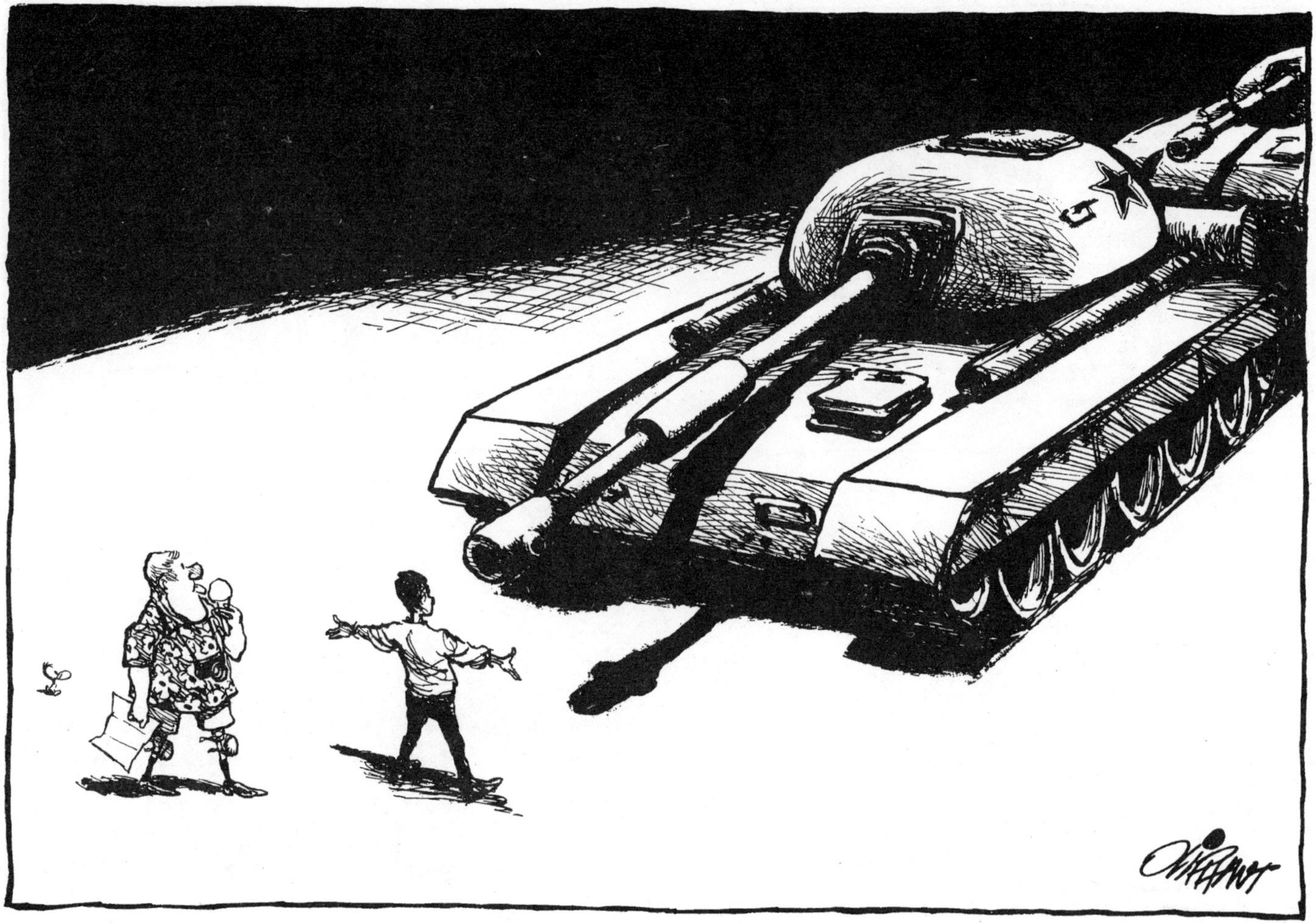

July 6, 1998

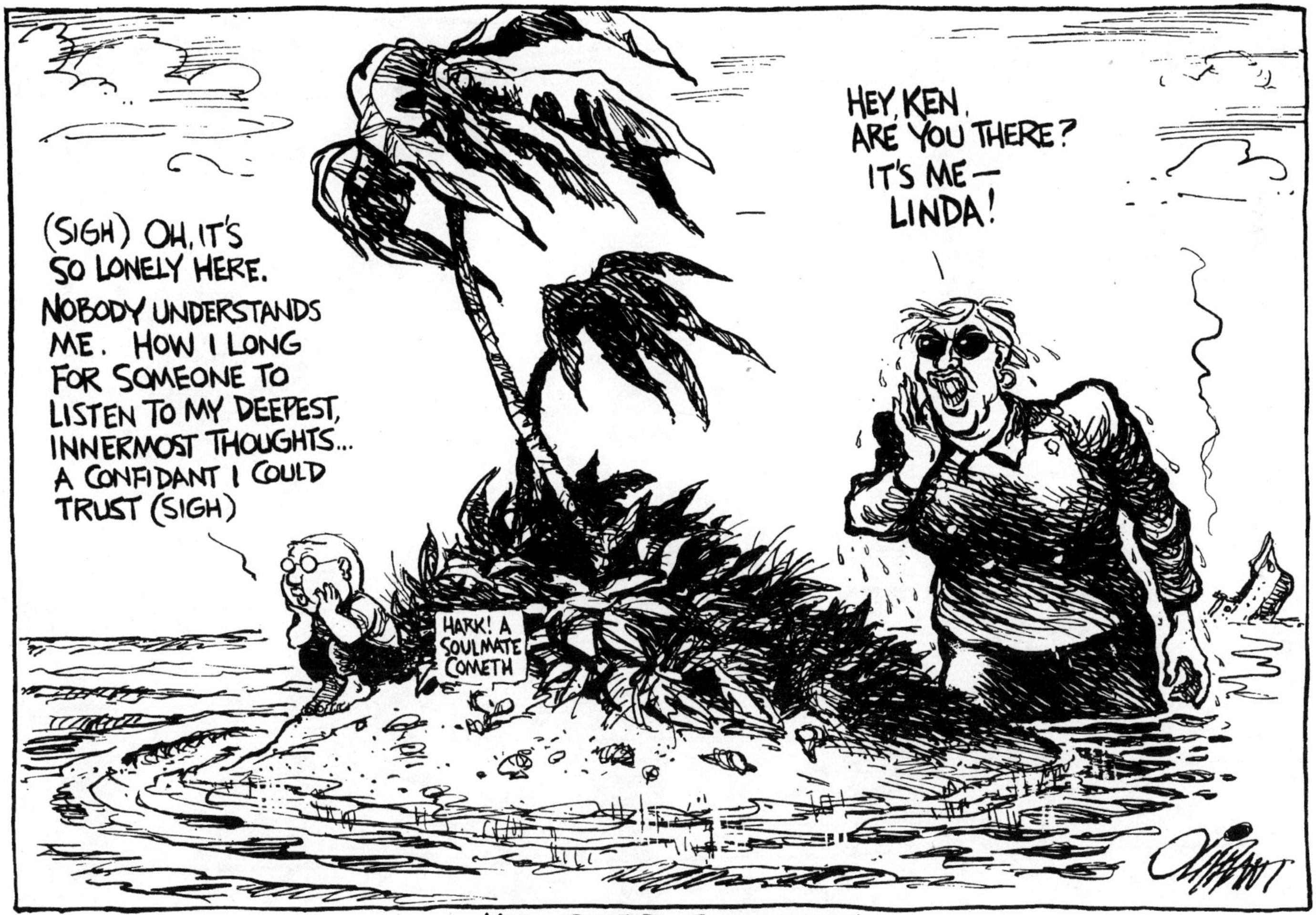
(SIGH) OH, IT'S SO LONELY HERE. NOBODY UNDERSTANDS ME. HOW I LONG FOR SOMEONE TO LISTEN TO MY DEEPEST, INNERMOST THOUGHTS... A CONFIDANT I COULD TRUST (SIGH)
HEY, KEN, ARE YOU THERE? IT'S ME— LINDA!
HARK! A SOULMATE COMETH

KEN STARR, SHIPWRECK.

July 7, 1998

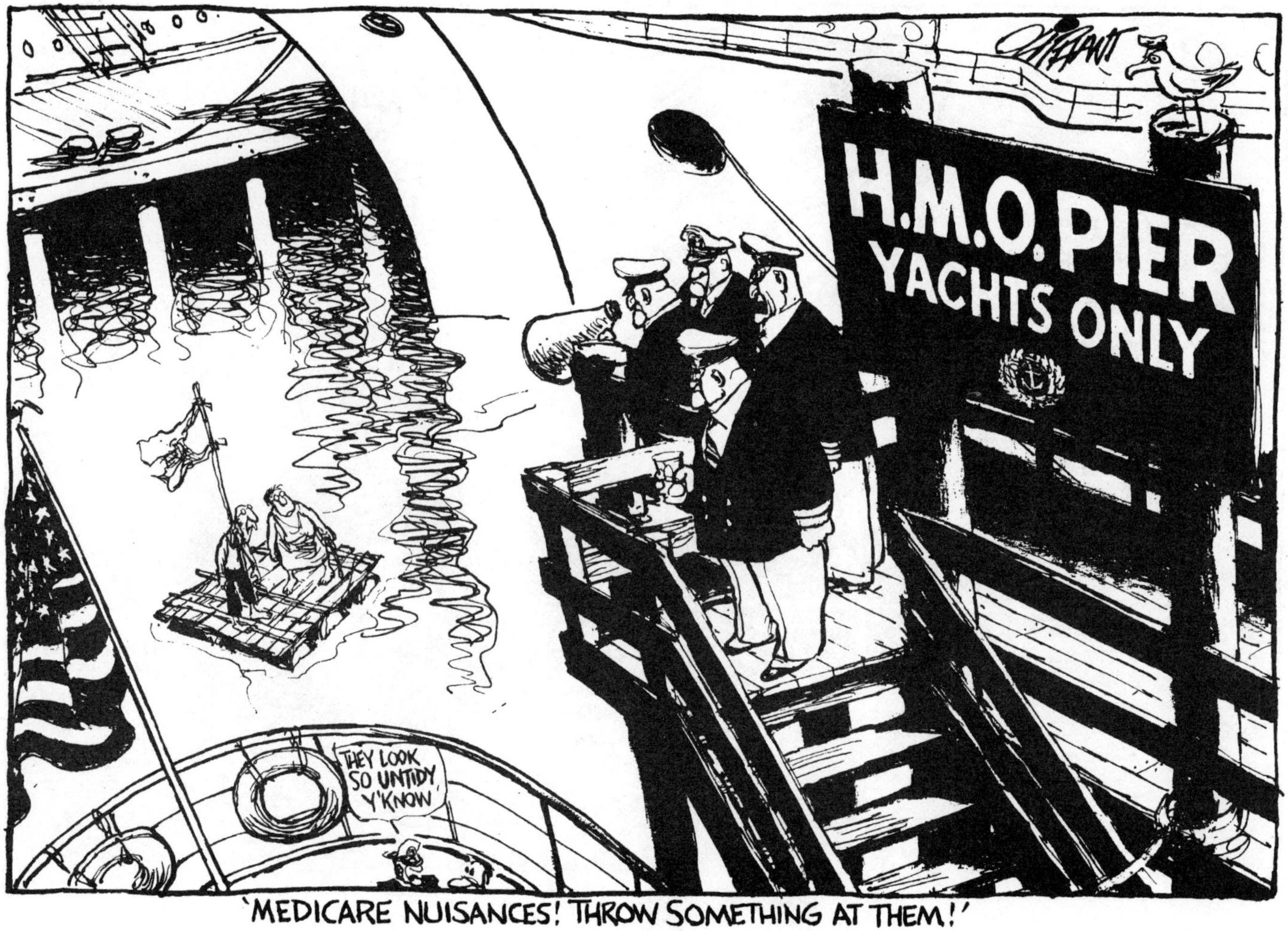
H.M.O. PIER
YACHTS ONLY
THEY LOOK SO UNTIDY, Y'KNOW

'MEDICARE NUISANCES! THROW SOMETHING AT THEM!'

July 8, 1998

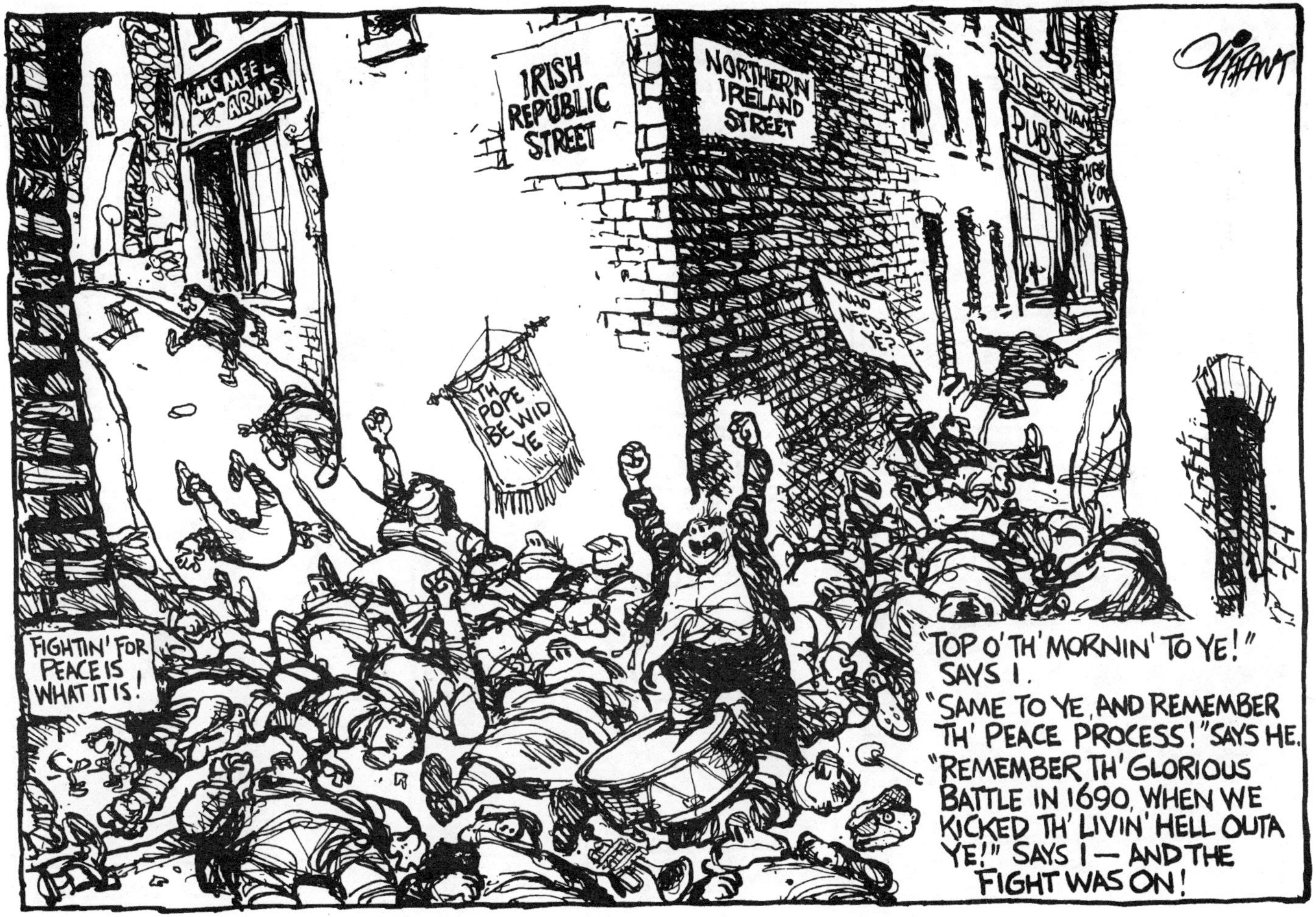

McMEEL ARMS
IRISH REPUBLIC STREET
NORTHERN IRELAND STREET
HIBERNIAN PUB
WHO NEEDS YE?
TH' POPE BE WID YE
FIGHTIN' FOR PEACE IS WHAT IT IS!
"TOP O' TH' MORNIN' TO YE!" SAYS I.
"SAME TO YE, AND REMEMBER TH' PEACE PROCESS!" SAYS HE.
"REMEMBER TH' GLORIOUS BATTLE IN 1690, WHEN WE KICKED TH' LIVIN' HELL OUTA YE!" SAYS I — AND THE FIGHT WAS ON!

July 9, 1998

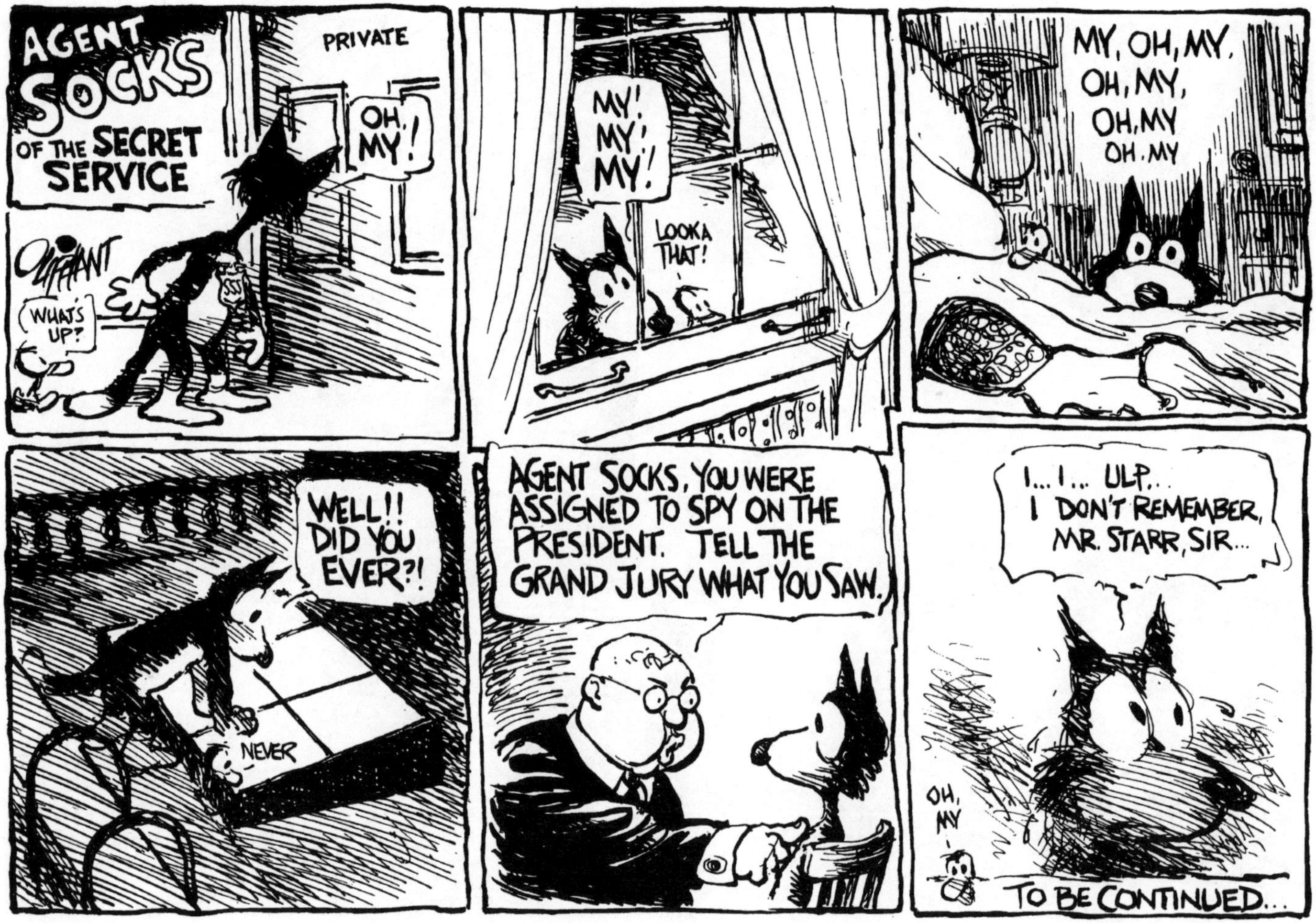
AGENT SOCKS OF THE SECRET SERVICE
OLIPHANT
PRIVATE
OH, MY!
WHAT'S UP?
MY! MY! MY!
LOOKA THAT!
MY, OH, MY, OH, MY, OH, MY OH, MY
WELL!! DID YOU EVER?!
NEVER
AGENT SOCKS, YOU WERE ASSIGNED TO SPY ON THE PRESIDENT. TELL THE GRAND JURY WHAT YOU SAW.
I... I... ULP... I DON'T REMEMBER, MR. STARR, SIR...
OH, MY!
TO BE CONTINUED...

July 13, 1998

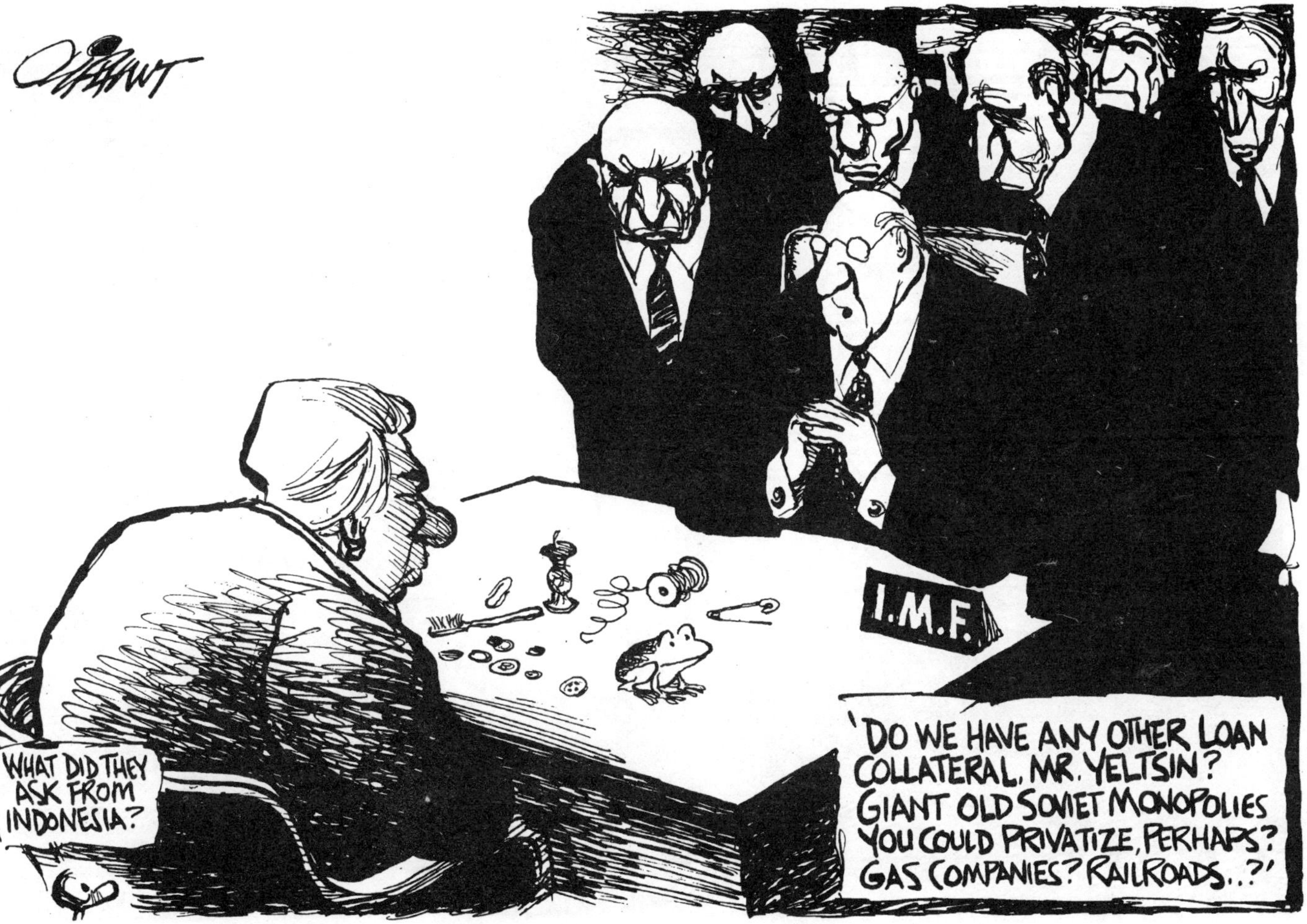
OLIPHANT
I.M.F.
WHAT DID THEY ASK FROM INDONESIA?
'DO WE HAVE ANY OTHER LOAN COLLATERAL, MR. YELTSIN? GIANT OLD SOVIET MONOPOLIES YOU COULD PRIVATIZE, PERHAPS? GAS COMPANIES? RAILROADS..?'

July 14, 1998

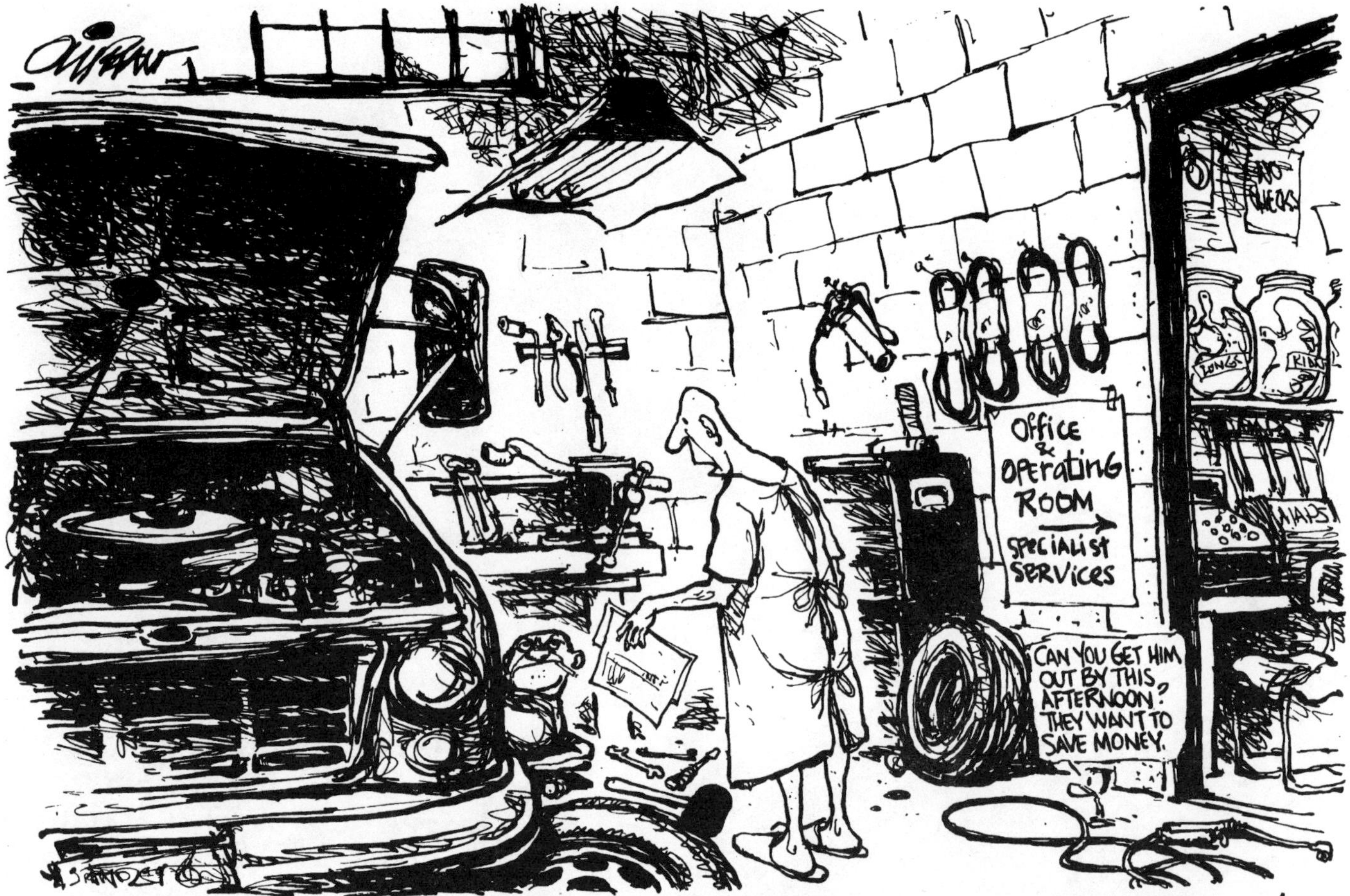
Office & Operating Room
Specialist Services
CAN YOU GET HIM OUT BY THIS AFTERNOON? THEY WANT TO SAVE MONEY.

'MY HMO SENT ME OVER FOR BRAIN SURGERY AND A LIVER TRANSPLANT.'

July 20, 1998

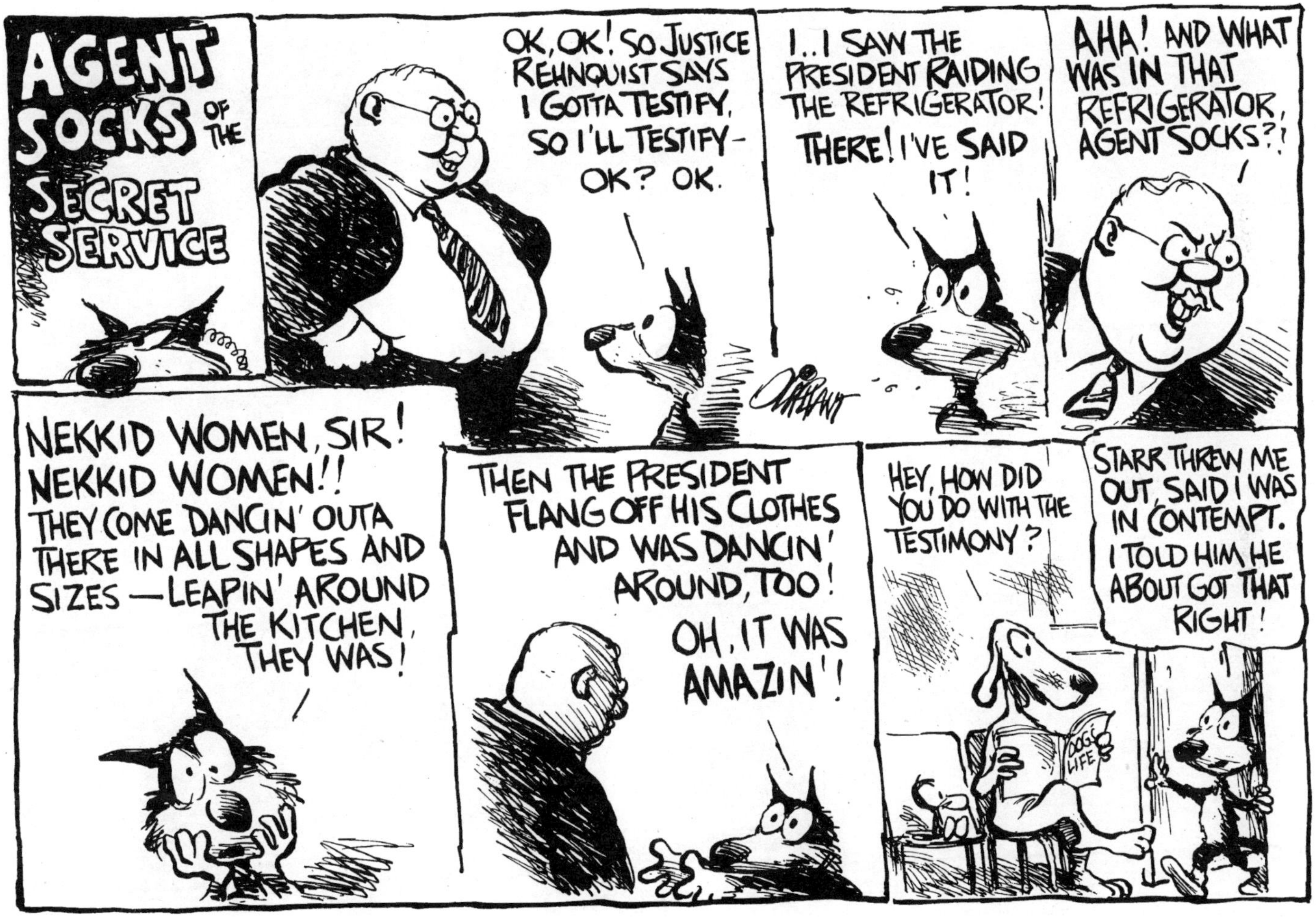
AGENT SOCKS OF THE SECRET SERVICE
OK, OK! SO JUSTICE REHNQUIST SAYS I GOTTA TESTIFY, SO I'LL TESTIFY- OK? OK.
I..I SAW THE PRESIDENT RAIDING THE REFRIGERATOR! THERE! I'VE SAID IT!
AHA! AND WHAT WAS IN THAT REFRIGERATOR, AGENT SOCKS?!
NEKKID WOMEN, SIR! NEKKID WOMEN!! THEY COME DANCIN' OUTA THERE IN ALL SHAPES AND SIZES—LEAPIN' AROUND THE KITCHEN, THEY WAS!
THEN THE PRESIDENT FLANG OFF HIS CLOTHES AND WAS DANCIN' AROUND, TOO!
OH, IT WAS AMAZIN'!
HEY, HOW DID YOU DO WITH THE TESTIMONY?
STARR THREW ME OUT, SAID I WAS IN CONTEMPT. I TOLD HIM HE ABOUT GOT THAT RIGHT!
DOG'S LIFE

July 27, 1998

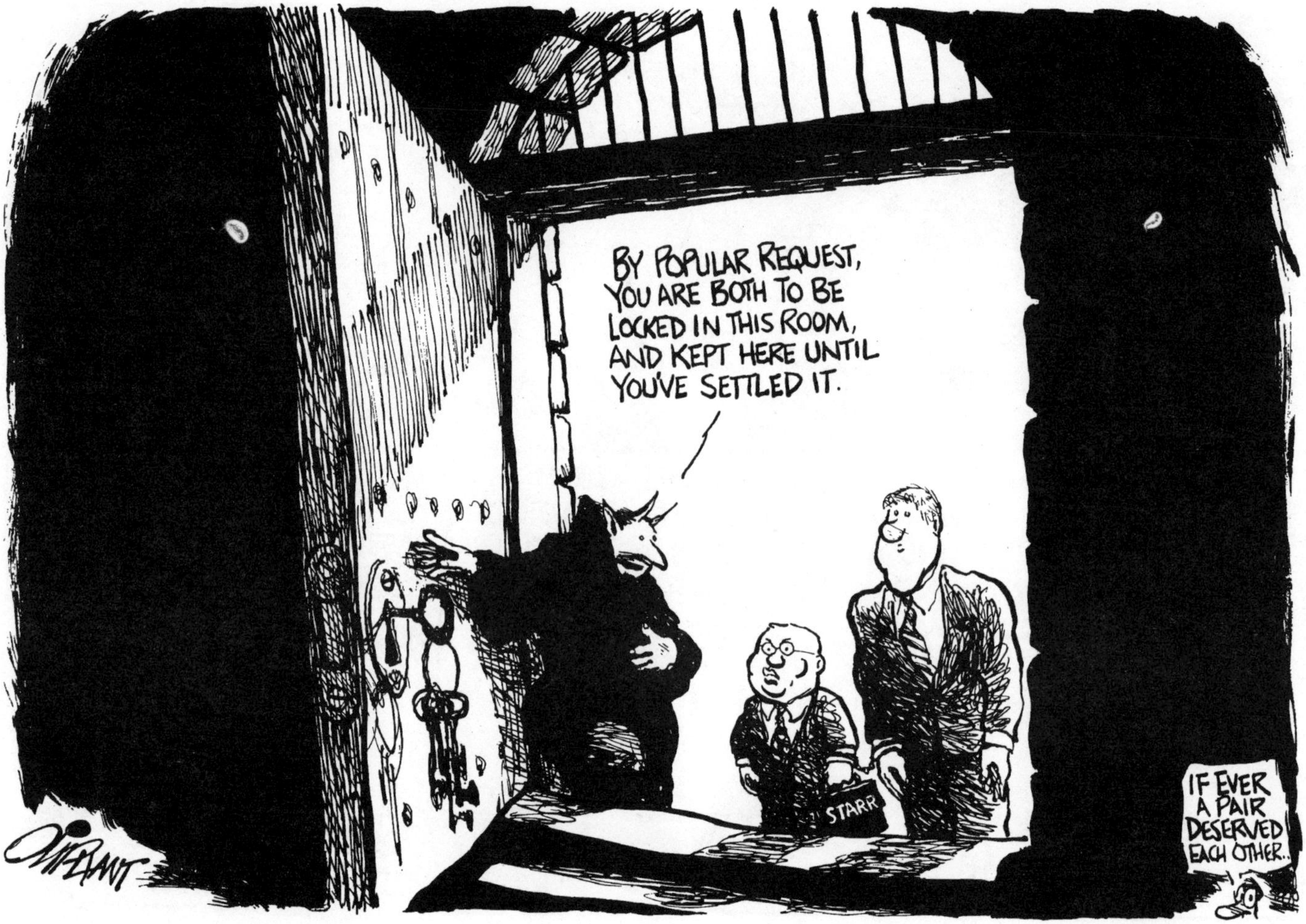
BY POPULAR REQUEST, YOU ARE BOTH TO BE LOCKED IN THIS ROOM, AND KEPT HERE UNTIL YOU'VE SETTLED IT.
STARR
IF EVER A PAIR DESERVED EACH OTHER..
OLIPHANT

August 3, 1998

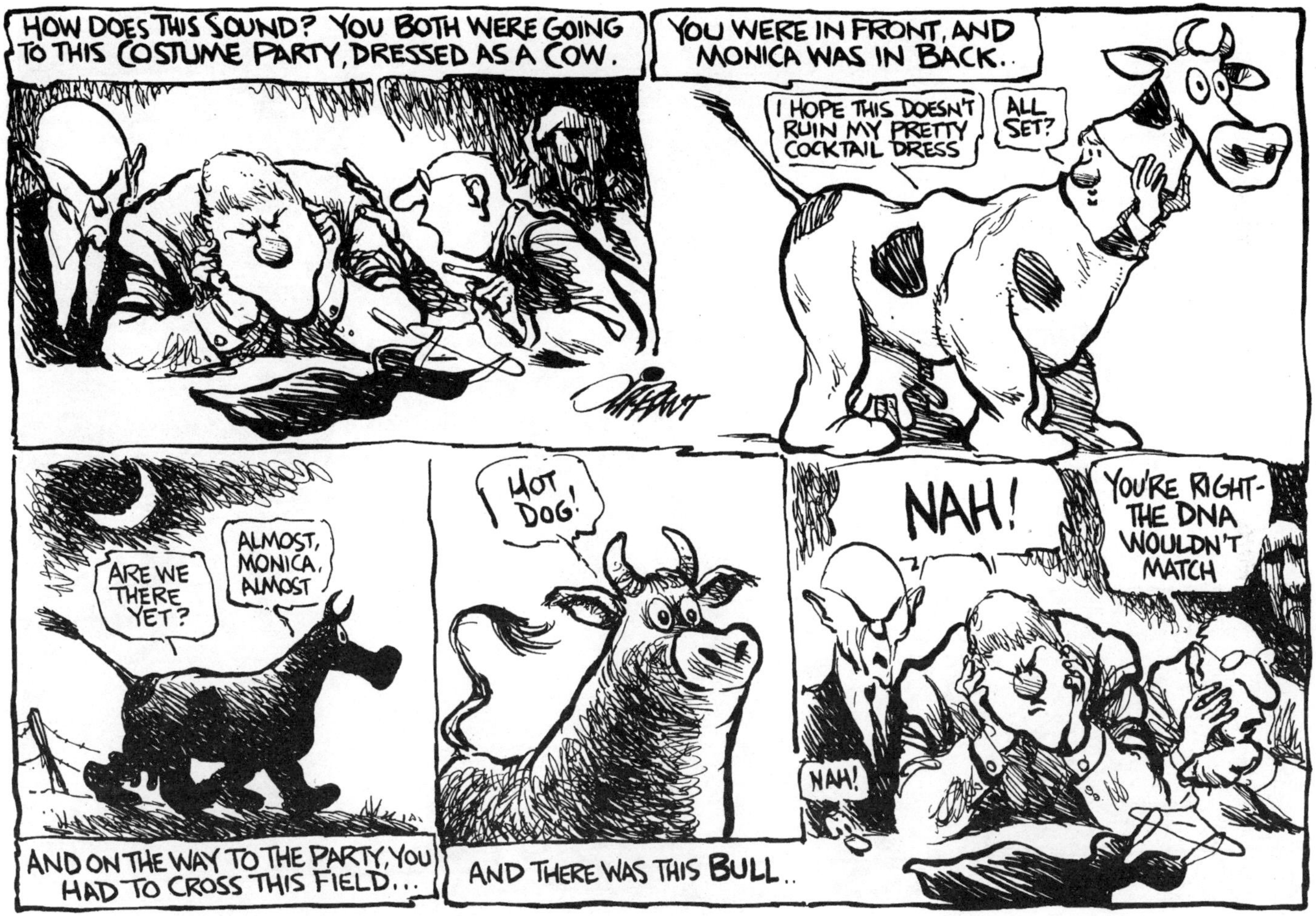
HOW DOES THIS SOUND? YOU BOTH WERE GOING TO THIS COSTUME PARTY, DRESSED AS A COW.
YOU WERE IN FRONT, AND MONICA WAS IN BACK..
I HOPE THIS DOESN'T RUIN MY PRETTY COCKTAIL DRESS
ALL SET?
ARE WE THERE YET?
ALMOST, MONICA, ALMOST
AND ON THE WAY TO THE PARTY, YOU HAD TO CROSS THIS FIELD...
HOT DOG!
AND THERE WAS THIS BULL..
NAH!
YOU'RE RIGHT- THE DNA WOULDN'T MATCH
NAH!

August 4, 1998

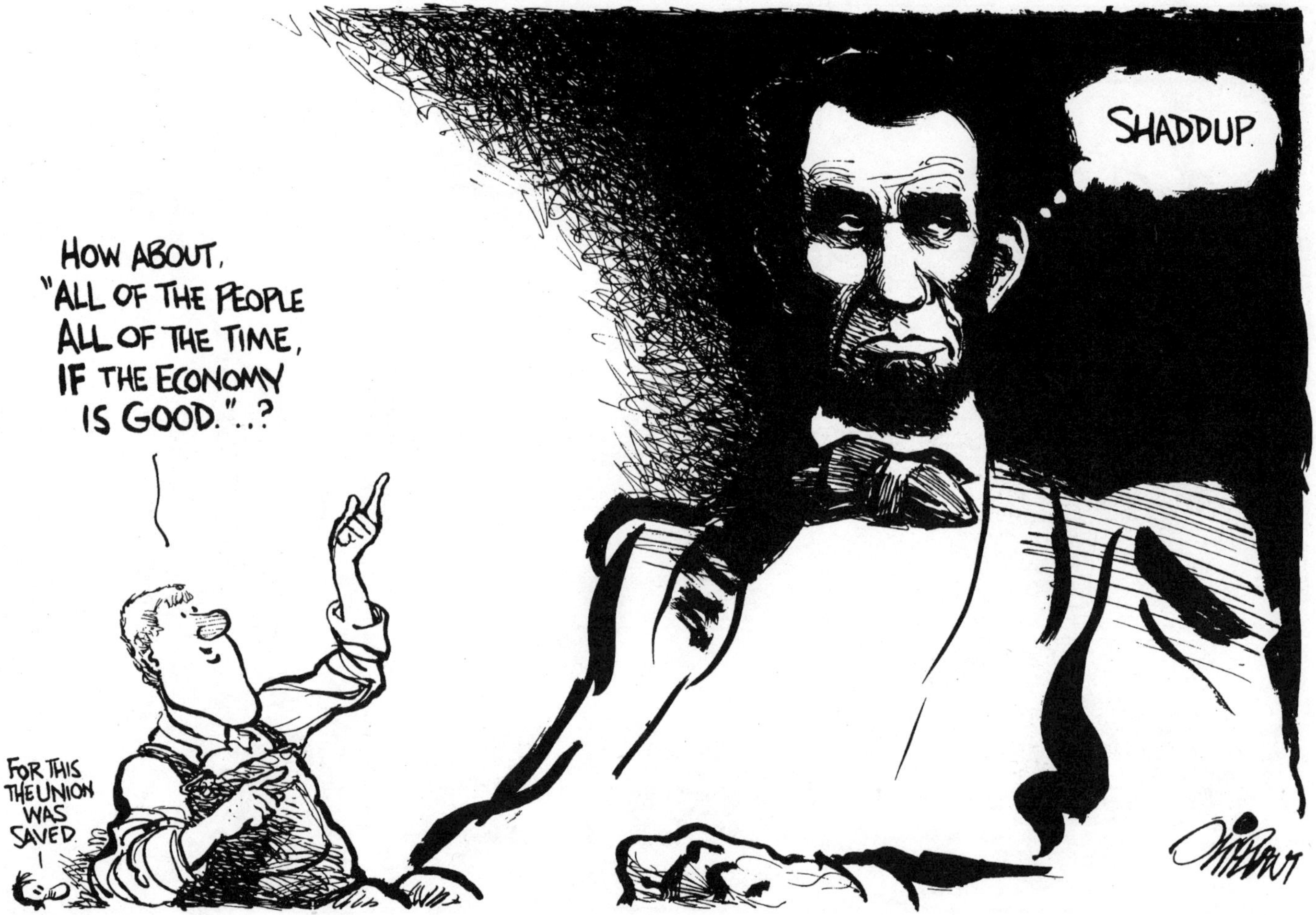
HOW ABOUT, "ALL OF THE PEOPLE ALL OF THE TIME, IF THE ECONOMY IS GOOD."..?
SHADDUP.
FOR THIS THE UNION WAS SAVED!

August 11, 1998

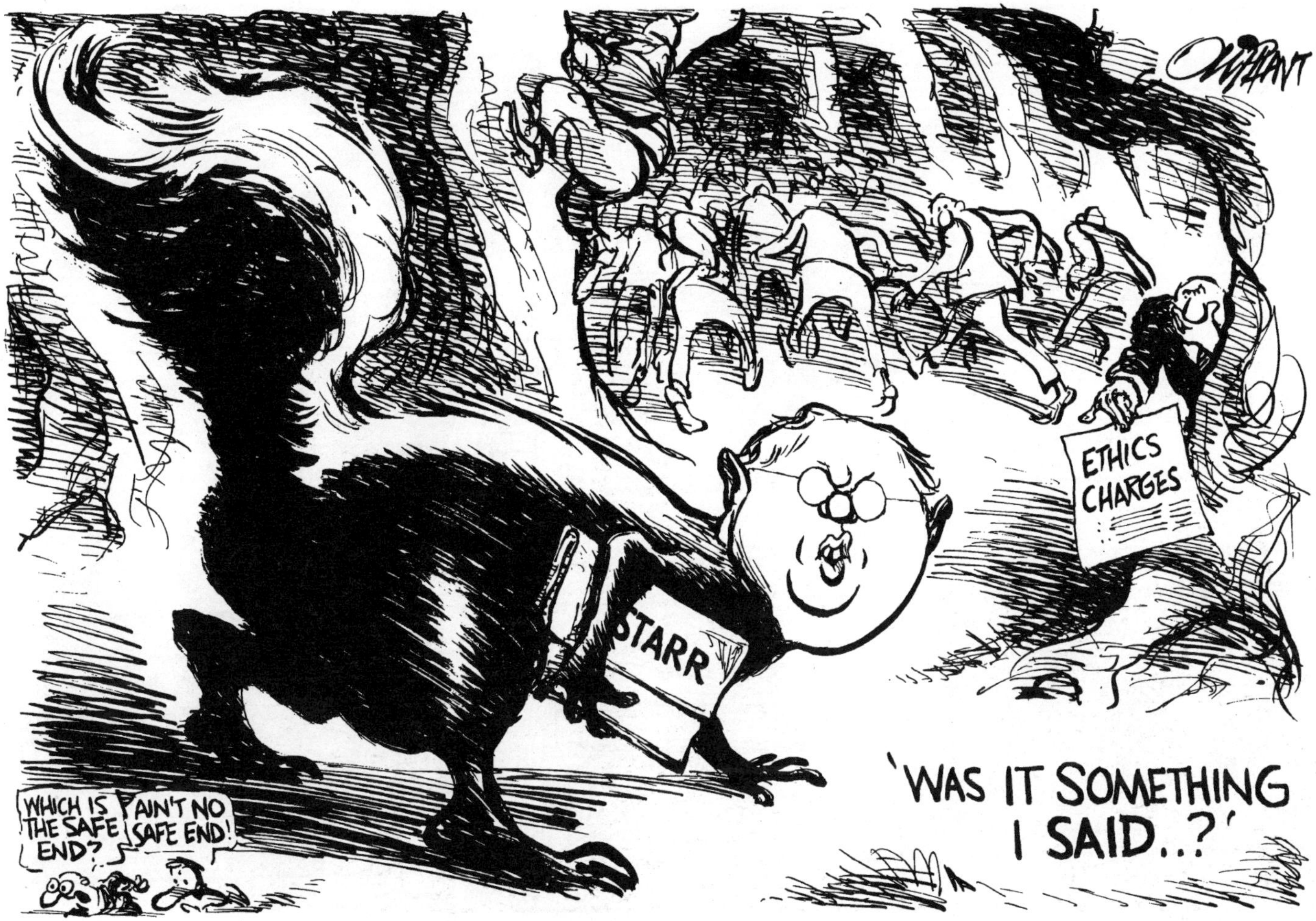

OLIPHANT
ETHICS CHARGES
STARR
'WAS IT SOMETHING I SAID..?'
WHICH IS THE SAFE END?
AIN'T NO SAFE END!

August 17, 1998

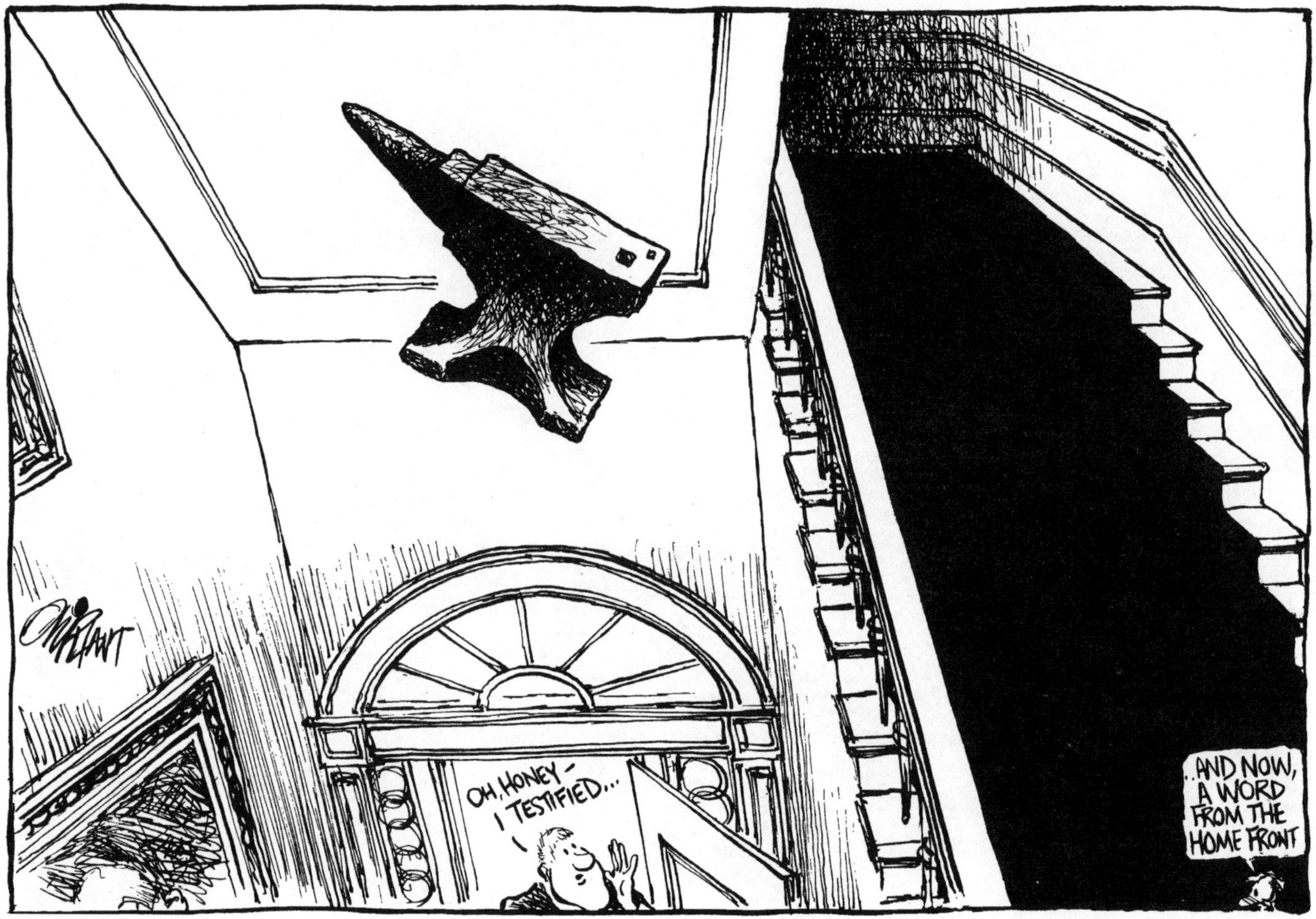
OH, HONEY-
I TESTIFIED...
..AND NOW,
A WORD
FROM THE
HOME FRONT

August 20, 1998

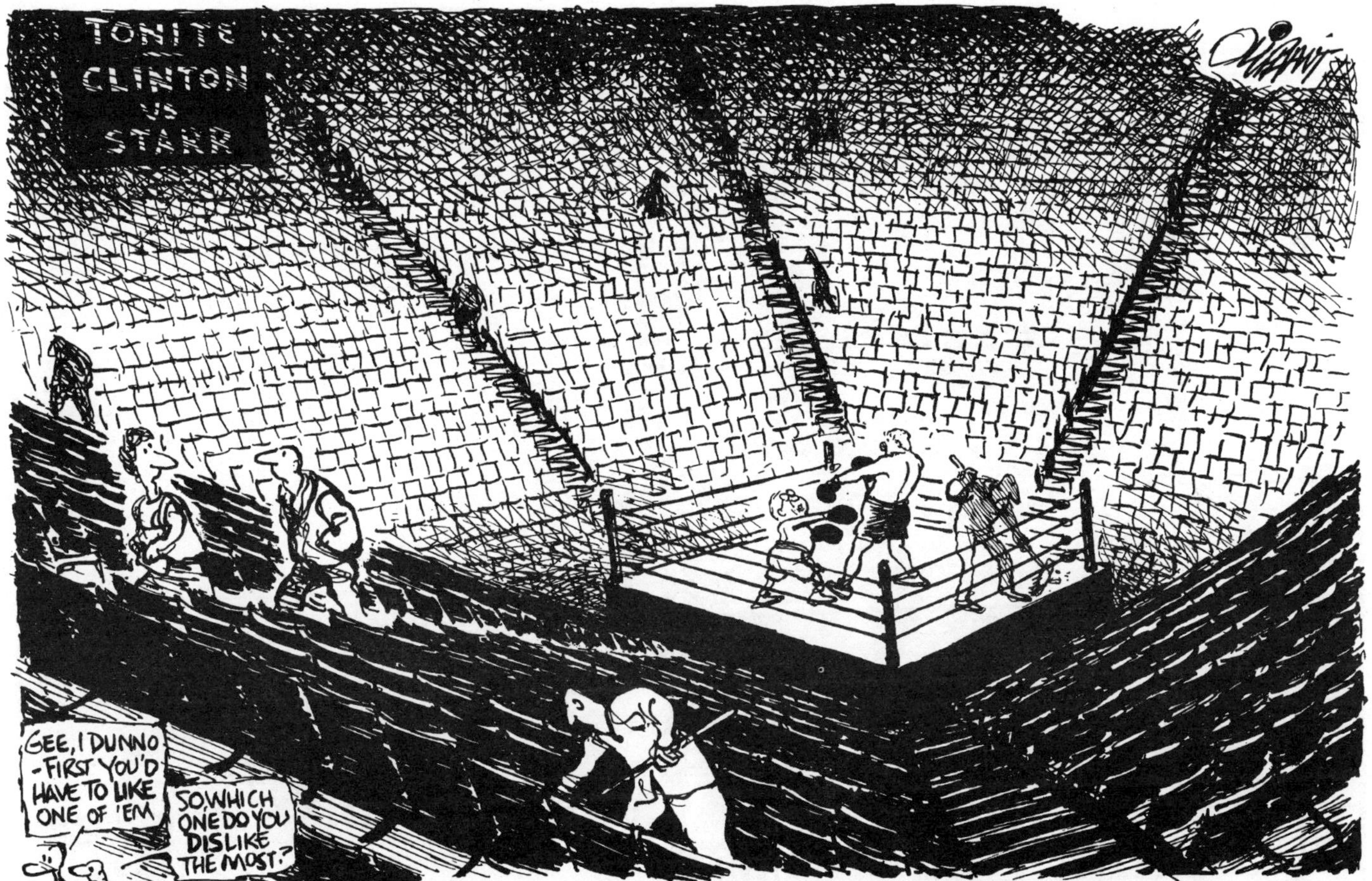
TONITE CLINTON VS STARR
GEE, I DUNNO -FIRST YOU'D HAVE TO LIKE ONE OF 'EM
SO WHICH ONE DO YOU DISLIKE THE MOST?

'.. BUT IF, SAY, YOU REALLY CARED, WHICH ONE WOULD YOU LIKE TO SEE WIN, IF, SAY, YOU CARED?'

August 31, 1998

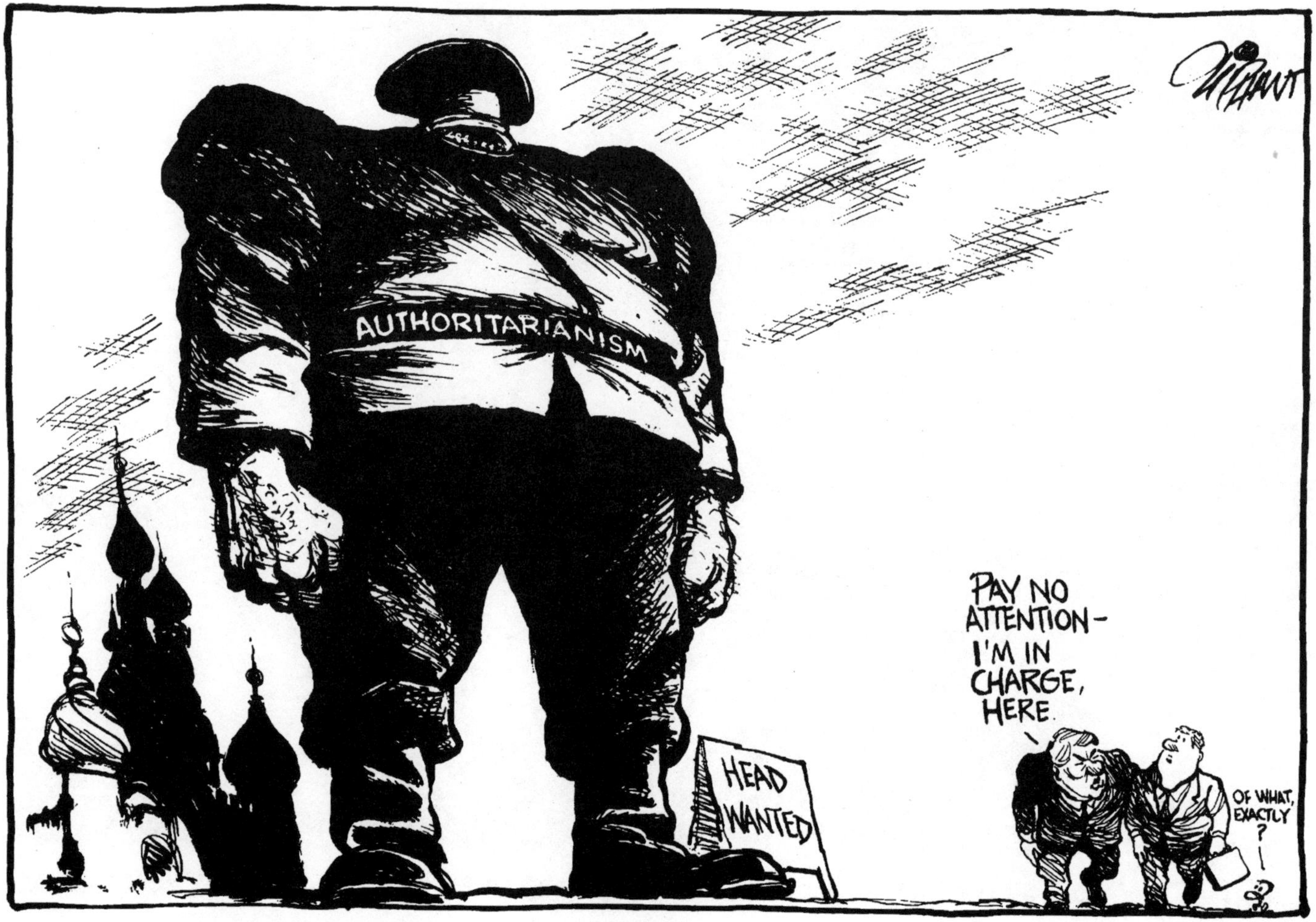
AUTHORITARIANISM
HEAD WANTED
PAY NO ATTENTION- I'M IN CHARGE, HERE.
OF WHAT, EXACTLY?

September 2, 1998

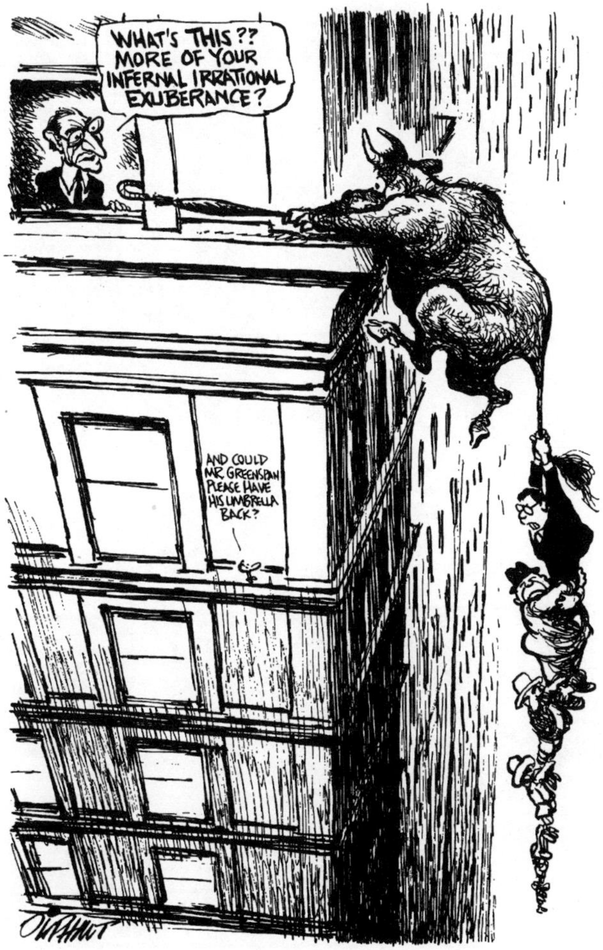
WHAT'S THIS?? MORE OF YOUR INFERNAL IRRATIONAL EXUBERANCE?
AND COULD MR. GREENSPAN PLEASE HAVE HIS UMBRELLA BACK?

September 2, 1998

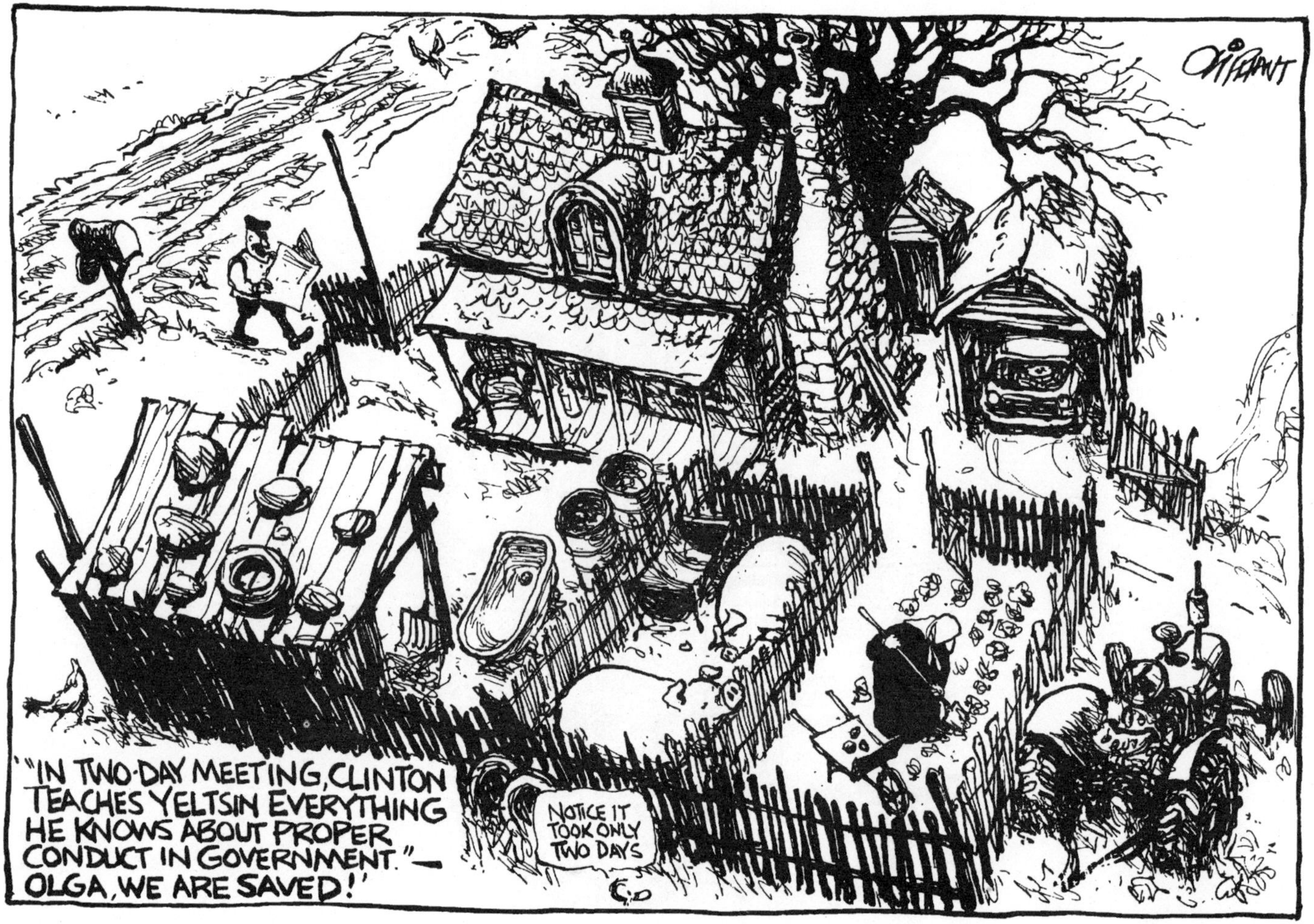
OLIPHANT
"IN TWO-DAY MEETING, CLINTON TEACHES YELTSIN EVERYTHING HE KNOWS ABOUT PROPER CONDUCT IN GOVERNMENT."— OLGA, WE ARE SAVED!"
NOTICE IT TOOK ONLY TWO DAYS

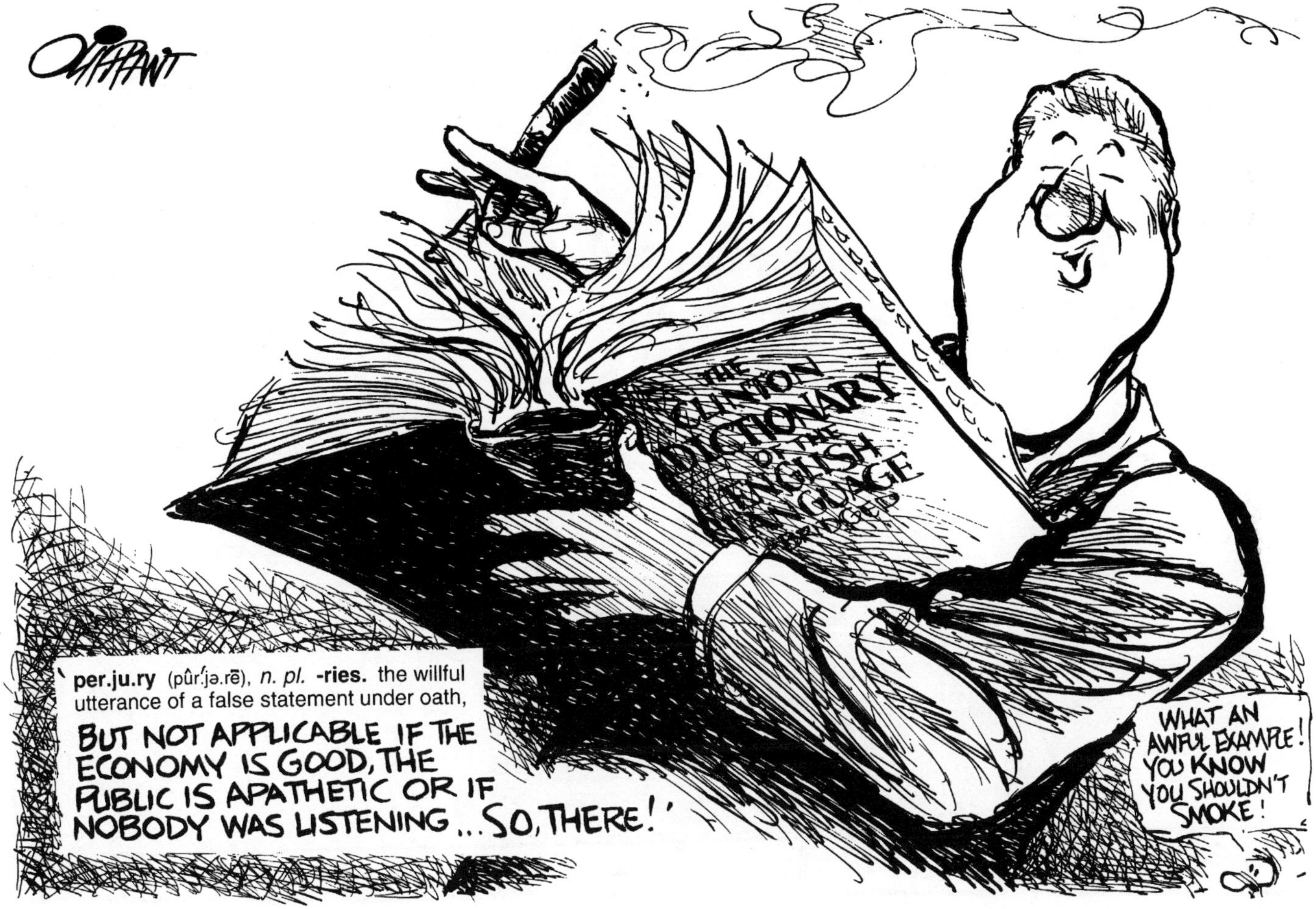
OLIPHANT
per.ju.ry (pûr′jə.rē), n. pl. -ries. the willful utterance of a false statement under oath,
BUT NOT APPLICABLE IF THE ECONOMY IS GOOD, THE PUBLIC IS APATHETIC OR IF NOBODY WAS LISTENING... SO, THERE!
DICTIONARY
WHAT AN AWFUL EXAMPLE! YOU KNOW YOU SHOULDN'T SMOKE!

September 25, 1998

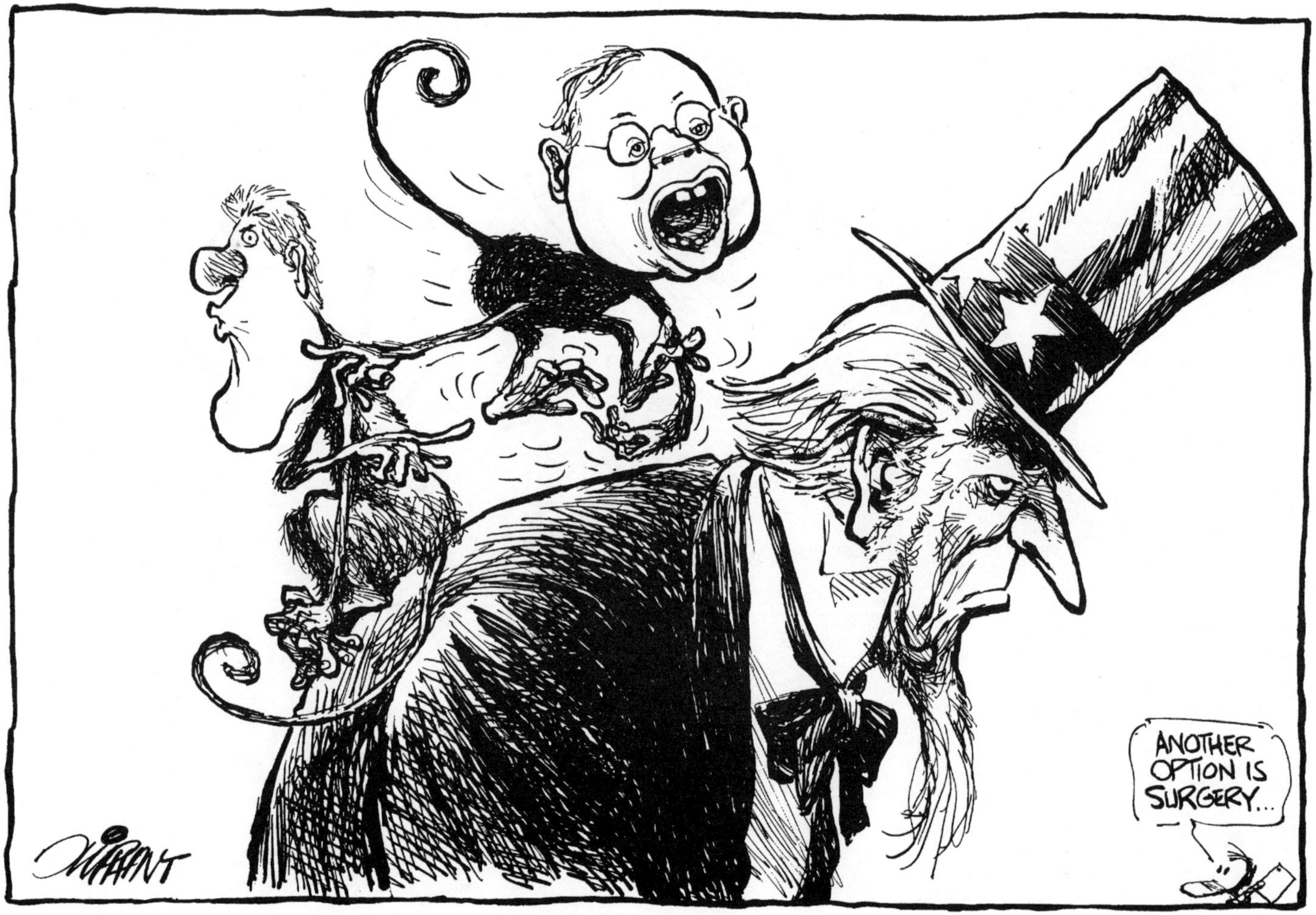
ANOTHER OPTION IS SURGERY...

September 30, 1998

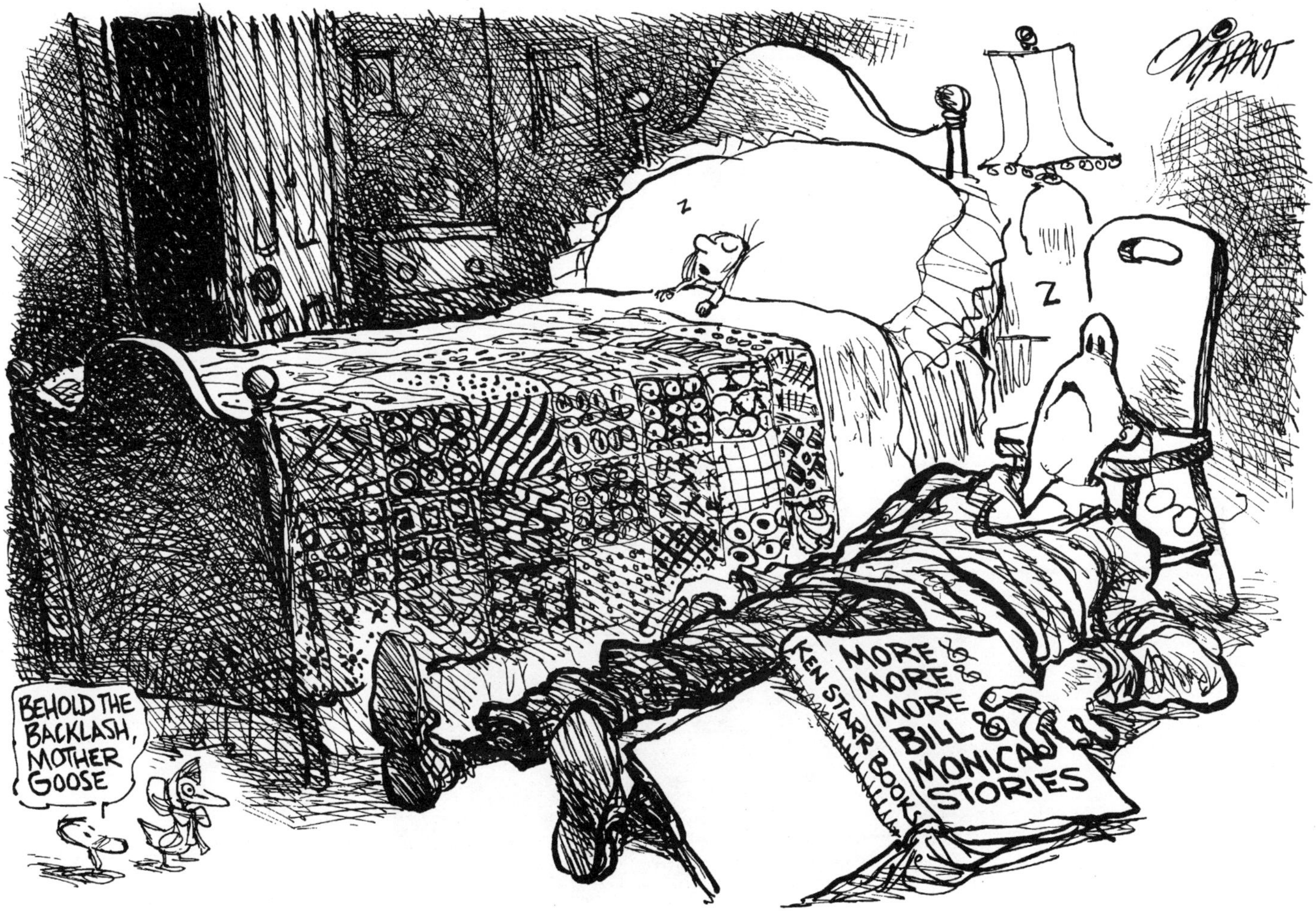
BEHOLD THE BACKLASH, MOTHER GOOSE
MORE & MORE & MORE BILL & MONICA STORIES
KEN STARR BOOKS

October 12, 1998

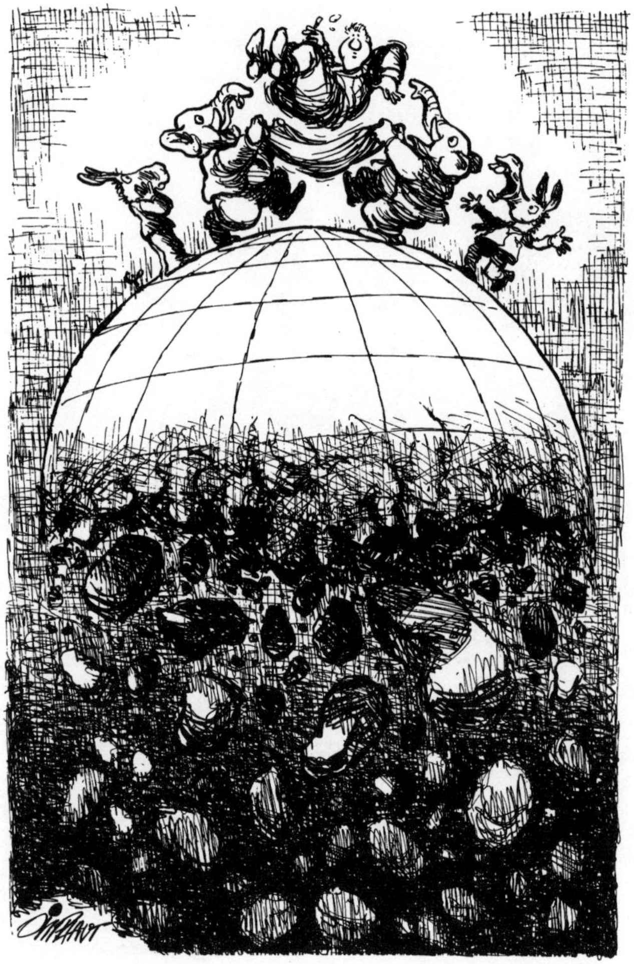

October 12, 1998

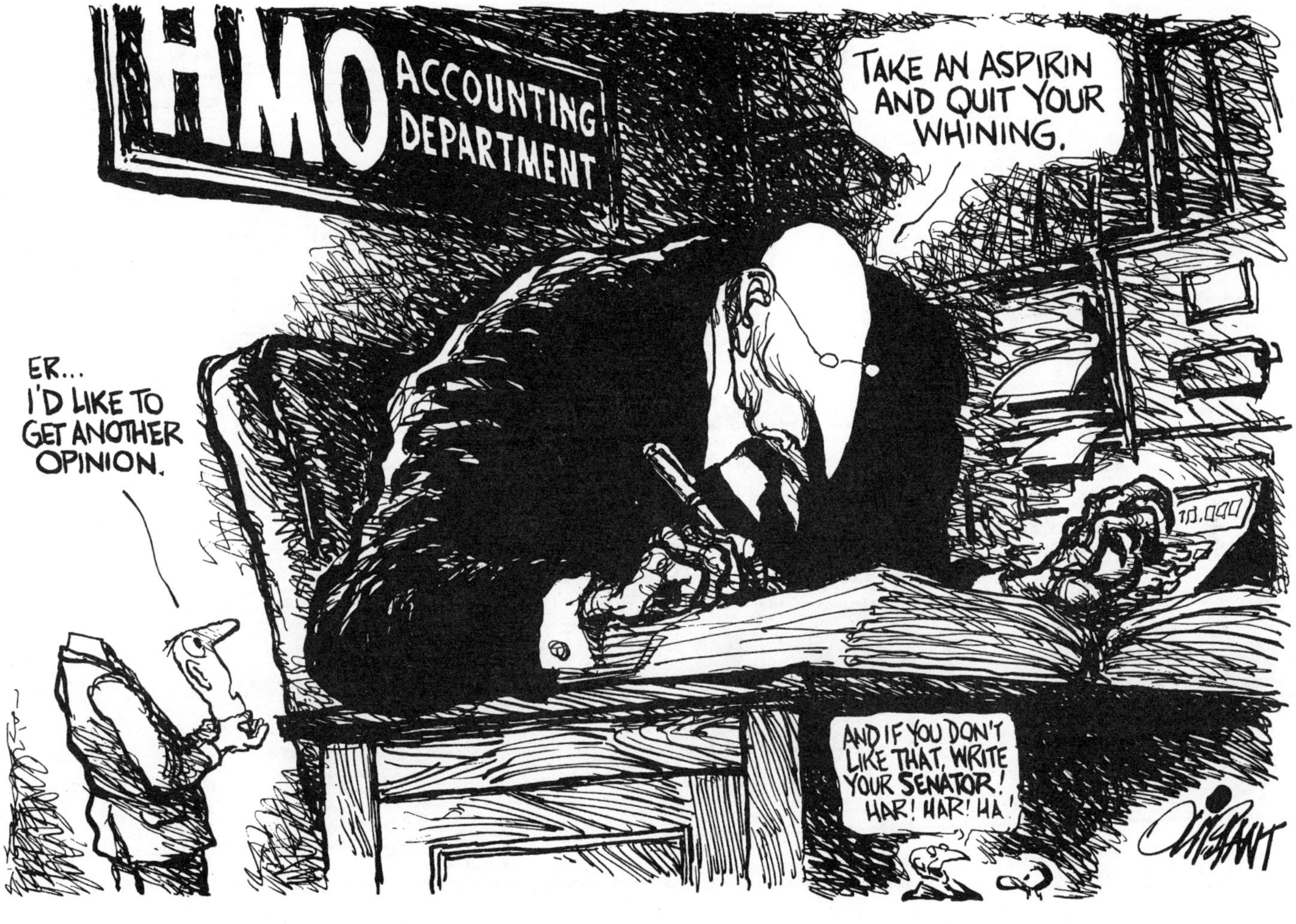
HMO ACCOUNTING DEPARTMENT
ER... I'D LIKE TO GET ANOTHER OPINION.
TAKE AN ASPIRIN AND QUIT YOUR WHINING.
AND IF YOU DON'T LIKE THAT, WRITE YOUR SENATOR! HAR! HAR! HA!
OLIPHANT

October 29, 1998

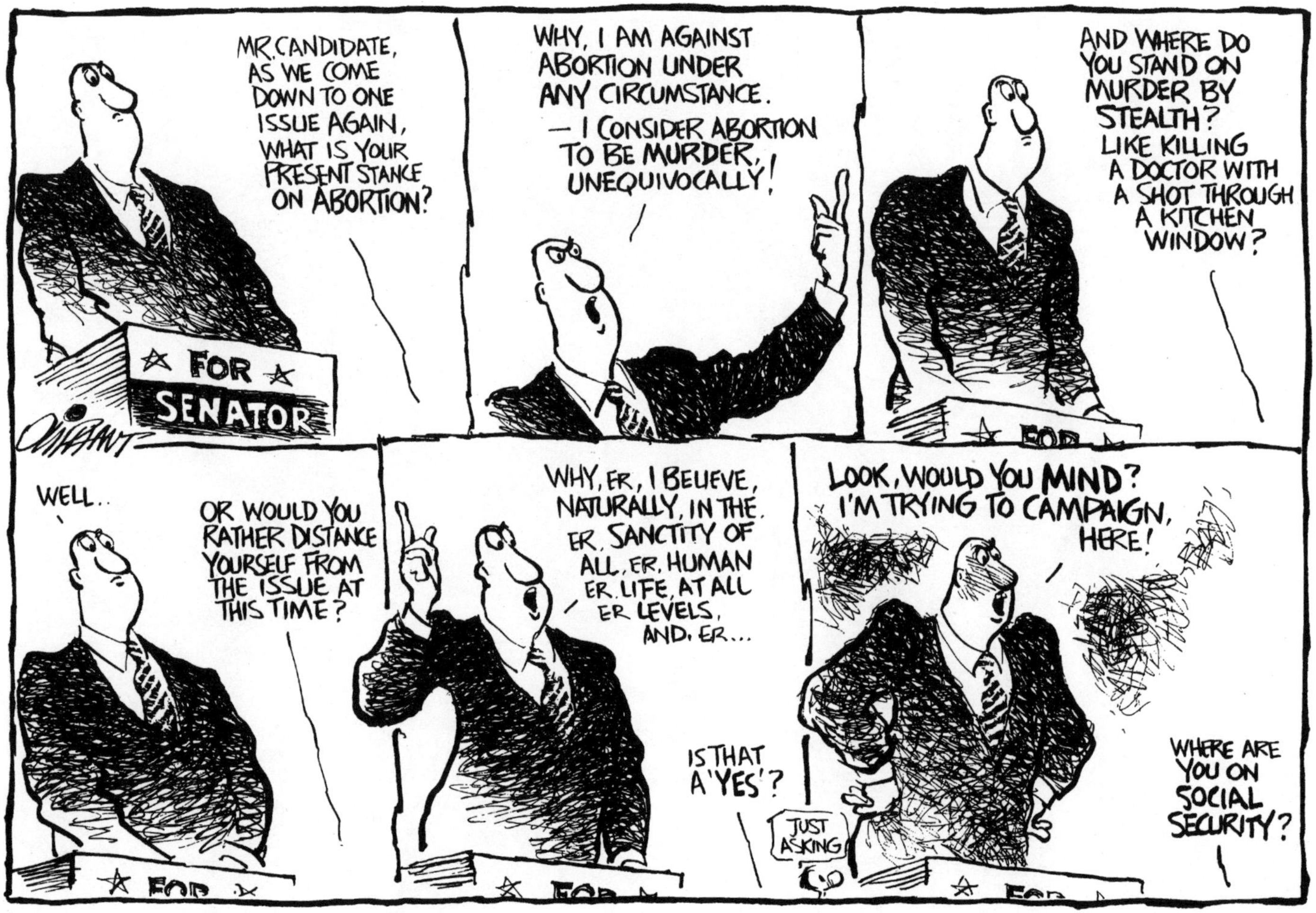
MR. CANDIDATE, AS WE COME DOWN TO ONE ISSUE AGAIN, WHAT IS YOUR PRESENT STANCE ON ABORTION?
FOR SENATOR
WHY, I AM AGAINST ABORTION UNDER ANY CIRCUMSTANCE. — I CONSIDER ABORTION TO BE MURDER, UNEQUIVOCALLY!
AND WHERE DO YOU STAND ON MURDER BY STEALTH? LIKE KILLING A DOCTOR WITH A SHOT THROUGH A KITCHEN WINDOW?
WELL..
OR WOULD YOU RATHER DISTANCE YOURSELF FROM THE ISSUE AT THIS TIME?
WHY, ER, I BELIEVE, NATURALLY, IN THE, ER, SANCTITY OF ALL, ER, HUMAN ER, LIFE, AT ALL ER LEVELS, AND, ER...
IS THAT A 'YES'?
LOOK, WOULD YOU MIND? I'M TRYING TO CAMPAIGN, HERE!
JUST ASKING
WHERE ARE YOU ON SOCIAL SECURITY?

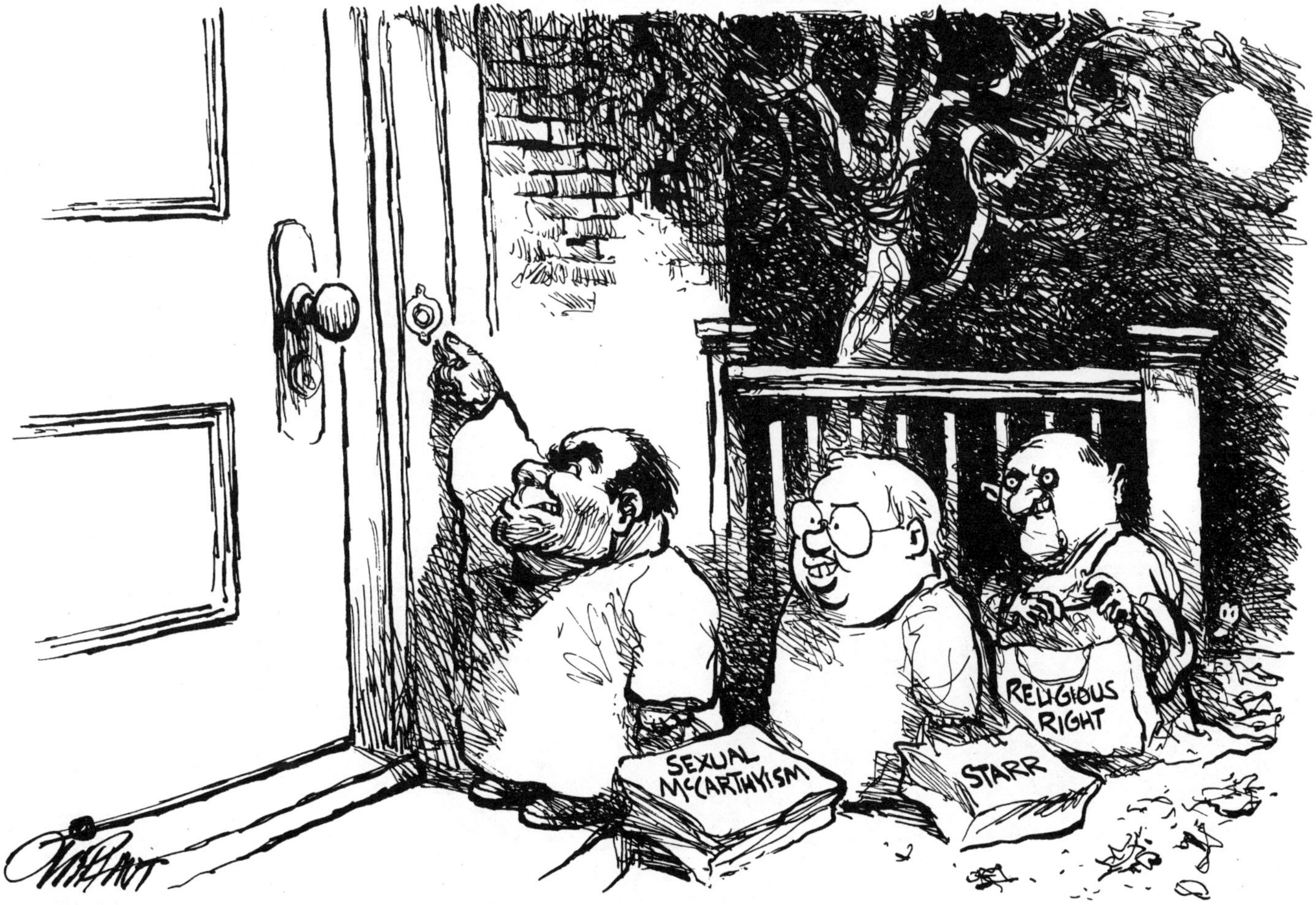
SEXUAL McCARTHYISM
STARR
RELIGIOUS RIGHT

November 5, 1998

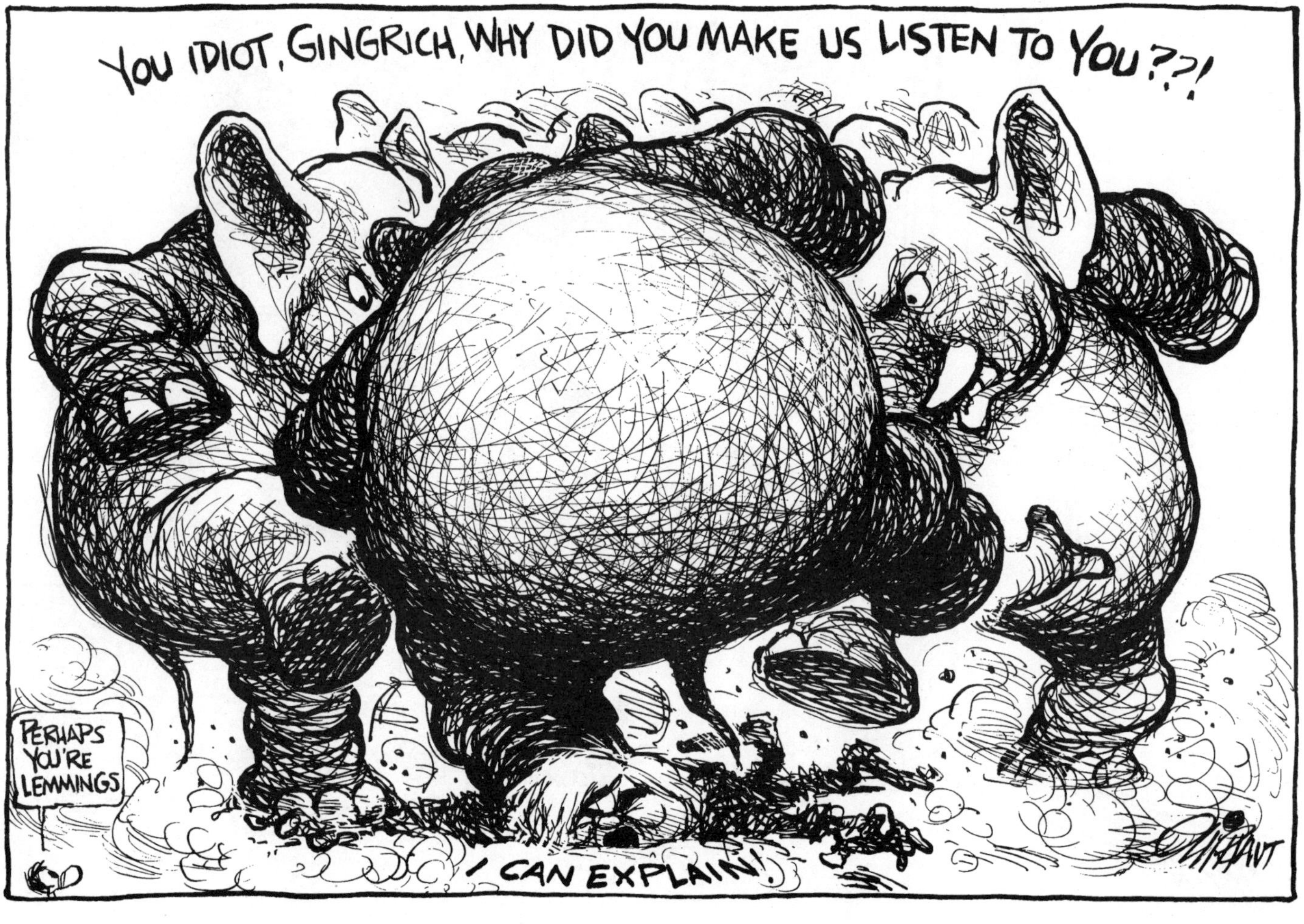
YOU IDIOT, GINGRICH, WHY DID YOU MAKE US LISTEN TO YOU???!
PERHAPS YOU'RE LEMMINGS
I CAN EXPLAIN!

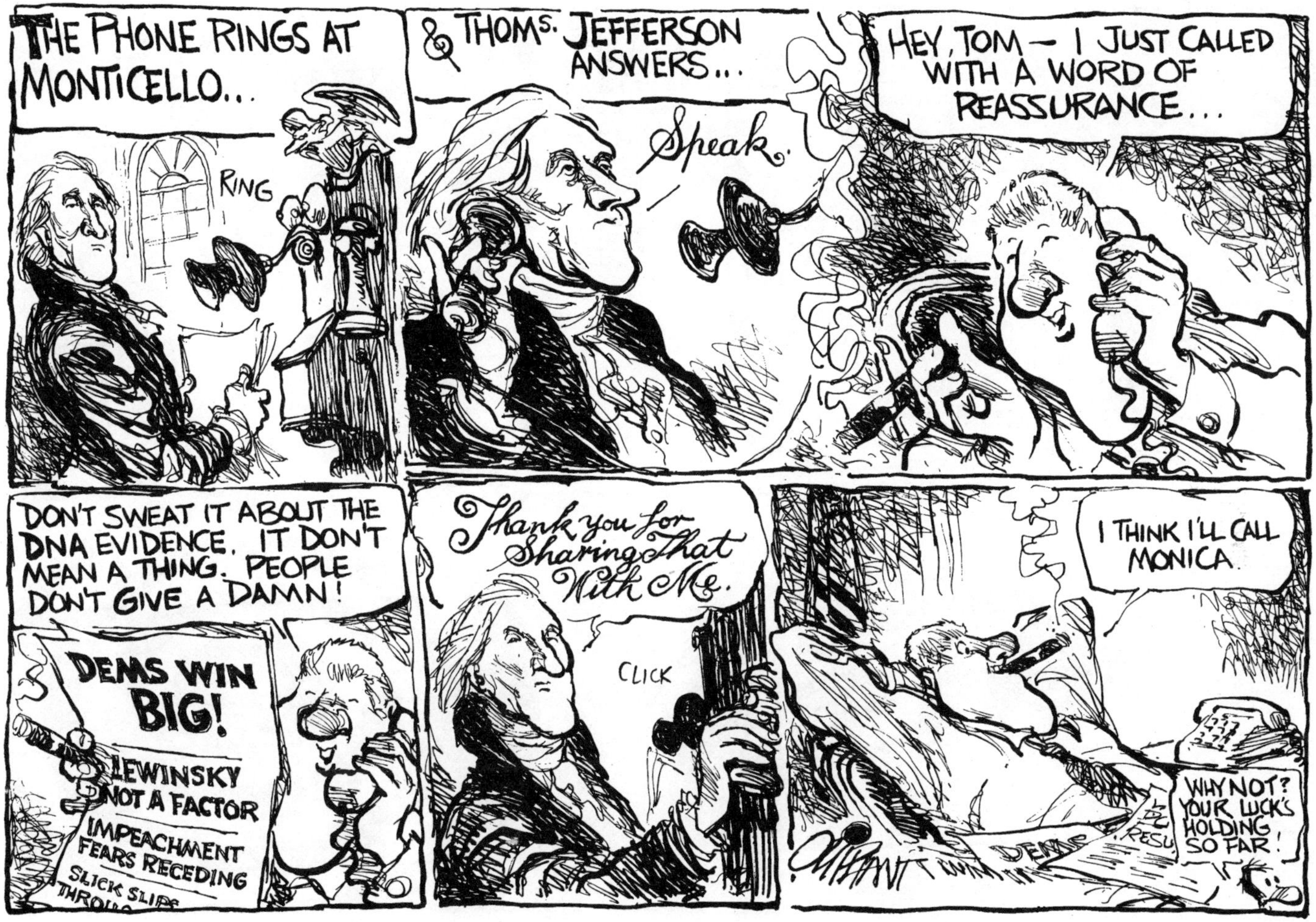
THE PHONE RINGS AT MONTICELLO...
RING
& THOMS. JEFFERSON ANSWERS...
Speak.
HEY, TOM — I JUST CALLED WITH A WORD OF REASSURANCE...
DON'T SWEAT IT ABOUT THE DNA EVIDENCE. IT DON'T MEAN A THING. PEOPLE DON'T GIVE A DAMN!
DEMS WIN BIG!
LEWINSKY NOT A FACTOR
IMPEACHMENT FEARS RECEDING
SLICK SLIPS
Thank you for Sharing That With Me.
CLICK
I THINK I'LL CALL MONICA.
WHY NOT? YOUR LUCK'S HOLDING SO FAR!
OLIPHANT

November 12, 1998

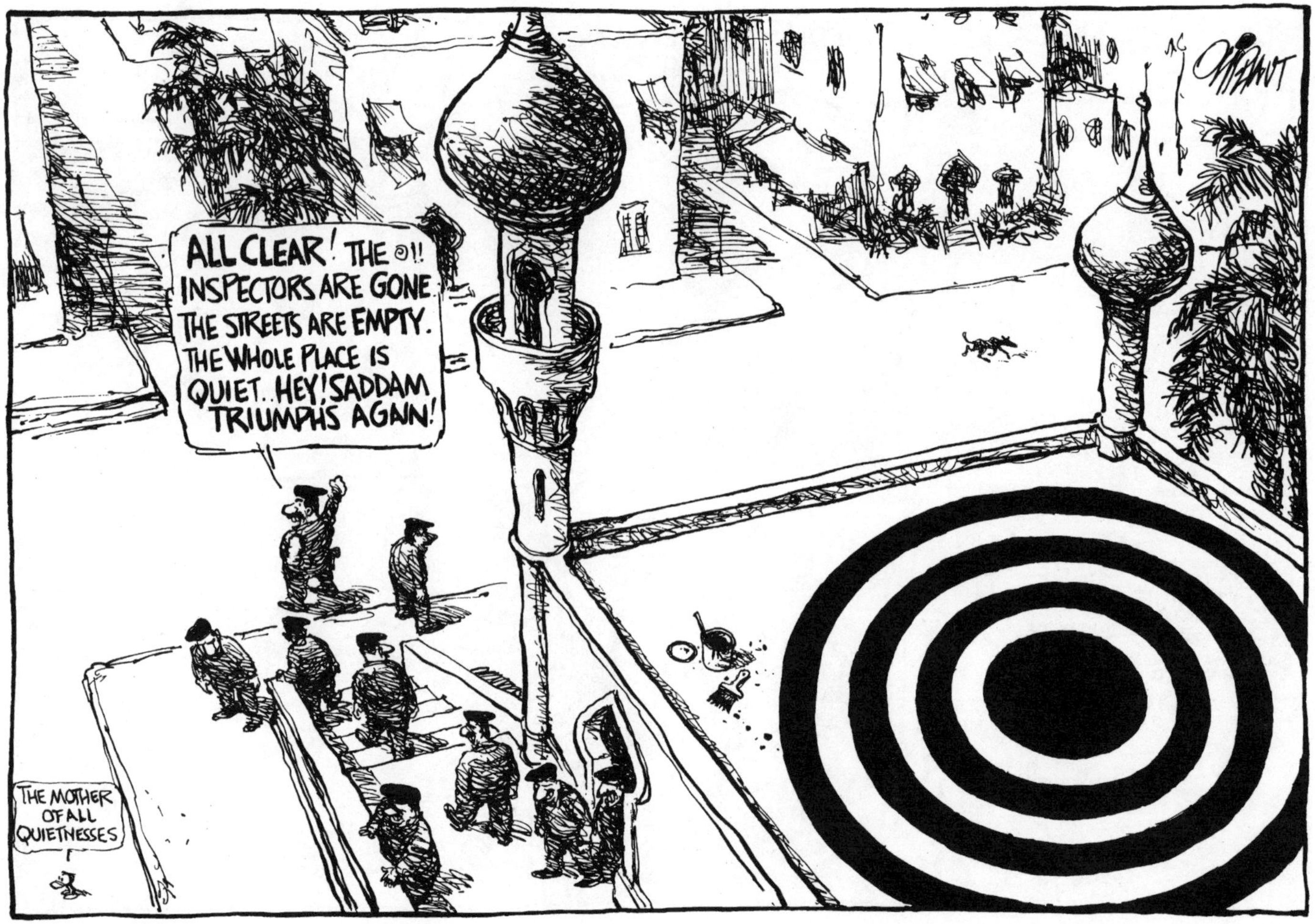
ALL CLEAR! THE @!! INSPECTORS ARE GONE. THE STREETS ARE EMPTY. THE WHOLE PLACE IS QUIET...HEY! SADDAM TRIUMPHS AGAIN!
THE MOTHER OF ALL QUIETNESSES
OLIPHANT

November 24, 1998

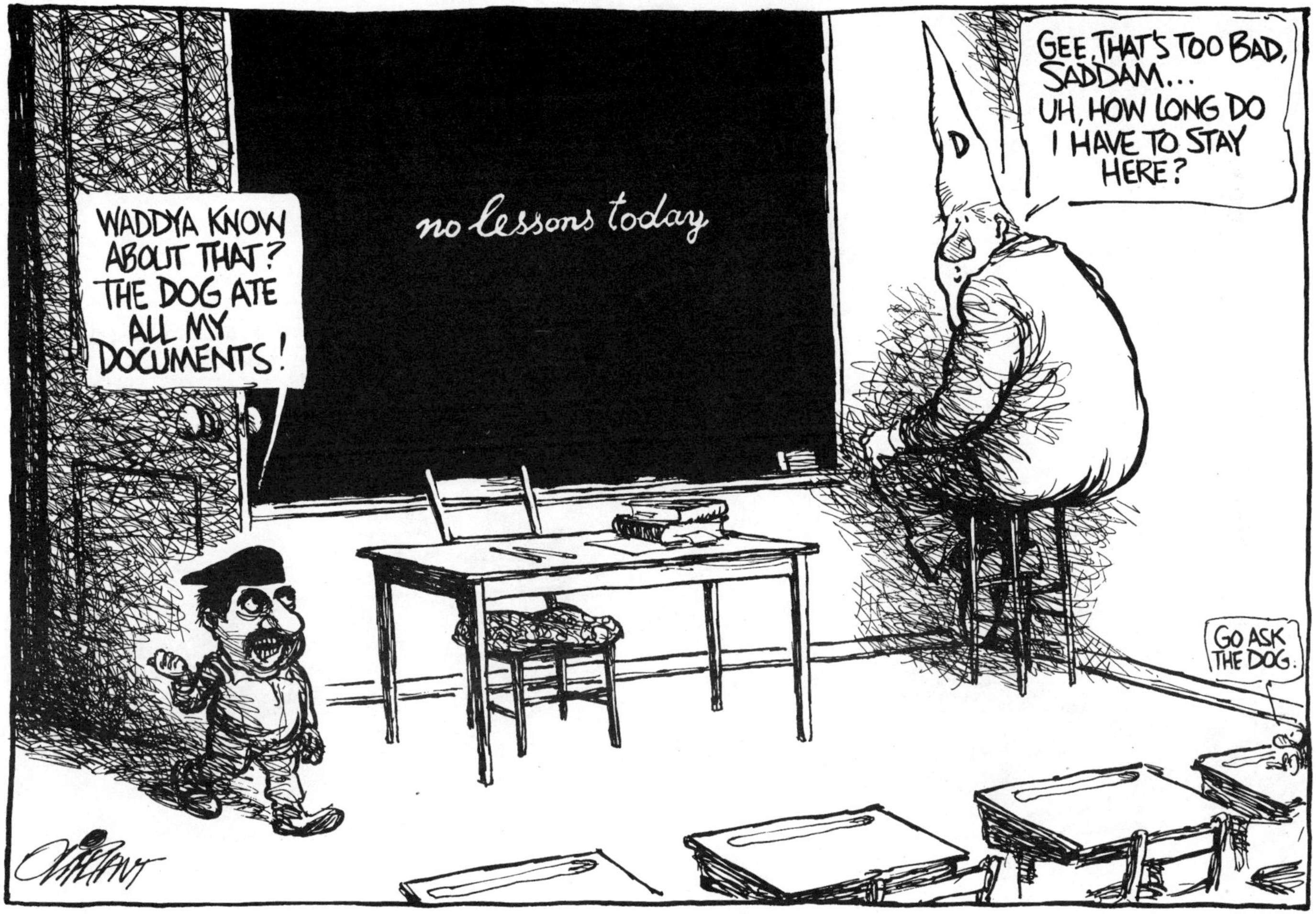
WADDYA KNOW ABOUT THAT? THE DOG ATE ALL MY DOCUMENTS!
no lessons today
D
GEE, THAT'S TOO BAD, SADDAM... UH, HOW LONG DO I HAVE TO STAY HERE?
GO ASK THE DOG.

November 25, 1998

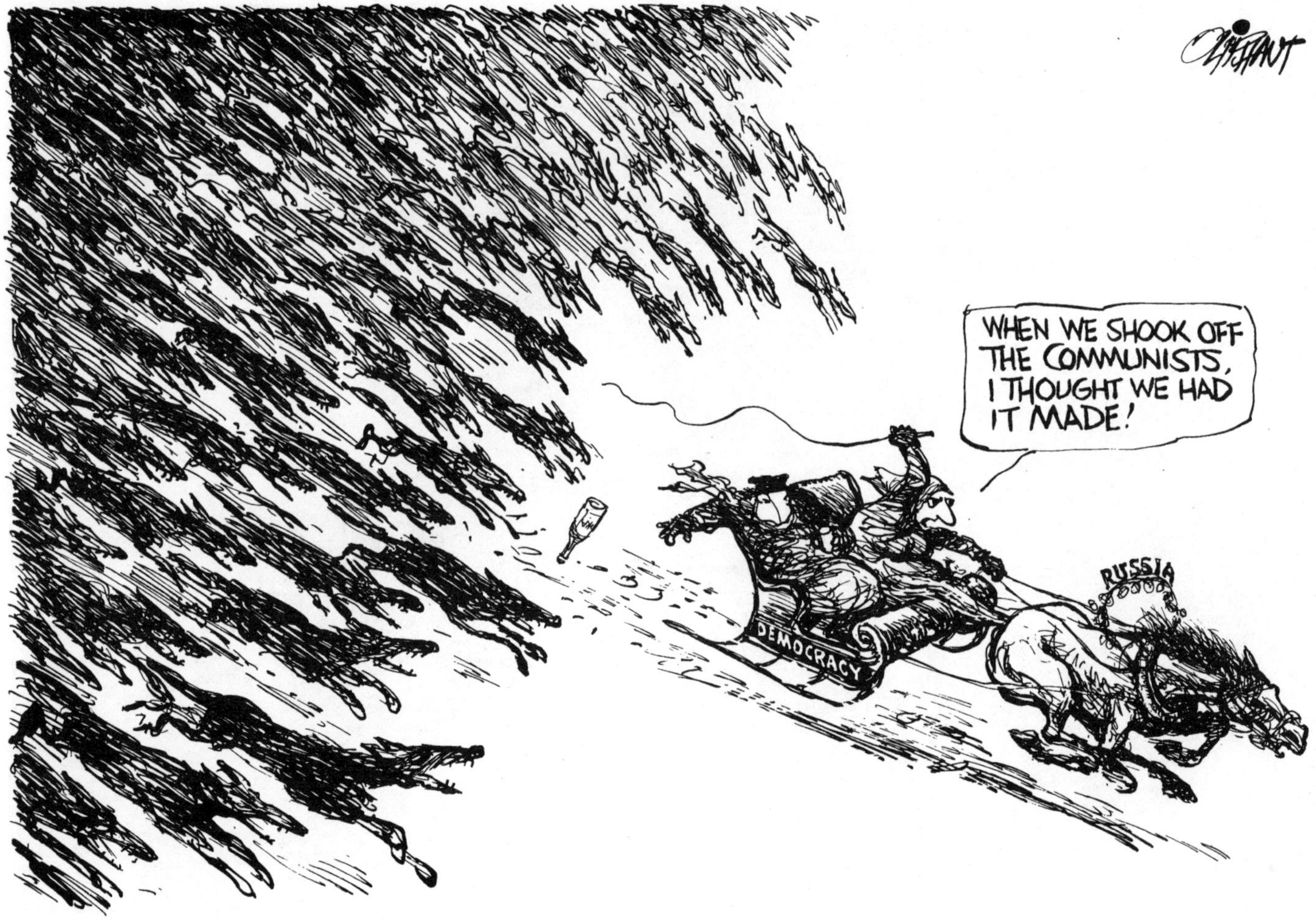
WHEN WE SHOOK OFF
THE COMMUNISTS,
I THOUGHT WE HAD
IT MADE!
DEMOCRACY
RUSSIA
OLIPHANT

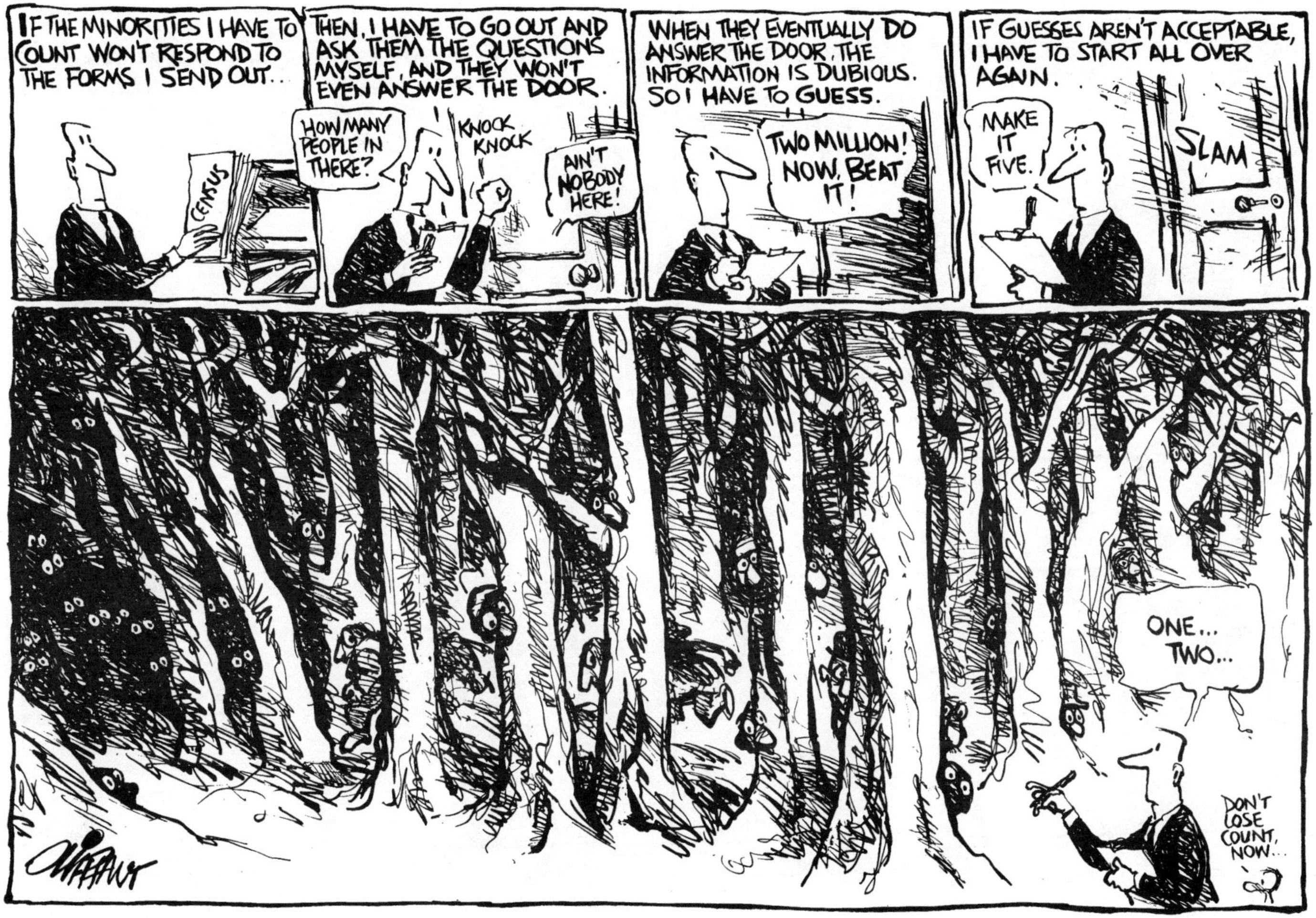
IF THE MINORITIES I HAVE TO COUNT WON'T RESPOND TO THE FORMS I SEND OUT...
CENSUS
THEN, I HAVE TO GO OUT AND ASK THEM THE QUESTIONS MYSELF, AND THEY WON'T EVEN ANSWER THE DOOR.
HOW MANY PEOPLE IN THERE?
KNOCK KNOCK
AIN'T NOBODY HERE!
WHEN THEY EVENTUALLY DO ANSWER THE DOOR, THE INFORMATION IS DUBIOUS. SO I HAVE TO GUESS.
TWO MILLION! NOW, BEAT IT!
IF GUESSES AREN'T ACCEPTABLE, I HAVE TO START ALL OVER AGAIN.
MAKE IT FIVE.
SLAM
ONE... TWO...
DON'T LOSE COUNT, NOW...

December 1, 1998

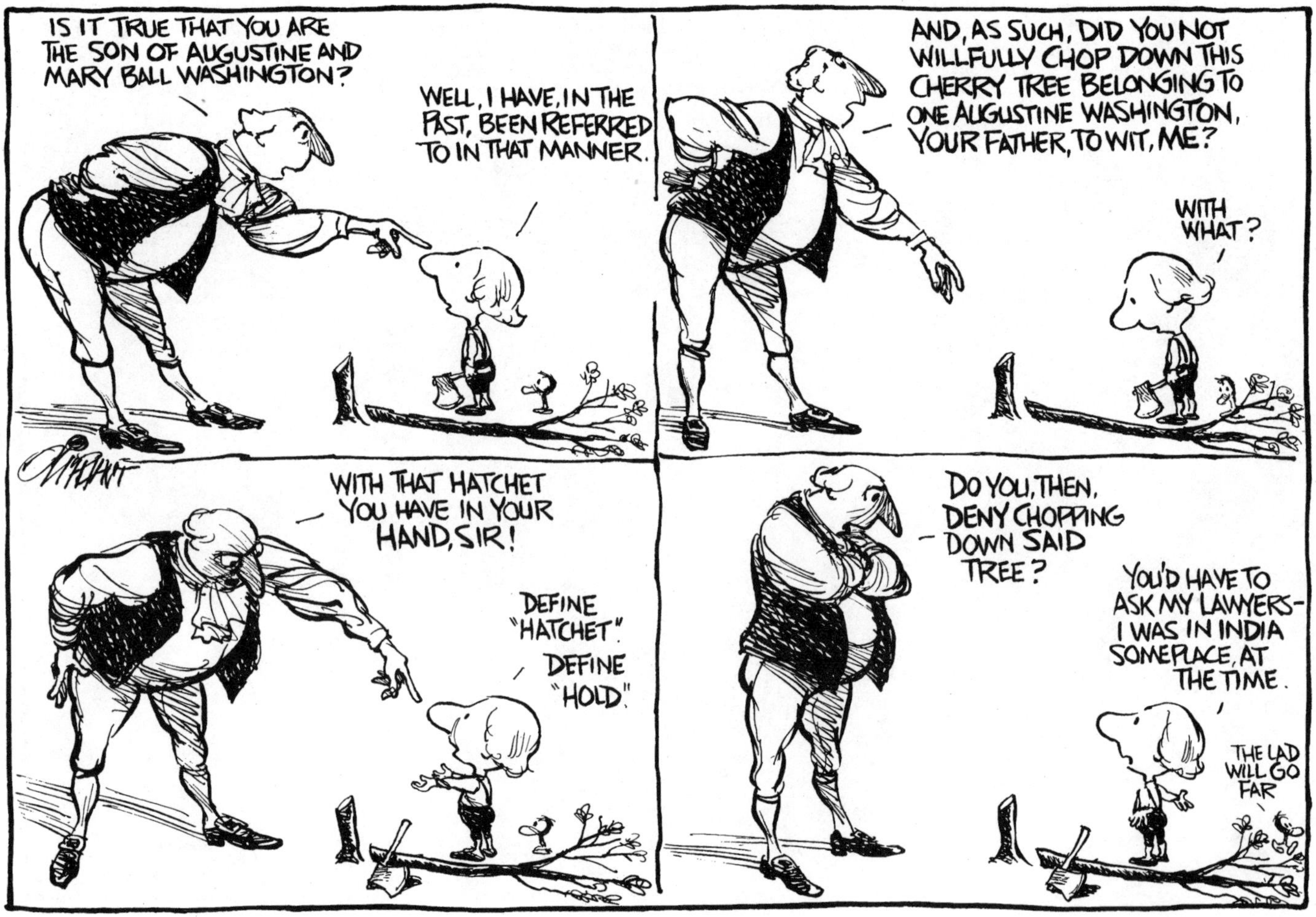
IS IT TRUE THAT YOU ARE THE SON OF AUGUSTINE AND MARY BALL WASHINGTON?
WELL, I HAVE, IN THE PAST, BEEN REFERRED TO IN THAT MANNER.
AND, AS SUCH, DID YOU NOT WILLFULLY CHOP DOWN THIS CHERRY TREE BELONGING TO ONE AUGUSTINE WASHINGTON, YOUR FATHER, TO WIT, ME?
WITH WHAT?
WITH THAT HATCHET YOU HAVE IN YOUR HAND, SIR!
DEFINE "HATCHET".
DEFINE "HOLD".
DO YOU, THEN, DENY CHOPPING DOWN SAID TREE?
YOU'D HAVE TO ASK MY LAWYERS- I WAS IN INDIA SOMEPLACE, AT THE TIME.
THE LAD WILL GO FAR

December 2, 1998

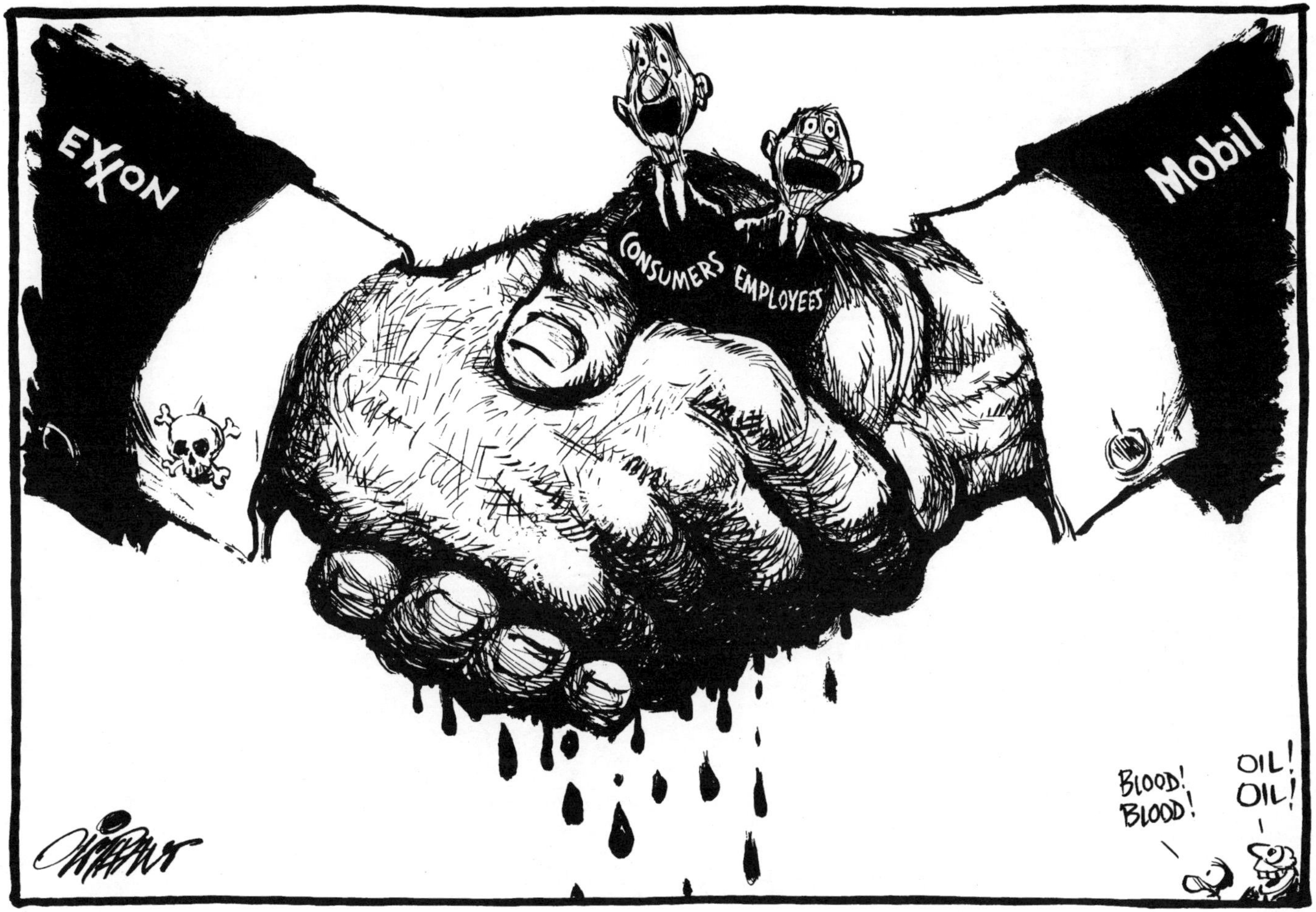
EXXON
Mobil
CONSUMERS
EMPLOYEES
BLOOD! BLOOD!
OIL! OIL!

December 8, 1998

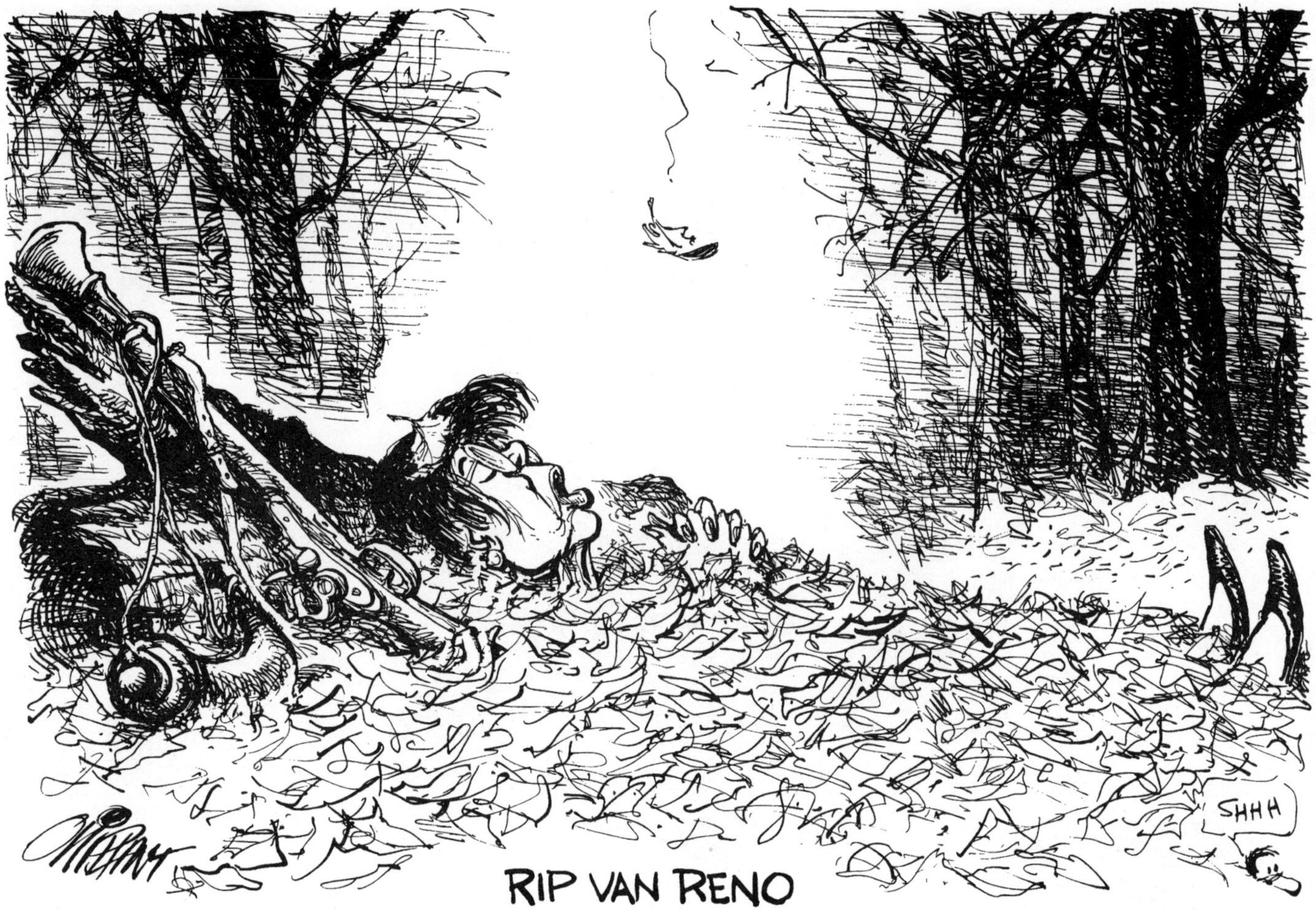
SHHH

RIP VAN RENO

December 10, 1998

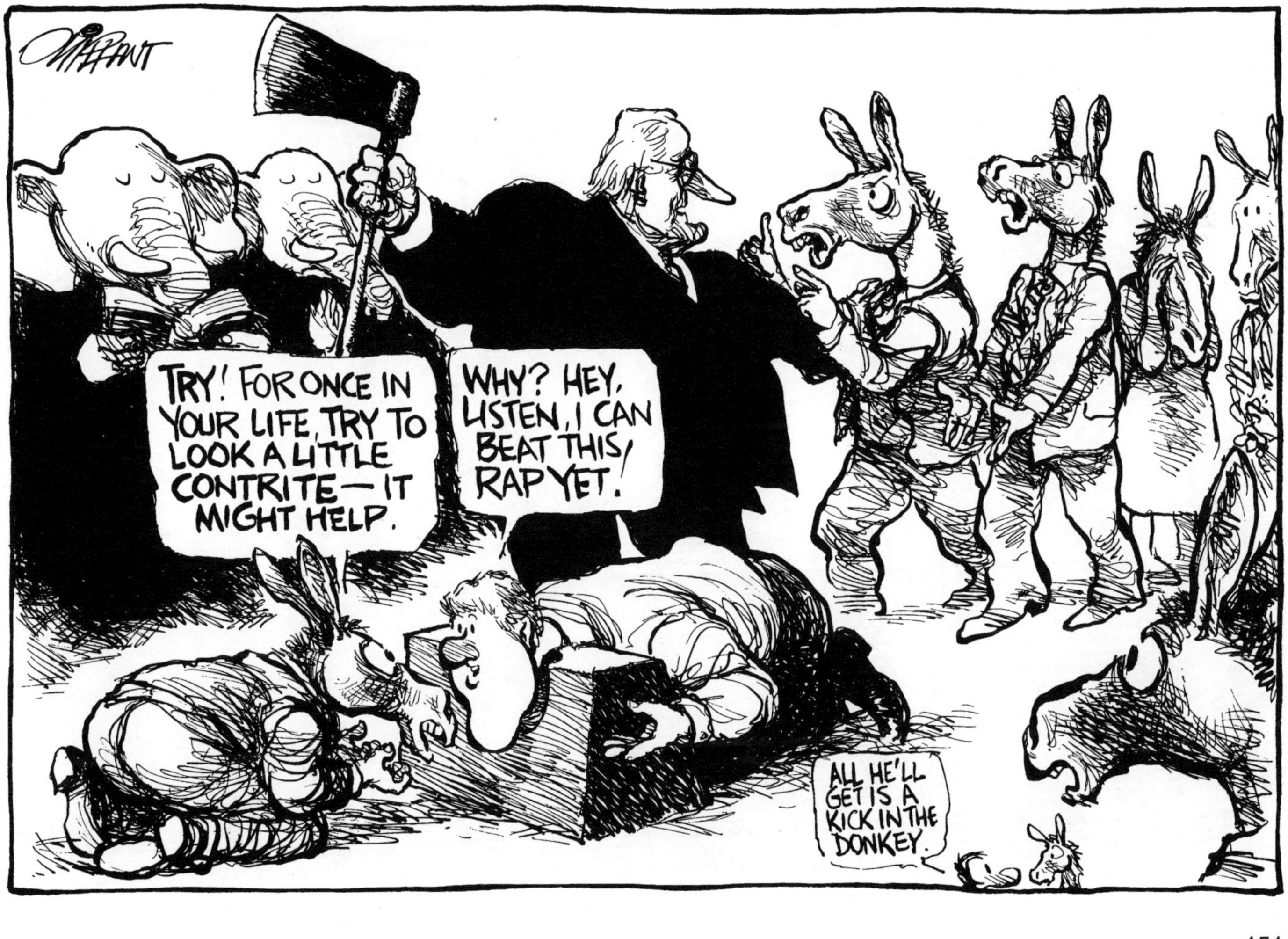
TRY! FOR ONCE IN YOUR LIFE, TRY TO LOOK A LITTLE CONTRITE—IT MIGHT HELP.
WHY? HEY, LISTEN, I CAN BEAT THIS RAP YET!
ALL HE'LL GET IS A KICK IN THE DONKEY.

December 14, 1998

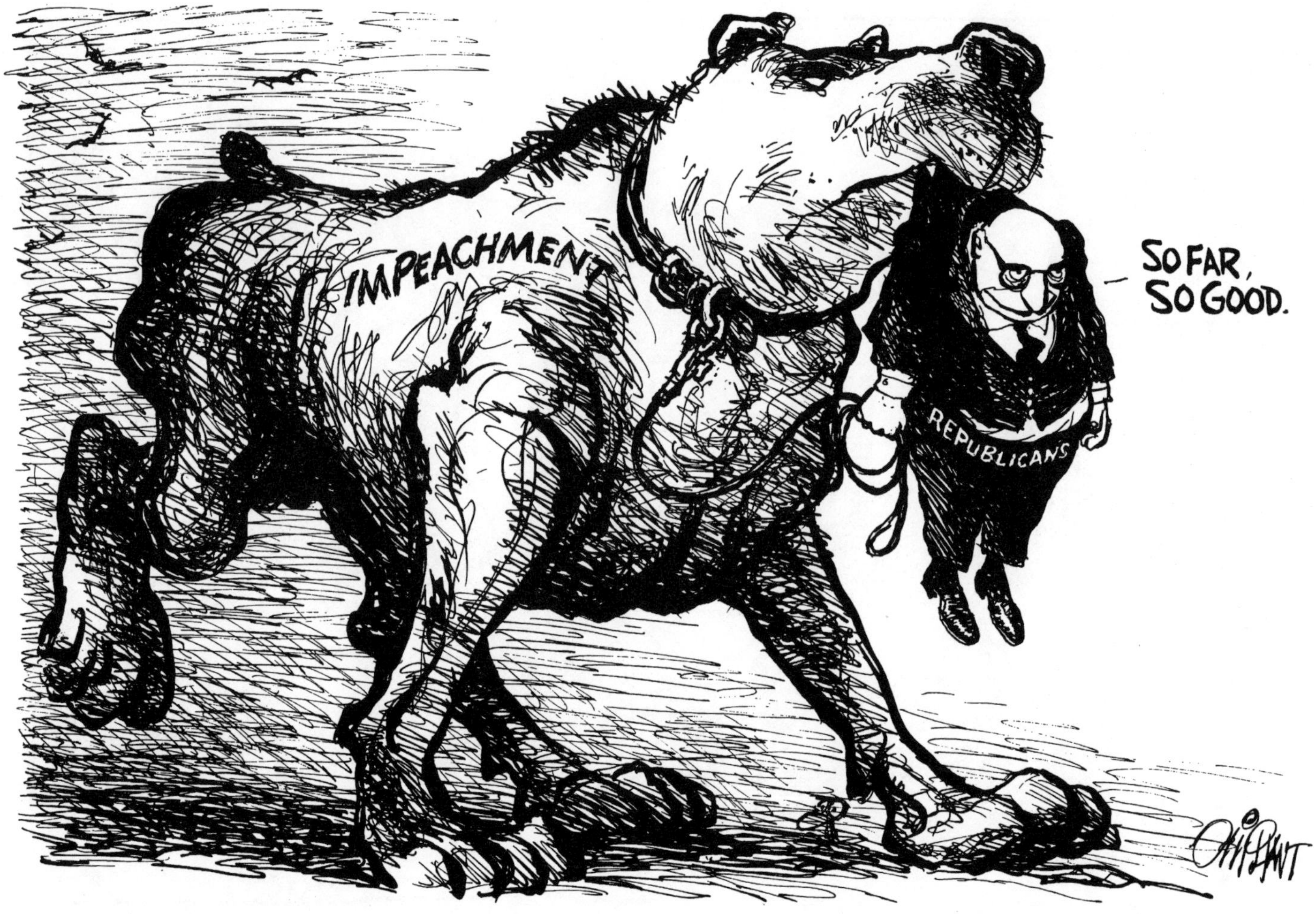
IMPEACHMENT
REPUBLICANS
SO FAR, SO GOOD.
OLIPHANT

December 15, 1998

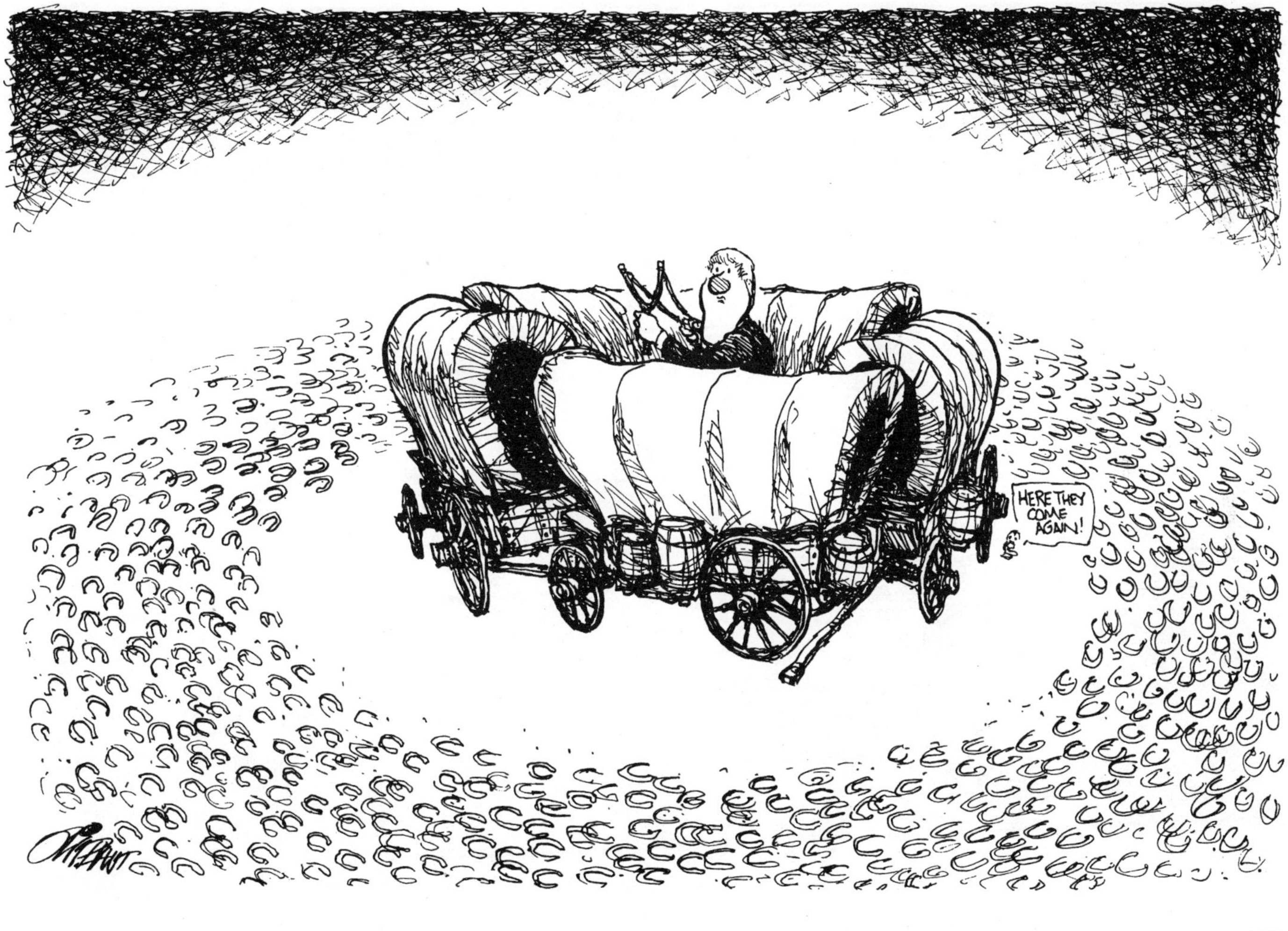
HERE THEY
COME
AGAIN!

December 16, 1998

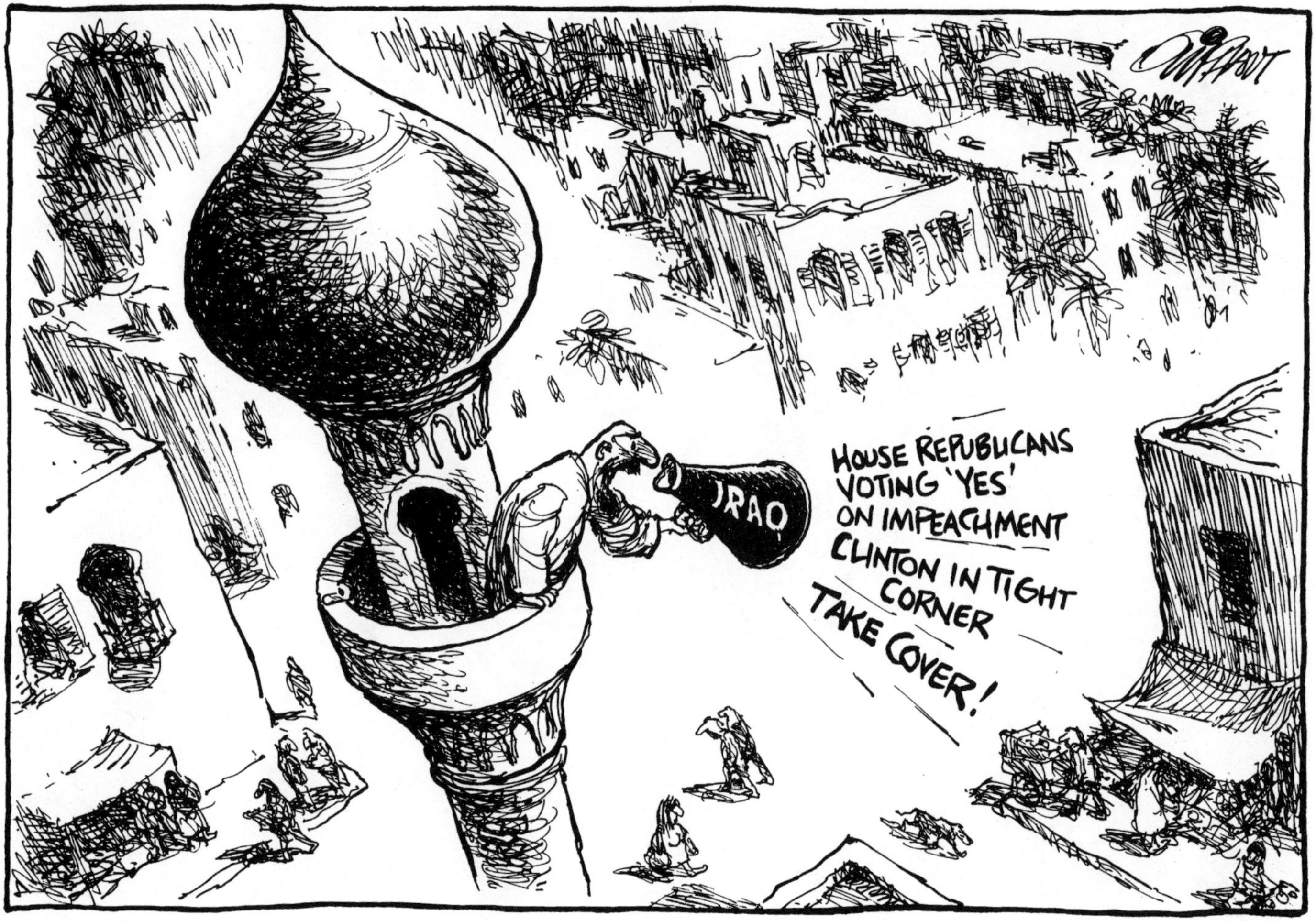
IRAQ
HOUSE REPUBLICANS VOTING 'YES' ON IMPEACHMENT
CLINTON IN TIGHT CORNER
TAKE COVER!

December 17, 1998

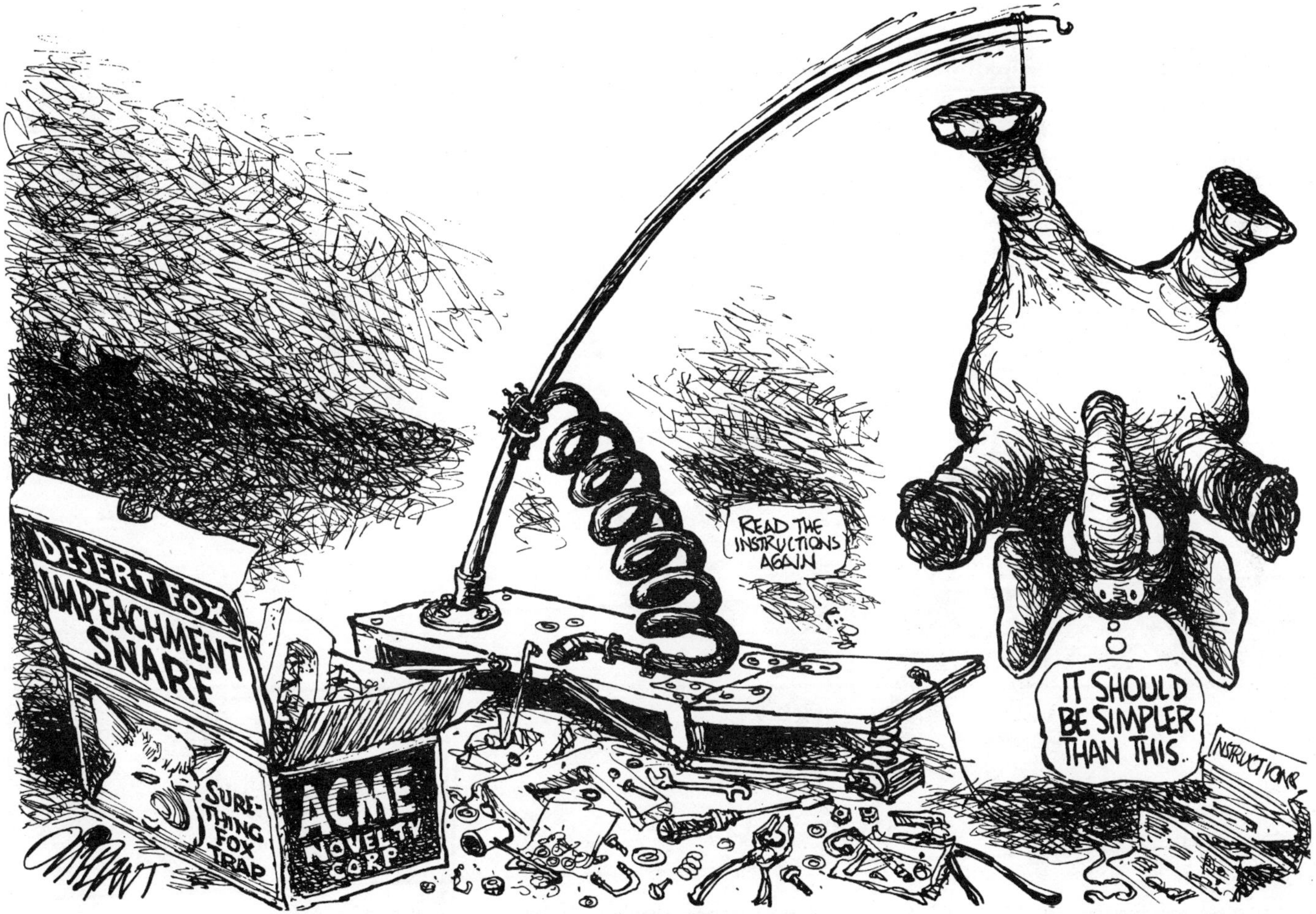
DESERT FOX
IMPEACHMENT
SNARE
SURE-THING FOX TRAP
ACME
NOVELTY CORP
READ THE INSTRUCTIONS AGAIN
IT SHOULD BE SIMPLER THAN THIS.
INSTRUCTIONS

December 21, 1998

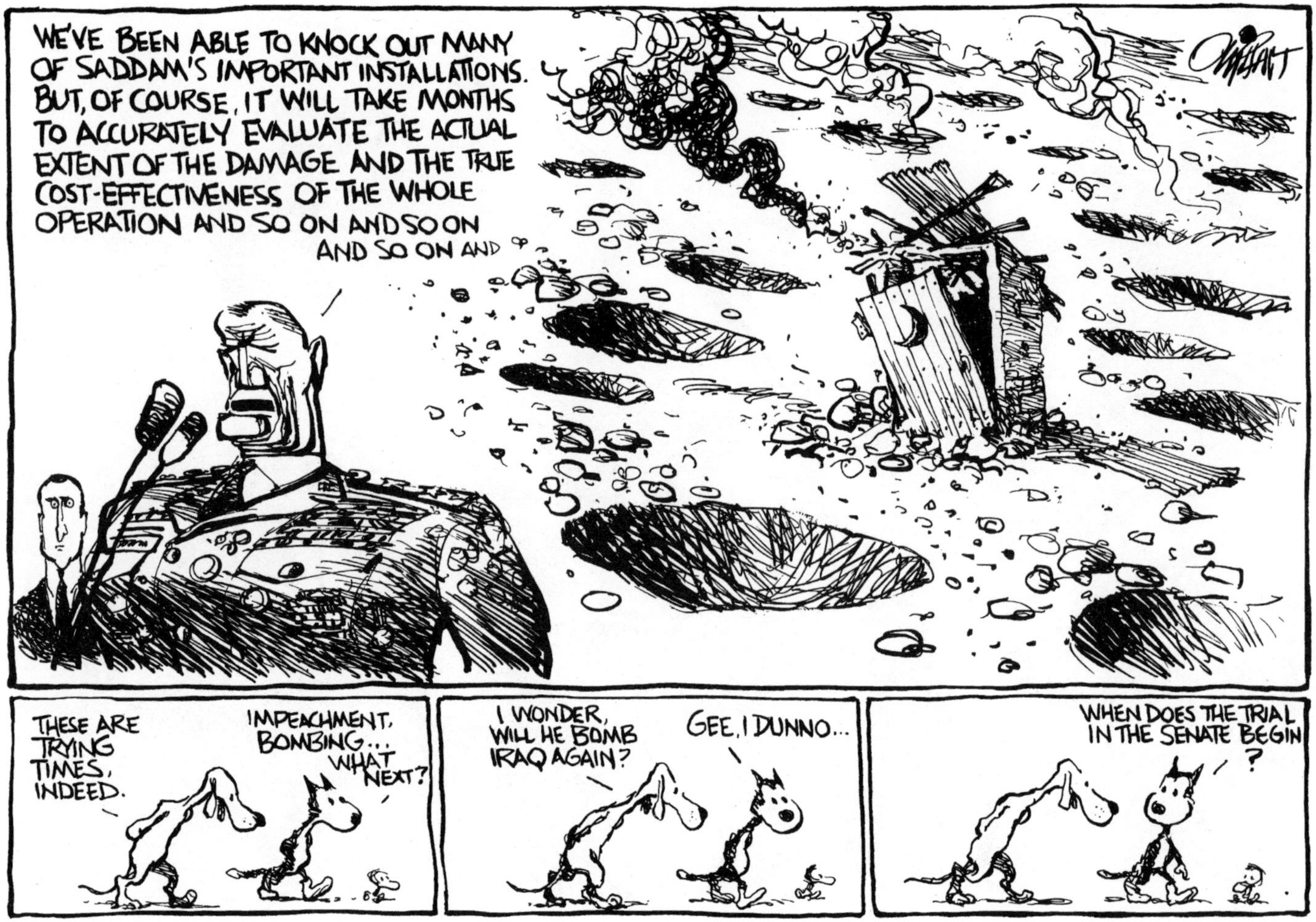
WE'VE BEEN ABLE TO KNOCK OUT MANY OF SADDAM'S IMPORTANT INSTALLATIONS. BUT, OF COURSE, IT WILL TAKE MONTHS TO ACCURATELY EVALUATE THE ACTUAL EXTENT OF THE DAMAGE AND THE TRUE COST-EFFECTIVENESS OF THE WHOLE OPERATION AND SO ON AND SO ON AND SO ON AND
THESE ARE TRYING TIMES, INDEED.
IMPEACHMENT, BOMBING... WHAT NEXT?
I WONDER, WILL HE BOMB IRAQ AGAIN?
GEE, I DUNNO...
WHEN DOES THE TRIAL IN THE SENATE BEGIN?

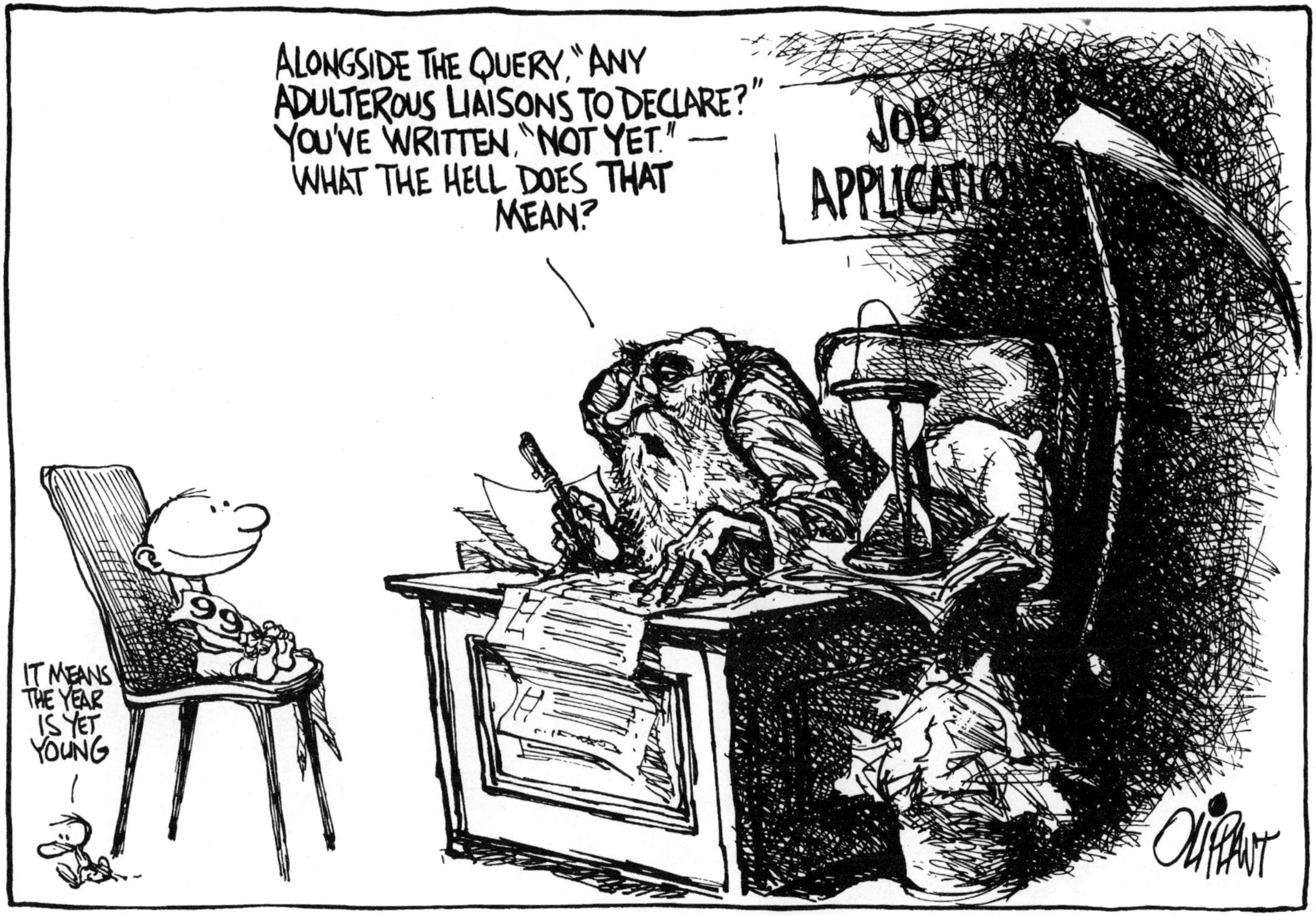
ALONGSIDE THE QUERY, "ANY ADULTEROUS LIAISONS TO DECLARE?" YOU'VE WRITTEN, "NOT YET." — WHAT THE HELL DOES THAT MEAN?
JOB APPLICATION
99
IT MEANS THE YEAR IS YET YOUNG
OLIPHANT

January 6, 1999

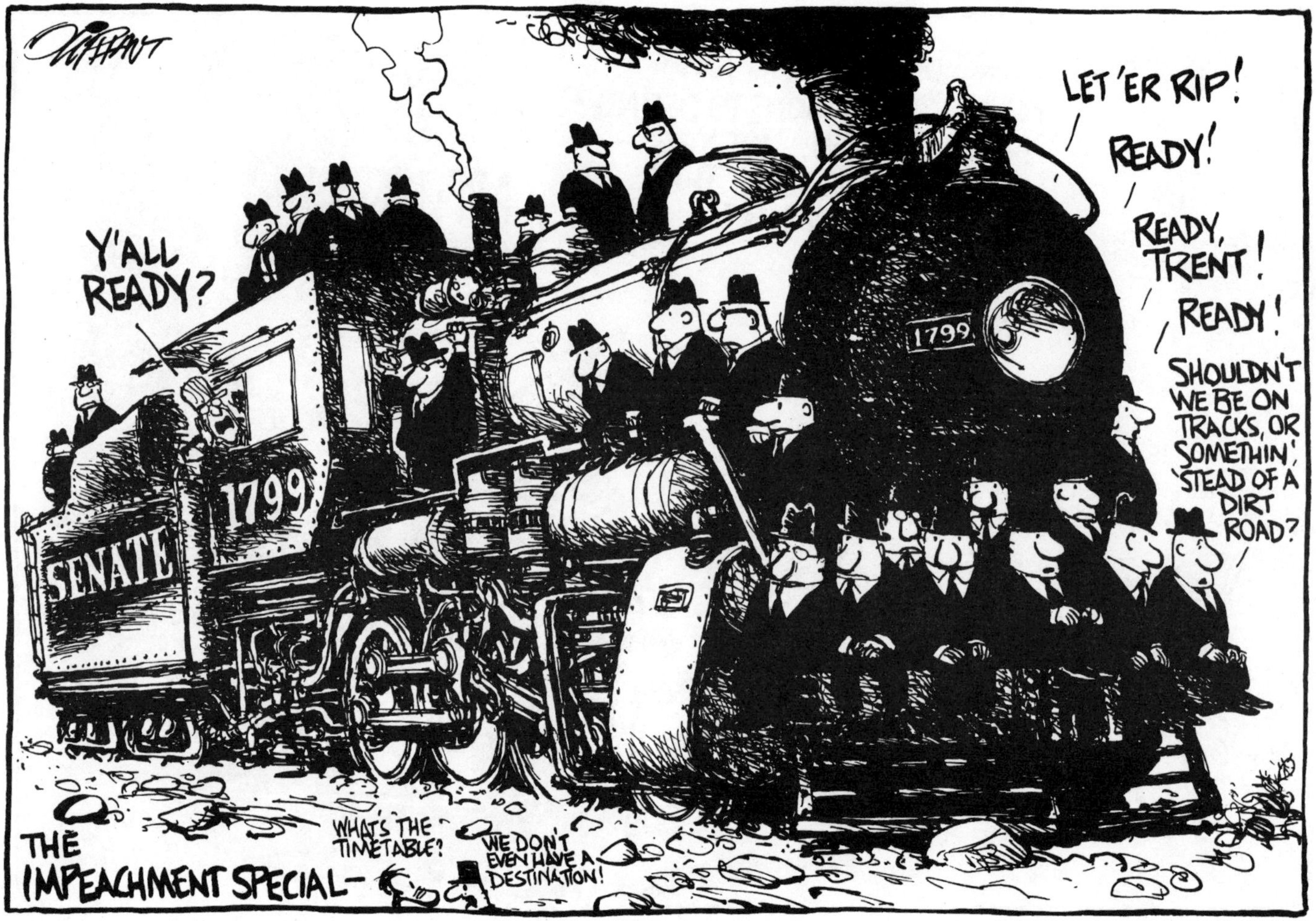
Y'ALL READY?
1799
SENATE
1799
LET 'ER RIP!
READY!
READY, TRENT!
READY!
SHOULDN'T WE BE ON TRACKS, OR SOMETHIN', 'STEAD OF A DIRT ROAD?
THE IMPEACHMENT SPECIAL–
WHAT'S THE TIMETABLE?
WE DON'T EVEN HAVE A DESTINATION!

January 11, 1999

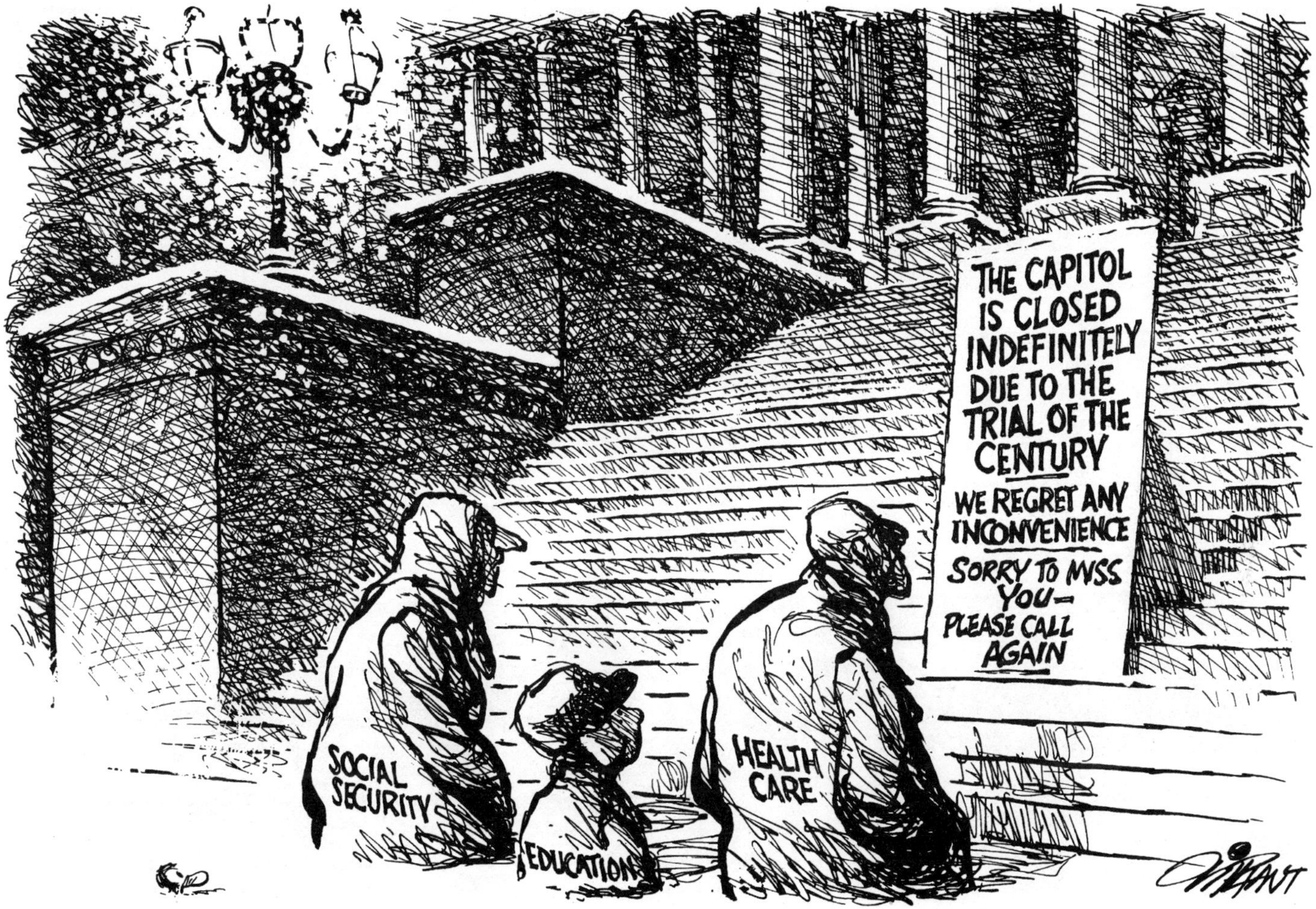
THE CAPITOL IS CLOSED INDEFINITELY DUE TO THE TRIAL OF THE CENTURY
WE REGRET ANY INCONVENIENCE
SORRY TO MISS YOU— PLEASE CALL AGAIN
SOCIAL SECURITY
EDUCATION
HEALTH CARE
OLIPHANT

January 19, 1999

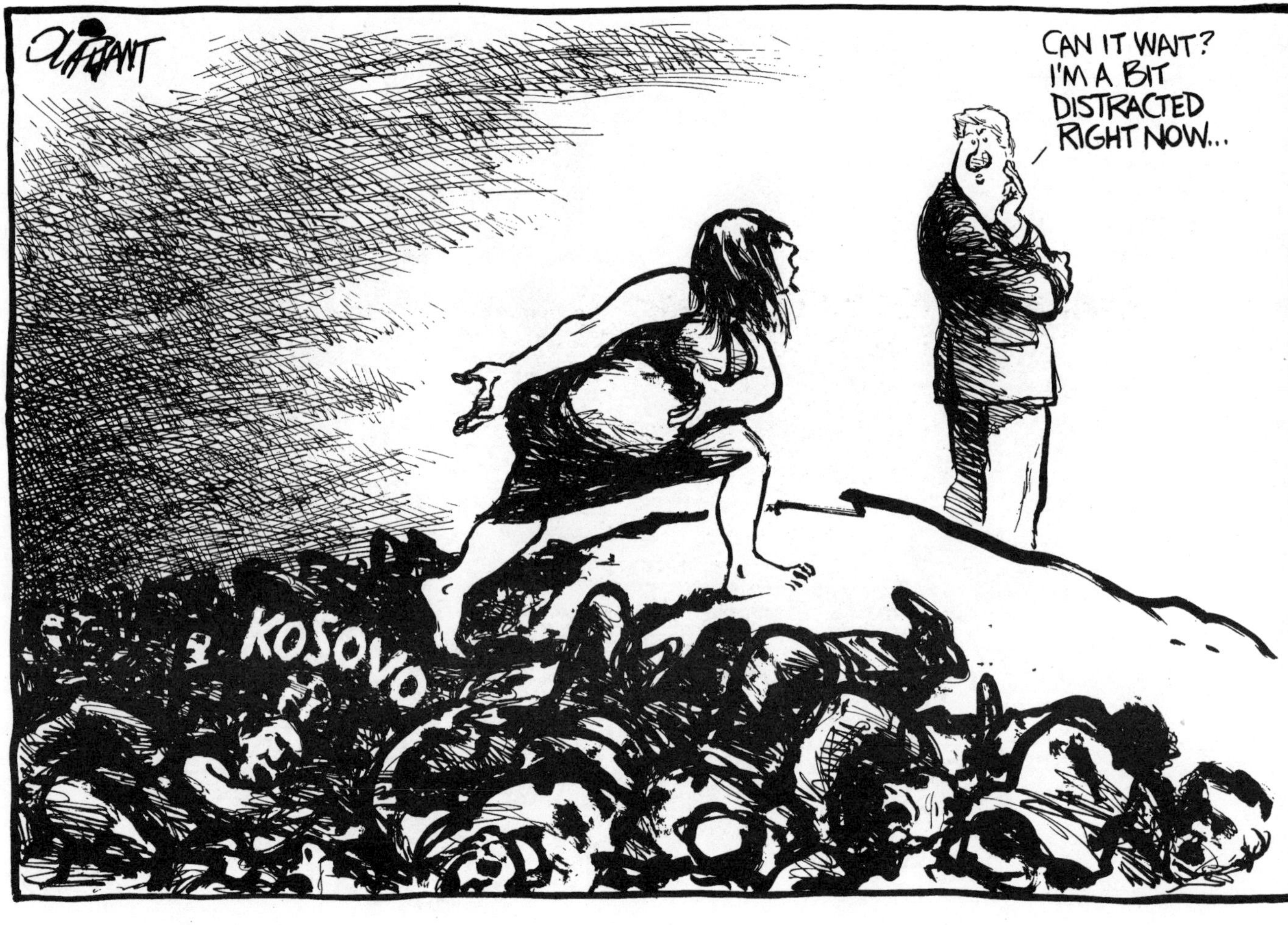
OLIPHANT
CAN IT WAIT? I'M A BIT DISTRACTED RIGHT NOW...
KOSOVO